Regulating Big Tech

Regulating Big Tech

Policy Responses to Digital Dominance

EDITED BY MARTIN MOORE

AND

DAMIAN TAMBINI

OXFORD
UNIVERSITY PRESS

OXFORD
UNIVERSITY PRESS

Oxford University Press is a department of the University of Oxford. It furthers
the University's objective of excellence in research, scholarship, and education
by publishing worldwide. Oxford is a registered trade mark of Oxford University
Press in the UK and certain other countries.

Published in the United States of America by Oxford University Press
198 Madison Avenue, New York, NY 10016, United States of America.

© Oxford University Press 2022

Library of Congress Cataloging-in-Publication Data
Names: Moore, Martin, author. | Tambini, Damian, author.
Title: Regulating Big Tech : policy responses to digital dominance /
Martin Moore and Damian Tambini.
Description: 1 Edition. | New York, NY : Oxford University Press, [2022] |
Includes bibliographical references and index.
Identifiers: LCCN 2021027068 (print) | LCCN 2021027069 (ebook) |
ISBN 9780197616109 (paperback) | ISBN 9780197616093 (hardback) |
ISBN 9780197616116 (updf) | ISBN 9780197616123 (epub) | ISBN 9780197616130 (oso)
Subjects: LCSH: High technology industries—Government policy.
Classification: LCC HC79.H53 M666 2022 (print) |
LCC HC79.H53 (ebook) | DDC 338.4/76205—dc23
LC record available at https://lccn.loc.gov/2021027068
LC ebook record available at https://lccn.loc.gov/2021027069

DOI: 10.1093/oso/9780197616093.001.0001

9 8 7 6 5 4 3 2 1

Paperback printed by LSC Communications, United States of America
Hardback printed by Bridgeport National Bindery, Inc., United States of America

CONTENTS

List of Contributors vii

Introduction 1
Damian Tambini and Martin Moore

PART I Enhancing Competition

1. Reshaping Platform-Driven Digital Markets 17
   Mariana Mazzucato, Josh Entsminger, and Rainer Kattel
2. Reforming Competition and Media Law—The German Approach 35
   Sarah Hartmann and Bernd Holznagel
3. Overcoming Market Power in Online Video Platforms 55
   Eli M. Noam
4. Enabling Community-Owned Platforms—A Proposal for a Tech New Deal 74
   Nathan Schneider

PART II Increasing Accountability

5. Obliging Platforms to Accept a Duty of Care 93
   Lorna Woods and William Perrin
6. Minimizing Data-Driven Targeting and Providing a Public
   Search Alternative 110
   Angela Phillips and Eleonora Maria Mazzoli
7. Accelerating Adoption of a Digital Intermediary Tax 127
   Elda Brogi and Roberta Maria Carlini

PART III Safeguarding Privacy

8. Treating Dominant Digital Platforms as Public Trustees 151
   Philip M. Napoli
9. Establishing Auditing Intermediaries to Verify Platform Data 169
   Ben Wagner and Lubos Kuklis
10. Promoting Data for Well-Being While Minimizing Stigma 180
    Frank Pasquale

PART IV Protecting Democracy

11. Responding to Disinformation: Ten Recommendations
    for Regulatory Action and Forbearance 195
    Chris Marsden, Ian Brown, and Michael Veale
12. Creating New Electoral Public Spheres 221
    Martin Moore
13. Transposing Public Service Media Obligations to Dominant Platforms 235
    Jacob Rowbottom

PART V Reforming Governance

14. A Model for Global Governance of Platforms 255
    Robert Fay
15. Determining Our Technological and Democratic Future: A Wish List 280
    Paul Nemitz and Matthias Pfeffer
16. Reconceptualizing Media Freedom 299
    Damian Tambini
17. A New Social Contract for Platforms 323
    Victor Pickard

Conclusion: Without a Holistic Vision, Democratic Media
    Reforms May Fail 338
    Martin Moore and Damian Tambini

Index 349

LIST OF CONTRIBUTORS

Elda Brogi is a part-time Professor at the European University Institute (EUI) and holds a Ph.D. in Public Law and Constitutional Law (University La Sapienza, Rome). At the EUI she is Scientific coordinator of the Centre for Media Pluralism and Media Freedom. She is a member of the Executive Board of the European Digital Media Observatory (EDMO) and teaches Communication Law at the University of Florence. She is also a member of the Council of Europe (CoE) Committee of Experts on Media Environment and Reform (MSI-REF), co-rapporteur on the recommendation on electoral communication and media coverage of election campaigns. She was previously a member of the CoE MSI-MED and MSI-JO Committees.

Ian Brown is visiting CyberBRICS Professor at Fundação Getulio Vargas (FGV) Law School in Rio de Janeiro, and an ACM Distinguished Scientist. He was previously Principal Scientific Officer at the UK government's Department for Digital, Culture, Media and Sport; Professor of Information Security and Privacy at the University of Oxford's Internet Institute; and a Knowledge Exchange Fellow with the Commonwealth Secretariat and UK National Crime Agency. His books include *Cybersecurity for Elections* (2020, Commonwealth Secretariat, with Marsden/Lee/Veale), *Regulating Code* (2013, MIT Press, with Marsden), and *Research Handbook on Governance of the Internet* (ed., 2013, Edward Elgar).

Roberta Maria Carlini is research associate at Centre for Media Pluralism and Media Freedom (CMPF), at the Schuman Centre of the European University Institute, where she contributes to the Media Pluralism Monitor covering the Market Plurality area and realizes the Italian Country Report for the MPM project. Her research in the CMPF focuses on the media economy, external pluralism, and the impact of the digital platforms on the media industry. Roberta joined the CMPF in 2019, after a career as economic journalist in Italy. As a journalist, she covered economic, social and political topics for Italian leading newspapers, magazines and radio. As an essayist, she has written several books, most recently "Come siamo cambiati. Gli italiani e la crisi" (Laterza, 2015).

Josh Entsminger is a PhD student in innovation and public policy, supervised by Professor Mariana Mazzucato and Professor Rainer Kattel. In addition to doctoral work, he currently serves as a fellow at the Center for Policy and Competitiveness at Ecole Des Ponts Business School, and fellow at IE School of Global and Public Affairs' Public Tech Lab. He was a research contributor on two World Economic Forum reports delivered at Davos in 2018 and 2020, concerning sustainable production systems and global technology governance. His writing and research can be found in Project Syndicate, MIT Tech Review Insights, WEF, RSA, The Conversation, The Decision Lab, and has been syndicated to over a dozen national newspapers in six languages.

Robert (Bob) Fay is the Managing Director of digital economy research and policy at CIGI. The research under his direction assesses and provides policy recommendations for the complex global governance issues arising from digital technologies. Prior to joining CIGI, Bob held several senior roles at the Bank of Canada, including as special assistant to Governor Mark Carney, serving as the Governor's chief of staff. Bob was also an economist at the Organisation for Economic Co-operation and Development and worked on a wide range of economic and labour market issues.

Sarah Hartmann is an academic counsellor and senior research associate at the Institute for Information, Telecommunications and Media Law (ITM) at the University of Muenster, Germany. After studying law in Bremen, Paris and Muenster, she was awarded her doctorate in law for her dissertation on the material scope of the European AVMS directive and regulation in convergent media environments in 2018. Her research focuses on German and European media regulation, human rights and data protection law. She is currently working on her habilitation.

Bernd Holznagel is the Director of the Institute for Information, Telecommunications and Media Law at the University of Muenster, Germany, where he is a Professor for Constitutional Law, Administrative Law, European Law and Administrative Science since 1997. He studied law and sociology in Berlin and Montreal, Canada (McGill University). He received his Ph.D. at the University of Hamburg (1990) and published his habilitation on "Broadcasting Law in Europe" in 1996. His main research areas are the regulation of platforms and algorithms, data protection, telecommunications, media and internet law.

Rainer Kattel is Professor and deputy director at Institute for Innovation and Public Purpose, UCL. He received his education from University of Tartu, Estonia, and University of Marburg, Germany, studying philosophy, political philosophy, classics and public administration. He has published extensively on innovation policy, its governance and specific management issues. His research interests include also public sector innovation, digital transformation in the public sector and financialization. His recent books include The Elgar Handbook of Alternative Theories of Economic Development (edited with Erik Reinert and Jayati Gosh; Elgar, 2016), Financial Regulations in the European Union (edited with Jan Kregel and Mario Tonveronachi; Routledge, 2016), and Innovation Bureaucracy (with Wolfgang Drechsler and Erkki Karo; Yale, forthcoming in 2021). In 2013, he received Estonia's National Science Award for his work on innovation policy.

Ľuboš Kukliš is Chief Executive at the Council for Broadcasting and Retransmission of Slovakia and Chair of the European Platform of Regulatory

Authorities (EPRA). In 2018 and 2019, he was Chair of European Regulators Group for Audiovisual Media Services (ERGA) and currently leads ERGA's work on disinformation.

Chris Marsden is Professor of Internet Law at the University of Sussex and an expert on Internet and new media law, having researched and taught in the field since 1995. Chris researches regulation by code - whether legal, software or social code. He is author of five monographs on Internet law including "Net neutrality: From Policy to Law to Regulation" (2017), "Regulating Code" (2013 with Prof. Ian Brown), "Internet Co-regulation" (2011). He is author of many refereed articles, book chapters, professional articles, keynote addresses, and other scholarly contributions. His current funded research is into Trusted Autonomous Systems (UKRI-EPSRC 2020-24).

Eleonora Maria Mazzoli is an ESRC-funded researcher in the data, networks and society programme of the Media and Communications Department of the London School of Economics and Political Science, after studying at Bocconi University (Italy), Utrecht University (Netherlands) and UC Santa Barbara (USA). Her most recent research focuses on online content policy and the political economic implications of digital platforms for the media industry. She also works as external consultant and policy advisor for various institutions, including Council of Europe, Journalism Trust Initiative, UCL Institute for Innovation and Public Purpose, and BBC.

Mariana Mazzucato is Professor in the Economics of Innovation and Public Value at University College London (UCL), where she is Founding Director of the UCL Institute for Innovation & Public Purpose (IIPP). She is winner of international prizes including the 2020 John von Neumann Award, the 2019 All European Academies Madame de Staël Prize for Cultural Values, and the 2018 Leontief Prize for Advancing the Frontiers of Economic Thought. She is the author of three highly-acclaimed books: The Entrepreneurial State: Debunking Public vs. Private Sector Myths (2013), The Value of Everything: Making and Taking in the Global Economy (2018) and the newly released, Mission Economy: A Moonshot Guide to Changing Capitalism (2021).

Martin Moore is a Senior Lecturer in Political Communication Education at King's College London, and Director of the Centre for the Study of Media, Communication and Power. He is the author of *Democracy Hacked* (Oneworld, 2018) and editor, with Damian Tambini, of *Digital Dominance: The Power of Google, Amazon, Facebook and Apple* (OUP, 2018). His research focuses on the political economy of big tech and the transformation of political communication.

Philip M. Napoli is the James R. Shepley Distinguished Professor of Public Policy at Duke's Sanford School of Public Policy; the Senior Associate Dean for Faculty and Research in the Sanford School of Public Policy; Director of the DeWitt Wallace Center for Media & Democracy; and an Associate of the Duke Initiative for Science and Society. A graduate of U.C. Berkeley (B.A.), Boston University

(M.S.) and Northwestern (Ph.D.), Professor Napoli's areas of expertise are media and democracy and his research focuses on media institutions, media regulation, and policy. He has provided formal and informal expert testimony on these topics to government bodies, such as the U.S. Senate, the Federal Communications Commission, the Federal Trade Commission, and the Congressional Research Service.

Paul Nemitz is the Principal Adviser on Justice Policy in the European Commission. He was appointed in April 2017, following a 6-year appointment as Director for Fundamental Rights and Citizen's Rights in the EU Commission. As Director, Nemitz led the reform of Data Protection legislation in the EU, the negotiations of the EU – US Privacy Shield and the negotiations with major US Internet Companies of the EU Code of Conduct against incitement to violence and hate speech on the Internet. He is the author of 'Constitutional democracy and technology in the age of artificial intelligence' (2018) and 'Prinzip Mensch – Macht, Freiheit und Demokratie im Zeitalter der Künstlichen Intelligence' (2020) with Matthias Pfeffer.

Eli M. Noam is Professor of Economics at the Columbia University Business School, and its Garrett Professor of Public Policy and Business Responsibility. He is the Director of the Columbia Institute for Tele-Information, a research centre focusing on management and policy issues in communications, internet, and media. Noam has published and over 350 articles and 37 books, most recently including: Who Owns the World's Media (Oxford 2016); Managing Media and Digital Organizations (Palgrave 2019); Media and Digital Management (Palgrave 2019); The Technology, Business, and Economics of Streaming Video (Elgar 2021); as well as The Content, Impact, and Regulation of Streaming Video (Elgar 2021). He served as a Commissioner of Public Services for New York State, and on the White House's President's IT Advisory Board. He was President of the International Media Management Academic Association, 2013-2015.

Frank Pasquale is an expert on the law of AI, algorithms, and machine learning. He is a Professor of Law at Brooklyn Law School, a Visiting Scholar at the AI Now Institute, an Affiliate Fellow at Yale University's Information Society Project, and a member of the American Law Institute. Before joining Brooklyn Law, he was Piper & Marbury Professor of Law at the University of Maryland. He is co-editor-in-chief of the Journal of Cross-Disciplinary Research in Computational Law (CRCL), based in the Netherlands, and a member of an Australian Research Council (ARC) Centre of Excellence on Automated Decision-Making & Society (ADM+S). His book The Black Box Society: The Secret Algorithms That Control Money and Information (Harvard University Press 2015) has been recognized as a landmark study on the law and political economy of information. His New Laws of Robotics: Defending Human Expertise in the Age of AI (Harvard University Press 2020) develops a new political economy of automation, in which human capacities are the irreplaceable center of an inclusive economy.

William Perrin is a practitioner and advisor at the interface of technology, the state and the voluntary sector. He is a trustee of several charities, the founder of tech start-ups and a community activist. In a wide-ranging public service career, which included being an advisor to Tony Blair, he was instrumental in creating OFCOM, reforming the regulatory regime of several sectors and kicking off the UK government's interest in open data. William founded community journalism start-up Talk About Local in 2012. He is a trustee of Good Things Foundation, Indigo Trust, The Philanthropy Workshop and 360Giving, a charity about charity data, which he co-founded.

Matthias Pfeffer is a journalist and TV producer, and founder of PfefferMedia, a production company based in Berlin. He has developed and produced TV formats including Future Trend, the first science format for RTL in private television (1997-2013) and with One-to-One for Sat.1 (2011-2013) a new kind of talk show format. With Focus Gesundheit (2005-2010) he created the first 24-hour health channel in Germany. Together with Paul Nemitz he published The Human Imperative, Power, Freedom and Democracy in the Age of AI. He publishes on AI among other newspapers in Frankfurter Allgemeine Zeitung.

Angela Phillips taught journalism and journalism studies at Goldsmiths, University of London where she is a Professor Emeritus. She is the co-author, with Eiri Elvestad, of *Misunderstanding News Audiences*, (Routledge) which considers the impact of digital media on news and news audiences; the author of *Journalism in Context*, and, with Omega Douglas, co-author of forthcoming book: *Journalism, Culture, Society*.

Victor Pickard is a Professor of Media Policy and Political Economy at the Annenberg School for Communication. Previously he taught at NYU and the University of Virginia and has held visiting appointments at Cornell, Goldsmiths, and LSE. He also worked on media policy in Washington, D.C. as a Senior Research Fellow at the media reform organization Free Press and the think tank New America, and as a Policy Fellow for Congresswoman Diane Watson. Pickard has published over 100 book chapters, articles, and essays in leading scholarly journals and anthologies. He also has written or edited six books, including, most recently, Democracy Without Journalism?: Confronting the Misinformation Society (Oxford University Press, 2020). Previous books include Net Neutrality: A New Deal for the Digital Age (with David Berman; Yale University Press, 2019) and America's Battle for Media Democracy: The Triumph of Corporate Libertarianism and the Future of Media Reform (Cambridge University Press, 2014).

Jacob Rowbottom is a Professor of Law at the University of Oxford and Fellow of University College, Oxford. He is the author of *Media Law* (2018) and *Democracy Distorted* (2010), and writes widely on issues relating to freedom of speech, political finance, constitutional law and media law.

Nathan Schneider is an Assistant Professor of Media Studies at the University of Colorado Boulder, where he leads the Media Enterprise Design Lab. He is the author of *Everything for Everyone: The Radical Tradition that Is Shaping the Next Economy*, published by Nation Books, and two previous books, *God in Proof: The Story of a Search from the Ancients to the Internet* and *Thank You, Anarchy: Notes from the Occupy Apocalypse*, both published by University of California Press.

Damian Tambini, author of *Media Freedom* (Polity 2021), is an academic researcher specializing in media and communications policy and law. He is Distinguished Policy Fellow at the London School of Economics. He has acted as an adviser to the Government of the United Kingdom and to the Council of Europe and the European Commission. From 2002 to 2006, he served as head of the Programme in Comparative Media Law and Policy at Oxford University, Humboldt University, Berlin (lecturer, 1997); and the European University Institute, Florence, Italy (Ph.D., 1996). His recent publications include numerous articles on media freedom and regulation and the power of the tech giants as well as Italian politics and social and political theory.

Michael Veale is Associate Professor in Digital Rights and Regulation at the Faculty of Laws, University College London. He researches in the spaces between computer science and technology law, particularly in the context of fundamental rights, machine learning and encrypted systems.

Ben Wagner is an Assistant Professor at the Faculty of Technology, Policy and Management at TU Delft, where his research focuses on technology policy, human rights and accountable information systems. He is Associate Faculty at the Complexity Science Hub Vienna and a visiting researcher at the Human Centred Computing Group, University of Oxford. He previously worked at WU Vienna, TU-Berlin, the University of Pennsylvania and European University Viadrina. He holds a PhD in Political and Social Sciences from European University Institute in Florence.

Lorna Woods is Professor of Internet Law in the School of Law at the University of Essex and a member of the Human Rights Centre there. She is Senior Associate Research Fellow at the Information Law and Policy Centre at the Institute for Advance Legal Studies, University of London, and a member of the Automatic Number Plate Recognition (ANPR) National User Group. Formerly a practising solicitor in the City of London in the technology, media and telecommunications sectors, she has both taught and researched in those fields. Her current research, with Carnegie UK Trust, is on regulation of social media platforms in which she proposed the introduction of a statutory duty of care.

Introduction

DAMIAN TAMBINI AND MARTIN MOORE ■

REGULATING BIG TECH

The Policy Toolkit

Digital dominance has intensified. In 2018, when the first volume in this series[1] was published, none of the GAFAM (Google, Apple, Facebook, Amazon, and Microsoft) had a market capitalization greater than $1 trillion. By mid-2021 four of the five had exceeded $1.5 trillion and one had surpassed $2 trillion. These five companies, along with two from China (Alibaba and Tencent) dominate— and in some cases monopolize—global markets in digital search, digital advertising, cloud infrastructure, social media, digital messaging, mobile operating systems, and other digital markets. Moreover, the GAFAM have been structurally dominant for long enough that they enjoy substantial incumbency advantages, including their ability to spot and absorb challengers, that insulate them from genuine competition. A series of cases brought by the European Commission and the US Department of Justice,[2] and an emerging set of reforms to competition law have yet to disturb this dominance, or to mitigate its corrosive impact on democracies.

The consequences are now clear: the Internet, whilst unleashing a storm of innovation and private value growth, has also enabled a paradigm shift in the development of capitalism and the global concentration of capital. It has also upset previous institutional balances in liberal democracy not only by increasing inequality but also by undermining established news and information ecologies. It has slowly dawned on citizens of democracies that the free circulation of information, democratic decision-making, and the nature of human autonomy will be increasingly compromised if the digital status quo is allowed to continue.

National governments and international policymakers can and should act. It is no longer feasible for them to do nothing. Leaving aside for a moment whether these policies are desirable, parliaments could pass laws to ban social media services or to block a search company. They could impose obligations on them or break them up, or require them to meet the terms of a licence. The use of data by dominant intermediaries could be made conditional on meeting new conditions. Equally, democratic governments could differentially tax their outputs, and use the receipts to mitigate harms they cause or facilitate. At the extremes, companies could be regulated as utilities or brought into public ownership. Regulation could constrain their use of the resources they rely on—such as data, patents, intellectual property, consumers, and advertisers. Alternatively, the dominant technology platforms could be held liable for new products or the misuse of existing ones. The overall regime of liability could be changed and strengthened. New competitors could be encouraged through adaptations to tax or ownership laws. The terms of trade between the platforms and content could be regulated to favour prosocial rather than antisocial content. The question is not whether any of these is possible (indeed many of these policies have already been proposed or introduced), but whether a given law or regulation is justified and necessary, how these laws and regulations complement or contradict one another, and what the adverse impacts—on global communication, user rights, the public interest, and economic activity, for example—might be. To address this complex policy problem requires states to make difficult choices. It is time to decide what kind of digital political economy we want.

In Europe, North America, and elsewhere a vibrant policy debate has engaged with all these proposals and more, though often as political slogans rather than considered policies. This book outlines some of the main policy proposals that are being considered, and some that are not yet being widely discussed. Given the wide range of interventions, real and proposed, it is useful to simplify the regulatory debate into distinct, but interrelated instruments, into what we will call a 'toolkit'. Each of the chapters in this book explores an element of this toolkit— either by setting out policies already in train or by detailing how a new intervention could work.

THE TOOLKIT

Hammer, Axe, and Chisel

Using competition and antitrust action and changes in competition law to shape market structure, reduce the size and limit the growth and market behaviours of dominant technology companies.

BREAK-UP
This would involve enforced structural separation of the largest technology companies into their constituent parts. It could include, for example, compelling Amazon to make Amazon Web Services (AWS) into a separate corporate entity, or

forcing Alphabet to do the same with YouTube. The US Department of Justice and various US attorneys-general have already started antitrust action against Google and Facebook—action that is expected to take years to play out but is likely to lead to the divestment of certain parts of each company by the parent. Whether this is sufficient to reduce either platform's market dominance is not clear.

GREATER LIMITATIONS ON TECH GROWTH AND ACQUISITIONS

Competition and antitrust regulation can be used to mitigate both dominance and the effects of dominance. It does this by structuring the market and setting down rules of behaviour, aiming to reduce the dominance of the most powerful companies and/or ensure they do not abuse it. A number of moves have already been taken in this direction. Pressure is building for divestment, for example, of WhatsApp or Instagram. A smarter approach could be to separate newsfeed from the other parts of the business: thus separating editorial and advertising in line with standard journalism ethics.[3] Or newsfeed could be subject to specific external oversight given its economic and social power.

The shorthand commonly used in relation to platforms is that there is a choice between permitting them a monopoly and regulating them tightly as a condition for this, or breaking them up in order to let consumer choice and market discipline protect consumer interests. Clearly, the notion of market power is only part of the problem: as Marianna Mazzucato, Josh Entsminger, and Rainer Kattel point out in Chapter 1 of this volume, the social and political power of platforms needs to be considered, and regulation should reflect a concern not only with measures of private value but with platforms as creators of public value. Therefore, a full revision of the competition law framework—one that is fully equipped to govern competition in the longer term in the platform economy, will require a reassessment of the underlying economic concepts that are applied. As Mazzucato et al. suggest, it should focus on value creation and public value. The German model has already attempted to develop new duties relating to media pluralism, as Bernd Holznagel and Sarah Hartmann show in Chapter 2, thereby addressing some of the potential for platforms to leverage their competitive position into political and social power.

Weights and Measures

To prevent dominant technology companies from abusing their power.

CONTROLS ON COMPETITIVE BEHAVIOUR

This can take the form of new approaches to measurement and the application of regulatory discretion, as illustrated by the German example. Or it can take the form of institutional innovation, such as the United Kingdom's new specialist digital competition regulator, the Digital Markets Unit (DMU), within the Competition and Markets Authority (CMA). This opens the way to sector-specific competition rules that build a bridge between the pure market objectives—of ensuring competition works better to enable consumer switching, data portability, and so forth—and public interest objectives such as promoting truth-seeking media and preventing harm. As a first step the DMU will oversee a statutory code of conduct setting out the 'do's and 'don'ts' of dominant platforms.

When it comes to behavioural regulation—and media law objectives such as 'online harms' and media pluralism, competition and antitrust can structure not only the shape of the market but also behaviour: for example by imposing conditions on mergers, or demanding higher standards of responsible behaviour of those platforms and services that occupy a dominant position in the market. In Germany, for example, the revised Federal Antitrust Act introduces a new notion of 'super-market dominance' and a number of updates to competition law that are designed to deal with the particular economic characteristics of multisided platform markets with strong 'winner takes all' features (as described by Barwise and Watkins 2018). The German experience is likely to be of wider interest because this is the broad approach of the European Union under the Digital Markets Act, which sets out a new range of constraints on the behaviours of the largest 'Gatekeeper' players, who will be obliged to offer open, interoperable access to their services and data.[4]

The gatekeeper role of intermediaries between consumers and news, and the extent to which the market power and position of social and search intermediaries enables them to extract value from news without paying for its production, has been a running sore for many years, although both parties have interests in creating policy solutions. The Australian News Media Bargaining Code regulates the terms of trade and revenue split between platforms and news producers and imposes strong transparency requirements on the platforms. This follows a number of attempts—such as in relation to Google News in Spain[5]—to shift the balance of power in favour of publishers. Platforms have ample opportunity to game these policy attempts by removing individual services from specific markets: another reason why an holistic approach is needed.

Methods to Prevent Moat-Building

Competition law and regulation is not only about price and quality: it has always engaged social goals to protect the public interest and these can be incorporated as general competition law is updated for the platform economy: companies can be obliged for example to protect media plurality, and the particular challenges of data dominance and super-market dominance can be addressed. From a consumer perspective, individual sector-specific regimes can do a great deal to increase levels of open competition, but may require a more proactive approach of legislators to design specific rules, for example in relation to the massively concentrated VOD sector (for an approach to this for online audio-visual content see Eli M. Noam in Chapter 3).

Mop and Bucket

Legislation to protect against misuse of platforms by malign actors and mitigate negative externalities.

INTRODUCTION OF NEW OFFENCES AND DEFINITIONS OF ILLEGAL CONTENT

One approach to what economists call 'negative social externalities' and policymakers increasingly call 'online harms' has been to seek to define new offences and codes to control 'bad actors' and 'bad conduct' through both criminal and civil law. This reflects a consensus that market incentives and pure self-regulation have failed to protect consumers from harm. The French law on manipulation of elections[6] is one such example, but particularly in Europe concern about hate speech and terrorism has led to a debate about whether new offences such as online gender-based violence should be included in order to restrict the worst harms online.

LIABILITY AND CONTENT

A new generation of legal and regulatory approaches to online harm involve providing legal and liability structures that create strong incentives for platforms to establish effective processes for identifying and removing harmful content in general. Through the European Union's proposed Digital Services Act, the United Kingdom's Online Harms legislation and Germany's Netz DG, Internet intermediaries are being migrated from a regime in which they were largely protected from liability until they had knowledge of content, to one in which they have a general 'duty of care' to protect people from harmful content. The *duty of care* concept and its application is discussed by its originators, William Perrin and Lorna Woods in Chapter 5.[7] Platforms can also be regulated to make public interest content more prominent, for example during elections (for more on this, see Jacob Rowbottom in Chapter 13). During the pandemic the tech giants were vocal in claiming that they were doing their best to promote trusted health information, but this ad hoc approach needs direction and accountability in addition to protection from censorship and propaganda.

COPYRIGHT AND PATENTS

The business ecology of content delivery in the data and advertising economy requires content businesses to contract with platforms and agree on a revenue split. This in turn requires legal structures and enforcement of intellectual property rights. Dominance enables platforms to set a price, and news providers attempts to bargain collectively have not been successful. At times, platforms have been criticized for exploiting and freeriding on the investment of news providers. Not only the terms of trade but also the enforcement of intellectual property rights by public authorities is contested, for example, when platforms are accused of selling advertising around news they do not fund or displaying snippets of news. Public authorities could choose to enforce existing laws more effectively or, as in the

Australian News Bargaining Code, they could empower news providers in that negotiation in light of their public value.

Safety Mask and Gloves

New protections for citizens and consumers from harms suffered on, or as a consequence of, dominant technology platforms.

INTRODUCTION OF NEW ETHICAL CODES AND RULES
At a level below the threshold for illegal content, which platforms increasingly refer to as 'lawful but awful' content, moderation codes and principles are constantly revised (Gillespie 2018). In the case of the most dominant platforms of all, users face huge switching costs. This has two implications, first they are unable to choose an alternative, perhaps a more liberal or more protective moderation policy, and second, decisions to remove speech under the policy tend to be irreversible. As a result, these codes have rightly been referred to as forms of privatized speech control and censorship. In Europe, the European Commission has been involved in a good deal of proactive coordination of codes on Hate Speech, Terrorism, and Disinformation, which are monitored (for example, the EU Code of Conduct on Disinformation). There are multiple ways of strengthening liability and changing the incentives on harms. Kornbluh and Goodman, for example, propose making liability exemptions conditional on ethical codes.[8]

NEW STRUCTURES AND LEGITIMACY STRATEGIES FOR SELF-REGULATION
The Facebook Oversight board is a valiant attempt to generate legitimacy for a form of self-regulation that has largely fallen into disrepute. The previous Right to be Forgotten Panel and the failed Google AI ethics Council show that platforms are prepared to sink resources into these exercises and are generating significant insight into the ethical dilemmas and responsibilities their position entails. Ultimately, the platforms are signalling that they think they can resolve the problems themselves, though they will—when pressed—admit that they need to do so in an economic and legal context that establishes the appropriate incentives. If those incentives are in place, there is no doubt that some progress towards ethical responsibility can be made, but if they are not, self-regulatory attempts will remain merely PR exercises. In the European Union, the European Commission and national governments have a long track record of developing and encouraging self-regulatory codes and institutions,[9] such as the codes on hate speech, disinformation, and terrorism, and the 2020 proposals for a Digital Services Act, if passed, would strengthen significantly the incentives to self regulate.

GREATER CONTROL OF PERSONAL DATA
Given the centrality of personal data to the new economic model of surveillance capitalism, the control of this input would be a critical means not only for protecting rights but also for introducing incentives that might genuinely change a

business model that is based on constant, intrusive, automated surveillance. One suggestion is that businesses should not in any sense own personal data, but they should be obligated to take proper care of it as public trustees (Philip Napoli, Chapter 8). Ghosh and Couldry have suggested that anonymity should be considered a 'conditional privilege'.[10] In Chapter 6 of this volume, Angela Phillips and Eleonora Mazzoli argue that effective implementation of the data minimization principle of the GDPR, together with other measures could create the conditions for the emergence of a new public service model for search.

User data is the key resource of the new surveillance capitalism model, and therefore the regulatory settlement for data is not only a means to protect user rights but also a means to shape the business model and behaviour of the new platforms. The intensifying threats posed by data to individual interests in the age of AI are highlighted by Frank Pasquale's discussion of health data in Chapter 10. Because the inferences made with regard to a growing range of personal data are growing, and potentially have both beneficial and negative implications for their subjects, it will be necessary to maintain careful control of that data. Ownership and control by the data subject, or information intermediaries, do not provide an easy answer, because the problem of actual and potential inferences nonetheless remains. In his chapter, Philip Napoli suggests a radical approach, reconceptualizing user data in order to reflect its position as a scarce public resource. Like spectrum to broadcasting, the use of user data under effectively a licensing regime would enable regulators to require benefits in return: not only in terms of how that data is protected and exploited and its consequences for individual users, but in terms of the wider implications for public value.

Scaffolding and Ladders

Reconfiguring technological and fiscal infrastructure to reduce the power of the platforms and enable a more mixed ecosystem.

DECENTRALIZATION THROUGH CODE AND TECHNOLOGICAL ARCHITECTURE
Part of the solution to digital dominance can come from technical solutions, standards, code, and design principles such as decentralization. Not only in the field of media law and policy, but in relation to AI ethics, recent years have seen a slew of publications of new principles for privacy by design, safety by design, leading to the wider notion of 'X' by design, in which 'X' stands for ethics.[11] Some of this relates to the structure of the Internet itself, in other words to the interdependent ecology of technical standards, software, numbering, and other resources and interconnection protocols which enable various forms of information exchange to occur.

But such standards and design questions belong firmly to the realm of private companies and multistakeholder coordination often working at a global level. The companies that hold sway within these multistakeholder bodies operate within company law in capitalist societies; companies, including those that form the subject of this book, are obliged to serve their shareholders, and thus there is only so much that they can do to reform themselves. The extent to which the design ethics movement can create forms of professional closure necessary to enforce a genuinely ethical design in a global market characterized by deep fragmentation in terms of the fundamental philosophy applied[12] remains unclear. Paul Nemitz and Matthias Pfeffer sketch out a technological wishlist that covers AI, decentralization, data, interconnectivity and other infrastructural issues in Chapter 15.

INCENTIVIZING NEW MODELS OF OWNERSHIP

Internet Governance 1.0 has emerged within a particular framework of capitalism that dates to the deregulation of the 1990s and a concern with economic growth based on deregulated 'neoliberal' corporations and private value (Mazzucato et al., Chapter 2). The companies that the two Digital Dominance volumes have been concerned with are joint stock companies, and therefore legally responsible primarily to their shareholders and to create maximum private value returns. These are not the only possible models for such institutions. Broadcasting, for example, evolved a plurality of models such as trusts, public ownership, ownership caps, limited liability companies, and community ownership. The same could be true for the new Internet ecology, and there is a strong argument that the public interest would be served by a mixed ecology of models, such as the cooperative model outlined by Nathan Schneider in Chapter 4.

There are a range of new approaches to company structures which have relevance for tech platforms in particular, in relation to their role in enabling free expression and democratic deliberation. Search and social media companies may have started with lofty objectives of connecting humans and knowledge, but their worthy ambitions were compromised when they needed to raise investment from private equity and form organizations consistent with existing company law and the contemporary framework of neoliberal capitalism. There are many alternatives, which are being promoted with increasing urgency. To take some examples: charity, trust, cooperative, and social enterprises, as well as benefit corporations would take some pressure away from the constant pressure to deliver short- to medium-term value to shareholders. Charity law offers beneficial tax and liability status, but only in exchange for measurable delivery on agreed charitable public purposes, trusts and cooperatives. B-Corp ownership[13] could build in an ethics—for example to serve truth, deliberation, and trust, for example—into the articles of association of a company, and enable a wider notion of responsibility to deliver public and social value and control externalities. As a long-term goal, public policy could foster the development of plural models—including for example public service search engines (see Mazzoli and Philips, Chapter 6) through application of fiscal incentives, charity law, competition law, data portability, and public subsidy.

STRATEGIC USE OF TAXATION

Taxation provides powerful incentive structures and can be used both to encourage best practice (for example by offering tax breaks to 'prosocial' platforms) and to mitigate harms. It can be used to recuperate revenue from the GAFAM companies; deployed effectively, it can also be a means to shape and incentivize their behaviours and in time to restructure their business models. In Chapter 7, Elda Brogi and Roberta Carlini review the range of 'news taxes' being considered around the world, including by the OECD and the US Biden administration.[14] There is a clear need for joining up policy silos here: these are obviously to be considered alongside alternative funding settlements on intellectual property and the terms of trade.

User Manuals

Coupling media literacy with consumer empowerment.

NEW MEDIA PROFICIENCY

Media literacy is proposed as a response to the challenges of digital dominance.[15] There are various versions of this argument: on the one hand users can be empowered to protect themselves from various forms of manipulation, be aware of propaganda and fakery, and even be aware of the wider business model of surveillance capitalism. In other versions, the emphasis is placed on the ability of users to switch away from those services that operate against the consumer interest and appeals to the altruism of users to take into account social value in their individual consumption choices. This is a well-travelled path in public policy, particularly as regards complex 'wicked' policy problems in economically strategic industries. The path of least resistance is to place some transparency obligations, deal with barriers to switching, and expect consumers to do the rest. This might work in some cases, but in general such an approach places too much pressure on consumers.[16] Switching costs may simply be too high, for example the economic and social costs of leaving a social network. In any case, the current decline in democratic legitimacy and trust might be too important to rely on consumers alone. Media literacy as a policy solution is also likely to enhance already existing inequalities—consolidating and enhancing the advantages of those with skills and resources, so any media literacy initiatives must be combined with other measures. The behavioural and economic incentives to stay with a platform are widely commented upon: and the switching costs and 'consumer lock-in' identified by Barwise et al. in the previous volume (2018) have intensified, given the lack of effect of the data portability obligations of the GDPR. Digital literacy ought to encourage consumer empowerment and switching, but only when combined with tougher new competition legislation—such as the German Antitrust Act described by Hartmann and Holznagel—can we have some confidence that they will work.

Scissors and Scalpels

Developing specific rules and obligations around critical political and social issues.

SPECIFIC RULES IN CRITICAL AREAS, SUCH AS ELECTIONS

we closed the first volume of Digital Dominance—in which we set out some of the impacts that Digital Dominance was having on society—on public interests, and above all on democracy—by highlighting the implications of Digital Dominance for elections. We argued then that the threat to election legitimacy makes digital dominance an existential issue for liberal democracies. Democracy and elections have been under threat, and arguably continue to be under threat, in a polarized and conflictual environment in which freedom of expression and the open Internet are seen as vulnerabilities that can be exploited. The years since that volume was published have seen a wave of new publications of standards and recommendations on elections, including those that are summarized in Chris Marsden, Ian Brown, and Michael Veale's chapter in this volume (Chapter 11). The 2020 legislation published by the European Union justified the new EU approach to regulation of platforms on the basis of the threat they pose to democracy.[17] Clearly, part of the response will be to ensure that dominant big tech companies are subject to effective regulation. But it may take time to turn around these tankers, and in the meantime elections as the site of democratic legitimacy must be protected (as highlights by the chapters by Marsden et al and Rowbottom). Moreover, we need to recognize that there are elements of these platforms that compromise their ability to act as democratic public spaces during election campaigns, and that we will need—in addition—alternative public spheres built on different principles, as Martin Moore sets out in Chapter 12.

PROMINENCE OBLIGATIONS

During the 2020–2021 pandemic all platforms actively sought to make trusted sources of health information prominent as part of the Covid response. Thus negative content regulation (broadly, taking stuff down or making it harder to find) is mirrored also by positive content regulation ('prominence' or promotion of content). In Europe, policymakers have actively sought to develop a public accountability framework for prominence, arguing that such sensitive decisions should be subject to checks and balances to ensure that they are not used for soft propaganda[18]. As with elections, such interventions represent the natural extension of the types of public interest obligations that existed in the broadcast world to the world of dominant platforms (see Moore; Rowbottom).

Universal and Multitools

Creating globally shared norms and methods of coordinated action.

DEVELOPING FUNDAMENTAL RIGHTS (SUCH AS PRIVACY AND FREEDOM OF EXPRESSION)

One of the complications of the role of intermediaries as regards fundamental rights is that they are both speakers and conduits for the speech of others. As such there is a good deal of international confusion as regards the application of fundamental rights categories to them (Tambini, this volume). Bodies like the Council of Europe and the UN Human Rights Committee should take a lead in resolving this, in coordination with the United States though not constrained by it, and in the longer-term drawing other countries into line with global standards (see also Marsden et al.'s recommendation number four). Central to the contemporary challenge within the international rules- based order is the lack of agreement on common frameworks between democracies. That is why the standards set by bodies such as the UN Human Rights Committee[19] and the Council of Europe have such an important role to play. As Damian Tambini points out in Chapter 16, at a time when democracy and free expression is threatened, it is time to end the narcissism of small differences between democratic countries and work purposefully towards agreed standards and definitions on the global level. As the platforms take on some of the functions of media but also deploy of powerful AI driven by personal data, it will be necessary to develop new standards of media freedom.

REGIONAL AND GLOBAL COORDINATION

In the European Union, the Digital Services Act attempts to coordinate these various levels into something like a coherent process. This process, which works within a framework of human rights and democracy, will prove crucial to protecting European democracy from challenges to its legitimacy from the new media barons of Digital Dominance. One aspect of this is innovation in coordination between existing regulatory agencies, which has already intensified in the case of European communications regulators in recent years. In Chapter 9, Ben Wagner and Lublos Kuklis argue that such coordination should focus on creating an auditing mechanism for the personal and other data accessed and used by regulators across Europe.

Coordination at the global level has been much less effective than intra-European cooperation due to national security considerations and the divergence both between democracies and non-democracies, and among democracies. Since the first World Summit on the Information Society in 2003, global Internet governance has embraced multistakeholder governance as a form of loose coordination of accountability mechanisms, standards bodies, private standard setters, and civil society organizations dealing with the Internet. The model has been effective in supporting communication during the initial phase of global Internet development, but it has not been effective in shaping an Internet business model that supports democratic deliberation and human well-being. It is time for more formal global coordination, and this should be achieved through bodies established within a human rights framework and according to UN values. As Bob Fay shows in Chapter 14, the first steps to such a global coordination framework are relatively simple, and urgent given the need for global standards on AI and personal data. The time has come to take positive steps to create new multilateral institutions, for example to establish a global Digital Standards Board as an intergovernmental organization to supplement the private/civil society work of bodies like the Internet Governance Forum.

This is of course an incomplete list: the key point here is that it is not the case that governments can do little or nothing in the face of platform power. The tools at the disposal of parliaments and governments are in fact immense and varied. As we discuss in the concluding chapter however, one reason that the move from proposals to actions has been slow is that there is a tendency to a silo approach with antitrust, data, content, and harm constituting separate policy streams and forms of institutionalized negotiation. In fact, these various forms of policy are interdependent in complex ways, and must be coordinated. The antitrust 'settlement', for example, might contain elements of undertakings and social policy in that dominant companies may undertake to mitigate negative externalities. Taxation policy might have a social policy element by attempting to incentivize behavioural change. And the future of a plural and democratic media depends on a combination of structural and behavioural rules. This is why a holistic policy overview is necessary.

A NEW SOCIAL CONTRACT

All in all, the growth and autonomy of large communication intermediaries, including liability protection, should no longer be treated as unconditional liberties. They should become conditional on certain ethics and norms of behaviour as the basis of a new social contract. This is too important to be left to the market, in light of the evidence that shareholder and individually owned companies are unable to respond to social pressures whilst maintaining their profit model.

The political will is building, and the European Union in particular offers a framework for a new social contract in its proposal for a Digital Services Act. But the United States lags behind and decisive action has yet to be taken. The sheer volume of government, parliamentary, civil society, and academic reports on the topic is overwhelming, so much so that only the well-resourced public policy departments of these huge companies are in a position to follow—and game—the various institutional responses.

It is therefore crucial to take short-term measures to protect the legitimacy of elections, as well as longer term thinking about how all of these aspects of media governance: competition, architecture, taxation, liability, taxation, and fundamental rights should develop. In the conclusion to this book we outline three potential routes forward, and the implications of taking of taking each of these paths. Eventually, as Victor Pickard writes in Chapter 17, democracies need to negotiate a new social contract with the technology platforms. In traditional regulatory theory, introduction of competition will lead to consumer welfare gains. But the problems associated with tech giants go beyond individual consumer welfare and relate to societal and public value, and in particular democracy and human autonomy. The challenge will be to shape a new design for a new settlement between the state, private actors and citizens.

NOTES

1. Moore, M and Tambini, D, (eds) Digital Dominance: The Power of Google, Amazon, Facebook and Apple. Oxford University Press 2018.
2. There has been an almost constant stream of litigation about dominance and abuse of dominant position. In the European Commission, Google was fined E1.49 bn in 2019 and E4.34 bn in 2018. Most of these related to google prioritizing its own services in search results. There has been a wide range of other platform competition including such cases as Microsoft/Skype. As yet such cases focus on consumer interests and price, rather than the social externalities and media pluralism implications of a merger.
3. https://blogs.lse.ac.uk/medialse/2018/05/02/how-to-break-up-facebook/.
4. European Commission. Proposal for a Regulation on Digital Markets (December 2020).
5. Wired (2014).
6. French Law no. 2018–1202.
7. The notion of duties of care is similar to the proposed concept of information fiduciaries (Balkin 2016; see also Khan and Posten 2019; Napoli in this volume).
8. Kornbluh and Goodman (2019).
9. Tambini et al. (2008).
10. See Digital Realignment. Rebalancing Platform Economies from Corporation to Consumer. Ghosh, Dipayan and Couildry, Nick. 2020. https://www.hks.harvard.edu/sites/default/files/centers/mrcbg/files/AWP_155_final2.pdf
11. See the discussion in Behavioural Insights Team and Doteveryone (2020).
12. Tambini (2021).
13. The B-Corp movement is campaigning for changes to company law that would encourage all corporations to incorporate deeper and wider notions of wider social benefit. See www.benefitcorp.net. In the UK context this would entail making changes to section 172 of the Companies Act in order to widen the duties of directors.
14. Politi et al. (2021).
15. See for example Marsden et al., this volume: recommendation 3.
16. Tambini (2012) http://eprints.lse.ac.uk/43054/
17. As outlined in the EU Democracy Action Plan (2020).
18. Mazzoli and Tambini (2020).
19. UN General Comment 34 on Freedoms of Opinion and Expression July 2011. https://www2.ohchr.org/english/bodies/hrc/docs/gc34.pdf.

REFERENCES

Balkin 2016. Balkin, Jack M., Information Fiduciaries and the First Amendment (February 3, 2016). UC Davis Law Review, Vol. 49, No. 4, 2016, Yale Law School, Public Law Research Paper No. 553, Available at SSRN: https://ssrn.com/abstract=2675270

Behavioural Insights Team and Doteveryone. 2020. 'Active Online Choices: Designing to Empower Users'. Centre for Data Ethics and Innovation. https://

www.bi.team/wp-content/uploads/2020/11/CDEI-Active-Online-Choices-Update-Report-FOR-PUBLICATION-2.pdf.

Khan and Posten. 2019.

Kornbluh, Karen, and Ellen Goodman. 2019. 'Bringing Truth to the Internet'. *Democracy Journal*. https://democracyjournal.org/magazine/53/bringing-truth-to-the-internet/.

Politi, James, Aime Williams, and Chris Giles. 2021. 'US Offers New Plan in Global Corporate Tax Talks'. FT.com, April 8. https://www.ft.com/content/847c5f77-f0af-4787-8c8e-070ac6a7c74f.

Tambini, Damian. 2012. 'Consumer Representation in UK Communications Policy and Regulation'. *Info* 14 (2): 3–16. http://eprints.lse.ac.uk/43054/.

Tambini (2021) Media Freedom. Polity.

Tambini et al. (2008). Codifying Cyberspace. Communications Self Regulation in the Age of Internet Convergence. Routledge.

Wired. 2014. 'Spain's Google News Shutdown Is a Silly Victory for Publishers', December 16. https://www.wired.com/2014/12/google-news-shutdown-spain-empty-victory-publishers/.

PART I

Enhancing Competition

Reshaping Platform-Driven Digital Markets

MARIANA MAZZUCATO, JOSH ENTSMINGER,
AND RAINER KATTEL ■

INTRODUCTION

Capitalism has always excelled at creating new desires and cravings. With digital platforms and algorithms, however, tech companies have both accelerated and inverted this process. Rather than just creating new goods and services in anticipation of what people might want, they already know what we will want and, more than simply catering to future desires, are attempting to sell us our future selves (Mazzucato 2019; Zuboff 2019). To change this will require focusing directly on the prevailing business model, and specifically on the source of economic rents, which have been naturalized as pro-consumer mechanisms and features, while disadvantaging supplier and content producers (O'Reilly 2019). Rather than simply assuming that economic rents are all the same, economic policymakers should be trying to understand how platform algorithms allocate value among consumers, suppliers, and the platform itself. While some allocations may reflect real competition, others are being driven by value extraction rather than value creation.

Creating an environment that rewards genuine value creation and punishes value extraction is the fundamental economic challenge of our time. Rather than talking about regulation, then, we need to go further, embracing concepts such as co-creation and market shaping towards value creation. Governments can and should be shaping markets to ensure that collectively created value serves collective ends. Likewise, competition policy should not be focused solely on the question of size of platform. Breaking up large companies would not solve the problems of value extraction and will remain insufficient for addressing rights or building innovation for consumer welfare.

We propose that policymakers should focus on understanding how platforms create and extract value, and how policymakers could conceive and build a digital economy which rewards platform value creation and marginalizes or removes value-extractive behaviour. We will look at the relationship between the economic power of platforms and new theories of how platform value is created—and the implications of contemporary framings of regulation and antitrust. We do so by first unpicking the embedded nature of innovation, and how its direction depends on the governance of the relationship between the public and the private sector, as well as governance relationships within both.

We do not intend to provide an exhaustive technical definition of what is and is not a platform; indeed, a core issue in antitrust and platform governance remains the lack of a singular accepted definition of platforms (Coyle 2018, 3). Rather, for our purposes a platform is a general market mechanism for building two-sided and multisided markets. As such, our concern is not with platforms per se, it is with the specific characteristics, conduct, strategies, ecosystems, and business models of the firms who have leveraged platform economics to their advantage in digital environments.

POLITICS OF INNOVATION IN PLATFORM ECONOMIES

Innovation is a cumulative process embedded in institutions and contractual relationships (Nelson 1993). This assumes that the value created through innovation is collectively generated by a range of stakeholders, including the private sector, the state, and civil society (Polanyi 1944; Mazzucato 2018). In other words, the market and the economy itself are an outcome of the interactions between these sectors.

This embedded nature of innovation and value helps us understand how platforms evolve. Platforms are increasingly taken to be hallmarks of innovative societies and entrepreneurial ecosystem development—not least because modern platforms are online ecosystems, implying a wide digital capacity in the social and corporate base to effectively use these platforms. Over the last two decades, firms which leverage aggregation and platform features have come to take a predominant place in the corporate landscape. The most commonly referenced of these firms, described as the tech giants relative to US-based firms—Alphabet/Google, Amazon, Apple, and Facebook—have gained established market positions, consolidating search, e-commerce, operating systems, and digital advertising markets internationally. While these are the key firms currently under debate, the scope of this chapter concerns the features of both existing dominant platforms and future models of platform dominance—where, beyond the existing theory of platform benevolence, or neutral agentive relationship to the ecosystem a platform supports, the dominance of a platform has both internal and external constitutive effects.

While the economics of platforms are well understood and capitalized upon, we cannot begin from the position that our relationships to platforms, and the transactions mediated by them, are without political implications or substantive information asymmetries. Whether subject to consolidated private ownership or peer production and cooperative frameworks, platform approaches are shaped by particular regulatory and legal environments, corporate governance models, user sentiments, market segmentation, and technological constraints as well as variations in the relationships among all such elements. In other words, platforms, like markets, are embedded in how we govern them. The key differentiation is that platforms serve as both agents and essential mechanisms, and how platforms not only exist in but also shape and compose the nature of modern digital markets renders them a unique analytic problem.

Modern digital capitalism is following the direction of extractive data capitalism (Zuboff 2019)[1] where platforms, as the primary agents enabling both primary data extraction and the demand for data-extractive and data-continent business models, are involved in an ecosystem of innovation to empower and improve such models. Modern platform varieties do not provide a neutral base for firm behaviour; rather, we pose that merchants in platform ecosystems increasingly comport to the requirements and means of best leveraging the tools provided by platforms, establishing a direct link between platform service provision, the larger market for data, and how merchants can feasibly build competitive strategies in platform-driven markets. Therefore, the scope of market shaping exceeds the primary extractive behaviour of platforms and involves the primary relationship between the aggregate impact of platform incentives for data extraction, and the market reliance and demand for such modes.

The embedded nature of platforms raises the question, what is the real distribution of risk and reward relative to the power and scale of such innovations? Credit card companies, as Harold Feld notes, achieved scale and monopoly potential through the publicly funded telecommunication networks (Feld 2019, 33). In parallel, the current platforms derive their advantage from the collective effects enabled by broad Internet access from public investment and continued development. In turn, we can attune the idea to the question of advancements in GPS and publicly funded intelligent infrastructure, relative to their exceptional usage by digital firms (Mazzucato 2013; 2018, 182).

There are three main arguments concerning the regulation of platform giants. The first posits that the platform giants have accrued too much market power, requiring antitrust measures (Warren 2019). In this analysis, antitrust metrics are suitable for evaluation and are warranted in the scenario. The second posits that while platform giants have gained broad strategic capacity and economies of scale, antitrust analysis may underevaluate or misevaluate the problem, leaving alternative regulatory tools and considerations as more viable (Khan 2018a, 100–101; O'Reilly 2019; Furman 2019, 4). The third posits that while platform giants have exceptional economies of scale and capacity, antitrust analysis effectively shows that regulatory intervention is not warranted and improved self- regulatory action from the market can suffice (Bourne 2019).

While all three positions recognize the complexity and importance of platform governance and regulatory discussions, all rely upon a common theoretical framework of market failure theory for designing, legitimizing, and critiquing government interventions (Kattel et al. 2018; Mazzucato 2013). Rather than acting as a functional model of analysis, market failure extends to serve as a theory to legitimize government intervention, framing a broader position on the identification of the desirable relationship between government and the market. The central idea here is that the point of regulation is to get markets to perform correctly, where this means to approach as closely as possibly 'competitive markets'. This model not only is foundational in common public choice and public management literatures but also informs the foundation of common policy and competition evaluation and accounting manuals (HM Treasury 2018, 12–39; OECD 2008, 2019) This approach emphasizes the idea that, given certain assumptions, individuals pursuing their own self-interest in competitive markets gives rise to the most efficient outcomes (Samuelson 1947; Mas-Colell et al. 1995, 539–40). Efficiency is understood in a utilitarian sense, whereby an activity is efficient if it enhances someone's welfare without making anyone else worse off (so-called Pareto efficiency). As already indicated by Arrow (1962), while a market failure approach can be used to understand why, for example, private firms underinvest in R&D, it is not so useful for guiding policy choices for public investment in R&D, because of the inherent uncertainty involved in the outcomes of such investment.

Under these conditions, the role of government intervention (such as regulation) is in practice often limited to addressing instances where the market is unable to deliver Pareto-efficient outcomes. Such 'market failures' arise when there are information asymmetries, transaction costs, and frictions to smooth exchange, or non-competitive markets (e.g., monopolies) or externalities, whereby an activity harms another agent not directly connected with the market transaction (e.g., pollution), or coordination and information failures that hamper investment (Rodrik 1996).

We argue that all prevailing approaches to platform governance referred to above aim to promote market efficiency without anticompetitive pricing, and to utilize data reintegration for service improvement without third-party manipulation. In our view, this does not satisfy the need to understand positive public value creation, which is left undertheorized and underdescribed in prevailing approaches. The starting point of analysis should not be the market condition relative to legitimate state intervention, but the nature of the state-market relationships as it shapes the behaviour of participants. In the context of the platforms, the problem is the limited restriction of the behaviour of a given platform, or a change in the system by which platform behaviour emerges, is incentivized, and spreads.

Platform governance concerns both the behaviour of specific market agents and the role of these agents in shaping the business models of a larger ecosystem of online players; to shape the business models of platforms is, by extension, to reshape the potential incentives for using and acquiring data from thousands of other firms. The remit of government questioning and investigation of these business models cannot be limited to the concern over short-run, anticompetitive pricing models. It must extend to asking, what kind of digital economy do we want?

What kinds of market characteristics of future digital economy are desirable, and which are not?

FROM MARKET POWER TO PLATFORM POWER

A primary issue facing the platform antitrust debate is whether, or to what extent, the nuances of platform economics and platform behaviour are effectively captured under existing analytic models and conventions for effective regulatory assessment. While improvements to market power analysis and anticompetitive behaviour assessments can help to improve the health of the digital economy as well as the market-shaping role of platforms in driving and building the future market characteristics of digital economies.

Platforms exhibit multiple functions and there is function-oriented competition between them. LinkedIn often functions as an employee-employer matchmaking service; however, it functionally serves as a social network, microblogging and content distribution platform, news and information dissemination platform, skill aggregation platform, and advertising distribution platform (Feld 2019, 38). These functions are reciprocally reinforcing to improve the amount of time a user spends on the platform, as well as the intensity and variety of engagement, improving overall data collection and platform development. Yet the question of function yields a deeper concern over potential misapprehension of competition by policymakers (Feld 2019, 38).

The main platforms are branching out beyond conventional improvements to the direct online service. In relation to the concern over data extraction and data hoarding, the question is the increasing scope of these firms' involvement in the otherwise offline elements of our daily lives through a new generation of smart devices and new models of interaction with them. The question regarding competition and development concerns improvements to the scope of the means for data collection—with increasing numbers of interactions, types of interactions, and interaction intensity—and the increasing oligopoly of data hoarding, both relative to and independent of primary service improvement, where the stakes concern the increasing remit of domains of viable consumption and information-gathering driving an exhaustion potential for the scope of digital intermediation. Platforms compete not simply over how much time you spend online but also over the increasing scope of including otherwise offline moments, practices, and institutions in digital domains; platforms compete over the creation of new markets for the total digitalization of everyday life. Furthermore, we can consider the reinvestment of data into interface and user experience for stickiness by design. As Christine Tucker notes relative to network effects, the strategic equation is not simply scale, but scale and stickiness (Tucker 2018). The drivers of stickiness are user-contingent and focus on the reinvestment of behavioural data into the nuances of user design. However, such addiction by design is not exhaustive for user behaviours relative to repeated use. The concern over stickiness is drivers of preferences relative to alternatives, and the non-existence of true alternatives.

Facebook has function-similar competitors, but it does not have a direct English-language competitor per se. This matters when considering the heterogeneous nature of network effects, as well as the nature of product- or service-specific assessment of competitive behaviour relative to firm size. In designed environments, it is increasingly unclear what counts as a free market.

Platforms are engaged in increasing verticalization of core digital services. Google is not simply a search engine but also provides video chat, email, and web browser services, among others. This means an increasing data collection remit and an increasing reliance on primary services, as well as the provision of public value through safety, privacy, and efficiency. The relative scope of digital services involved in such verticalization serves two additional concerns. The first is the friction of user experience across functions, helping to improve stickiness. The second is the consolidation of power over meta-functions, such as the privacy and security which all these services demand, thus increasing the power of the decisions Google makes relative to these features.

The specifics of platform features create unique challenges for assessing how competitive effects serve as countervailing forces to check the market power, as well as the prominence, of specific market characteristics. Two-sided markets do not compete with one another in the same fashion as one-sided markets. Improvements to specific market power metrics may help to improve how regulators understand the competitive dynamics of platform-driven markets, as well as the theoretical suitability of antitrust. Such metrics, however, will remain non-advantageous for assessing the additional functions which platforms maintain.

The features posed in this section were selected to show that while market power and strategic market status help to distinguish potential anticompetitive behaviours in the classic sense, multisided market-attuned versions of analysis are in need of a more progressive analysis to better assess the nuances and implications of how platform features relate to desirable market states and evolve independently. This latent concern over the suitability of existing analytic tools has generated a division between appealing to market power and appealing to platform power (Khan 2017; Lynskey 2017, 7), wherein platform power is a distinct formulation of the competitive and social attributes of modern platforms relative to the nuances of digitally literate and platform-reliant markets and users, which themselves suffer from inconsistent framing (Lynskey 2017, 4). The question of power holds a double usage, as the concern is not simply market manipulation through the properties listed previously, but the social and political implications of the increasing consolidation of function and usage in these platforms (Lynskey 2017, 28).

The issue can be extended further, for even if we accept that Google, Facebook, or Amazon can be displaced, what will be more difficult to displace is the reliance on platform intermediaries, for which the verticalization of services and the increase in size hold increasing returns and high value for consumers. So, just as the power concern is for market analysis and sociopolitical implications, the latter demands further consideration of the power of existing platforms, as well as the power of the platform model independent of the current set of platform giants. Firms which leverage platform economics in their favour can enable value creation while also interacting more directly with the direction of the digital economy—the behaviour of modern platforms composes a disproportionate amount of the value created in direct digital economic environments, serving to shape how business models of other firms in such environments relate to directionality of markets.

Market power is intended to call attention to consumer harm as well as anticompetitive behaviour, causing market inefficiencies leading to decreasing aggregate welfare. Market power theories and tests tend to be user- and consumer-focused. However, such theories tend to underdefine the specific problems and properties of platform-mediated user behaviour and different kinds of digital harms. Like market power, platform power helps to attune attention to precise anticompetitive elements, such as arguments on the nature of the verticalization of seemingly non-competitive services in the case of Google and Facebook. More directly, multisided markets are insufficiently described and assessed by competition tools built on considerations of single-sided markets and firms (Evans 2013; Feld 2019).

The competing critiques from market power and platform power approaches to one another show both the promise and the limits of expanding analysis within those frameworks. A more attuned model of market power can reduce ad hoc considerations of conventional and unconventional market dynamics; improvements to platform power can retool understandings of platform behaviour and multisided market-specific considerations for potentially unique anticompetitive behaviour and incentives, as well as the constituent features of innovation within platform moderated ecosystems. Each theory can be approached as a mutually exclusive concept, or they can be considered as analytic lens, which, by layering, can help to further differentiate competing claims on the nature of platform impact on market and innovation dynamics.

However, both market power and platform power theories are insufficiently descriptive of how value is created, extracted, and distributed, as well as of the role of platforms in collective value creation processes among public, private, and civic sectors. Such a value theory can help to attune not only whether platform regulation might shape innovation relative to platform-driven ecosystems but also the kind of innovation that can enable the kind of positive market ecosystems deemed desirable. Where in many policy arenas the concern for policymakers is to improve the rate of digital economic development and investment, the question of platform governance must concern both the rate and direction, as the model of platform behaviour currently shapes how market characteristics in digital environments emerge, evolve, and become dominant.

VALUE CREATION AND VALUE EXTRACTION

Platforms have consolidated enormous wealth and valuations by improving allocative efficiency through the reorganization of information asymmetries (Feld 2019, 22). The value-creating capacity invites parallel concerns that any such dominant position in resolving these informational problems provides disproportionate opportunity and means for value extraction. The consolidation of decision-making power in allocative mechanisms influences what users see when they search, perform online purchases, and pursue online services (O'Reilly 2019). While technology changes frequently and is therefore difficult to establish as the primary focus of regulatory concern, the function which technology performs may serve as a focal point of attention. In this case, the question of value creation relative to the dominance in allocative functions derived by multisided markets at scale can help to reorganize regulatory attention in terms of potential value extraction from suppliers and consumers. As such, to help expand such a position, we intend to leverage a theory of rents to help improve the differentiation between value creation and value extraction.

Value creation is our primary concern, but each generation of economists has a different relationship to the assessment and analytics of value. For classical economists the question of value concerns three separate categories of income: these concern profits for capitalists derived from production, wages distributed to labour by virtue of production, and rents distributed to owners of assets critical to production (Mazzucato et al. 2020). The latter points to the idea that such assets often had little to no cost of production and thereby marginal or non-existent opportunity costs. The classic example concerns the ownership of land and natural resources, for which an individual can achieve natural monopoly, charging a price for use without adding anything to the essential productive value of the resource itself.

Modern capitalist systems are encumbered by rent- and value-extraction activities (Mazzucato 2018; Mazzucato et al. 2020). The two most noted cases remain the executive pay gap and the increasing financial allocation of resources away from the real economy towards unproductive activities. Yet the real economy, beyond the housing sector, is not inexperienced with rents. Network monopolies in telecoms, monopolies in natural resources, natural and artificial monopolies in pharmaceuticals and knowledge-driven enterprises and increasing reward for share buy-back schemes represent critical issues facing modern competitiveness agendas (Mazzucato et al 2020). Such concerns over value go to the heart of inequality analysis as well as deeper concerns over how to assemble accurate theories of why some kinds of distributive arrangements succeed and others fail—either in aligning value creation with appropriate models of risk and reward, or with direct improvements to value and social surplus redistribution mechanisms. In turn, we propose that a modern theory of rents, building out a model of digital economic rents, can help to improve the reasoning of policymakers on the kinds of value and allocative capacity which function to resolve fundamental social problems.

For our purposes, we will treat rents for the rest of this chapter under the following hypothesis—that rent is income earned in excess of the reward corresponding to the contribution of a factor of production to value creation (Mazzucato et al. 2020), wherein rent generally corresponds to a specific price-cost margin. However, in the context of platforms this conventional price-cost margin exercise can be insufficient and probably even misguided for assessing how value is extracted. Rather, a more careful awareness of risk and reward relative to their matchmaking systems helps to elicit just how value is created and destroyed among platforms (Mazzucato 2019). A platform which defers risk to suppliers while leveraging a demand-side economy of scale can multiply rewards without the comparable investment into risk reduction—a claim brought on by concerns against the policies of Uber and Lyft, which defer car ownership, maintenance, and benefits to individual suppliers. While such platforms privatize collectively generated rewards, the question is how risks are distributed and socialized relative to the distribution of those rewards.

Just as different rent practices exist, the conditions and models of rent extraction vary among sectors, industries, and even firms. While we cannot deal here with a full treatment (see Mazzucato et al. 2020), we intend one further clarification relative to the Schumpeterian rent and monopoly apologists. In this view rents and monopolies are productive when temporary—with rents being exceptional profits derived from increasing returns to technological innovation (Burlamaqui 2011). For instance, how platforms defer risk to their suppliers relative to the conservation of a demand-side economy of scale demands continuous attention (O'Reilly 2019). Such a problem is heavily tied to evaluations of major tech firms such as Google, Amazon, and Apple. For the purposes of this chapter, however, we can focus on two models of digital economic rents: network rents and algorithmic rents.

Network rents, although not unique to platforms, are profits derived from artificial monopoly creation and monopoly-independent gatekeeping functions through network effects (Mazzucato et al. 2020). Rather than monopoly advantages, network effects in digital markets mean platforms can more feasibly experience increasing marginal returns, at least in early-to-mid stages of scaling (Langley and Leyshon 2017; Srnicek 2017; Zuboff 2019). As exhibited by telecommunications, modern network rents concern the domination of e-commerce and search, and online distribution more broadly. These rents and monopoly phenomena are well understood—although the specific anticompetitive pricing and predatory pricing models pursued by platforms exhibiting monopoly conditions is a different concern (see Khan 2017, 791). In digital environments, network effect and heterogeneous network effect, contingent on monopoly status, create and extract rents differently than parallel offline agents. This uniqueness can be minimally attributed to the marginal cost properties and low-cost advantage of network creation in digital environments and with digital products. However, what is more interesting relative to our present concerns is the algorithmic form of rents. Algorithmic rents concern profits derived from the allocative power exercised by matchmaking systems (Mazzucato et al. 2020). Uber's surge and dynamic pricing, as Lina Khan notes, has normalized a perception of varying price to match supply and demand. However, Uber likely manipulates the in-app availability of both riders and users, while simultaneously selectively distributing coupons to users, effectively creating a differential charging scheme (Khan 2017, 763, 786). Yet more notably, the concern over algorithmic rents is expressed by search and display functions, and platform-produced product beneficence. This includes concern over whether Google, Amazon, and Apple uniquely privilege their own services to the detriment of suppliers, as well as exercising pricing over top positions (O'Reilly 2019). There are similar concerns over how Facebook and Google exert non-transparent algorithmic capacity in the allocation of advertising budgets for merchants. The concern is the distribution of risk and reward; the distribution of value-creating power relative to the valued feature of products, given the centralization of data capability as well as flows of consumer attention.[2] While the question of allocative power invites concern, allocative power is not in itself negative nor undesirable. However, when that power is non-transparent, or blatantly distributes rewards according to rent maximization, regulators should be more concerned and attentive. As such, the first concern from algorithmic rents for platforms is the embedding of such allocative power as an inherent, invisible mechanism.[3] While this behaviour is well-known, the suitability of existing regulatory tools and market heuristics to respond to non-Schumpeterian rents remains underdetermined. Rent helps to crystallize the concern over extractive practice relative to this allocative function, whereby the decisions by which value and income are allocated among users, merchants, and the platform itself becomes critical (O'Reilly 2018). In the decision process itself, these decisions are increasingly non-transparent—for instance, the relative opaqueness of value to small firms with a given advertising budget leveraging an advertising service such as Google or Facebook, as well as the real value to consumers. With the increasing feasibility of rent derivation from accrued allocative and algorithmic power, the distribution of platform and merchant incentives relative to improving means for further rent extraction, and relative to primary service improvement, needs awareness and more careful attention. Yet such potential rents are non-exhaustive with regard to the harm and undesirable scenario for social relations. We pose that the stakes of such centralization of allocative power are not simply the allocation of value among users, with potential platform beneficence. Rather, we should concern ourselves with the precise nature and variety of power as it derives from the control of markets and non-market information asymmetries.

We can consider the more troubling position of behavioural reinvestment of data for profiling and predictive analysis (Zuboff 2019). The irony of this position is that the models which function to perform this analysis are powered by collective user-driven activity, from individual searches to photo labelling to Mechanical Turk functions, and related improvements to machine learning systems. While this collective user activity is centralized in platforms, the question emerges as to the distribution of benefits from this activity. Zuboff poses a clear divide between firms which leverage data for investment into service improvement as opposed to firms which divide incentives for data use from service improvement to advertising improvement or data aggregation for sale (Zuboff 2019). This position can be further extended to consider precise questions of how alternative algorithmic models relative to business models establish the incentives for what, precisely, platforms tend to optimize for—a position which Larry Page and Sergey Brin infamously noted in their 1998 paper, stating, 'We expect that advertising-funded search engines will be inherently biased towards the advertisers and away from the needs of the consumers' (Brin and Page 1998).

Advertiser incentive-driven divergence is one category of a larger problem of algorithmic governance which rents serve to help expose, where mixed motives in outcome optimization can establish incentives for a broader range of self-servicing activities, rather than expanding benefits in favour of consumers (O'Reilly 2020). The parallel position is that while algorithmic rents currently exist by virtue of the centralization of allocative and algorithmic power, the redistribution of such power, while desirable, may not be inherently free of rent-seeking behaviour. Breaking up prior Google and Facebook mergers, as well as more extensive internal division of data and service ownership, may help to drive positive selection effects to reduce pricing, as well as dropping the cost of being excluded from any one platform. However, this does not automatically imply that the model of competition is not data- and value-extractive, or that such platform competition cannot give way to further concentration. Rather, it defers the problem to market selection, while ignoring the fundamental association between rent extraction and data-driven platform business models.

The power and de facto authority to set the outcomes for which algorithmic capacity is optimized is now one of the most important platform governance questions (O'Reilly 2020), as the concern is both whether the centralization of reward from collective user behaviour is served by the existing governance model and whether the outcomes can be effectively shaped to be, or become, dedicated to improving human capacity and flourishing (O'Reilly 2020). It is unclear whether, in terms of trust and conservation of asymmetric agency, there is any such thing as a neutral allocative decision-making system.

When allocative and automated decisions become entrenched in non-transparent algorithmic conditions, we should consider what kinds of decisions we are actually deferring to the platform leveraging that power. We should not simply pose these as economic harms but rather as extraction of value under-determined by competition assessment. To build a more competitive economy predicated on data extraction, or to merely improve the avoidance of the anti-competitive practices of existing data-extractive business models, is not to build an economy free of rents; rather it is to decentralize and diffuse rent-extractive features.

GOVERNING PLATFORMS AS INNOVATION SYSTEMS

Public values are expressions of the properties of social, political, and economic relations that we prefer.[4] Where value, relative to our assessment of rents, tends to be confined to understanding wealth creation; public value concerns the improvement of means for advancing and sustaining the kind of environment in which that wealth is created. Our concern for public value in this context is not simply the improvement in aggregate welfare from allocative efficiency gains but also the change in the kinds of social relations we want embedded in or enabled by specific market features.

As digital environments are increasingly consolidated into private hands, there are few positions on public value more important than the need to understand that such value is not produced by the public sector alone (Bozeman 2002). Indeed, as calls for Facebook and Twitter to monitor the quality of information in their feeds grow, we should better understand these calls are implying not only the means but also the functional demand that private actors bear the primary responsibility in delivering such value, independent of concurrent regulatory action or public sector delivery. From the market side, we can rephrase the position in terms of what kinds of functions should not be subject to competition or what kinds of competition over online privacy and security best enable the creation of public value? More directly, does having a market, or the current market structure, for social data count as a public value failure overall? What kind of relationship between data creation, allocative decision-making and ecosystem behaviour constitutes a healthy system, and which does not? As such, to effectively govern platforms to deliver public value, policymakers need to maintain a clear awareness of the mechanisms and incentives shaping how value is allocated among users, the platform and merchants (O'Reilly 2019). Such allocative decisions involve a wide distribution of actors and data-gathering among those actors. As such, the structural problem of the distribution of data and the rights regarding its access, ownership, and the transparency of analytics thus inform this primary allocative concern as well as the broader consolidation of decision-making on how relations, social and economic, are mediated (Feld 2019, 202). Platforms organize an ecosystem of related actors to effect broad changes in how information is arranged in society. However, the initial relationship of platforms being shaped by users has, as predicted, established a world where the conditions of using platforms means that users and firms comport to the model and structure of a platform-driven economy (O'Reilly 2020, 20). This extends to a continual demand to understand platforms on the terms of the ecosystem they create by virtue of the mix of unique mechanisms leveraged, and, as such, to understand the varieties of different ecosystem-level relationships which could exist—for instance, the relationship between Google and content providers by virtue of a change in ad placement and direct answers could improve consumer gains, but at the expense of content producer business models (O'Reilly 2020, 19).

We pose that just as platform power diverges in nuance from market power, a corollary theory of value creation relative to allocative scenarios is needed to better attune regulatory attention to the extractive behaviours and harms that exist both within and independent of economic and income implications. Such a theory is needed to help differentiate between the kinds of scenarios which yield not only market failures from the complex relationship with platforms but also the kinds of public failures that can ensue from underdeveloped and inappropriate visions. This is not simply to understand effectively and curtail the power of dominant platforms but also to better articulate the alternative domains of practices that we want public and private sector to co-create. Such concerns are embodied less in the ethical approaches of various institutions, and more in the different kinds of structure and infrastructure by which digital rights are made integral and basic to all platforms.

In effect, beyond regulating platforms from the perspectives of antitrust and competitiveness, governments face the daunting task of building countervailing power and innovation dynamics into the digital economy. Particularly in the European context, there is an emerging discussion around technological sovereignty. We propose that this should be largely an innovation and industrial policy agenda. For this we need a positive theory of public value that begins with a notion of the public good not as a correction to a failure, but as an objective in itself.

This public-value approach, however, does not presume a single model of market shaping, nor indeed that markets are always the necessary mechanism. As data trusts show, non-market mechanisms for management may satisfy a number of desirable governance scenarios. Directionality and public value are inherently normative claims. As such, with multiple distinct contexts regarding public sector capabilities, the agency and ecosystem assessment relative to the distinct data capitalism model, and the distribution of platform business models impose a unique analytic demand on each scenario relative to assembling both a coherent analysis of the direction and the specific policy tools to shape it.

One such problem regarding directionality concerns the expanding scope of data activities. Platforms are increasingly predicated on further reaches for data capture and creation, where the increasing digitalization of everyday life and the intermediation through platforms establish a universal scope of concern to any given business or individual leveraging online resources (Zuboff 2019). The reach of digital infrastructure and improved means of data capture are further contingent on additional legal conditions regarding data management, research and development for infrastructure, research and development for analytics, and the increasing market absorption of analytic demand by firms. The distribution of agency in the operational model of data capitalism, the data-extractive predicate of platform business models, and the increasing operational incentives for data-engagement from platform merchants establishes the primary problems facing the future of platform-driven economies.

Platform giants advance allocative efficiency in their respective sectors and cross-sector activities. By controlling the mechanisms by which allocative efficiency and market intelligence for a large number of firms are maintained, however, they shape the predominant business models of competitors and entrants. By extension, they shape the distribution of technology relative to operational models of use. Our concern is not simply with dominant platforms and giants but also with platforms as technology model diffusers, validators, and maintainers—the way the model of dominance translates into shaping the model of user and firm behaviour in the digital economy through fear of exclusion and the dependency on platform-offered services. The nature of the relationship between platform business models and the prominence of data-extractive business models needs to be denormalized as the only, or best, operational framework for digital economic growth.

We have intentionally overfocussed on data-extractive or data-intensive questions of platform behaviour, relative to their prominence in privacy, security, and power concerns in the digital economy. However, this normative position enables a consideration of alternative directions relative to the identification of different sets of public values—where, for instance, the deference of data governance to private sector may in some contexts be more desirable. In each, the question of the characteristics of the desired market in question and the distribution of agency involved in shaping that market should be the key focus of policymakers. The question is, what kind of (sub-) innovation system should public policies foster and co-create? A targeted policy needs to be investigated, which fully addresses the unique distribution of agency for collective value creation in a given context of governance, so an appropriate model of coordinated policy and the requisite public sector dynamic capabilities can be built. The value creative opportunity that a platform-driven economy can provide when disassociated from data-extractive business models is what needs clarification and elaboration. This should be where the parallel investment and incentivization of an ecosystem of actors to support an alternative model, as well as the disincentivizing of platform and firm behaviour relative to the extractive model establishes a joint demand on ecosystem creation and funding, infrastructure assessment, and assembly for technical provision of privacy coherent models, among other features.

CONCLUSION

Any exhaustive analysis of the economic, political, and social implications of big tech that does not account for the extractive behaviour will provide limited, and potentially misguided, policy. We can accept that such polices may improve the level of innovation of the system but will likely not improve the direction of such innovation, although as algorithmic rents proceed, the likelihood that improvements to services balance with improvements to the extractive features of those services and drive innovation may be a dubious proposition. The target of policymakers needs to be bolder, aiming towards a transformative approach to the nature of the platform-dominated online environments.

Our concern is not simply to effectively and precisely leverage antitrust, but to orient broader coordination among policy programmes to reward a platform innovation ecosystem which prioritizes value creation and marginalizes or removes value extraction. However, the scope of such a move exceeds regulatory improvements, as it demands rethinking an industrial policy approach to the digital market features which platforms create and diffuse, such as data-extractive business models. Such an approach considers platforms less as monopoly agents in one sector or for one product, but as horizontal market agents. Data portability, interoperability, and social graph portability arguments extend to these features. However, the concern remains that targeted changes may effectively reduce lock-in effects but may be insufficient to reorganise incentives regarding data-extractive and rent-seeking features, or fail to assess them entirely.

Targeted antitrust moves, such as opening up the data use to third-party players through splitting advertising from search or analytic functions within Google and Facebook, while attempting to minimize anticompetitive data use within Google, or at least the availability of such opportunities, demands further focus and attention on reorganizing algorithmic capacity ownership and reshaping means of access to that capacity. The ultimate consideration is whether such improvements constitute an adjustment to a data-extractive norm, or an opportunity to shape how a market can marginalize the extractive features of modern advertising-driven economies. This struggle between such reformist and revolutionary visions of digital economy growth directions is growing, but the question is whether the discursive relationship among these visions can move the window of viable policy considerations and the domain of feasible options. Platforms are not simply allocative agents, working to organize market participants to resolve a number of information asymmetries, among other things; they function as primary controllers of data aggregation and data flows.

The features of multisided platforms demand more scrutiny over supplier or merchant health, where the nature of internal competition dynamics among merchants within a given platform, as well as between the platform and merchants, requires more regulatory scrutiny (O'Reilly 2019). This scrutiny extends to the allocative power exercised over how value is distributed among users, merchants, and the platform itself. While the requirements for this allocation and its monitoring are data-intensive, the concern must extend beyond existing big tech to platforms more generally—as well as the nuances of platform-mediated digital economies. This implies both the need for a dedicated assessment agency and a consideration of the institutional remit of regulatory oversight for assessing the relationship between platform growth and other digital economy features and practices. However, as the scope and reach of platforms extend, the remit of assessment demands a larger consideration of the direction of digital economy growth as a collective policy and research agenda.

Policymakers have the larger burden of considering how to cultivate and incentivize a privacy-coherent digital economy relative to the barriers to scale provided by the existing centralization of data, as well as the relationship between broader digital business models and the data-extractive, rent-pursuing models which are currently predominant.

Antitrust measures against monopolies will underdetermine a change in market characteristics. As such, we are not opposed to antitrust; rather we are opposed to antitrust without both the additional coordinated policy programmes to crowd in investment, reshape standards, and identify appropriate institutional mixes for enabling innovation ecosystems as well as the capacity to effectively target and assess a number of value-extractive behaviours at the algorithmic and ecosystem level. We pose that such approaches demand a parallel expansion to a broader industrial policy and innovation policy approach to consider not only the rent-extractive features of platforms, and their economic harms, but also the kind of system which could effectively replace those behaviours.

NOTES

1. Platforms' data-driven function relative to the current advertising business model remains a primary concern. However, suppose data capture incentives exceed advertising-driven business models. The concern is not simply with the violation of privacy, but the incentives by which privacy violations occur. Tech giants are single, individuated entities only in name; functionally, they are predicated on the consolidation of agency from both the larger ecosystem of innovation and the collective input of users and citizens.
2. The counter push to such centralization has been the position that, absent such rents, alternative marketplace models serving as essential digital infrastructure should be further considered.
3. The difference, as Lina Khan notes, is the 'scale and sophistication of data collection. Whereas brick-and-mortar stores are generally only able to collect information on actual sales, Amazon tracks what shoppers are searching for but cannot find, as well as which products they repeatedly return to, what they keep in their shopping basket, and what their mouse hovers over on the screen' (Khan 2017).
4. The first concerns public value theory as articulated by Mark Moore, wherein, just as private agents yield private value when capturing market opportunities in their interest, public agents or civil servants can yield public value when managing regulations, services, laws, and public resources in the collective, public interest (Moore 2013). Such a theory primarily serves as a legitimation of the increased scope for neutral civil servants to act as public entrepreneurs (Bryson et al. 2014, 449). The second concerns public value theory as articulated by Barry Bozeman, wherein he states that public values are those: 'providing normative consensus about (a) the rights, benefits and prerogatives to which citizens should (and should not) be entitled; (b) the obligations of citizens to society, the state and one another; and (c) the principles on which governments and policies should be based' (Bozeman 2007, 132). Bozeman further poses that public value does not correspond to a theory of public policy, nor does it hold that a normative consensus is demanded for public values to be realized (Jorgensen and Bozeman 2007).

REFERENCES

Bozeman, B. 2002. 'Public-Value Failure: When Efficient Markets May Not Do'. *Public Administration Review* 62(2): 145–61. doi: 10.1111/0033-3352.00165.

Bozeman, B. 1988. 'Exploring the Limits of Public and Private Sectors: Sector Boundaries as Maginot Line'. *Public Administration Review* 48(2): 672. doi: 10.2307/975772.

Bozeman, B., and D. Sarewitz. 2005. 'Public Values and Public Failure in US Science Policy'. *Science and Public Policy* 32(2): 119–36. doi: 10.3152/147154305781779588.

Brin, S., and L. Page. 1998. 'The Anatomy of a Large-Scale Hypertextual Web Search Engine'. Retrieved July 15, 2020. http://infolab.stanford.edu/~backrub/google.html.

Culpepper, P. D., and K. Thelen. 2019. 'Are We All Amazon Primed? Consumers and the Politics of Platform Power'. *Comparative Political Studies* 53(2): 288–318. doi: 10.1177/0010414019852687.

Dewey, John. 1954. *The Public and Its Problems*. Athens, OH: Swallow.

Evans, D. S. 2019. 'Basic Principles for the Design of Antitrust Analysis for Multisided Platforms'. *Journal of Antitrust Enforcement* 7(3): 319–38. doi: 10.1093/jaenfo/jnz012.

Evans, D., and R. Schmalensee. 2013. 'The Antitrust Analysis of Multi-Sided Platform Businesses'. NBER Industrial Organization. doi: 10.3386/w18783.

Feld, H. 2019. 'The Case for the Digital Platform Act: Market Structure and Regulation of Digital Platforms'. Roosevelt Institute; Public Knowledge.

H. M. Treasury. 2018. 'The UK's Treasury Green Book: Central Government Guidance on Appraisal and Evaluation'. https://assets.publishing.service.gov.uk/government/uploads/system/uploads/attachment_data/file/685903/The_Green_Book.pdf.

Keynes, J. M. 1942. *The General Theory of Employment, Interest and Money*. London, UK: Palgrave Macmillan.

Kattel, R., and M. Mazzucato. 2018. 'Mission-Oriented Innovation Policy and Dynamic Capabilities in the Public Sector'. UCL Institute for Innovation and Public Purpose, Working Paper Series (IIPP WP 2018-5). http://www.ucl.ac.uk/bartlett/public-purpose/wp2018-05.

Kattel, R., M. Mazzucato, J. Ryan-Collins, and S. Sharpe. 2018. 'The Economics of Change: Policy Appraisal for Missions, Market Shaping and Public Purpose'. UCL Institute for Innovation and Public Purpose, Working Paper Series (IIPP WP 2018-06).

Khan, Lina. 2017. 'Amazon's Antitrust Paradox'. *Yale Law Journal* 126: 710–805.

Khan, Lina. 2018a. 'Amazon: An Infrastructure Service and Its Challenge to Current Antitrust Law'. In *Digital Dominance*, edited by Martin Moore and Damian Tambini. Oxford University Press.

Khan, Lina. 2018b. 'The New Brandeis Movement: America's Antimonopoly Debate'. *Journal of European Competition Law and Practice* 9(3): 131–32. doi: 10.1093/jeclap/lpy020.

Laplane, A., and M. Mazzucato. 2019. 'Socialising the Risks and Rewards of Public Investments: Economic, Policy and Legal Issues'. UCL Institute for Innovation and Public Purpose, Working Paper Series (IIPP WP 2019-09).

Lynskey, Orla. 2017. 'Regulating 'Platform Power'. LSE Law, Society and Economy Working Papers. https://papers.ssrn.com/sol3/papers.cfm?abstract_id=2921021.

Mas-Colell, A., M. D. Whinston, and J. R. Green. 1995. *Microeconomic Theory*. New York, NY: Oxford University Press.

Mazzucato, M. 2013. *The Entrepreneurial State: Debunking Public vs. Private Sector Myths*. London: Anthem Press.

Mazzucato, M. 2018. *The Value of Everything: Making and Taking in the Global Economy*. London: Allen Lane.

Mazzucato, M., and C. Perez. 2015. 'Innovation as Growth Policy'. In *The Triple Challenge for Europe*, edited by Jan Fagerberg, Staffan Laestadius, and Ben R. Martin, 229–64. Oxford University Press. doi: 10.1093/acprof:oso/9780198747413.003.0009.

Mazzucato, M., J. Ryan-Collins, and D. Giorgos. 2020. 'Mapping Modern Economic Rents'. UCL Institute for Innovation and Public Purpose, Working Paper Series.

Mazzucato, M., and J. Ryan-Collins. 2019. 'Putting Value Creation Back into 'Public Value': From Market Fixing to Market Shaping'. UCL Institute for Innovation and Public Purpose, Working Paper Series (IIPP WP 2019-05).

Meade, A. 2020. 'Google and Facebook Ordered to Pay for Content in Australia after Negotiations Failed'. *The Guardian*, April 28. https://www.theguardian.com/media/2020/apr/29/google-and-facebook-ordered-to-pay-for-content-after-negotiations-failed.

Mcafee, A., and E. Brynjolfssonn. 2018. *Machine, Platform, Crowd: Harnessing Our Digital Future*. New York: W. W. Norton.

Moore, M., and D. Tambini, eds. 2018. *Digital Dominance*. Oxford, UK: Oxford University Press.

Moore, M. H. 2014. 'Public Value Accounting: Establishing the Philosophical Basis'. *Public Administration Review* 74(4): 465–77. doi: 10.1111/puar.12198.

O'Reilly, T. 2019. 'Antitrust Regulators Are Using the Wrong Tools to Break Up Big Tech', July 18. https://qz.com/1666863/why-big-tech-keeps-outsmarting-antitrust-regulators/.

O'Reilly, T. 2020. 'We Have Already Let the Genie Out of the Bottle'. Rockefeller Foundation. Blog post, July 8, 2020. https://www.rockefellerfoundation.org/blog/we-have-already-let-the-genie-out-of-the-bottle/.

Perez, C. 2003. *Technological Revolutions and Financial Capital*. Cheltenham, UK: Edward Elgar Publishing.

Polanyi, K. 1944. *The Great Transformation*. Boston, MA: Beacon Press.

Tucker, C. 2018. 'Network Effects Matter Less Than They Used To. That's a Really Big Deal', June 27. https://hbr.org/2018/06/why-network-effects-matter-less-than-they-used-to.

Tucker, C. 2018. 'Network Effects and Market Power: What Have We Learned in the Last Decade?' http://sites.bu.edu/tpri/files/2018/07/tucker-network-effects-antitrust2018.pdf.

Wachter, S., and B. Mittelstadt. 2018. 'A Right to Reasonable Inferences: Re-Thinking Data Protection Law in the Age of Big Data and AI'. doi: 10.31228/osf.io/mu2kf.

Zuboff, S. 2020. *The Age of Surveillance Capitalism: The Fight for a Human Future at the New Frontier of Power*. New York: PublicAffairs.

2

Reforming Competition and Media Law

The German Approach

SARAH HARTMANN AND BERND HOLZNAGEL ■

INTRODUCTION

The search for responses to digital dominance has led to tangible legal proposals in Germany. In 2019, major revisions were made to competition law and to sector specific media regulation. These included measures targeted towards digital platforms and intermediaries.

Competition law (addressing market structures) and media law (establishing specific behavioural duties) traditionally have no overlap. While the former is restricted to economic considerations and regulation takes effect ex post, the latter deals with matters of content with the overall aim of preserving plurality in the marketplace of opinions ex ante. Still, there are undeniable interdependencies between the economic market status and opinion-forming powers of the regulated entities. Likewise, the phenomena emerging in connection with dominant digital players affect the respective objectives of both competition and media law. With their recent initiatives, the German legislators have attempted to gradually adapt the existing frameworks to these challenges.

German competition law shares many similarities with European competition law, which in turn has taken inspiration from the US-American Sherman Act. The foundations of contemporary German media law were established by the allied forces in the aftermath of the Second World War and are primarily based on British press and broadcasting regulation. Because of these connections and structural similarities, the German legal proposals make suitable points of reference for media and competition policy in other EU states and beyond.

In this chapter we will examine the German approaches in both areas individually before integrating them into an overall proposal. Our main focus will be the preservation of plurality, not economic competition. We argue that a combination of formerly independent legal instruments and safeguards could solve a number of inherent shortcomings, both on a substantial and on an institutional level. Namely, our proposal will address the central questions of how to determine the content that should benefit from plurality measures and how to target these safeguards to the most impactful platforms.

RESPONSES TO DIGITAL DOMINANCE IN GERMAN COMPETITION LAW

Part of the political agreement between the governing parties in Germany was the modernization of competition law towards the challenges of globalization and digitalization (CDU et al. 2018, 61) especially in reaction to dominant digital services, like Google and Facebook, with market shares above 90% in Germany. In this situation, the *preservation of market structures* is tackled with instruments of antitrust law. Therefore, the current legislative proposal[1] for the tenth amendment to the federal antitrust act (GWB) of January 2020 (BMWI 2020) specifically targets platforms, enhancing and adapting instruments already introduced with the last reform from 2017[2] for digital market conditions and incorporating the results of several national and international studies.[3]

Three components of the proposal are relevant to the discussion at hand: (1) lowering the thresholds for intervention in two-sided and network markets (earlier and more proactive intervention), (2) the introduction of sector-specific abuse control for those markets (expanding the regulatory toolkit), and (3) the introduction of new criteria for market status assessments tailored to the unique position of intermediaries (redefining market dominance).

Measures to Prevent Market Tipping

(Digital) network markets are especially vulnerable to tipping effects, resulting in high market concentration with 'winner takes it all' structures. Market tipping is often fostered by exclusionary strategies and is extremely difficult to reverse. The new GWB proposal redefines two elements of the intervention threshold, enabling earlier and more effective competition policy (BMWI 2020, 85 ff.). Instead of requiring the established market dominance test, 'superior market positions' are sufficient[4] in two-sided markets and network markets.[5] Prohibited behaviours include the obstruction of positive network effects for competitors, for example by restricting multi-homing[6] or platform migration (BMWI 2020, 86). Obstructions of interoperability, on the other hand, are not subject to this rule because they do not relate to autonomous network effects (BMWI 2020, 86).

In addition to the lower market position threshold, the required level of threat to competition is also decreased. Regulatory authorities can now take action in cases where a disruption of the market has not yet occurred if there is a serious threat of substantial restrictions to competition.[7] Unfortunately, the proposal fails to clarify what constitutes a 'serious' threat. A non-exhaustive listing of examples would be beneficial in this case, while still allowing for discretion in accounting for innominate restrictive behaviours on a case-by-case basis.[8]

To further enhance the regulator's ability to react promptly and flexibly to changes and threats to the market, the proposal also facilitates the use of provisional measures.[9]

Abuse Control for 'Super-Market Rulers'

The traditional categories of German competition law do not account for the kind of market conditions characteristic for digital platform economies. Single-homing and log-in effects often facilitate the capture of neighbouring markets, resulting in even greater volumes of user data to be merged and used to strengthen the platform's position in its original market (Höppner 2020, 72). The complex economic and technical operations and related data at the heart of intermediary services are often kept obscure (BMWI 2020, 80). In contrast to infrastructure-bound telecommunications companies, no sector-specific abuse control currently applies to platforms like Amazon, Apple, Facebook, and Google.

The GWB proposal now introduces a two-tiered system of abuse control specifically targeted at large digital companies.[10] The system depends on a constitutive determination of 'paramount cross-market significance' in two-sided and network markets[11] by the German Federal Cartel Office[12] (first step). The criteria for this new superlative among market statuses are:[13] the company's dominant position in one or several markets, financial strength or access to other resources, vertical integration or other activities in connected markets, access to relevant data, and the overall significance of its activities for third parties' access to procurement and sales markets.

Companies that meet these criteria and are determined to be 'super market rulers' by the Cartel Office are subject to case-by-case behavioural prohibitions (second step).[14] The most important provision relates to the kind self-preferment that has been at the centre of the Google-Shopping controversy (see also Höppner and Weber 2020, 31).[15] To counteract tipping effects, the remedies also include a general prohibition of obstructive behaviour in neighbouring markets[16] and a more specific prohibition of obstructive use of relevant user data to create or heighten barriers to entry in neighbouring markets.[17] Finally, the Cartel Office can bar the obstruction of interoperability of products and services or data portability[18] as well as insufficient transparency of extent, quality, and effort of the services offered that would impede evaluation of the services' value.[19]

It seems doubtful that the new provisions are proactive enough to impact dominant players' market behaviour. Even after the potentially time intensive determination of paramount market status has been concluded, the catalogue of prohibitions must also be individually applied on a case-by-case basis, since it is not self-executing. This is a deviation from the traditional rationale of German competition law, where dominant companies are barred from certain behaviours by default, without the need for individual orders by the regulatory authority. It would be preferable for the new prohibitions to be directly applicable, as well.

New Criteria for Intermediary Market Power

Currently, the GWB's evaluation criteria for market dominance do not account for the specific intermediary services of major digital platforms. Their strategic position as gatekeepers between suppliers and customers (Höppner and Weber 2020, 42; Schweitzer et al. 2018, 73) and suppliers' dependence on beneficial ranking in the intermediary's service (BMWI 2020, 71) are not reflected or considered in the market status assessment that only focusses on immediate procurement and sales markets. The proposal now introduces the concept of intermediary market power as a separate category of market power (Höppner and Weber 2020, 42), which is based on the intermediary's impact on third parties' access to these markets.[20] This concept is more familiar to media content regulation, where the inherent threat of gatekeeper positions has been recognized and mediated by platform regulation for two decades.[21]

Another aspect addressed in the proposal is access to data as a crucial factor for market success. While data access rules exist in several sector-specific regulations,[22] general competition law so far did not reflect its importance. Data access is now introduced as a general criterion[23] in the market status assessment for all areas, not limited to two-sided or network markets (BMWI 2020, 70).

Evaluation

The legislator's effort to update competition law for new digital environments is commendable. The issues identified and targeted by the GWB proposal show general awareness of the central problems posed by dominant digital platforms. However, the execution of possible solutions to these problems lacks substance and assertiveness.

Both the new intervention threshold of 'serious threats' of market disruptions and the concept of intermediary market power would benefit from substantial clarification (Höppner and Weber 2020, 40 ff.). In the case of intermediary market power, the criteria to assess and quantify a company's impact on third parties' market access should be further elaborated in the provision itself (Höppner and Weber 2020, 42).

On the other hand, the behavioural duties for 'super market rulers' would need to apply by default after the market status determination is completed and not depend on subsequent decisions and orders by the regulatory authority. Likewise, the introduction of intermediary market power should have been accompanied by a general prohibition of preferring the intermediary's own services over those of outside parties (Kommission Wettbewerbsrecht 4.0 2019, 53; Höppner and Weber 2020, 44). This would not only heighten the rule's impact but also streamline the regulatory process and accelerate countermeasures against market distortions.

Although the proposal takes certain steps towards sooner and faster intervention, it remains rooted in the ex post approach of general competition law. Legislative processes, such as the current reform, tend to lag several steps behind the highly dynamic market developments. Higher flexibility and swift responses can be achieved by delegating competences to the regulator. The challenges of digital dominance could potentially be addressed more adequately within a sector-specific ex ante regulatory framework (Höppner 2020, 72), comparable to telecommunications law. Instead of promoting better cooperation and exchange of information between competition, media and data protection authorities, as the proposal attempts to do,[24] a single sector-specific regulatory body could potentially reconcile the different fields into a one authority with expertise in the different fields (Höppner 2020, 72).

RESPONSES TO DIGITAL DOMINANCE IN SECTOR-SPECIFIC MEDIA REGULATION

Outside of competition law, measures addressing intermediaries and platforms to promote diversity and regulate opinion forming power are implemented as *behavioural duties* in media regulation. The central instrument relating to content is the Rundfunkstaatsvertrag (RStV) or Interstate Broadcasting Treaty, which has been updated and rebranded as the Interstate Media Treaty (MStV).[25] In the course of the latest reform, the Treaty has been amended to include rules for internet platforms and other intermediaries.

The Evolution of Platform Regulation—It Is Not as New as You Might Think

Contrary to the narrative of early reactions within and outside of Germany, this is not the first inclusion of 'platforms' in the scope of the Treaty. 'Platform regulation' has actually been a part of the Interstate Broadcasting Treaty for over twenty years at this point,[26] albeit referring to different platforms than the ones that come to mind today and that are the focus of the present discussion. A basic understanding of the Treaty's legal history is important to put the newly introduced rules into context.

Intermediary regulation in Germany began in 1999, with the fourth amendment to the Interstate Broadcasting Treaty.[27] Previously, the Treaty only applied to TV and radio broadcasters, as its name would suggest. Broadcasting media is traditionally conceptualized to have a higher impact on the formation of public opinion than other media,[28] while relying on scarce and cost-intensive technical resources to distribute content.[29] In essence, this is the main justification for the strict regulation of broadcasting as opposed to print media. In addition to broadcasters, the Treaty from 2000 also sought to regulate cable TV operators as redistributors. While these intermediaries do not produce content, broadcasters depend on them to actually deliver their programmes to large parts of the audience. Cable providers control the bottleneck of access to consumers over their respective (closed) infrastructure. In this position they impact broadcaster's chances to influence the process of public opinion formation. As cable TV became more prevalent, legislators recognized the necessity to establish a framework to regulate broadcasters' admission into cable provider's bundles and thereby guarantee 'communicative equal opportunities'. This is reminiscent of the newly introduced concept of intermediary market power in competition law.[30]

With the tenth amendment to the RStV in 2008, the rules were broadened to digital offers on all channels of distribution (cable, satellite, and terrestrial, at the time) and the term 'platform regulation' was introduced. The definition was designed to apply to aggregators in gatekeeper positions for limited transmission capacities. The legislator was especially concerned with TV on mobile (cell phone) devices in the DMB-standard, which later proved to be economically inviable. In practice, cable TV operators overwhelmingly remained the sole subject of the regulation.

Platform regulation in Germany has both negative and positive safeguards to secure pluralism: non-discrimination and must-carry rules. Platforms have to facilitate access to their interfaces and interoperability with any technical specifications and treat and price[31] all content providers in a way that is non-discriminatory.[32] This obligation explicitly also applies to user interfaces that are used to navigate the platform and has been further specified by the regulatory authorities (see ZAK 2016).

The second cornerstone of platform regulation is known as the must-carry rules. These specify the allocation of the platform's available technical capacity to groups of linear TV or radio broadcasting programmes, as provided by Art. 31 of the European Universal Service Directive.[33] The provider's free selection of TV or radio channels is limited to one-third of the platform's overall capacity. Another third is reserved for public service broadcaster's channels, regional and community channels that are by default considered to particularly contribute to plurality. The last third of the capacity can be attributed to channels according to the choice of the platform provider as long as it results in an overall diverse offer.

Both the non-discrimination rules and the must-carry regime are meant to ensure an adequate level of plurality in bundled broadcasting offers. However, they are also expressions of very different approaches: non-discrimination prohibits interference with user's choices on the part of the platform provider[34] and is supposed to result in a neutral representation of programmes available (plurality through equal opportunity and neutrality); the must-carry rules, on the other hand, establish a system of positive safeguards in order to strengthen diversity (plurality through selective preference). Certain services, that are deemed to positively impact plurality, are treated preferentially by their obligatory inclusion into platforms' offers. This is especially true for public service broadcaster's programmes that are subject to internal plurality requirements and generally have to comply with higher (journalistic) standards of quality and objectivity than private broadcasters.[35]

However, the must-carry and non-discrimination obligations did not apply to all aggregator platforms. They were ultimately designed to mitigate the effects of closed networks, such as cable TV infrastructure. Platforms in open networks like the Internet were excluded if they did not have a dominant market position,[36] because it was assumed that content providers had alternative means of accessing the network's users and for lack of a bottleneck did not depend on platforms in these networks.[37] The regime was still rooted in its origin as regulation of access to and allocation of scarce (physical) resources.

Introduction of New Categories of Media Services

Keeping in mind the legislative history of German platform regulation, the newly introduced rules for Internet platforms and other intermediaries can be understood as a logical continuation of the same regulatory approach. The final version of the new MStV proposal, officially signed by representatives of the federal states in 2020, introduces three new categories of services into the Treaty—'media platforms', 'user interfaces', and 'media intermediaries'.

Both 'media platforms' and 'user interfaces' are mostly an extension of the previously addressed platforms and navigators. The definition of media platforms calls for incorporating broadcasting content and similar editorial media services of third parties into a *bundled offer* according to the selection of the platform provider.[38] However, the previous exclusion of services in open networks was abandoned. The definition and subsequent obligations thereby can be applied beyond cable TV providers to different types of Internet services, as long as they reach a threshold of 20,000 average monthly users.[39]

User interfaces, as defined in the new Treaty, are the navigational layers for users to access content or applications on media platforms,[40] for example on Amazon's Fire TV stick. They are usually incorporated into the platforms. Acoustic systems, such as the voice-assisted Amazon Echo, are also included.

Finally, 'media intermediaries' are the only genuinely new category. They are defined as aggregators of third-party editorial content.[41] Unlike on media platforms, the aggregated content is *not incorporated into a bundled offer*. Media intermediaries that do not reach a threshold of 1 million average monthly users are excluded.[42] Intermediaries' navigator functions are not specifically addressed and do not constitute 'user interfaces' in the meaning of the Treaty if they are not linked to a media platform.

At first glance, these definitions seem to encompass streaming services like Netflix or Amazon Video as media platforms. There are important caveats to the definitions, though. Services like Netflix, Amazon Video, or catch-up libraries of broadcasters are excluded due to the exception for services that are completely under the editorial control of their provider.[43] In short, all services that constitute audiovisual media services according to the definition in the AVMS directive[44] and their text- or audio-based equivalents are outside of the scope of the new provisions. These services, characterized by editorial control over their content, are not regulated as media platforms but are subject to the rules for AVMS and other editorial media.

What about services without editorial control, like YouTube? They do not meet the criteria of 'selective bundled' platforms with an element of selection by the platform provider. Rather, 'indiscriminate unbundled' services fall within in the scope of 'media intermediaries' (Hönig d'Orville 2019, 106 ff.). Other examples of intermediaries in the sense of the Treaty's definition include social networks and search engines (Hönig d'Orville 2019, 106 ff.).

To understand the scope of the proposal, it is helpful to consider the history of platform regulation summarized earlier. Despite ambitious claims, the legislation is not designed to address all types of prevalent online platforms, but rather to mostly extend the previous rules for cable TV to new over-the-top (OTT) services, that are offered via Internet instead of proprietary networks. The most prominent example of an OTT bundling service in Germany is Zattoo, which provides live streaming of most linear German and Swiss TV channels on devices connected to the Internet. In contrast to streaming platforms like Netflix or catch-up libraries, Zattoo does not control the individual content on its service. In contrast to user-generated-content services like YouTube, however, it does select and admit the content providers.

Another example of media platforms are the systems integrated into smart TV devices that allow users to access content through third-party software applications over the Internet. These systems are now explicitly included[45] in the definition of media platforms as the 'bundling of software applications used to access broadcasting and editorial content'.[46] Similar to OTT TV-services, the device manufacturer does not directly control the selection of content but acts as a gatekeeper for content providers wanting to access the system with their applications (Schütz 2018, 38).

Obligations: Neutrality, Transparency, and Must-Be-Found

NEGATIVE BEHAVIOURAL DUTIES

Similar to the extension of the material scope, the services' respective obligations can also be traced back to the previous platform regime of the RStV. At its core, the new regulation relies on transparency and non-discrimination rules for media platforms, user interfaces, and intermediaries. Both platforms and intermediaries have to communicate the conditions for access of content to their services as well as the criteria for the content's presentation and organization in their services (ranking).[47] They are also obligated to explain the criteria for personalized recommendations[48] and the implemented algorithms.[49]

The safeguards against discrimination are gradual depending on the type of service and only apply to editorial content. For media platforms, the previous obligation to facilitate access to interfaces and interoperability and employ non-discriminatory pricing practices was extended to the new scope.[50] For user interfaces, the legislator has adopted a more detailed approach.[51] The rules explicitly address the prominence and discoverability of content, where similar content must be treated equally and its discoverability must not be obstructed.[52] A neutral search function must be available. Content may be sorted according to neutral criteria, i.e., by alphabet, genre, or popularity.

Media intermediaries also have to adhere to non-discrimination rules that apply to the conditions for access and the treatment of editorial content.[53] Discriminatory practices are indicated by deviations from the principles communicated by the provider under its transparency obligation.[54] However, intermediaries are only subject to this rule if they are 'essential to the perception of editorial content'. An essential function is supposedly indicated by market shares of around 40%, similar to the definition in the GWB.[55]

POSITIVE SAFEGUARDS
Must-carry obligations, as one of the integral components of platform regulation, were not directly extended to media platforms or intermediaries. They continue to apply only to infrastructure platforms in closed networks.[56] Instead of implementing both neutrality and positive safeguards, the new approach is limited to neutrality and transparency. However, some aspects of the must-carry obligations were adapted for media platform's user interfaces. They do not address the allocation of capacities but rather deal with the prominence of content as 'must-be-found' rules with two tiers of selective preference. All broadcasting content must be prominently placed and easily accessible within the interface (preference for broadcasting content over other types of content).[57] Within the available broadcasting content, programmes of public-service broadcasters and private programmes that particularly contribute to plurality must again be placed more prominently than other broadcasting programmes (preference for broadcasting content of public interest [PI] over other broadcasting content).[58] A similar rule exists for non-linear content.[59] The determination of PI content is delegated to the media regulatory authorities, with considerations such as the proportion of political and regional news, accessibility, and the quota of European works.[60] In contrast to the must-carry regime, there is no obligation on the part of the service provider to include specific content. Rather, the must-be-found rules only apply to content that is already included in the user interface.

Evaluation

The Treaty's rules for platforms are not a global solution for the various challenges of digital dominance. From the offset, they were only designed to address concerns of plurality, not economic competition. Due to the strong path dependency of German broadcasting and media law, which is shaped and determined by the constitutional court's interpretation, old concepts are now being applied to new situations and players.

The interpretation of media freedom in the German constitution is unique. It does not solely restrict state action, but rather (by its so-called objective dimension) obligates the state to act in certain situations to create and sustain an open and pluralistic public sphere. The German Federal Constitutional Court (BVerfG) has upheld the constitutional mandate to proactively ensure media plurality in online media environments despite their quantitative variety of services and content. The court reasoned that this quantitative variety does not necessarily result in qualitative plurality.[61] The financial incentive for platforms to select, promote, and rank content purely according to mass appeal needs to be counterbalanced through regulatory plurality measures.[62] This (legislative) obligation rests with the federal state's parliaments. The media regulatory authorities, on the other hand, are bound by the legislator's decisions and have little room to influence overall media policy.

Platforms and other (modern-day) intermediaries are treated as descendants of traditional redistributors of media content. As such, their regulation is roughly governed by the same principles that were once introduced for cable TV providers: non-discriminatory access and obligatory inclusion of PI content. Media outlets depend on physical or virtual infrastructures in order for their content to reach consumers. The concept of the traditional platform regime, applying to physical infrastructures, can be broken down into two core factors. Protecting content creator's *equal opportunities* (access and treatment) to safeguard *overall plurality* in the market and protecting *consumer's access to a diverse offer of media content* on each individual platform through *positive must-carry requirements*.

Operating within these boundaries, however, the Treaty's system for virtual platforms is neither coherent nor sufficient. While it aspires to broadly address these new and dominant players in the digital sphere, the negative and positive safeguards they are ultimately subjected to are incomplete. Transparency and equal treatment requirements are meant to guarantee neutrality, falling short of the more ambitious goal of plurality. Even the baseline obligation of non-discrimination only applies to intermediaries with significant market status.

In terms of positive safeguards, the must-be-found system has severe limitations when compared to the traditional must-carry regime and appears to be the result of many political compromises. Its most obvious shortcoming is the very limited scope. Must-be-found obligations do not extend to intermediaries, as their navigational functions do not constitute user interfaces in the meaning of the Treaty. As explained earlier, few services actually meet the definition of media platform, even without considering the additional territorial limitation of the scope. Not one of the core services immediately associated with the discussion on dominant platforms is addressed by the positive content regulation. Google's search engine and its video service YouTube are both 'media intermediaries' in the meaning of the treaty,[63] Amazon's Prime Video is excluded as an audiovisual media service just like the Apple TV streaming service,[64] and Facebook and

Apple's Appstore both lack the selective bundling required for media platforms[65] and constitute 'media intermediaries', as well.[66] Even if the model was adopted on a broader, European level it would only apply to fringe services in its current form.

Where they apply, the criteria for privileged content under the must-be-found obligation are also outdated. The preference for linear broadcasting content over non-linear editorial content does not reflect the reality of the services' impact on public opinion in this day and age.[67] The individual determination of 'content that particularly contributes to plurality' and is therefore granted the must-be-found privileges[68] by the media regulatory authorities is both highly problematic and ineffective. The concept of a state authority hand-picking 'quality' media sources among all German editorial content has the connotation of a conspiracy theory in the making.

This criticism is not directed at the larger policy goal of mitigating the effects of platforms' and intermediaries' gatekeeper positions in digital media environments, which has been included in the constitutional plurality mandate by the BVerfG.[69] However, the specifics of how the German legislature has chosen to implement its countermeasures cause the approach to be ineffective. As an overall result of the fragmented regulation, online content, which plays a vital part in the democratic process of opinion forming, will continue to be disseminated, ranked and promoted according to economic reasoning with no regard for plurality.

PROPOSAL: MERGING MEDIA REGULATION WITH ELEMENTS OF COMPETITION LAW

Having examined the German proposals and pointed out their respective innovations as well as their shortcomings, we see potential in interconnecting the approach of competition law with sector-specific media regulation. Our proposal is based on two cornerstones: PI content should be subject to privileged discoverability to promote plurality. The determination of PI content, however, must be left to an independent self-regulatory body instead of state authorities (1). Second, instead of addressing all services that disseminate editorial content of third parties, regulation should be targeted to the most influential players with the highest (potential) impact on public opinion (2). This can be achieved by incorporating market status criteria into the material scope. Our concept is not meant to 'fix' the shortcomings of the German system, but should rather be understood as a model to be adopted on a supranational level, drawing inspiration from and enhancing the national approach.

The Interstate Media Treaty applies roughly the same (low) level of obligations to all services within its new scope. Certain services' significant impact on public opinion would, however, warrant a higher level of regulation, including rules to actively promote plurality. Positive safeguards in the form of 'must-be-found' rules should be introduced for both platforms and intermediaries (see also Schwartmann et al. 2019, 501 ff., for the so-called dual-model). While the new GWB provisions are not designed to achieve media plurality, they can be an important instrument in specifying the scope of these more extensive rules. Referencing services' market status is not only an adequate and tangible indicator of their potential impact on public opinion but also ensures proportional differentiation between services.

Both texts already incorporate elements traditionally found in the respective other area of law. The Interstate Media Treaty requires intermediaries to be 'essential for the perception of editorial content' in order for the non-discrimination rule to apply, referencing their market share. The GWB, on the other hand, has developed instruments to facilitate faster intervention at a lower threshold[70] as well as provisional measures,[71] abandoning the traditional strict ex post character of competition law and converging towards the pre-emptive nature of sector specific regulation. Both texts reference the impact of intermediaries' gatekeeper positions on competitors and third parties in the value chain, albeit from the inherently different perspectives of economic competition and communicative competition.[72]

Introducing Gradual Positive Safeguards for Public Interest Content

To counteract negative effects of dominant platforms on diversity and ensure plurality, the Treaty's instruments must be enhanced towards more robust positive safeguards.

As a baseline, the new transparency and non-discrimination requirements should be upheld. They should be extended to all intermediaries, irrespective of their market status. Navigational layers of intermediaries, which are currently not included in the definition of user interfaces, should also be subject to the non-discrimination rules.

Concerning the must-be-found privileges, we propose a model based on two categories of privileged PI content providers. The first category would consist of media outlets that provide high quality content with major relevance to the public discourse and public opinion (absolute PI content). This category is based on a concept similar to that currently employed in the Treaty. It would include both linear and non-linear providers that are either inherently subject to strict requirements of internal plurality and quality control (such as public service media) or otherwise meet objective quality criteria. These criteria could be proportion of current news and affairs content, accessibility, and cooperation with external fact checking organizations, for example. Inclusion in this group of PI content providers should be subject to the constitutive determination of an independent self-regulatory institution and not the media regulatory authorities.

The second category of privileged providers should be determined through a system of self-accreditation (relative PI content). Any media outlet willing to partake in this group would be required to commit to predetermined journalistic standards and duties of care, such as those laid out in the press code of conduct[73] issued by the self-regulatory German Press Council.[74] The status of relative PI content provider would be granted after accreditation and commitment and not depend on further ex ante determinations. However, if the provider is found to be in violation of the standards according to the decision of an independent self-regulatory body, the status could be revoked.

Both categories of PI content providers would have to be granted prominence in user interfaces of platforms and intermediaries in the category of platforms with potential impact on plurality, which is laid out in what follows. In practice, this would have to be implemented by specifying the relative and absolute PI status as factors for ranking, recommending and personalising content. For example, when recommending content based on user's previous choices of topic (as opposed to source), PI content relevant to the same topic must be granted a positive boost, and be considered in addition to neutral ranking criteria, such as relevance and popularity. The boost for absolute PI content would be higher than that of relative PI content. To clarify, we do not propose an absolute preference for PI content, where it would be required to rank among the top results in any situation, but rather a flexible adjustment of ranking criteria.

Defining the Material Scope According to Market Status

One of the major obstacles in introducing the kind of positive content obligation proposed above is the adequate definition of the rules' scope. The Treaty currently uses a broad scope to cover many different types of 'platform' and 'intermediary' services (mostly) irrespective of their size, audience share, or impact, while only applying very basic obligations to these services. The alternative approach proposed here would shift the weight of obligations to a much narrower subset of digital services, whose significance justifies stricter measures to safeguard plurality (for a similar approach concerning access, see also Noam this volume).

Referring back to our evaluation of the GWB proposal, the updated scope for companies with 'paramount cross-market significance'[75] and the new criteria for 'intermediary market power'[76] should also be used to determine the market participants with the highest (potential) impact on public opinion. Among the services that meet the Treaty's definition of media platforms, user interfaces and media intermediaries, those above a certain threshold should be categorized as platforms with potential impact on plurality, or PIP, for short (see also Noam this volume, on 'significant media market power'). The positive safeguards would thereby be expanded beyond 'media platforms' to the larger group of 'media intermediaries', which includes services like YouTube and Facebook, for example. While we fully acknowledge that market status and opinion forming power are not interchangeable, they are interdependent. This is especially true in the case of intermediaries, who act as distributors and multipliers of third-party content. Their impact on public opinion is not characterized by editorial activity but rather by economic decisions about the distribution, ranking, and promotion of other people's content. The criteria relevant to assess intermediaries' market status, such as market share, financial strength, vertical integration,[77] impact on third parties' access to markets, and access to relevant data,[78] are also an adequate representation of their relevance as gatekeepers of virtual infrastructures for content creators.

The proposed PIP category would act as an intersection between market data-based assessment and media law regulatory measures. It could be complemented by additional criteria, such as the proportion of editorial content on the service and be subject of a constitutive determination of the competent regulatory authority, ideally a digital agency comprising both competition and media authorities.

(Voluntary) Plurality Measures as a Factor in Competition Law

The obligatory plurality measures for PIP services could be complemented by in-centives for non-PIP platforms and intermediaries to implement the system on a voluntary basis.

Non-PIP platforms or not-yet-determined PIP platforms could chose to im-plement the promotion of absolute and relative PI content. This would in turn be considered as a counter-indicator in the assessment of anticompetitive agreements and coordinated practices between companies,[79] to enable more flexible cooper-ation (as proposed for media outlets by Gostomzyk et al. 2019, 15 ff.) between (smaller) services. The proposed integration of plurality aspects is similar to how data protection aspects have recently factored into competition law assessments.[80]

Legislative efforts to facilitate cooperation between media outlets have already been made with regard to the press,[81] where national publishers are supposed to 'join forces' in response to the overwhelming dominance of US-American new media services and the economic challenges facing traditional press outlets.[82]

The concept is not completely foreign to German media law, either. Media-specific antitrust law includes a prohibition of dominant impact on public opinion by individual programmes and broadcasters. If broadcasters exceed an audience share of 30%, they lose the ability to apply for additional programme licenses, are subject to regulatory countermeasures, and can have their licence revoked if they fail to comply.[83] However, the broadcaster can also take voluntary countermeas-ures, namely the inclusion of time frames for independent third-party broad-casting, and is in turn granted an additional 5% allowance towards the audience share threshold.[84]

Institutional Implementation—Digital Agencies

Due to the connected considerations rooted in both competition law and media regulation proposed in this model, a singular authority, specializing in digital markets, would have to be created or integrated into one of the previously separ-ated regulators. Similar proposals for a 'Digital Markets Unit' have already been made in the United Kingdom (Furman et al. 2019), and the establishment of a 'Digitalagentur' has been discussed in Germany (BMWi 2017, 101 ff.; Höppner

2020, 72 ff.) for years. This would have a number of positive side effects, bundling expertise of media markets in a specialized unit and making the intervention processes more efficient. The implementation as a separate spin-off agency or dovetail to already existing entities should take into account respective national circumstances. On the territorial side of things, a supranational implementation of this model would be preferable to singular national approaches.

SUMMARY AND CONCLUSION

As discussed, individual aspects of the German approaches in competition and media law are innovative. They can serve as interesting case studies or models for other states in their efforts to regulate digital dominance. Germany shares legal traditions with the European Union and many of its Member States. This is exemplified by the GWB proposal, which has been drafted in cooperation with the European Commission's Directorate-General for Competition and bares close resemblance to pertinent discussions on a European level. The safeguarding of media pluralism is also part of the European common constitutional traditions, illustrated by Art. 11 para 2 of the EU Charter of Fundamental Rights. Non-discrimination rules and must-be-found regimes for intermediary services should therefore be compatible to other state's media regulations that serve the same objective of facilitating an equal opportunities public discourse and promoting PI content, e.g., public broadcasting content. Transparency requirements similar to those in the new MStV will most likely be introduced on a European level by the highly anticipated Digital Services Act.[85]

Other legislatures, looking to take inspiration from the German proposal or adopt a similar approach should, however, be mindful of its limitations and inconsistencies. The concepts as are whole are not sufficiently coherent and assertive to mediate the phenomena they are addressing. The limited and cautious approach chosen by the German legislature will ultimately fail to prevent further damage to content plurality and competition online. Already dominant platforms will continue to grow even more influential. Their gatekeeper status is not mitigated by the proposed changes. In essence, the conditions for the communicative process online are like a train cart rolling downhill at the moment. It is continuously picking up speed. The proposed reforms are meant to act as a track switch to change its course back uphill. However, what is lacking are effective brakes required to slow the cart down enough to stay on track.

Intermediaries' gatekeeper position impacts both economic competition and media plurality. Targeted measures should therefore include elements of media regulation and competition law and ideally be entrusted to the same sector-specific comprehensive authority (Höppner 2020, 72 f.). In summary, our proposal would broaden the scope of the baseline obligations of neutrality and transparency to all platforms and intermediaries, while simultaneously introducing additional positive measures for the prominence of PI content for a subset of services with the highest potential impact on plurality. This PIP category of services is determined according to market status assessment and includes important intermediaries like social networks and user-generated-content sites. The content providers privileged within the system are distinguished as absolute and relative PI content, according to either a determination of objective quality criteria by an independent self-regulatory body or self-accreditation and commitment to journalistic standards and duties of care. No state authority should be involved in this qualitative assessment. The privilege associated with PI status entails a ranking boost, which must be considered in addition to neutral ranking criteria. Platforms and intermediaries can also implement the system voluntarily, which would be factored into cartel assessments.

These are the key aspects of the kind of measures needed to ensure and strengthen plurality in digital environments with dominant intermediaries. The proposal is not meant to be exhaustive and instead only focusses on certain regulatory issues. We hope it can provide a foundation for further discussion across Europe and elsewhere.

NOTES

1. The proposal has been passed and entered into force in January 2021, Gesetz zur Änderung des Gesetzes gegen Wettbewerbsbeschränkungen für ein fokussiertes, proaktives und digitales Wettbewerbsrecht 4.0 und anderer Bestimmungen (GWB-Digitalisierungsgesetz) of January 18, 2021, BGBl. I p. 2.
2. Neuntes Gesetz zur Änderung des Gesetzes gegen Wettbewerbsbeschränkungen of June 1, 2017, BGBl. I p. 1416, https://www.bmwi.de/Redaktion/DE/Downloads/Gesetz/neuntes- gesetz- zur- aenderung- des- gesetzes- gegen- wettbewerbsbeschraen kungen.pdf?__ blob=publicationFile&v=4.
3. The proposal (p. 58) references Schweitzer et al. (2018); Kommission Wettbewerbsrecht (2019); Furmann et al. (2019); Crémer et al. (2019); Australian Competition and Consumer Commission (2019).
4. § 20 para 3a of the GWB proposal.
5. As defined by § 18 para 3a GWB.
6. Multi-homing is the parallel use of multiple platforms.
7. § 20 para 3a of the GWB proposal.
8. In contrast to the proposal's (p. 86) argument of insufficient flexibility of enumerative examples.
9. § 32a para 1 of the GWB proposal.
10. § 19a of the GWB proposal.
11. As defined in § 18 Abs. 3a GWB.
12. Bundeskartellamt.
13. § 19a para 1 of the GWB proposal.
14. § 19a para 2 of the GWB proposal.
15. European Commission, Case AT.39740—Google Search (Shopping).
16. § 19a para 2 No. 2 of the GWB proposal.
17. § 19a para 2 No. 3 of the GWB proposal.
18. § 19a para 2 No. 4 of the GWB proposal.

19. § 19a para 2 No. 5 of the GWB proposal.
20. § 18 para 3b of the GWB proposal; for a US approach to defining platform's market power as 'cost of exclusion' to third parties see Feld (2019), 42 ff.
21. See section 'Evolution of Platform Regulation'.
22. E.g., Regulation (EC) No 715/2007 on type approval of motor vehicles with respect to emissions from light passenger and commercial vehicles (Euro 5 and Euro 6) and on access to vehicle repair and maintenance information, OJ L 171/1; Directive 2010/40/EU of July 7, 2010, on the framework for the deployment of Intelligent Transport Systems in the field of road transport and for interfaces with other modes of transport, OJ 2010 L 207/1; Directive (EU) 2015/2366 of November, 25, 2015 on payment services in the internal market, OJ 2015 L 337/35.
23. § 18 para 3 No. 2 of the GWB proposal.
24. § 50f para 1 of the GWB proposal.
25. Staatsvertrag zur Modernisierung der Medienordnung in Deutschland, April 2020 (entered into force November 7, 2020), https://www.rlp.de/fileadmin/rlp-stk/pdf-Dateien/Medienpolitik/Medienstaatsvertrag.pdf; English version available at https://ec.europa.eu/growth/tools-databases/tris/de/index.cfm/search/?trisaction=search.detail&year=2020&num=26&dLang=EN.
26. See §§ 52 ff. RStV.
27. Vierter Staatsvertrag zur Änderung rundfunkrechtlicher Staatsverträge, July 20, 1999, LT-Drs. BW 12/4568, 30.
28. BVerfGE 90, 60 (87); 114, 371 (387).
29. BVerfGE 12, 205 (261).
30. § 18 para 3b of the GWB proposal.
31. § 52d RStV.
32. § 52c para 1 RStV.
33. Directive 2002/22/EC, now incorporated into directive (EU) 2018/1972 as Art. 114.
34. Gesetz zum Zehnten Rundfunkänderungsstaatsvertrag, LT-Drs. BW 14/2705, p. 45.
35. See e.g. § 11 RStV.
36. §52 para 1 No. 1 RStV.
37. Gesetz zum Zehnten Rundfunkänderungsstaatsvertrag, LT-Drs. BW 14/2705, p. 41.
38. § 2 para 2 No. 14 MStV.
39. § 78 No. 2 MStV.
40. § 2 para 2 No. 15 MStV.
41. § 2 para 2 No. 16 MStV.
42. § 91 para 2 No. 1 MStV.
43. § 2 para 2 No. 14 lit b MStV.
44. Art. 1 para 1 lit. a of Directive 2010/13/EU.
45. It was unclear under the previous platform regime, whether OTT services and smart TV portals could even constitute platforms, since they hold no control over the delivery infrastructure and usually provide access to applications rather than content, see Fuchs and Försterling (2018), 293; Chardon and Heyeckhaus (2015), 22 f.
46. § 2 para 2 No. 14 MStV.
47. For media platforms see § 85 MStV, for intermediaries see § 93 para 1 MStV.
48. § 85 MStV.
49. § 93 para 1 MStV.

50. § 82 para 2 MStV.
51. While incorporating some aspects of the regulatory authorities' previous specifications, see ZAK (2016).
52. § 84 para 2 MStV.
53. § 94 MStV.
54. § 94 para 2 MStV.
55. § 18 para 4 GWB.
56. § 81 MStV.
57. § 84 para 3 MStV.
58. § 84 para 3 MStV.
59. § 84 para 4 MStV.
60. § 84 para 5 MStV.
61. BVerfGE 149, 222 (261).
62. BVerfGE 149, 222 (261).
63. § 2 para 2 No. 16 MStV, see also explanatory memorandum to the MStV, LT-Drs. NRW 17/9052, p. 127.
64. § 2 para 2 No. 14 lit. b MStV.
65. Explanatory memorandum to the MStV, LT-Drs. NRW 17/9052, p. 125, 127.
66. § 2 para 2 No. 16 MStV, see also explanatory memorandum to the MStV, LT-Drs. NRW 17/9052, p. 127.
67. For non-linear services' impact on public opinion see Hartmann (2019), 341 ff.
68. § 84 para 3, 4 MStV.
69. BVerfGE 149, 222 (261).
70. § 20 para 3a of the GWB proposal.
71. § 32a para 1 of the GWB proposal.
72. 'Intermediary market power' in §18a para 3b of the GWB proposal; intermediary and platform obligations in §§ 84, 85, 94 MStV.
73. An English version of the press code is available at https://www.presserat.de/en.html?file=files/presserat/dokumente/download/Press%20Code.pdf.
74. The German Press Council is similar to the British Press Council.
75. § 19a para 1 of the GWB proposal.
76. § 18 para 3b of the GWB proposal.
77. § 18 para 3 GWB.
78. § 18 para 3b of the GWB proposal.
79. The general prohibition of restrictive and anticompetitive agreements and practices is codified in § 1 GWB.
80. On the recent case of the German Cartel Office involving Facebook see Buttarelli (2019), for the subsequent judgement see BGH, decision of June 23, 2020, KVR 69/19.
81. See § 30 GWB, introduced with ninth amendment to the GWB in 2017, which exempts certain agreements and cooperation in the press sector from the general prohibition of restrictive and anticompetitive agreements and practices in § 1 GWB.
82. Entwurf eines Neunten Gesetzes zur Änderung des Gesetzes gegen Wettbewerbsbeschränkungen, BT-Drs. 18/10207, p. 54.
83. § 26 RStV.
84. § 26 para 2 RStV.

85. As was explicitly mentioned by the Commission during the notification procedure for the State Treaty.

REFERENCES

Australian Competition and Consumer Commission. 2019. 'Digital Platforms Inquiry—Final Report'. https://www.accc.gov.au/system/files/Digital%20platforms%20inquiry%20-%20final%20report.pdf.

Buttarelli, Giovanni. 2019. 'This Is Not an Article on Data Protection and Competition Law'. *CPI Antitrust Chronicles*, February 2019. https://edps.europa.eu/sites/edp/files/publication/19-03-11_cpi_buttarelli_en.pdf.

BMWI. 2020. 'Referentenentwurf [draft bill] GWB-Digitalisierungsgesetz', January 24. https://www.bmwi.de/Redaktion/DE/Downloads/G/gwb-digitalisierungsgesetz-referentenentwurf.pdf?__blob=publicationFile&v=1061.

BMWI. 2017. 'Weissbuch Digitale Plattformen'. https://www.de.digital/DIGITAL/Redaktion/DE/Publikation/weissbuch.pdf?__blob=publicationFile&v=8.

CDU/CSU/SPD. 2018. 'Koalitionsvertrag [coalition agreement]', March 12. https://www.bundesregierung.de/resource/blob/975226/847984/5b8bc23590d4cb2892b31c987ad672b7/2018-03-14-koalitionsvertrag-data.pdf?download=1.

Chardon, Carin, and Katrin Heyeckhaus. 2015. 'Plattformregulierung aus Sicht der Unterhaltungselektronik'. *Zeitschrift für Urheber- und Medienrecht* 59(1): 21–26.

Crémer, Jacques, Yves-Alexandre de Montjoye, and Heike Schweitzer. 2019. 'Competition Policy for the Digital Era'. Final report. https://ec.europa.eu/competition/publications/reports/kd0419345enn.pdf;.

Feld, Harold. 2019. 'The Case for the Digital Platform Act'. Roosevelt Institute. May 2019. https://rooseveltinstitute.org/wp-content/uploads/2020/07/RI-Case-for-the-Digital-Platform-Act-201905.pdf.

Fuchs, Thomas, and Matthias Försterling. 2018. 'Neue Entscheidungen in der Plattformregulierung—Plattformrechtliche Relevanz von Live-Streaming-Portalen und Zero-Rating-Angeboten'. *Multimedia und Recht* 21(5): 292–96.

Furmann, Jason, Diane Coyle, Amelia Fletcher, Derek McAuley, and Philip Marsden. 2019. 'Unlocking Digital Competition'. Report of the Digital Competition Expert Panel. March 2019. https://assets.publishing.service.gov.uk/government/uploads/system/uploads/attachment_data/file/785547/unlocking_digital_competition_furman_review_web.pdf.

Gostomzyk, Tobias, Ottfried Jarren, Frank Lobigs, and Christoph Neuberger. 2019. 'Kooperationsorientierte Weiterentwicklung der Medienordnung'. https://www.vbw-bayern.de/Redaktion/Frei-zugaengliche-Medien/Abteilungen-GS/Planung-und-Koordination/2019/Downloads/19-11-20-Kooperationsorientierte-Weiterentwicklung-der-Medienordnung.pdf.

Hartmann, Sarah. 2019. *Die europäische Regulierung audiovisueller Medien*. Berlin: Peter Lang.

Hönig D'Orville, Melanie. 2019. 'Die Perspektive der Länder: AVMD-Richtlinie, der 22. Rundfunkänderungsstaatsvertrag und der 'Medienstaatsvertrag'—Angemessene Instrumente für die Regulierungsherausforderungen?' *Zeitschrift für Urheber- und Medienrecht* 63(2): 104–9.

Höppner, Thomas. 2020. 'Plattform-Regulierung light—Zum Konzept der Unternehmen mit überragender marktübergreifender Bedeutung in der 10. GWB-Novelle'. *Wirtschaft und Wettbewerb* 69(2): 71–79.

Höppner, Thomas, and Jan Markus Weber. 2020. 'Die Modernisierung der Missbrauchskontrolle nach dem Referentenentwurf für eine 10. GWB-Novelle'. *Kommunikation und Recht* 23(1): 24–51.

Kommission Wettbewerbsrecht 4.0. 2019. 'Ein neuer Wettbewerbsrahmen für die Digitalwirtschaft'. https://www.bmwi.de/Redaktion/DE/Publikationen/Wirtschaft/bericht-der-kommission-wettbewerbsrecht-4-0.pdf?__blob=publicationFile&v=12.

Schütz, Raimund. 2018. 'Regulierung in der digitalen Medienwelt—Fünf aktuelle Herausforderungen'. *Multimedia und Recht* 21(1): 36–39.

Schwartmann, Rolf, Maximilian Hermann, and Robin L. Mühlenbeck. 2019. 'Eine Medienordnung für Intermediäre—Das Zwei-Säulen-Modell zur Sicherung der Vielfalt im Netz'. *Multimedia und Recht* 22(8): 498–503.

Schweitzer, Heike, Justus Haucap, Wolfgang Kerber, and Robert Welker. 2018. 'Modernisierung der Missbrauchsaufsicht für marktbeherrschende Unternehmen'. Projekt im Auftrag des BMWI, Nr. 66/17. August 2018. https://www.bmwi.de/Redaktion/DE/Publikationen/Wirtschaft/modernisierung-der-missbrauchsaufsicht-fuer-marktmaechtige-unternehmen.pdf?__blob=publicationFile&v=15.

ZAK. 2016. 'Satzung über die Zugangsfreiheit zu digitalen Diensten und zur Plattformregulierung gemäß § 53 Rundfunkstaatsvertrag', April 26. https://www.lfk.de/fileadmin/media/recht/Zugangs-und_Plattformsatzung_14.06.2016.pdf.

3

Overcoming Market Power in Online Video Platforms

ELI M. NOAM ■

THE MARKET STRUCTURE OF ONLINE VIDEO

Few questions are fraught with more long-term implications than the way we shape our communications system. If the medium is indeed the message, and if these messages influence people and institutions, then tomorrow's media, and today's media policies, will govern future society, culture, and economy.[1]

It is therefore important to recognize that we are on the verge of an enormous leap in media and communications, and consequently also of one of its major disruptions of social and economic arrangements. It is the transition of TV media into its third generation—following broadcasting and multichannel—online video. There are many positive aspects to this emerging online video system, but also troubling ones. In no particular order, the latter include privacy, security, morality, piracy, accessibility, affordability, national culture, consumer protection, and antisocial behaviour. All these—and others—are significant problems. And yet, arguably, the major policy issue is *digital dominance*. Many other problems flow from such market power. (Conversely, several problems might be alleviated by it.)

It is complex and expensive to do digital platforms and services well. Multiple systems need be in place and be integrated. Processes must operate at almost lightning speed, with great reliability, easy scalability, user friendliness, and flexibility of configuration. They must be secure, with marketing and branding advantages, and able to implement technologies for content and advertising such as individualization. They must integrate several core competencies and operations in what might be called a 'video cloud': running a video platform facing the user and filling it with content; operating an infrastructure platform to store, process, connect, and deliver content; and extracting and deploying data. This favours large providers that have the advantage of economies of scale and scope, and the related factors of network effects, economies of distance and of data, and the synergies of vertical integration.

There are significant advantages to scale in digital platforms. The largest providers have the greatest choice in applications, content, and advanced technology, which attracts users. Users, in turn, attract other users through network effects. A large user base attracts applications providers (at a lower price), advertisers (at a higher price), and still more users (at a higher price.) At the same time, it also lowers its unit cost. Thus, large providers have a distinct advantage, for example, in generating the functionalities of interactivity, individualization, or peer-to-peer (P2P) operations, all of which require high capital outlays to create but are relatively cheap to operate subsequently. There are also major advantages of connection to data, to advertising, and to content aggregation. In combination, economies of scope, scale, and verticality create winner-takes-all scenarios for infrastructure and for usage on platforms, leading to a highly concentrated digital industry.

When the market structure of digital platforms is uncompetitive, the results are likely to be:

- Market power over users who could not easily switch ('consumer lock-in').
- Reduced competition, higher prices, and lower innovation ('monopoly power').
- Difficulty for users of one platform to interact with users and elements of other platforms ('fragmentation').
- A vertical chain of service elements closed to most outside providers ('walled garden').
- The reduced diversity of applications and content sources ('narrowcasting').
- A constricted access to users by content providers, often domestic ones, and a resultant stronger economic, cultural, and political influence of the platform ('gatekeeping').
- Market power over outside providers of hardware, software, transmission, and content, who fear exclusion ('foreclosure').

While such dynamics apply to just about all aspects of digital platforms, they raise special concern when it comes to media applications. Media concentration, of course, is nothing new (Noam 2016). What is different in the digital economy is its extreme global extension by the top providers. In consequence, the focus of this chapter is the market power of digital media, specifically in video entertainment, and what to do about it.

First, some empirical data to quantify the issue. Table 3.1 provides our calculations of the concentrations of various submarkets of online video in the United

Table 3.1 MARKET SHARES OF VIDEO PLATFORMS (USA)[a]

Media Type	HHI	Market Leaders
Internet Service Providers, 2018[b]	2,259	Regional Cable Operator (30%)
		Regional Telecom Wireline Operator (16%)
		National Mobile Operators (53%: Verizon: 23.5%, AT&T: 15.3%, T-Mobile/Sprint: 14.2%)
Public Content Delivery Networks, 2017/18[c]	1,828	Akamai (31%)
		Amazon/Fastly (16%)
		Google (16%)
Public Online Infrastructure Platforms, 2017[d]	2,611	Amazon Web Services (41.5%)
		Microsoft Azure (29.4%)
Subscription-Based Streaming Video Content Platforms, 2019		
USA[e]	3,097	Netflix (49.4%)
		Disney (Hulu and ESPN) (20.2%)
		Amazon Prime Video (10.1%)
Europe (18 Countries)[f]	3,221	Netflix (52%)
		Amazon Prime Video (21%)
Advertising-Supported Video Platforms, 2018[g]	1,916	Google YouTube (33.2%)
		Verizon Media (16.4%)
		Facebook (15.2%)
Live TV Streaming Services, 2019[h]	2,218	Disney Hulu Live TV (29.1%)
		Dish/Sling TV (29%)
		Google YouTube TV (17.3%)
Social Media Streaming Platforms, 2018[i]	3,537	Facebook (incl. Instagram) (41.9%)
		Google YouTube (38.7%)
		Amazon Twitch.tv (16.6%)
US Online Advertising Market, 2019[j]	1,940	Google (37.1%)
		Facebook (20.6%)
Content Platforms for User-Generated Content, 2015[k]		
USA	2,968	Google YouTube (54%)
UK	2,651	Google YouTube (51%)
France	3,258	Google YouTube (52%)
		Vivendi Dailymotion (23%)
Japan	3,633	Google YouTube (53%)
		NicoNico (28%)
Content Production and Acquisition, 2019[l]	1,238	Disney (23%)
		Comcast, Netflix, Viacom, each 12.4%
		AT&T 11.7%
Consumer Streaming Devices, 2019[m]	2,829	Apple (37.5%)
		Samsung (14.3%)
		Amazon (1.2%)
Total Weighted Average	2,473	

(continued)

Table 3.1 CONTINUED

[a] Full data tables are available (Noam 2021a and 2021b.)

[b] Based on reported 'Data Revenues' from company annual reports. Telecom wireline and cable companies in the United States operate regionally, and a regional market concentration is therefore more instructive than national figures, since there is almost no intraindustry overlap. The two major telecom wireline ISPs are also the major nationwide wireless providers, and their national wireless market shares are added to their regional wireline shares. Their market shares are based on reported revenues for wireless 'Data Services'.

[c] Developed from company reports.

[d] Calculated with data from McAfee (Coles 2018).

[e] Calculated from market shares developed using 2019 revenue data. Where revenue data were not directly available, they were calculated by multiplying the number of subscribers by annual subscription price.

[f] Calculated with data from Kagan Research (O'Halloran 2019).

[g] Calculated from market shares developed by obtaining 2018 unique monthly visitors to various streaming services (Statista 2018).

[h] Calculated from market shares developed from 2019 subscription and user numbers. Data from *Variety* (Spangler 2019) and *The Motley Fool* (Sun 2019).

[i] Calculated from market shares developed from 2018 minutes spent watching particular advertising supported outlets (also used: Tran 2017).

[j] Calculated with transnational data from Nikki Wardle (2018).

[k] Calculated with data from Ofcom (2015), also using data from Statista (2015).

[l] Based on Variety Intelligence Platform (Bridge 2020). Allocation of general media companies to online video 33%.

[m] Consumer streaming device subsegments are smartphones, tablets, laptops, and TV streaming devices. Market shares and revenues for each subsegment from Statista. Allocated 30% of smartphone revenues and 20% of laptop revenues to video, based on usage. Overall segment market shares and HHI weighted averages based on revenues.

States, as measured by the Herfindahl-Hirschman Index (HHI). (An index over 2,500 is considered to indicate a highly concentrated market.)

Thus, we observe a high market concentration in most online media activities. Weighted by the size of the subindustry, the average sector market concentration is at an HHI figure of 2,437, just about at the threshold of 'highly concentrated' by the US Government's definition of 2,500.

This high number is not surprising. Concentration has always been extreme in telecom-type infrastructure networks, which were considered, for a long time, a 'natural' monopoly. It has also been high in TV networks, film distribution, major websites, and information technology (IT). The same is true for newer Internet activities such as social media, web browsers, search engines, etc. Given all the incidence of market power in the sub elements of online video, it would be surprising if such power did not emerge for online video as a whole.

OPTIONS TO REDUCE DIGITAL DOMINANCE IN ONLINE VIDEO PLATFORMS

Given the passion over a concentration in the digital sector, it is predictable that market power in the online video area will lead to regulatory responses. The obvious reason for the stronger concern over concentration in media and information is that most people desire a greater diversity in their information sources than in their computer hardware. They wish more choices for themselves and for the political process. They consider media to be a different category from other industries and functionalities, with a key role in politics and culture. And of media, none is more broadly influential than video. In consequence, regulatory approaches to deal with digital dominance are quite likely to emerge first for video media operations. From there, they might spread. Wherever digital interventions are going, video media are likely to be there first.

There are several basic approaches to deal with market power, especially in an essential service:

- Separation of infrastructure and distribution from the production of the good and service itself.
- Market share ceilings.
- Governmental or public service provision.
- Licensing subject to conditions.
- Restrictions of extensions to other product lines.
- Unbundling of product elements.
- Regulation of prices and of firm behaviour.
- Nonapproval of mergers, and divestitures/break-ups of parts of existing firms.
- Ownership and cross-ownership restrictions.
- Foreign ownership limitations and quotas on foreign imports.
- Establishment of a public utility status for dominant firms.
- Interoperability and access requirements to the bottleneck facilities of dominant firms.

Each of these approaches has some advantages but is also problematic in one way or another. For example, a vertical break-up or separation would reduce foreclosure but still leave intact the main source of market power, the domination in one segment. A behavioural regulation would limit conduct harmful to consumers and other providers, but requires constant governmental intervention in a fast-moving field. A public utility status would reduce the exercise of monopoly power but entrench it. Space does not permit an analysis.[2] We do, however, discuss a proposal based on the last option, that of access. While the analysis focuses on streaming video, it is similarly applicable to most situations of digital dominance.

THE OPEN VIDEO SYSTEM

Overview

The option proposed here is to establish an *open video system*. It is based on access, not on break-up. It incorporates aspects of several other approaches. There are three basic elements to this system. All can be applicable to other segments of the digital economy.

1. There are access rights to infrastructure and platform elements, where significant media market power (SMMP) exists. Such access rights exist for the users/consumers and for the users' delegated *information intermediaries*.[3]
2. Such access would be accomplished through interfaces that must be offered by platforms that possess SMMP. These are known as Applications Program Interfaces (APIs), a way to let software by other parties interoperate with the platform's software.
3. Conditions of access would be governed by the nondiscriminatory principle of 'most favoured nation', subject to arbitration by a self-regulatory process.

We now discuss these elements, starting with a key element, the information intermediaries.

Information Intermediaries

The key to dealing with market power is to give users a meaningful choice among providers[4] and, where some large companies hold advantages that are insurmountable in the short term, to give smaller providers the opportunity to compete. A meaningful user choice requires an enabling of a new type of operator, namely 'information intermediaries' that would act on behalf of customers to seek the best options. Most consumers are busy and technically unsophisticated. To make the option of choice practical for them, they should be able to delegate the implementation of their digital activities to professional intermediaries. Figure 3.1 shows this schematically. Intermediary 1 operates between the end user and the several video platforms, A and B. (There would be multiple intermediaries for an end user to choose from, but they are not charted so as to reduce clutter.) The figure also shows the access of other providers, such as an Independent, to those platforms, enabling such a firm to access a bottleneck facility held by the platform.

For example, an information intermediary could recommend and select content, if it could access and review the content catalogues of several platforms and their price for viewing. Based on the intermediary's own information about the films, plus the user preferences communicated to it, plus past user choices, its own algorithms would make choices or recommendations.

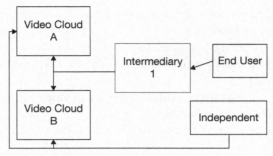

Figure 3.1 Information Intermediaries

For online video, the information intermediary's functions might include:

- Search for content following instructions and parameters set by the end user.
- Find the most favourable option in terms of content and price, and negotiate on behalf of the end user for favourable terms.
- Filter out undesirable videos, such as those with profanity, sex, violence, or hate, per end user instructions.
- Deal with payments to platforms for subscriptions and single videos, and bill the end user periodically.
- Set data privacy settings on behalf of its clients, monitor what happens to that data subsequently, and collect royalties for the use of customer data, where such use was agreed upon.
- Deploy its own algorithms, or those of independent algorithm providers.
- Set up and update technology tools, such as encryption, anonymization, and other techniques to enable users to create electronic moats around their information.
- Select infrastructure elements of the pathway from the video provider to the end user.
- Play a role in selecting advertisements, based on instructions by users in which products and types of ads they are interested in.

Such a system would create user choice in search, algorithms, data control, content filtering, and infrastructure.

Business Models for Information Intermediaries

There could be a variety of business models for the information intermediaries:

- A for-profit company offering subscriptions.
- A charitable provision by an NGO such as a church organization.

- An ideological provision by organizations with a definite perspective, as a service to its adherents.
- A community effort by an open-source cooperative.
- An advertising-based service, with the ability to insert ads that reach its consumer clients.
- A vendor-oriented service, with commission payments from platforms for mediating access to buyers.
- A subsidized service, as an offshoot of public service broadcasting or of a public university.
- An offering by a large tech or media company as part of its more general applications suite, for example by Google as part of its search functionalities. (In that case, the company would have to demonstrate that it would not give any preference to its own content platform.)
- A feature offered by a consumer electronics company such as Samsung, and baked into its TV set to attract buyers.
- A collaborative operation by rival smaller platforms as a way to divert some viewers from the dominant platform with SMMP.
- A service by an infrastructure network company such as Verizon or Vodafone as a feature of its transmission network.
- A feature by credit card companies as a supplementary service to their customers.
- Commissions for the authorized sale of anonymized user data or bulk data to third parties (data brokerage).
- Commissions from app developers for app sales through the intermediary (similar to other 'app stores').
- Fees by third parties for extra services, such as analytics-as-a-service, for example on how video products are appreciated by customers.
- A membership model in which the users of a platform, such as an organization of independent film-makers, become participants in a cooperative data management operation, supported by their membership fees plus possible additional fees.
- An industry-wide cooperative of multiple for-profit service providers and platforms.[5]

Most likely are hybrid models that combine several of these approaches. For example, a 'freemium' model with the free use of basic functionalities, but additional service level requiring payment. More generally, the wide variety of business models and types of organizations indicates a potentially vigorous presence of intermediaries. They require, however, a mechanism to interoperate with dominant platforms.

Access Arrangements

Video platforms with significant market power (SMP) would be potentially open to rival providers of content or services in several ways, including through the proprietary interoperation arrangements. These APIs are designed to allow out-side programmers and companies access to a portion of the system, without giving them full access. Netflix used to provide a free public API which gave such access to its film and TV series catalogue. This allowed independent programmers to plug in and develop consumer products. An example was the app 'A Better Queue', which made recommendations of movies worth watching on Netflix. This service, and others like it, were ended when Netflix closed off the API in 2014, limiting access to select partners.[6]

There have been no regulatory requirements for API access arrangements. But nothing on a constitutional level (in the United States) prevents govern-ment regulation of APIs.[7] [8] In several cases, companies with market power have been compelled to open up their information and share it in the past (European Commission 2007).[9] [10] On a practical level, cybersecurity is an issue to consider. API access makes it easier to hack the platform. To deal with that, there could instead be a list of acceptable third parties that can gain these APIs, as long as no favouritism is provided to allies of the platform company.

The overall principle should be that companies with SMMP need to give an API access that is sufficient to achieve the remediation of their dominance by pro-viding consumers with realistic alternatives.

Administration

The administration of access arrangements would be based on basic principles set by a governmental regulator. But the implementation and specifics would be by a consortium of stakeholders, both from the private sector, and importantly, also from the NGO sector. Thus, the third element of the system is *self-administration and arbitration*. To the extent that no agreement is reached, it would be taken up by the regulatory agency.

User choice does not mean that all options will be available. Regulators could set ceilings or floors on certain transactions. For example, child porn or cyberbul-lying might be restricted on any platform and through any intermediary. These regulated limits need not be identical globally but can vary by jurisdiction.

Market Definition

One of the main tasks for the self-regulatory mechanism would be to delineate market definitions. A key question to determining the market share is how that market is defined. It cannot be defined too narrowly or else just about every com-pany would have SMMP in its sliver of a market. But if the definition is too wide, none would have more than a minor share of a huge market. What makes sense is to match the 'significant' media market power with 'significant segments' of the media market that make economic and intuitive sense. For example, the mar-kets could be the major links in the chain of the online video market: content

production, aggregation, content platforms, data operations, infrastructure platforms, Internet Service Providers (ISPs), and consumer media devices.

Access Provision by Whom?

Which companies must offer access? Requiring every last tiny operator to do so
would be a regulatory overkill. And what purpose would it serve? For a company,
having a small market share means, by definition, that there are important alternatives for users, suppliers, or customers.[11]

What should a test for market power be? It should be based on a clear standard
that is based on empirical and analytical observations of the behaviour of dominant firms and of tight oligopolies. In the United States, the Department of
Justice's Merger Guidelines define a concentrated industry rather than a single
firm's market power. The HHI[12] sets 2,500 as a 'highly concentrated industry'. This
measure would occur, for example, in a market with four firms, each holding 25%
of the market; or with one firm with 40% and two with 21%. In Europe, market
share is one factor of several, but the unofficial shorthand number is often given
as 30%. In most industries, a firm with a market share of more than 30% would
be considered to have SMP. However, for the media sector, a special sensitivity to
high market concentration and gatekeeping power applies, and it might result in a
stricter standard. Such a threshold can be termed 'significant *media* market power',
or SMMP. A company with a market share of over 25% would be considered to
have SMMP. Even this is a fairly high threshold, considering that it means that two
such companies could together control half of the market. A high market share
alone is not sufficient to establish the possession of SMP (dominance), but it is
unlikely that a firm without a significant share of the relevant market would be
in a dominant position. The market share threshold number would therefore be a
rebuttable presumption for SMP.

A company with SMMP in a particular market segment would have to provide
access in that specific segment, in an unbundled fashion.[13]

The Pricing of Access

How much a dominant firm could charge for the access to its segments is a per-
ennially difficult question. One approach would be to establish, in effect, regulated public utility pricing based on some formula, such as that of rate of return,
or on avoided cost, or on benchmarks set by others, or on past prices. A second
approach is that of straight cost engineering, including that of 'forward-looking
long-run incremental cost pricing'. One calculates the extra cost for the company to create and build the segment given new technology, and adds a reasonable profit margin on top (Deloitte 2014; Noam 2001). A third approach is to
require 'nondiscrimination' in pricing (Wu 2003). A version of this approach is a
'most-favoured nation' model, which means that similarly positioned customers,

intermediary information curators, or rivals must be treated similarly in terms of price and service conditions.[14] The approach originates in the world of trade negotiations, where countries agreed that a tariff rate set by a country on a product from a second country would have to apply to the same product exported by a third country.

Nondiscrimination does not solve the problem of a provider of an element charging *all* rival users a monopoly price—as long as the same price is extracted from all. To deal with that one would have to add a test for 'fair and reasonable' on top of the nondiscrimination test. In the IT world this process is known as 'Fair, Reasonable, and Non-Discriminatory' (FRAND) pricing. It originated as a way to set the price charged by company A to its rival B for a patent license. FRAND pricing is most commonly seen in situations in which some users benefit from the technology developed by others, e.g., for video codecs or for mobile telecommunications. It is established through an industry organization or industry standards committee that would include the major stakeholders, including users. They set up a process for determining FRAND conditions. Even more important, this sets up a self-regulatory mechanism to adjudicate complaints and have its decisions adhered to (Lewis 2014; Rypka 2018).

Accessibility

Access rights (or 'accessibility') can operate in several directions: *upstream* (towards the content creation); *downstream* (towards the user); and *sideways* (towards parallel elements; for example, an infrastructure network operator may want access to another infrastructure network operator in order to expand its geographical range; in an interactive game, users want access to other users.)[15]

ACCESSIBILITY TO CONTENT PRODUCERS AND AGGREGATORS
Content products cannot usually be accessed as a right. The speech rights of content producers mean that they can control whom they speak to. There are exceptions, however, in traditional TV media. In some countries, highly important sports events are accessible to all distribution networks that wish to do so.[16] This reduces the ability of a rights holder to extract monopoly profits from pay-viewers or advertisers.

More significant is the system of 'compulsory licenses'. For music, anyone has rights, without any special permission, to song compositions and lyrics created and copyrighted by others, to perform them freely, and to sell recordings. A governmentally set fee must be paid, however. That is an extraordinary right, nonexistent in other media. Should there also be a compulsory license for online video content? To software applications? That would mean that another platform could retransmit the content as long as it pays a regulated fee.[17] Under normal circumstances, the principles against compelled speech would protect the content owner or licensee from being forced to let others use and sell their programs, especially if they are competitors. But suppose, hypothetically, that Netflix has 50%

of the subscription video streaming market and insists that a Hollywood major studio had to license all of its output to Netflix alone and to no one else. Such exclusivity would be most likely held by American courts to be an exercise of monopoly power and to constitute a market foreclosure. The remedy would likely be to require nonexclusive licenses. This is not quite the same as full accessibility by compulsory license. It would still require a license negotiated by the platform with SMMP with the content provider, with the presumption that the terms of such license would be governed by FRAND principles.

There is even less of an access right *into* content. Control over a channel or a program is part of its editorial prerogative, and there are no rights to be included in, e.g., a news program or a game show.[18]

A more nuanced access arrangement would be to require a subscription platform with SMMP to offer its content also in an unbundled form, i.e., 'à la carte'. A user would be able to access a piece of content by buying a single-event ticket, without having to buy a subscription. The ticket price would be set by the platform. But it would be a 'most-favoured nation' price, i.e., nondiscriminatory. And while such a price might be set prohibitively high to discourage such use altogether, it would not make sense in commercial sense to prevent all one-time users altogether if they can be charged a fee that is net profitable to the platform. Publishers of popular magazines offer single-issue as well as subscription sales. Requiring such an unbundling would not be a restriction of a platform's speech rights—it already distributes the content to everyone who wants to subscribe—but rather only on the manner it bundles.

Such seller-required bundling (known as 'tying') has, in other cases, been cut down by courts or by laws, for example for Hollywood studios' packaging of films offered to movie theatres. To find a tying requires market power in one or several of the tied items. In the case of a subscription platform with market power, this would be true by definition. Thus, there should be no fundamental impediment to mandate an à-la-carte option, and there are good antitrust grounds for a governmental or private challenge of a take-it-or-leave-it subscription bundle.

The implication of an à-la-carte option would be that a user's delegated information intermediary could find a film through its search function across multiple platforms, and, if desired by the end user, purchase it on behalf of that user, at the price set by the platform, without requiring a full subscription.

In conclusion, the protections of intellectual property rights and of speech rights are fairly firm in denying mandated access rights to content created by others, especially with the intent to redistribute such content to third parties for profit. Where such rights exist, they are coupled with a mechanism of compulsory license payments. But where a platform holds significant media market power, it could not require exclusive licenses from content providers, and it might have to offer content also on an unbundled basis, at prices it sets, as long as these are not discriminatory.

ACCESSIBILITY TO CONTENT PLATFORMS

We now move to the accessibility onto content platforms themselves. When it comes to content platforms such as Netflix, Amazon, Hulu, or Dailymotion, what should be the access rights of others? Normally, such a platform should not be required to carry content it finds commercially uninteresting, or objectionable in content terms, or created by rivals. However, if it holds SMMP, its judgments on politics and morality as well as its business interests would create a significant society-wide gatekeeping role over content. That role would create an endless set of disputes. It would also create an opening for governments to mandate the company to become a private censor by imposing responsibility and liability. To some, therefore, content platforms with market power are like public utilities, with a requirement to serve every provider of content on equal terms. A mechanism of compulsory licensing could conceivably be used for the access by rival content onto a platform with SMMP. This would resemble a common carrier obligation that exists for several infrastructure industries such as telecom or airlines. But to others, the platforms are more like publishers who curate content and shape it into branded packages, and whose judgment is protected under free speech rules.

Fortunately, there is a middle ground. First, platforms without SMMP need not carry any content they do not wish to carry. That is pretty obvious. Second and more importantly, platforms with SMMP would also not be required to carry content they do not wish to carry, but they would have to make it possible for their users to conveniently reach such outside content. To do so, the dominant platforms must provide the information intermediaries with API access to their content catalogue. This enables the information intermediaries to help end users in their selection function, by enabling them to conveniently find and access a particular item of content, on whatever platform it is stored.

ACCESSIBILITY TO INFRASTRUCTURE PLATFORMS
Normally, there would be no requirement for an infrastructure platform to provide transmission, storage, or processing service to independents or third-party rivals, or to collocate the independents' hardware servers in its data centres. But where the infrastructure platform holds SMMP, the same principles apply, to offer APIs to the Independent, such as accessibility to its transmission networks and data centres at reasonable points, and at FRAND pricing.

ACCESSIBILITY TO LAST-MILE TRANSMISSION SERVICE
The last-mile transmission segment—the communications link that connects the end user to a core network further upstream—is provided by the ISPs, which use several types of links, mostly phone lines, cable lines, and mobile wireless. These links are either operated by the ISP itself, or leased from a telecom infrastructure network company. 'Access' can mean two things:

- *Access to an ISP* by any content, content provider, or platform. This is the basic issue addressed in the net-neutrality debate. The principle of nondiscrimination would operate where SMMP exists, just as it would when it comes to other parts of the online video. And while this might restrict ISPs with such market power, it also gives them stronger bargaining power where they operate content platforms and intermediate content distribution networks, which many of them do. (In the United States content platforms are operated by AT&T, Comcast, and Verizon, which are also the three largest ISPs.) The ISPs would not be restricted in network management functions, as long as these are applied to all similar types of data streams.

- *Access by an ISP to the last-mile infrastructure.* A 'virtual' (facilities-less) ISP may seek to operate on top of the infrastructure. To picture this, imagine, in an analogy, a transportation company operating trains, but using the tracks of another company, which may be a rival for transportation customers. What kind of access would the train company have to those tracks? For ISPs, this kind of access is often implemented in Europe and Japan by regulations that require unbundled access by telecom operators and set a pricing system. This arrangement gives consumers additional options in choosing ISPs. But it also reduces incentives for additional infrastructure. Access rights by a virtual ISP to the local infrastructure of a communications network company would exist solely where there exists SMMP. Where no such market power exists, or where the SMMP exists on both sides, access would be negotiated on a commercial basis.

ACCESSIBILITY TO DATA

Data give competitive advantage in individualizing content, recommending content, and supporting effective advertising platforms. To be consistent in concept, where there is SMMP, consumer data should be accessible to competitors and independents.[19] However, the problem is the protection of privacy. Making that user data accessible to everybody willing to pay an access price will spread personal information widely. There is thus a clash between the goals of protecting user information and reducing media platform power. In that situation, privacy should take priority. In consequence, the data would not be accessible to rivals as a matter of right, and in fact should even be pre-cluded from being passed on. It should be available to others, if at all, only in broad aggregates.

The protection of user data from wide access does not mean that market power should prevail in the exploitation of user data. There is another way to deal with that problem, based on the of the information curators described earlier. Users should be able to control subsequent use of personal information generated in a transaction with them. First, for all data operations above a certain size, they should be offered access to a menu of data-usage preferences. User permission requires full disclosure, and with an easy ability to stop such usage. Users could be compensated by the platform company for various permissions, or they can offer data to other companies, thus creating competition by data brokers. Where market power exists in an activity level where such data is generated, there would be further protections. In these transactions, the end users would be represented by their information intermediaries.

CONCLUSION

This chapter proposes and develops an 'open video system' to deal with digital dominance in the online video sector. The basic principles apply to other segments of digital platforms. Accessibility to a segment of an online video media company's service or facility should exist where that company holds significant media market power. Where such market power is found, the company must provide access to such a segment through an API or similar arrangement, priced under the principle of a most-favoured nation arrangement, and administered through industry self-regulation. Standing behind the self-regulatory mechanism is the governmental regulatory agency. Thus, it is a system of 'regulated self-regulation'.

Access would be given to end users and to information intermediaries who act on their behalf, and to rivals without SMMP. Access would not be to every element, only to those where significant media market power exists. Even where such market power exists, the system does not require a break-up of such platforms. And it does not tie a forbearance from regulation to a requirement for dominant platforms to act as the policemen for governments to restrict content in ways that governments have no legal right to do themselves.

There are no access rights, however, to a rival platform's content. Nor is there is an access right by rival content to be placed on a content platform. Instead, there is an API access for intermediaries to the content catalogue of platforms with SMMP, and they can provide links to rival online video providers. Similarly, there is no access right to personal data, but an intermediary may have control over data re-use when delegated by a user as its information intermediary.

Together, these approaches would assure a dynamic content industry and user involvement, while operating on infrastructure that operates with considerable openness to all users and content providers. In doing so, the proposed open video system reduces the need to fall back on detailed governmental control and oversight.

Next-generation video media must be open and diverse in technology, content, and participants. An access to segments where a platform holds digital dominance would

- create a more competitive and open system;
- protect free speech, intellectual property, and data privacy;
- reduce gatekeeping power over content and its origin;
- strengthen technology innovation;
- lower prices and increased consumer choice.

But it will leave or exacerbate other issues. It is easier, for example, to control for user privacy when the number of participants in the data collection field is small. Therefore, for remaining or additional issues such as privacy, consumer protection, security, etc., there could be governmentally set floors and ceilings. And different countries could set them differently.

The proposed access-based system does not solve all issues, and adds complexity, but it reduces the problem of digital dominance of the platforms and its global extension, which otherwise would lead to still more complex and restrictive behavioural regulations, structural breakups, and ownership segmentations and ceilings. We should give our attention and thought to establishing such an access-based system for video media, since it will be the foundation of media policy for a long time. And it may well be a model for other parts of the digital environment with similar dominance. The time to start working on this is here and now.

NOTES

1. This article is based on the recent volumes by the author: *The Content, Impact, and Regulation of Streaming Video: The Next Generation of Media Emerges* (Noam 2021a); and *The Technology, Business, and Economics of Streaming Video: The Next Generation of Media Emerges* (Noam 2021b).
2. Noam discusses them in detail in his recent volumes (Noam 2021a, 2021b).
3. In Germany, platform-oriented market power criteria were established in 2020, targeting the so-called super market rulers (Hartman and Holznagel, in this volume).
4. In the United Kingdom, the 2019 Report of the Digital Competition Expert Panel, appointed by the government, recommended more competition rather than breakups or restrictiveness. It proposed a new regulatory body to force firms to restructure themselves so as to enable users to control their data and switch among providers (Economist 2019).
5. An example was the company Respect Network, which created the world's first trusted personal cloud network. All members subscribed to the Respect Trust Framework as a model for personal data sharing.
6. The proposed open video system would restore such alternative program recommendation guides, thus resolving the European concerns with 'prominence' and searchability of domestically oriented or public service video.
7. The European Union enabled, in its Payment Services Directive 2 (PSD2), open banking (through the access to banks' APIs). The United Kingdom required the nine largest banks to give government-licensed startups access to the banks' APIs and user data down to the transaction level. However, this regulation applies only to banking.
8. Arguments have been made that requiring the granting of APIs and access to program listings amounts to 'compelled speech' and thus violates the First Amendment of the US Constitution (Fiest 2020).
9. Microsoft, in order to get EU regulatory approval of its purchase of LinkedIn, agreed to give other companies access to certain APIs related to Microsoft Office's integration with social media services.
10. APIs can be designed to give as much or as little functionality or access as the programmer determines. For example, they can be designed to only give access to a database of information. Similarly, the access via API could be for a simple yes-no click action from the outside, or to a more complex interaction with the software. That might include the ability to use an independent algorithm, for example to

affect user selection of content, both inside one platform and across multiple platforms (Wenger 2018).

11. Many companies in the chain of online video are vertically integrated across multiple stages. In that case, the test would be for the element where they hold market power, and not for those stages where they do not.

12. An HHI is the sum of the squares of the market shares of the firms in an industry.

13. In order to make the transition from non-SMMP to SMMP smooth, there could be a phasing-in of regulatory requirements corresponding to increasing market shares. The governmental regulatory body to make the determination whether SMMP exists would be the competition authority. That agency could delegate its authority to a more specialized agency, such as the media regulator.

14. A related version is for the price to be the same as the one the dominant provider with SMMP charges to itself. This is conceptually a nice way to think, but practically the internal pricing of operations (transfer pricing) can be set at just about any rate. To determine its reasonableness would then require again some form of rate utility-style analysis.

15. Game players' connectivity to each other would be an 'indirect' sideways access that passes through several other downstream stages.

16. Strictly speaking, the access is to the event, not to a video production by a rival.

17. Or, should there be a narrowly targeted compulsory license that gives such rights only to certain platforms, in the same way that cable channels could be retransmitted in the United States but only by recognized multichannel video programming distributors (MVPDs) such as cable and satellite platforms? In 2015, the FCC expanded the definition of MVPD to a category of online channel package providers. The major US television networks fought the online video platform providers on that status issue, because they did not want to be forced to give out a compulsory license under non-discriminatory conditions, which would have reduced their control and bargaining strength. In 2017, a federal Court of Appeals agreed, and held that an over-the-top video service does not classify as a 'cable system' as defined in the US Copyright Act, and thus did not get a compulsory license to retransmit the broadcasters' content. There is, symmetrically, a question of access rights for others, such as 'virtual MVPDs' operating online, to content that is offered by VOD platforms such as Netflix, Amazon, YouTube, and Hulu. MVPDs in the United States are, in particular, Sling TV, DirecTV Now, PlayStation Vue, Fubo, Philo, YouTube TV, PlutoTV, and Hulu Live.

18. In the United States, a 'Fairness Doctrine' rule, which existed for several decades, required access to opposing perspectives on issues of public importance. However, this requirement was abolished in 1987. That rule existed as a condition for receiving a scarce and valuable license for a TV channel. It never applied to the print media. Although newspaper journalists often bemoan the abolishment of the Fairness Doctrine rule for TV, they would not tolerate it for their own publications, even on a voluntary basis. *In re Complaint of Syracuse Peach Council against Television Station WTVH Syracuse, New York*, 2 FCC Rcd 5043 (1987).

19. In the United Kingdom, the Open Banking approach creates access rights by third parties to a consumer's information, with the latter's consent.

REFERENCES

Bridge, Gavin. 2020. 'Entertainment Companies Spend $121 Billion on Original Content in 2019', January 6. https://variety.com/2020/biz/news/2019-original-content-spend-121.

Coles, Cameron. 2018. 'Cloud Market in 2018 and Predictions for 2021'. *McAfee*, July 30. https://www.skyhighnetworks.com/cloud-security-blog/microsoft-azure-closes-iaas-adoption-gap-with-amazon-aws/.

Deloitte. 2014. 'Costing Methodology for Next Generation Networks'. https://www2.deloitte.com/content/dam/Deloitte/sg/Documents/technology-media-telecommunications/sea-tmt-costing-methodology-next-generation-networks.pdf.

The Economist. 2019. 'Competition, Not Break-Up, Is the Cure for Tech Giant's Dominance', March 13. https://www.economist.com/business/2019/03/13/competition-not-break-up-is-the-cure-for-tech-giants-dominance.

European Commission. 2007. 'Antitrust: Commission Ensures Compliance with 2004 Decision against Microsoft', October 22. http://europa.eu/rapid/press-release_IP-07-1567_en.htm?locale=en.

Fiest, Max. 2019. 'Why a Data Disclosure Law Is (Likely) Unconstitutional'. *Columbia Journal of Law and the Arts* 43: 518–69.

Lewis, Jeffrey I. D. 2014. 'What Is "FRAND" All About? The Licensing of Patents Essential to an Accepted Standard'. *Cardozo Law*, June 11. https://cardozo.yu.edu/what-"frand"-all-about-licensing-patents-essential-accepted-standard.

Noam, Eli. 2001. *Interconnecting the Network of Networks*. Cambridge, MA: MIT Press.

Noam, Eli. 2016. *Who Owns the World's Media?* New York: Oxford University Press.

Noam, Eli. 2021a. *The Content, Impact, and Regulation of Streaming Video: The Next Generation of Media Emerges*. Cheltenham, UK: Edward Elgar Publishing.Noam, Eli. 2021b. *The Technology, Business, and Economics of Streaming Video: The Next Generation of Media Emerges*. Cheltenham, UK: Edward Elgar Publishing.Ofcom. 2015. 'International Communications Market Report 2015', December 10. https://www.ofcom.org.uk/__data/assets/pdf_file/0020/31268/icmr_2015.pdf.

O'Halloran, Joseph. 2019. 'Five Services behind 89% of European Subscription Streaming Revs'. RapidTVnews, March 6. https://www.rapidtvnews.com/2019030655357/five-services-behind-89-of-european-subscription-streaming-revs.html#axzz5hPM2I6dE.

Rypka, Ryan. 2018. 'FRAND Royalties Will Impact the Cost of Your Next Smart Phone'. *Michigan Technology Law Review*.http://mttlr.org/2018/11/frand-royalties-will-impact-the-cost-of-your-next-smart-phone/.

Spangler, Todd. 2019. 'Hulu Live TV Tops Sling TV as No.1 Streaming Pay-TV Service, Analysts Estimate'. Variety, November 15. https://variety.com/2019/digital/news/hulu-live-tv-beats-sling-top-streaming-pay-tv-research-1203406138/.

Statista. 2015. 'Active Reach of Selected Online Video Websites as of August 2015, by Country', December 10. https://www.statista.com/statistics/284801/active-online-reach-of-selected-online-video-sites-by-country/.

Statista. 2018. 'Most Popular Online Video Properties US 2018'. https://lh6.googleusercontent.com/xAwi6vaYS77JLLqTdRyScgQxOD-kyP0_dVzJeH0_h-vVZEeevwWWvmwqVyPPWLMMf_uu8zClioj7CCFyimPkSFlS1P8563ST-PslwruzE7I8tG9Qji6p5TS7JplbioQiQZVI0kJ7.

Sun, Leo. 2019. '3 Reasons Sony Wants to Sell PlayStation Vue'. *The Motley Fool*, October
    29.7373https://www.fool.com/investing/2019/10/29/3-reasons-sony-wants-to-sell-
    playstation-vue.aspx.

Tran, Kevin. 2017. 'Millennials Still Watch TV Despite Cord-Cutting Increases'. *B
    usiness Insider*, November 1. https://www.businessinsider.com/millennials-
    still-watch-tv-despite-cord-cutting-increases-2017-11?r=UK&IR=T.

Wardle, Nikki. 2018. 'Amazon Advertising vs. Google Ads'. *Tribute Media*, November
    2. https://www.tributemedia.com/blog/new-kid-on-the-block-amazon-ads.

Wenger, Albert. 2018. 'World after Capital: Bots for All of Us (Informational Freedom)'.
    Continuations, December 10. https://continuations.com/post/180985743645/
    world-after-capital-bots-for-all-of-us.

Wu, Tim. 2003. 'Network Neutrality, Broadband Discrimination'. *Journal of
    Telecommunications and High Technology Law* 2: 141. https://papers.ssrn.com/sol3/
    papers.cfm?abstract_id=388863.

4

Enabling Community-Owned Platforms

A Proposal for a Tech New Deal

NATHAN SCHNEIDER ■

Economic crises highlight not just pre-existing failures of distribution—the bread lines, the shantytowns—but also failures of production: the blindness among allocators of capital to vast terrains of opportunity and human potential. Times of crisis have therefore compelled governments not just to mobilize redistributive measures but also to adopt more sensible forms of productive allocation, forms that usually had long seemed necessary at the margins but were ignored at the centre until the centre itself began to buckle.[1]

The crisis brought on by the COVID-19 pandemic, for one, has surfaced many such failures—although for people experiencing them directly they come as no surprise. The platform-guided gig workers making deliveries and caring for elders have become 'essential workers', a designation that stands in stark contrast to the platforms' refusal to afford them employee status or basic protections. Public health orders to work from home don't compute in rural and urban communities where telecom companies have long refused to deploy modern connectivity. The regime of 'social distancing' further deepens the reliance of many on apps that treat surveillance as the price of connecting with friends, family, and co-workers—offering few guarantees about what might or might not be done someday with all the data.

At a time when regulators are seeking new responses to the dilemmas of world-spanning digital platforms, cooperative ownership has been a matter of growing discussion and experimentation (Scholz and Schneider 2016; Schneider 2018b). A cooperative of gig-economy workers could distribute profits more equitably than has been the case, as investor-owned platforms have tended towards a race to the bottom in terms of wages and working conditions (Scholz 2017; Schor

2020). A social-media cooperative could give users the power to oversee how their personal data can be monetized and prevent abuses (Pasquale 2015; Zuboff 2019). Through cooperative federations, platforms could reduce their antitrust exposure by balancing local control with global network effects (Vaheesan and Schneider 2019). In turn, rather than relying solely on external regulation within territorial jurisdictions, platforms could be subject to internal regulation from their user communities. Aligning business and participant interests through co-ownership could meanwhile introduce new efficiencies (Albæk and Schultz 1998; Bogetoft 2005; Mikami 2011; Molk 2014; Blasi et al. 2018). Policymakers in several countries have expressed formal or informal interest in the idea, including the British Labour Party (Corbyn 2016), the German Social Democratic Party (Scholz 2018a), the Innovation Committee of the Italian Parliament in Rome (Sifry 2016), the city of Barcelona (Morell and Espelt 2018; Bria 2019), and US senator Kirsten Gillibrand (Scholz 2018b).

The market share of actually existing platform cooperatives remains close to negligible (Schneider 2018a, 155–62). They have rarely been able to access external financing, and thus they lack the infrastructure of advisors, incubators, and accelerators that are typically tied to such financing (Lloyd et al. 2019). Even when tech giants such as Airbnb and Uber have sought to practice equity compensation with their user-workers, they have encountered regulatory barriers (Robbins et al. 2018). For all the near-magical properties ascribed to the platform economy—notably, rampant disintermediation and negligible marginal costs (Rifkin 2014; Parker et al. 2016)—why have platforms not transcended the conventional corporation into a utopia of co-ownership?

The answer lies in the recognition that what can and cannot be done in private enterprise depends on public policies that lurk in the background, often unnoticed and uncredited. Silicon Valley–style venture capital, for instance—however much its doyens might like to declare independence from the *ancien régime* of offline government (Barlow 1996)—owes a considerable portion of its success to the US Congress's 1979 amendment to the 'prudent man' rule, opening the door to investment from pension funds (Nicholas 2019, 176).

Success in most arenas of community-owned business has also relied on dedicated policy. To consider US history again, the Great Depression–era New Deal legislation included mechanisms for financing cooperatives in the Farm Credit Act (1933), the Federal Credit Union Act (1934), and the Rural Electrification Act (1936); programs around retirement and homeownership further encouraged widespread capital ownership. Where community ownership has flourished internationally, it has come with similar litanies of such provisions (Mayo 2017; Pentzien 2020). It thus stands to reason that economic democracy for the online economy will require an appropriate policy framework, an outline of which I offer here.

The solution, however, is not simply to carve out the Internet as yet another special case in which a distinct and bounded cooperative sector might emerge. Investor-owned businesses, across wildly diverse sectors, operate under general-purpose methods of incorporation and financing; community ownership could do the same. It could be a means of discovering latent value in our networks, data, and work, which the investor-oriented models are not able to notice.

I will draw on successful cooperative policies in various countries and industries, and propose ways of generalizing them broadly across the economy—including to the online economy. The New Deal era was an especially generative time in the United States for visionary, targeted policies for democratizing ownership, from housing to financial institutions. These, in turn, took inspiration from earlier, small-scale experiments (Knapp 1973; Curl 2012). The 'Tech New Deal' I propose here draws on the New Deal and related policy legacies as test runs for a more ambitious agenda, one capable of undergirding economic democracy for a time of global networks that are at once embattled in controversy and pregnant with possibility. But as a generalized framework, the Tech New Deal should be considered of a piece with related undertakings, such as calls for a Green New Deal or large-scale economic recovery programs. Policy should use community ownership not just to solve specific problems but also as a universal means of organizing innovation. It should also seek to repair past injustices to communities marginalized through underinvestment. This agenda sets out to ensure that community ownership is at least as available to the online economy as investor ownership has been.

I employ the spacious frame of 'community ownership' to include a variety of relevant legal mechanisms, such as cooperatives, stock-owning trusts, and democratic non-profits. Community members might be workers, users, or businesses, depending on who happen to be the central stakeholders in a given context. Yet community ownership should be 'broad-based' among all or most members of any stakeholder class (Blasi et al. 2018), rather than including only an elite subset of stakeholders. The imprecision of *community* reflects the respects in which online platforms have unsettled familiar notions of stakeholdership in economic life. In each case, however, a given firm would define its community of stakeholders precisely to ensure clear lines of ownership and governance. Appropriate community stakeholders might include those most responsible for the firm's behaviour (e.g., employees and other workers) and those who contribute value to it (e.g., users contributing original content and personal data).

In what follows, I begin by reviewing the constraints that community ownership faces under present conditions, which limit its capacity to compete fairly with investor ownership. I will then introduce three 'vectors of democratization', drawing on earlier legacies to propose an agenda for radically emboldening community ownership in an age of global networks. Finally, I conclude by considering the political strategies that might advance such an agenda.

CONSTRAINTS ON AND FOR COMMUNITY OWNERSHIP

The startups that have come to dominate the online economy have a peculiar relationship with regulation. In the spirit of John Perry Barlow's 'Declaration of the Independence of Cyberspace' (1996), tech startups established markets seemingly immune to the rules imposed on foregoing businesses through grey-area operations and regulatory arbitrage. Ride-sharing apps in many jurisdictions operate outside of taxi regulations; communications platforms help themselves to kinds of user surveillance unavailable to earlier phone companies and parcel services; social networks can distribute news items without bearing the news producers' liability for the content. It is as if Barlow's Silicon Valley friends made good on his warning to the governments of the world: 'You have no moral right to rule us nor do you possess any methods of enforcement we have true reason to fear'. Meanwhile, the old rules keep on inhibiting the startups' incumbent competitors.

To pay for the risks of such grey-area, winner-takes-all business models, Internet startups typically rely on venture capital financing—a kind of Faustian bargain that pays for risk tolerance with a demand for growth at all costs and the prospect of lavish rewards for early bets. This arrangement has produced a critical mass of the world's most valuable companies, though it has also earned critics among startup founders for failing to serve diverse aspirations and leaders (Griffith 2019). Venture capital has thus far been ill-equipped to invest in community-owned enterprises, which tend to avoid the risks of regulatory arbitrage and refuse the degrees of investor power that venture capital needs in order to compensate for failed investments. The lower risk profile found in community ownership (Molk 2014; Blasi et al. 2018), however, could be attractive in economies outside the relatively rare urban tech hubs where venture capital concentrates and flourishes (Florida 2017). But thus far, cooperative and other community-owned Internet startups have struggled to access necessary capital. While they reject the growth-at-all-costs logic that venture demands, they still present risks that legacy cooperative banks, credit unions, and public financing were not built to tolerate.

Policies to promote community ownership have often included provisions for 'technical assistance' grants to support startups in business processes (Kerr 2015). Yet support tends to become scalable and sustainable only when there a viable means of capital access that businesses can aspire towards. When investment opportunities are present, entities such as accelerators and incubators arise around them. Without proper investment infrastructure, the infrastructure for entrepreneur education and mentoring will not persist long after the grant periods end.

In addition to what policy does and doesn't enable, policy has the power to restrict. Certain well-placed inhibitors of rampant platform capitalism are needed, and there has been no lack of discussion on what those should be. For example, robust privacy regulations could threaten the dominance of surveillance-based platforms and benefit competitors that prioritize users' ownership and control over their data. Labour enforcement could undermine the current gig-economy business model and spur the development of platforms premised on more secure employment. Without restrictions on exploitative practices, higher-road alternatives will have a hard time competing.

For better or worse, the most effective resistance to Silicon Valley giants has come through protectionist regulatory enforcement. The case of China stands out; its 'Great Firewall' has served the dual purpose of aiding in political censorship and keeping out certain US platforms so that local alternatives could gain market share and flourish (Chu 2017). There are less drastic examples as well. Austin, Texas, for instance, saw the rise of a non-profit ride-sharing platform after officials drove Uber and Lyft out of the city by requiring the companies to abide by safety regulations required of taxis (Davidson 2017). Other cities, from London (Spicer 2019) to Seoul (Moon 2017), have similarly barred platforms from operating above the law—while facilitating the development of their own platforms in the process.

As with any other sort of alternative to dominant platforms, community-owned platforms are unlikely to gain a foothold unless there are barriers in place to constrain better-capitalized competitors that lack community accountability. But along with such constraints must come strategies that enable healthier, more democratic ownership to take hold.

VECTORS OF DEMOCRATIZATION

This section presents vectors for advancing community ownership for the online economy and beyond. I refer to them as vectors to emphasize that, in each case, these policies for the future share lines of continuity with narrower but well-tested policies of the past and present. They set out to universalize access to community ownership for the networked age in three directions:

- Versatile statutes for firm incorporation and membership
- Access to scalable financing for diverse communities
- Enablers of coordination and collective voice

Incorporation: From Localities to Networks

According to George Jacob Holyoake, an early chronicler of the British cooperative movement, the 1846 Friendly Societies Act presented working people with 'an advantage so great that the most sanguine despaired of living to see its enactment' (Holyoake 1908, 290). Just two years after the birth of the Rochdale cooperative store, a foundational success story, Parliament enabled this nascent kind of business to incorporate with limited liability. Within a few years, similar stores were appearing throughout England, which joined forces through federations to manage joint factories, warehouses, and supply chains. From the 1840s to today's Delaware C Corporation—a favourite for Internet startups thousands of miles away in Silicon Valley—people's organizational imaginations live within the boxes of what policy regimes happen to enable.

Statutes for cooperative incorporation vary worldwide (Cracogna et al. 2013). Within the United States alone, the state of Mississippi does not allow for even basic worker-owned or consumer-owned cooperatives, while Colorado's Limited Cooperative Association statute can handle complex, multi-stakeholder structures with arbitrary member types, including a role for investor members. (Colorado lawyers Wiener and Phillips [2018] have called their state 'the Delaware of co-operative law'.) By and large, statutes for cooperatives and other forms of community ownership were designed for local or regional organizations with relatively stable memberships, not transnational networks whose users come and go with ease. So long as such statutes remain limited in scale and scope, community-ownership efforts will remain at a disadvantage compared to the tools available for investor-owned companies.

Corporate law need not be custom-made for online platforms. Colorado's Limited Cooperative Association is a 'uniform law' enacted in several other states, originally for the purpose of rural development (Uniform Law Commission 2013); the law itself, however, does not limit its provisions to rural cooperatives, making it serviceable for many other applications, and it has been popular with platform startups. German cooperatives of any type similarly incorporate under a common statute (Pentzien 2020). A proposed Cooperative Platform Economy Act in California (Upside Down Consulting n.d.) would establish a new type of co-operative to handle employment for gig-economy platforms, but it could also address long-standing abuses in older, offline gig economies. The European Union, meanwhile, established in 2003 the Statute for a European Cooperative Society, which provides for cooperatives among citizens of more than one EU member state, facilitating cross-border collaboration—again, a boon for platforms whose constituencies are not nationally bounded. When such intergovernmental agreements are not forthcoming, there should be provisions for virtual membership, in which a platform's international users might hold de facto profit-sharing and governance powers, even if short of de jure company ownership.

Community ownership need not require distinctive company structures. The US Employee Stock Ownership Plan (ESOP), which achieved federal recognition and favourable tax treatment beginning in 1974, employs a trust that can hold shares in several different types of companies on employees' behalf; similar structures could be employed to hold platform assets for other kinds of communities (Schneider 2020b). Perpetual purpose trusts, although originally created for estate planning (Antoine 2013), are beginning to prove useful in conjoining community ownership with organizational mission (Michael 2017; Peters 2018), although this approach is little-tested and may not yet be sufficiently enforceable. Trust-mediated ownership could also provide the benefits of co-ownership for platform users who do not want a formal, ongoing stock-holding relationship with the company. Whether through direct or mediated means, community ownership should ensure that members can speak with a collective voice and counteract exploitation by managers and investors.

Recommendations in Brief

- Enable the incorporation of flexible legal mechanisms for community ownership.
- Mechanisms should support international membership and multiple member classes.
- Ensure purpose trusts are available and legally enforceable.

Financing: From Sectoral to Universal

Community-owned enterprises face consistent and even crippling disadvantages in accessing capital. Compared to firms designed for investor ownership, community ownership by definition restricts the rights of outside capital providers. This goes a long way towards explaining, for instance, what Molk (2014) refers to as 'the puzzling lack of cooperatives'. When cooperatives have arisen historically, it has been due either to communities' ability to mobilize collective action and fill 'missing markets' (Hueth 2014) or to tailor-made policies that carved out exceptions to the general bias for investor ownership. Smaller cooperatives have often relied on member investment to start and grow; they could be considered the original crowdfunding, long before the likes of Kickstarter. But capital-intensive businesses—whether they are laying power lines or coding tech platforms—can't easily be built this way. There is promise in recent developments around 'equity crowdfunding' through the USA JOBS Act (Catalini et al. 2016), the UK's Community Shares model (Community Shares 2016), and blockchain-based token offerings (Rohr and Wright 2017), but none of these appears poised to supplant the need for institutional finance.

In the United States, policy interventions have been essential (and effective) in bringing community ownership to scale, such as through the Farm Credit System (Knapp 1969), credit unions (Taylor and Goodman 2019), rural electric cooperatives (Doyle 1979; Spinak 2014), and widespread employee ownership (Speiser 1977; Kroncke 2018). Each of these interventions involved either direct government financing or indirect inducements for private capital markets, such as insurance guarantees and tax incentives. Yet each case serves only very particular kinds of markets. As part of the Farm Credit System, the country's largest cooperative bank—CoBank—can only invest in rural cooperatives; credit unions are typically restricted to a certain 'field of membership'; tax benefits for employee ownership occur only within the context of a particular type of retirement program. As with incorporation statutes, financing provisions for cooperatives around the world tend to revolve around certain sectors and lines of business, particularly in farming and small-scale finance (Cracogna et al. 2013).

There have been understandable reasons for keeping policy interventions narrow. Doing so reduces risks for the public purse by targeting tested, replicable business models and judging investments according to uniform standards. Limiting interventions to specific, low-margin sectors also mitigates the political threat from the investor class, which could perceive (and often has) policy accommodations for community ownership as unfair competition; in the wake of the 1936 Rural Electrification Act, for instance, investor-owned electric companies built 'spite lines'—power lines intended to divide and sabotage prospective cooperatives (Doyle 1979). Such reasons, however, need not forever constrain the potential of community ownership to isolated cases.

Examples of past successes in financing community ownership can inform an array of generalized policies capable of putting cooperatives and their ilk on par with investor ownership throughout the economy, including in the realm of online platforms. In order to do so, it will be necessary to update earlier risk-mitigation strategies—generally, the replication of tested, local models—in order to protect public investments. This might be done, for instance, through more strenuous diversification or the use of revenue-based financing to recoup greater returns from successful efforts.

Louis Kelso, inventor of the aforementioned ESOP, proposed an intriguing strategy for making community ownership more widely available: a government agency called the Capital Diffusion Reinsurance Corporation (Kelso and Kelso 1986; Schneider 2020a). Akin to public insurance for credit unions and agricultural cooperatives, this entity would vet and underwrite community-ownership financing or conversions in order to encourage investment. It would especially encourage lending to groups of undercapitalized people, while enabling access to capital ownership in the enterprises that they participate in as workers, customers, neighbours, and more. In this way, community financing could be part of a broader package of reparations for past historical injustices, such as the New Deal's underinvestment in US communities of colour.

Whether through insurance pools, direct lending, or tax inducements, the critical challenge of community-ownership finance is to counteract the conventional expectation of personal guarantees to secure capital, which favours small numbers of wealthy people. Collective ownership needs mechanisms to enable collective guarantees.

A further theme in Kelso and Kelso (1986)'s proposals is using public investment to enable community-owned, revenue-producing infrastructure. Such practices are in some respects common, ranging from the aforementioned electric cooperatives to indigenous tribal corporations, the sovereign wealth funds that many countries maintain, and the Alaska Permanent Fund, which distributes cash dividends to residents. Likewise, community ownership could help correct power imbalances in the digital economy, such as through user-owned data repositories and broadband networks. Already, some rural electric and telecom cooperatives in the United States have used public and private financing to create successful fibre-to-the-home projects, often in areas that investor-owned providers avoid serving (Talbot et al. 2017). The European Union has meanwhile adopted policies that aid in financing community-owned renewable power generation (Friends of the Earth Europe 2018)—an initiative inspired, in part, by Louis Kelso's legacy (Lowitzsch 2018, 164).

With appropriate policy support, financing could be at least as available for community-owned enterprises as for investor ownership. By drawing on global lessons in targeted sectors such as agriculture and energy, financial mechanisms for community ownership can be generalized across the economy—making them available to help address the accountability crises of the digital economy in particular. It should be at least as attractive for entrepreneurs seeking growth capital or an 'exit' (Schneider 2019) to be able to access capital by partnering with their stakeholder communities as through outside investors.

Recommendations in Brief

- Universalize financing mechanisms that have been successful in specific sectors—such as with insurance pools, direct government lending, and appropriate taxation.
- Develop digital infrastructure on the basis of ownership by participant communities.
- Target incentives towards capital acquisition for communities historically marginalized through undercapitalization.

Coordination: From Niche to Commonwealth

Cooperativism, like organized labour, is a phenomenon that often refers to itself as a 'movement' without always behaving like one. National cooperative associations and the International Co-operative Alliance use the rhetoric of representing a unified community, while in practice the reality is much more fragmented. In the United States, for instance, the operations of the National Cooperative Business Association, which represents all cooperatives, are dwarfed by those of both the rural electric association and the credit union association. This inversion, like so much else, is a product of policy; since US cooperatives depend on industry-specific regulation, they organize and lobby on the basis of industry. In contrast, one might consider a context like Italy, where cooperative legislation is cross-industrial and constitutionally protected (Menzani and Zamagni 2010; Fici 2015). There, a small percentage of a cooperative's profits are expected to be pooled for investing in other cooperatives, and tax benefits encourage retaining 'indivisible reserves' that go towards future cooperative development upon a company's liquidation. In Germany, association membership is mandatory for cooperatives (Pentzien 2020). Spanish law formalizes multiple forms of 'intercooperation' (Sánchez Pachón 2018), and the Basque region's famous Mondragón cooperative is in fact a cluster of tightly integrated but distinct businesses. Thus the international cooperative principle of 'cooperation among cooperatives' (Alliance n.d.) can become not merely rhetoric but is enshrined in and encouraged by law.

A broader frame for community ownership could extend beyond just cooperatives to include such entities as ESOPs, non-profit community land trusts, and equity crowdfunding as part of a bloc working to strengthen alternatives to investor ownership. With a shared policy framework, such entities might then coordinate mutual support and shared policy agendas. And while narrower, industry-specific associations might prefer to take a defensive posture towards emerging innovations, broader associations stand to benefit by helping to seed member businesses in new markets. The Italian cross-industrial federation Legacoop called for a 'Cooperative Commons' for digital data in 2012—several years before talk of cooperative platforms began in earnest elsewhere (Maffettone 2012; Schneider 2018a).

If recent advocacy is a guide, broad community-ownership blocs might seek preferred access to government contracts. Alongside existing preferences for women-owned and minority-owned businesses, worker cooperative proposals in the United States have proposed a preference for worker-owned businesses (Kerr 2015); advocates in the United Kingdom have redirected local pension funds and other public capital investments (Singer 2016). In the digital economy specifically, such preferences might build on efforts to adopt non-proprietary software independent of Silicon Valley tech giants; this has led, for example, to the French government's investment in open-source projects like the Matrix communication protocol and the file-sharing platform NextCloud (Hodgson 2018; Poortvliet 2019). Demands for preferred procurement have extended to non-governmental organizations, such as in efforts to enlist hospitals and universities as 'anchor institutions' for local cooperatives (Serang et al. 2013).

Community-owned enterprises could also serve as their own anchor institutions by leveraging network technology to better coordinate their supply chains. Bauwens and Niaros (2017) have called for digitally enabled 'open and contributory value accounting', a paradigm for enabling organizations to make their processes and needs radically transparent, so that other organizations can more readily collaborate. To begin with, open accounting could be contained among community-owned entities to prevent outside exploitation. Such practices may also become obligatory for all; momentum is growing behind policy proposals that would require all online platforms to enable greater interoperability with application protocol interfaces (Crémer et al. 2019) or data trusts (McDonald 2019), which third parties could use to build services of their own.

Coordination should spread not just among businesses but also among workers and other kinds of platform users. Consider the 1922 Capper-Volstead Act, which protected US farmer co-op members from becoming targets of antitrust enforcement when wielding legitimate collective power. New Deal labour legislation extended similar protections to unions. Extending this logic to online platforms could empower vulnerable groups to build collective power of their own, from small-business sellers on Amazon to drivers for ride-sharing platforms (Vaheesan and Schneider 2019). While the current resurgence of interest in antitrust policy has focussed on dismembering large tech companies (e.g., Hughes 2019), antitrust wields broad powers over coordination rights (Paul 2020). It determines not only when companies abuse their power but also who can organize.

A further form of necessary coordination is cultural policy. Various governments have encouraged alternatives to investor ownership through their powers of information dissemination and narrative building—in contexts ranging from worker cooperatives in Perónist Argentina to the solidarity economy in Quebec. The US Department of Agriculture has long supported conferences, academic centres, publications, and research on cooperatives (Knapp 1973; Anonymous 2019). A strong movement could also hold private institutions accountable. It is an irony that the educational nerve centre of investor-powered Silicon Valley,

Stanford University, had among its three founding principles 'the establishment of cooperative effort in the industrial systems of the future'—by which the founder very explicitly meant community-owned enterprise (Altenberg 1990). Perhaps, if the university had listened, the online economy would already practice community ownership as a matter of course.

Recommendations in Brief

- Encourage cross-industrial associations for community-owned enterprises.
- Protect legitimate collective power to counteract corporate power.
- Use government resources to study and promote community ownership alongside other forms of business.

ORDER OF OPERATIONS

The goals outlined in this chapter are ambitious, significantly more so than what previous generations have achieved. But such ambition is necessary, particularly if the challenge at hand is to equip community-owned enterprise to confront the market power of the investor-owned online platforms, which include some of the most valuable companies in the world. In each vector, I have sought to ground ambition in tangible precedents. By simply generalizing local or industry-specific policies of the past, radical change may be possible through familiar mechanisms—so familiar that by now we might take them for granted.

To conclude, I will consider political strategies for achieving the goals outlined here. In the spirit of the extending past achievements, it is worth reflecting on some of the means by which past policy advances for community ownership have been won. These provide a palette of options for future conditions and opportunities.

Community ownership can be uncommonly cross-partisan. There have been times when it became highly identified with one ideology or another, of course; from the collectivized factories of communist Yugoslavia (Ward 1958) to Tony Benn's advocacy of worker ownership through Britain's Labour government of the 1970s (Tomlinson 1980), the association can stick in the public mind. But minds—and alignments—also tend to change. US Republicans, who once regarded the New Deal's rural electric cooperatives as a type of 'creeping communism', turned far friendlier once rural areas served by cooperatives became their electoral base (Doyle 1979; Case 2013). Kenya's powerful agricultural cooperatives began as a segregated institution of British imperialism, then a method for African Socialism, then a tool of capitalist structural adjustment (Wanyama 2008). Italy's apex cooperative associations, founded more than a century ago by Catholics and communists respectively, now seem so indistinct that they are likely to merge (Fici 2015). Louis Kelso courted both Republican and Democratic politicians in his efforts to establish the ESOP (Speiser 1977), and in 2016 expanding employee ownership was on both parties' platforms. Two years later, despite fever-pitch polarization, President Donald Trump signed the Main Street Employee Ownership Act, the most important US legislation on the issue in decades, whose sponsors were nearly down-the-middle bipartisan (Dubb 2018).

Legacy community-ownership institutions represent a further variable. These can be quite strong. For instance, the US rural electric and credit union associations wield considerable lobbying power in Washington. But their interests tend to be confined to industry-specific needs, attuned to industry-specific policies. They could even see efforts to build on and expand their own policy successes as a potential threat. Then again, if a new generation of policy proposals improves on legacy arrangements while expanding them to new participants, the legacy institutions could provide decisive political heft. If they hope to see a new generation of success stories in community ownership, these institutions should invest not just in preserving what they have but in enabling what they have yet to envision.

Achieving the New Deal came at the cost of a racist compromises with segregationists, harming the prospects of millions for home-ownership and labour rights for generations. No strategy for community ownership would be worth the name if it accepted such terms. Yet, wherever their loyalties generally lie, advocates of policies to advance community ownership should expect unexpected allies.

NOTE

1.   The author is grateful for substantive feedback on drafts from Fred Freundlich, Pete Davis, Martin Moore, Doug O'Brien, and Jonas Pentzien. Work on this essay was supported in part by a fellowship with the Open Society Foundations. The opinions expressed herein are the author's own and do not necessarily express the views of the Open Society Foundations.

REFERENCES

Albæk, Svend, and Christian Schultz. 1998. 'On the Relative Advantage of Cooperatives'. *Economics Letters* 59(3): 397–401. https://doi.org/10.1016/S0165-1765(98)00068-8.

Alliance, International Co-operative. n.d. 'Co-Operative Identity, Values & Principles'. Accessed May 27, 2018. https://ica.coop/en/whats-co-op/co-operative-identity-values-principles.

Altenberg, Lee. 1990. 'Leland Stanford's Forgotten Vision'. *Sandstone and Tile* 14(1): 8–20. https://dynamics.org/Altenberg/PAPERS/BCLSFV/.

Anonymous. 2019. 'USDA's Division of Cooperative Marketing: An Examination of the Dismantling of the Only Federal Support Program for Cooperatives'. https://cooperativecurriculum.org/resources/White-Paper-on-USDA-Co-op-Program's--decline.pdf.

Antoine, Rose-Marie. 2013. *Offshore Financial Law: Trusts and Related Tax Issues*. 2nd ed. Oxford, United Kingdom: Oxford University Press.

Barlow, John Perry. 1996. 'A Declaration of the Independence of Cyberspace'. *Wired*, June 1. https://www.wired.com/1996/06/declaration-independence-cyberspace/.

Bauwens, Michel, and Vasilis Niaros. 2017. 'Value in the Commons Economy: Developments in Open and Contributory Value Accounting'. Heinrich Böll Foundation and the P2P Foundation. http://commonstransition.org/value-commons-economy/.

Blasi, Joseph, Douglas Kruse, and Richard B. Freeman. 2018. 'Broad-Based Employee Stock Ownership and Profit Sharing: History, Evidence, and Policy Implications'. *Journal of Participation and Employee Ownership* 1(1): 38–60. https://doi.org/10.1108/JPEO-02-2018-0001.

Bogetoft, Peter. 2005. 'An Information Economic Rationale for Cooperatives'. *European Review of Agricultural Economics* 32(February): 191–217. https://doi.org/10.1093/eurrag/jbi010.

Bria, Francesca. 2019. 'Barcelona Digital City: Putting Technology at the Service of People'. Barcelona: Ajuntament de Barcelona. https://ajuntament.barcelona.cat/digital/sites/default/files/pla_barcelona_digital_city_in.pdf.

Case, Ted. 2013. 'Power Plays: The U.S. Presidency, Electric Cooperatives, and the Transformation of Rural America'. http://tedcaseauthor.com/product/power-plays/.

Catalini, Christian, Catherine Fazio, and Fiona Murray. 2016. 'Can Equity Crowdfunding Democratize Access to Capital and Investment Opportunities?' MIT Innovation Initiative Lab for Innovation Science and Policy Report. Cambridge, MA: MIT. https://papers.ssrn.com/abstract=2780551.

Chu, Cho-Wen. 2017. 'Censorship or Protectionism? Reassessing China's Regulation of Internet Industry'. *International Journal of Social Science and Humanity* 7(1): 5.

Community Shares. 2016. 'A Guide to Investing in Community Shares'. https://communityshares.org.uk/guide-investing-community-shares.

Corbyn, Jeremy. 2016. 'The Digital Democracy Manifesto'. https://d3n8a8pro7vhmx.cloudfront.net/corbynstays/pages/329/attachments/original/1472552058/Digital_Democracy.pdf?1472552058.

Cracogna, Dante, Antonio Fici, and Hagen Henrÿ. 2013. *International Handbook of Cooperative Law*. Berlin: Springer.

Crémer, Jacques, Yves-Alexandre de Montjoye, Heike Schweitzer, European Commission, and Directorate-General for Competition. 2019. 'Competition Policy for the Digital Era'. Brussels: European Commission Directorate-General for Competition. http://publications.europa.eu/publication/manifestation_identifier/PUB_KD0419345ENN.

Curl, John. 2012. *For All the People: Uncovering the Hidden History of Cooperation, Cooperative Movements, and Communalism in America*. Oakland, CA: PM Press.

Davidson, John Daniel. 2017. 'The Saga of RideAustin'. *Texas Monthly*, June 30. https://www.texasmonthly.com/the-daily-post/the-saga-of-rideaustin/.

Doyle, Jack. 1979. *Lines across the Land: Rural Electric Cooperatives, the Changing Politics of Energy in Rural America*. Washington: The Rural Land & Energy Project, Environmental Policy Institute.

Dubb, Steve. 2018. 'Historic Federal Law Gives Employee-Owned Businesses Access to SBA Loans'. *Non Profit News | Nonprofit Quarterly*, August 14. https://nonprofitquarterly.org/employee-owned-businesses-sba-loans/.

Fici, Antonio. 2015. 'Cooperation among Cooperatives in Italian and Comparative Law'. *Journal of Entrepreneurial and Organizational Diversity* 4(2): 64–97. https://doi.org/10.5947/jeod.2015.011.

Florida, Richard. 2017. 'Venture Capital Remains Highly Concentrated in Just a Few Cities'. CityLab. October 3. https://www.citylab.com/life/2017/10/venture-capital-concentration/539775/.

Friends of the Earth Europe. 2018. 'Unleashing the Power of Community Renewable Energy'. Brussels, Belgium. http://foeeurope.org/unleashing-power-community-energy.

Griffith, Erin. 2019. 'More Start-Ups Have an Unfamiliar Message for Venture Capitalists: Get Lost'. *New York Times*, January 13. https://www.nytimes.com/2019/01/11/technology/start-ups-rejecting-venture-capital.html.

Hodgson, Matthew. 2018. 'Matrix and Riot Confirmed as the Basis for France's Secure Instant Messenger App'. Matrix.org Blog. April 26. https://matrix.org/blog/2018/04/26/matrix-and-riot-confirmed-as-the-basis-for-frances-secure-instant-messenger-app.

Holyoake, George Jacob. 1908. *The History of Co-Operation*. London: T. F. Unwin. http://archive.org/details/cu31924002593816.

Hueth, Brent. 2014. 'Missing Markets and the Cooperative Firm'. Workshop on Producers' Organizations in Agricultural Markets, 22. Toulouse, France.

Hughes, Chris. 2019. 'It's Time to Break Up Facebook'. *New York Times*, May 9. https://www.nytimes.com/2019/05/09/opinion/sunday/chris-hughes-facebook-zuckerberg.html.

Kelso, Louis O., and Patricia Hetter Kelso. 1986. *Democracy and Economic Power: Extending the ESOP Revolution Through Binary Economics*. Cambridge, MA: Ballinger Publishing. http://books.google.com?id=_R5XDQAAQBAJ.

Kerr, Camille. 2015. 'Local Government Support for Cooperatives'. Austin, TX: Austin Cooperative Business Association & Democracy at Work Institute. https://community-wealth.org/sites/clone.community-wealth.org/files/downloads/paper-kerr.pdf.

Knapp, Joseph G. 1969. *The Rise of American Cooperative Enterprise: 1620–1920*. Danville, IL: Interstate Printers & Publishers.

Knapp, Joseph G. 1973. *The Advance of American Cooperative Enterprise: 1920–1945*. Danville, IL: Interstate Printers & Publishers.

Kroncke, Jedidiah J. 2018. 'ESOPs and the Limits of Fractionalized Ownership'. *University of Chicago Legal Forum* 201(12): 40. https://legal-forum.uchicago.edu/publication/esops-and-limits-fractionalized-ownership.

Lloyd, Jenni, Tom Symons, and Simon Borkin. 2019. 'Platform Co-Operatives—Solving the Capital Conundrum'. Nesta and Co-operatives UK. https://www.nesta.org.uk/report/platform-co-operatives/.

Lowitzsch, Jens. 2018. *Energy Transition: Financing Consumer Co-Ownership in Renewables*. New York, NY: Springer Berlin Heidelberg.

Maffettone, Sebastiano. 2012. 'Manifesto'. Cooperative Commons. 2012. https://web.archive.org/web/20170313041935/http://www.cooperativecommons.coop/index.php/en/manifesto.

Mayo, Ed. 2017. *A Short History of Co-Operation and Mutuality*. Co-operatives UK. https://www.uk.coop/sites/default/files/uploads/attachments/a-short-history-of-cooperation-and-mutuality_ed-mayo-web_english.pdf.

McDonald, Sean. 2019. 'Reclaiming Data Trusts'. Centre for International Governance Innovation. March 5. https://www.cigionline.org/articles/reclaiming-data-trusts.

Menzani, T., and V. Zamagni. 2010. 'Cooperative Networks in the Italian Economy'. *Enterprise and Society* 11(1): 98–127. https://doi.org/10.1093/es/khp029.

Michael, Christopher. 2017. 'The Employee Ownership Trust, an ESOP Alternative'. *Probate and Property* 31(1): 42–47.

Mikami, Kazuhiko. 2011. *Enterprise Forms and Economic Efficiency: Capitalist, Cooperative and Government Firms*. New York: Routledge.

Molk, Peter. 2014. 'The Puzzling Lack of Cooperatives'. *Tulane Law Review* 88(5): 899–958.

Moon, M. Jae. 2017. 'Government-Driven Sharing Economy: Lessons from the Sharing City Initiative of the Seoul Metropolitan Government'. *Journal of Developing Societies* 33(2): 223–43. https://doi.org/10.1177/0169796X17710076.

Morell, Mayo Fuster, and Ricard Espelt. 2018. 'A Framework to Assess the Sustainability and the Pro-Democratization of Platform Economy'. *Urban Science* 2(3). https://www.mdpi.com/2413-8851/2/3/61.

Nicholas, Tom. 2019. *VC: An American History*. Cambridge, MA: Harvard University Press.

Parker, Geoffrey G., Marshall W. Van Alstyne, and Sangeet Paul Choudary. 2016. *Platform Revolution: How Networked Markets Are Transforming the Economy and How to Make Them Work for You*. New York: W. W. Norton & Company.

Pasquale, Frank. 2015. *The Black Box Society*. Cambridge, MA: Harvard University Press.

Paul, Sanjukta. 2020. 'Antitrust as Allocator of Coordination Rights'. *UCLA Law Review* 67(2). https://www.uclalawreview.org/antitrust-as-allocator-of-coordination-rights/.

Pentzien, Jonas. 2020. 'Political and Legislative Drivers and Obstacles for Platform Cooperativism in the United States, Germany, and France'. Working Paper submitted for publication to the Institute for the Cooperative Digital Economy.

Peters, Adele. 2018. 'This Company Pioneered a New Business Structure to Preserve Its Mission'. *Fast Company*, July 13. https://www.fastcompany.com/90201663/this-company-pioneered-a-new-business-structure-to-preserve-its-mission.

Poortvliet, Jos. 2019. 'EU Governments Choose Independence from US Cloud Providers with Nextcloud'. Nextcloud Blog. August 27. https://nextcloud.com/blog/eu-governments-choose-independence-from-us-cloud-providers-with-nextcloud.

Rifkin, Jeremy. 2014. *The Zero Marginal Cost Society: The Internet of Things, the Collaborative Commons, and the Eclipse of Capitalism*. New York, NY: St. Martin's Press. http://books.google.com?id=L6afAgAAQBAJ.

Robbins, Robert B., Cindy V. Schlaefer, and Jessica Lutrin. 2018. 'From Home Sharing and Ride Sharing to Shareholding'. Pillsbury Law. October 25. https://www.pillsburylaw.com/en/news-and-insights/rule-701-revision-uber-airbnb.html.

Rohr, Jonathan, and Aaron Wright. 2017. 'Blockchain-Based Token Sales, Initial Coin Offerings, and the Democratization of Public Capital Markets'. Cardozo Legal Studies Research Paper 527. https://www.ssrn.com/abstract=3048104.

Sánchez Pachón, Luis Ángel. 2018. 'Los acuerdos de intercooperación como mecanismo jurídico de integración de cooperativas'. *Revesco: Revista de Estudios Cooperativos*, no. 126 (January). https://doi.org/10.5209/REVE.58616.

Schneider, Nathan. 2018a. *Everything for Everyone: The Radical Tradition That Is Shaping the Next Economy*. New York: Nation Books.

Schneider, Nathan. 2018b. 'An Internet of Ownership: Democratic Design for the Online Economy'. *Sociological Review* 66(2): 320–340.

Schneider, Nathan. 2019. 'Startups Need a New Option: Exit to Community'. Hacker Noon. September 16. https://hackernoon.com/startups-need-a-new-option-exit-to-community-ig12v2z73.

Schneider, Nathan. 2020a. 'Digital Kelsoism: Employee Stock Ownership as a Pattern for the Online Economy'. In *Reimagining the Governance of Work and Employment*, edited by Dionne Pohler. Ithaca, NY: Cornell University Press. Pp. 234–246. https://osf.io/7wrab/.

Schneider, Nathan. 2020b. 'User Trusts: Broad-Based Ownership for Online Platforms'. *Informatik Spektrum*, no. 43: 9–14. https://osf.io/puy5d/.

Scholz, Trebor. 2017. *Uberworked and Underpaid: How Workers Are Disrupting the Digital Economy*. New York: John Wiley & Sons. http://books.google.com?id=0pNNDwAAQBAJ.

Scholz, Trebor. 2018a. 'Andrea Nahles, Head of Social Democratic Party of Germany, Commits to Support Platform Co-Ops'. Platform Cooperativism Consortium. August 31. https://platform.coop/blog/andrea-nahles-democratic-party-of-germany/.

Scholz, Trebor. 2018b. 'A New Bill of Rights for American Workers Building Support for Cooperatively-Owned Businesses That Are Democratically-Owned and Governed'. Platform Cooperativism Consortium. November 30. https://platform.coop/blog/policy-recommendations-for-united-states/.

Scholz, Trebor, and Nathan Schneider. 2016. *Ours to Hack and to Own: The Rise of Platform Cooperativism, a New Vision for the Future of Work and a Fairer Internet*. New York: OR Books.

Schor, Juliet. 2020. *After the Gig: How the Sharing Economy Got Hijacked and How to Win It Back*. Berkeley: University of California Press. https://www.ucpress.edu/book/9780520325050/after-the-gig.

Serang, Farzana, J. Phillip Thompson, and Ted Howard. 2013. 'The Anchor Mission: Leveraging the Power of Anchor Institutions to Build Community Wealth'. College Park, MD: The Democracy Collaborative. https://democracycollaborative.org/content/anchor-mission-leveraging-power-anchor-institutions-build-community-wealth.

Sifry, Micah. 2016. 'A Conversation with Trebor Scholz on the Rise of Platform Cooperativism'. Civic Hall. October 25. https://civichall.org/civicist/conversation-with-trebor-scholz-platform-coop/.

Singer, Clifford. 2016. 'The Preston Model'. The Next System Project. September 9. https://thenextsystem.org/the-preston-model.

Speiser, Stuart M. 1977. *A Piece of the Action: A Plan to Provide Every Family with a $100,000 Stake in the Economy*. New York: Van Nostrand Reinhold Co.

Spicer, André. 2019. 'Uber's London Woes Show the Need for a Taxi App Owned by Drivers | André Spicer'. *The Guardian: Opinion*, November 26. https://www.theguardian.com/commentisfree/2019/nov/26/uber-london-taxi-app-drivers-cities.

Spinak, Abby (Abby Elaine). 2014. 'Infrastructure and Agency: Rural Electric Cooperatives and the Fight for Economic Democracy in the United States'. Thesis, Massachusetts Institute of Technology. http://dspace.mit.edu/handle/1721.1/87519.

Talbot, David A., Kira Hope Hessekiel, and Danielle Leah Kehl. 2017. 'Community-Owned Fiber Networks: Value Leaders in America'. Berkman Klein Center for Internet & Society Research Publication. Harvard University. https:// dash.harvard.edu/handle/1/34623859.

Taylor, Keith, and Nathan P. Goodman. 2019. 'The Stakeholder-Empowering Philanthropy of Edward Filene'. *Journal of Institutional Economics* (October): 1–15. https://doi.org/10.1017/S1744137419000675.

Tomlinson, Jim. 1980. 'British Politics and Co-Operatives'. *Capital and Class* 4(3): 58–65. https://doi.org/10.1177/030981688001200104.

Uniform Law Commission. 2013. 'The Uniform Limited Cooperative Association Act (UCLAA): A Summary'. Chicago, IL: National Conference of Commissioners on Uniform State Laws. https://www.uniformlaws.org/HigherLogic/System/ DownloadDocumentFile.ashx?DocumentFileKey=2b40106d-9905-860b-dd4a-847960751b7a&forceDialog=0.

Upside Down Consulting. n.d. 'Cooperative Platform Economy Act'. Accessed January 3, 2020. https://cooperativeplatform.org/.

Vaheesan, Sandeep, and Nathan Schneider. 2019. 'Cooperative Enterprise as an Antimonopoly Strategy'. *Penn State Law Review* 124(1): 1–55. http:// www.pennstatelawreview.org/print-issues/cooperative-enterprise-as-an-antimonopoly-strategy/.

Wanyama, Frederick O. 2008. 'The Qualitative and Quantitative Growth of the Cooperative Movement in Kenya'. In *Cooperating Out of Poverty: The Renaissance of the African Cooperative Movement*, edited by Patrick Develtere, Ignace Pollet, and Frederick O Wanyama. Geneva: International Labour Office.

Ward, Benjamin. 1958. 'The Firm in Illyria: Market Syndicalism'. *American Economic Review* 48(4): 566–89.

Wiener, Jason, and Linda Phillips. 2018. 'Colorado—"The Delaware of Cooperative Law"'. Fifty by Fifty Blog. July 11. https://medium.com/fifty-by-fifty/colorado-the-delaware-of-cooperative-law-babedc9e88eb.

Zuboff, Shoshana. 2019. *The Age of Surveillance Capitalism: The Fight for a Human Future at the New Frontier of Power*. New York: PublicAffairs.

PART II

Increasing Accountability

5

Obliging Platforms to Accept a Duty of Care

LORNA WOODS AND WILLIAM PERRIN ■

INTRODUCTION

Services delivered over the Internet pervade modern life in countless ways, bringing many benefits. As with much human behaviour, there are also pervasive downsides. While the 1990s saw a period of optimism about the potential of the Internet, from the early 2000s, as Internet use became mainstream, concerns about harms caused through online services arose, especially as regards child protection. These concerns have increased with the development of social media platforms. While platforms could have done something about these concerns, in the main they have not done so but have sought to ignore the problem. The regulatory environment has not only facilitated but encouraged this failure, as some forms of engagement with user interactions (at least in some regimes) endangered platforms' immunity (Woods 2012). The problem is exacerbated by the consolidation of the market into a small number of super-dominant providers who have little incentive to compete on the basis of safety.

Around the world governments are starting to consider regulation amidst significant and growing user concern about harmful conduct and behaviours. In 2016 the authors of this chapter worked with Anna Turley MP on a Private Members Bill to limit online harms—the Malicious Communications (Social Media) Bill. It was clear even then that all such projects face the same underlying question: the best approach to regulation. Regulatory solutions based on the traditional assumptions from media regulation seemed ill-suited to the online environment given how the platforms work, the scale of the main social media platforms, and the transnational nature of those businesses (Ofcom 2018, 25–26). Regulation of online harm by providing each category of harm with its own palliative rule would create a regulatory quagmire comprising a complex if not conflicting set of rules, unworkable in practice.

Experience of other complex sectors suggests that process-based regulation oriented towards preventing harmful outcomes, which puts responsibility on companies to design services safely, will work better. The polluter pays approach puts the burden back on the company that enables the harm and is economically efficient as well as appealing to some felt sense of justice.

Drawing on their work with Turley, the authors in late 2017 began to develop a more general regulatory approach for online harms. Carnegie UK Trust, an independent foundation and think tank, agreed to publish the authors' work, and by April 2018 the outlines of what we term a systemic approach for online harms was published on the Carnegie UK Trust website. This approach constitutes a conceptual reformulation of the problem, focused on the underpinning systems for communication across the Internet rather than content itself and leading to a new understanding of this area. In so doing, it opens the way to a solution—even if not perfect—for this major policy problem. Because of this potential, Carnegie UK Trust, as part of its policy work on 'digital futures', supported the authors to develop a fuller policy proposal, working with civil society groups, technology companies, government, regulators, and commentators. Three UK Parliamentary Select Committees endorsed a *duty of care* approach based on our work, by then also supported by Luminate. The UK government announced in April 2019 that it would implement a systemic statutory duty of care enforced by a regulator based in part on the model the authors originally set out and reiterated that it proposed to introduce a statutory duty of care in its Full Government Response of December 2020. It is anticipated that a bill will come before Parliament in 2021.

The systemic approach has two aspects: a recognition that the platform (software system and business system) should be the focus of regulation; and that the primary required response from the operators is that of risk management. The authors envisaged a statutory duty of care backed up by an independent regulator as the vehicle by which these obligations could be imposed. By adopting a systemic approach, the proposal sought to develop a future-proof and flexible scheme, that protects the rights of users while allowing space for service and technological innovation. This chapter sets out our reasoning justifying this approach and outlines how such a duty could be imposed in practice based in the UK legal context.

PLATFORM NOT CONTENT

The first element of our proposal suggested that the focus of regulation should not target content directly but focus on the design of the service, its business model, the tools the platform provides for users, and the resources it devotes to user complaints and user safety, as each of these aspects influences information flows across the platform.

In looking to the system and services provided, this proposal recognizes the role of software in constituting online environments, and consequently on user choices, a recognition already found in the work of, for example, Reidenberg and Lessig. Reidenberg (1997, 554) argued that'[t]echnological capabilities and system design choices impose rules on participants'. Lessig (1999) characterized this as 'architecture' which constrains behaviour physically so that 'code' (software) affects what people do online. It permits, facilitates, and sometimes prohibits.

While Lessig suggests that code could be used as a mechanism in regulating the Internet, we look at the issue of code and design in the context of business choices made by platform operators. The design choices made by the companies in constructing these platforms are not neutral; they have an impact on content and how it is shared (see, for example, Herzog 2018; Norwegian Consumer Council 2018), even if we recognize that users have some choice in how they respond to technology (see criticism of Lawrence Lessig on this, among others). Insofar as these design choices, deliberately or otherwise, exploit cognitive biases and nudge users towards one set of behaviours or another, the rationality and even autonomy of each user may be compromised (Costa and Halpern 2019). As Mark Leiser suggests, some of the theoretical models in this area that emphasize that users are not just passive 'dots' have fallen into a common trap: that of assuming that all users are rational and underplaying the role of cognitive weaknesses most humans exhibit which are exploited by the platform design choices (Leiser 2016). The provision of information through terms and conditions is not the answer, even accepting that nudges do not render individuals complete zombies. These policies may be lengthy, written in appalling legalese, the implications of which are obscure, and spread often across several documents. Not everyone has the time, energy or intellectual capacity to read and understand them. Moreover, they operate at the entry point to the services rather than as those services as used; they engage the brain differently from design choices and therefore have little mitigating effect against nudges. Indeed, some have suggested that legal concepts such as user consent based on these policies are little more than the attempt to legitimate the manipulation of users through choice architecture (Hartzog 2018).

Recognizing that the system design has an impact on what happens online suggests that a relevant, if not the most appropriate, point for regulation is at the point of construction of these synthetic landscapes. In sum, the platforms which affect user behaviour reflect choices made by the people who create and manage them and those who make choices should be responsible for, at least, the reasonably foreseeable risks of those choices. This test originally derives from the duty of care found in the common law and is discussed later. This duty of care does not equate to direct liability for the publication of content or for its distribution, but rather constitutes a recognition that the consequences of design and business choices should be taken into account and, where practicable, dealt with.

Some commentators have suggested that currently many platforms are designed to modify user behaviour so as to maximize revenue, and that users are encouraged to make choices that are not in their best interest in furtherance of this goal. Zuboff termed this model 'surveillance capitalism' (Zuboff 2015). This 'manipulation' machine is not inherent to the services it underpins (Lanier 2019). That this is about business choice becomes apparent when we consider that not all platforms suffer the same issues. While much may be about size, significant aspects may derive from design and business model. A number of commentators have noted this point (Moore 2018); Beyer pointed to the different communities and their interaction in respectively World of Warcraft and 4Chan (Beyer 2014). This reminds us that technology is not inherently bad, but nor is it neutral. Significantly, these structures and business models are not inevitable or immutable.

In terms of design choices, there are three main points of influence which will have an effect on the occurrence of harm before reaching the question of whether individual items of content should be taken down. These are: the point at which a user engages with the platform (including sign up processes including the possibility of anonymity/pseudonymity, means of finding others in a group, and tools to communicate for example augmented reality filters/overlays); the mechanisms by which content is disseminated (e.g., search engines, hashtags, recommender algorithms, newsfeeds); the mechanisms by which recipient users engage with content, including choosing not to engage with it, but also mechanisms such as tools for sharing/forwarding/demonstrating approval or disapproval. In relation to all of these, defaults and ease of use are important. Examples of this category include retweeting, liking, and forwarding tools.

Finally, complaints mechanisms and take-down processes play a role in affecting users' online behaviour. While this is not a matter of choice architecture, enforcement of community standards still has a role in affecting user behaviour and there are risks from slow, erratic, or unequal enforcement, as there are for non-enforcement. The visibility of enforcing such standards is an important aspect of reinforcing community norms. Handling of complaints is also an important part of harm reduction—a company's complaints process should function as an early warning of systemic problems. By contrast with the software-based features, the existence of terms and conditions and some form of community standards is common to all platforms.

Selecting a Statutory Duty of Care Model

Historically, in media regulation control over content and its public availability has been exercised through the imposition of responsibility (and liability) for content on the creators and publishers of the content. By contrast, although the focus of the traditional media regulation remains liability for content, distributors (such as broadcast transmitter owners) tend not to attract such liability. Distributors have no impact on the content—indeed they are likely unaware of that content; nor do they choose its distribution strategy. As noted earlier, this publisher/distribution model, with its focus on content, is difficult to apply to platforms. The boundary between creation/publication and distribution is not so clear-cut (as demonstrated in the previous section), and there are questions of the speed and scale of the content posted. Finally, but significantly in the context of global companies, views as to the acceptability of particular types of content vary from one jurisdiction to another and, more generally, the understanding of meaning may be context-specific.

If we accept that the traditional binary boundary between content and transmission is not helpful, and that a better analogy is that of architecture and spaces, we might look beyond the current regulatory frameworks for communications and media for regulatory models. We can look to the regulatory approaches to public, quasi-public, and even some private spaces to see this. There is little regulation as to what goes on in these spaces; what is said and done there. These spaces, however, need to reach a certain threshold in safety. In general, there should be adequate lighting and ventilation, fire extinguishers, and exits. Other safeguards may relate to the specific context: the risks in a swimming pool are different from a football ground; different behaviours might be expected in a coffee shop than in a pub. The risks posed by the activities of visitors might also be taken into account. In *Everett v. Comojo* (2011), the Court of Appeal noted in relation to an obligation under the Occupier's Liability Act 1957 (OLA) that:

> it requires the occupier to take such care, as in all the circumstances of the case is reasonable, to see that the visitor will be reasonably safe in using the premises for the purposes for which is he invited or permitted to be there. It would be surprising if management could be liable to a guest who tripped over a worn carpet and yet escape liability for injuries inflicted by a fellow guest who was a foreseeable danger—for example in that he had previously been excluded on account of his violent behaviour and who on this occasion had been allowed in carrying an offensive weapon. (para 33)

The statutory duty of care we propose is inspired by the UK approach to regulating the broad landscape of workplace health and safety. Workplaces are a quasi-public space in which many different types of activity take place and all sorts of different people engage with one another. By the late 1960s industrial disasters forced parliament to reform radically hundreds of years of detailed rules about workplace safety, which by tackling the issue of safety piecemeal left gaps in protection. The Health and Safety at Work Act (HSWA) clarified the beneficiaries of the duty owed by employers. Section 2(1) HSWA specifies:

> It shall be the duty of every employer to ensure, so far as is reasonably practicable, the health, safety and welfare at work of all his employees.

This is very broad, and s. 3(1) extends the category of beneficiaries to include 'persons not in his employment who may be affected' by the business, seeking to close the gaps in protection. While the nature of the obligation is wide, it is limited in that the steps required to be taken are those that are 'reasonably practicable'. A duty of care does not require absolute protection from harm. The question is whether sufficient care has been taken and 'reasonably practicable' does not require all actions that are theoretically possible. In this professionals are held to industry standards, which may include the responsibility to undertake a risk assessment (Threlfall v. Hull 2011). The foreseeability of a risk is a relevant factor too. So—looking at existing case law—an employer would not in breach of a duty of care in failing to take precautions against an unknown danger (Heyes v. Pilkington Glass Ltd 1998). The risk should not be insignificant in relation to the sacrifice. Perfection is not required.

Further, the HSWA gives examples of specific issues about which the employer must take action, at least as regards employees, although these do not replace the general duty. Examples include: provision of machinery that is safe (and has been tested to be safe); the training of relevant individuals; and the maintenance of a safe working environment. Additionally, HSWA includes a specific obligation 'to prepare and as often as may be appropriate revise a written statement of his general policy with respect to the health and safety at work': this is the beginnings of formalizing a preventative approach, based on an assessment of risks posed. Lord Young's 2010 review of the HSWA found the regime to be working well. Its longevity, and the fact it can be deployed in a wide range of circumstances, suggests the model to be flexible and, to some extent, future-proof.

OVERVIEW OF THE DUTY

Against this background, our report for Carnegie UK Trust proposed a statutory duty of care, similar to that found in the HSWA, but addressed to social media platforms (see what follows for definition). As noted earlier, social media platforms through their design choices are not neutral as to the flow of information and may be said to have a role in the creation or exacerbation of problems arising. This singles them out from other Internet service providers who may be necessary in the flow of information and could therefore act as gatekeepers but do not have such a constitutive effect. The duty would be owed to their users but also to those people who might be affected by the operation of the platform, such as victims of revenge pornography who may not use a service that is being used to harm them. The statutory duty is generic, focussed on reducing risk of harm, and is neutral as to how that harm is caused. When establishing the regime, legislators will want to ensure that the harms of greatest concern are addressed by companies and the regulator, so (as in the HSWA) specific heads of harm would be listed in statute. The proposal identified the following categories of harm:

1. terrorism;
2. dangers to persons aged under 18 and vulnerable adults;
3. racial hatred, religious hatred, hatred on the grounds of sex, or hatred on the grounds of sexual orientation;
4. discrimination against a person because of a protected characteristic;
5. fraud or financial crime;
6. intellectual property crime; and
7. threats which impede or prejudice the integrity and probity of the electoral processes.

Most of these terms are already defined in domestic law and are not open-ended categories. We emphasize that the statutory duty of care is not about whether a particular civil of criminal offence has occurred, or even that harm has arisen in a particular instance; rather, the question is whether this sort of harm is likely to arise on or be exacerbated by the service or a feature in the service, as we discuss later. The proposal also envisaged that there should be a mechanism whereby the categories of harm could be reviewed and, if necessary, updated.

The regime would be run (including through the provision of advice as to best practice) and enforced by an independent regulator. The regulator would, of course, be bound by the Human Rights Act so, when exercising its powers, it should have regard to fundamental human rights and the need to maintain an appropriate balance between conflicting rights. The regulator would not be a censor; the regime is about the choice architecture and other business choices at the systems level rather than the regulation of specific items of content.

Central to the duty of care is the idea of risk, specifically identifying and managing risk, and we proposed that there should be a specific obligation on an operator to carry out a thorough assessment of the risks posed by the operation of the platform or any aspect of the service, especially as regards vulnerable groups. There are three questions relating to risk of harm.

The first question is whether a harm can eventuate from certain conditions. This implicates the current evidence base, which is incomplete. Here, we propose that the precautionary principle approach, developed for use in assessing indicative evidence, is taken to whether harms may eventuate. The second question is whether there is a risk of that harm on a particular platform, in the light of available evidence. This is a question of a reasonable assessment, not perfect hindsight; wilful blindness is not permissible. We suggested that risks include the foreseeable risks of 'misuse' of the platform by actors—especially where that behaviour has happened elsewhere. Platforms should take into account any guidance on this question provided by the regulator. The third question asks about the nature of the response to mitigate the risk to determine what are appropriate measures. The response should be effective but take into account the risk: both the nature of the harm and the likelihood it would occur.

Likelihood of a particular harm arising or being exacerbated will vary from platform to platform, depending on—amongst other things—the nature of the user-base and the types of services and features offered. So, a mass membership, general purpose service should manage risk by setting a very low tolerance for harmful behaviour, in the same way that some public spaces take into account that they should be a reasonably safe space for all. Specialist audiences/user-bases of social, media services may have online behavioural norms that on a family-friendly service could cause harm but in the community where they originate are not harmful. Examples might include sports-team fan services or sexuality-based communities. This can be seen particularly well with Reddit: its user base with diverse interests self-organizes into separate subreddits, each with its own behavioural culture and moderation. We proposed that services targeted at children and young people are high risk, particularly where the services are designed to be used on a mobile device away from immediate adult supervision.

The duties of care are expressed in terms of what they aim to achieve—a desired outcome (i.e., the prevention of harm) rather than necessarily specifying the steps to get there. The measure of compliance is not about whether a certain numerical target is reached in terms of types of content existing or taken down, but it is about processes within the company and a focus on product safety in terms of services deployed, tools provided, and resources allocated to particular aspects of the business—and an assessment of whether they are appropriate given an appreciation of what is reasonably foreseeable in terms of the occurrence of harm at all stages of the communication chain where the platform connects with content or affects information flows. It is possible for a platform operator to satisfy the duty of care even if some harmful content and behaviours are found on the platform; the regime does not impose liability for individual instances of content. It is on the likelihood of harm occurring that the Carnegie proposal focusses. While heads of harm need to be identified in the underpinning legislation, the understanding of risk factors related to those harms, which can be filled in—as in other regulatory regimes—through guidance from the regulator, is key.

It has been suggested that the obligations on platforms should be limited to content which is criminal under national law. In our view, while the liability of platforms for the content of third parties is affected by the distinction between civil and criminal law, that distinction has less relevance here. The criminal law in particular deals with culpability of the speaker, and rules designed with punishment are not well adapted for focussing on the harm suffered by victims; indeed, the requirement of Mens Rea may exclude some actors from a criminal offence while including others, although the impact on the victim in both sets of cases is the same (Kyd et al 2017, paras 2-129–2-132). Moreover, the criminal law is tightly focussed and, as the Law Commission has noted, this might mean that behaviours which are similarly harmful from the view of a victim are not equally criminalized; upskirting is now a criminal offence in England and Wales, down blousing is not. While the Law Commission's review has identified some anomalies (Law Commission (2018, 2020, 2021), it is unlikely that all have been found. Moreover, revision of the criminal law might not deal with all issues arising from the differences between the respective legal systems of the home nations. There is an additional concern that if a regime focussed on the categorization of speech, too much regulatory attention would be diverted into understanding those categories. Moreover, there is a risk that this would lead to a limitation of the types of possible interventions, with a focus on ex post measures (essentially take-down) rather than the wider range of possibilities in play were the entire service and its features to be considered. We note that the Full Government Response contains an internal boundary between platforms in general and those perceived to be particularly risky based on the difference between criminal and 'harmful but legal' content. We maintain that the legal characterization of the content, while pertinent for the attribution of liability to the speaker is not the best tool for determining the obligations of the platform.

SCOPE OF SERVICES WITHIN THE REGIME

The proposal suggested that the duty should be imposed on social media platforms rather than Internet services more broadly, reflecting the fact that social media platforms affect the content environment in a way other levels of the distribution chain (e.g., CDN, DDoS mitigation), do not. Insofar as this level of the distribution chain is a material factor in creating the problem, it should have a responsibility (and not off-load its business expenses) to other levels in that chain, the users themselves, or society in general.

We identified two central characteristics defining services to be regulated (and the Full Government Response [DCMS, 2020] takes a similar approach—see para 19). They should:

- Have a strong multiway communications component; and
- Display user-generated content publicly or to a large member/ user group.

Operators would be obliged to notify the regulator of their operations. Failure to do so would be an offence.

On this basis, services such as Facebook and Twitter would be included, as would closed messaging services that allow communications to large groups, and gaming platforms such as Twitch. As regards messaging services, the size of groups on these services suggests that much communication mediated via the service is neither private nor confidential. Other characteristics also indicate the non-private nature of the communication, notably the growing practice of public groups, sharing of group links and browsers and search apps for groups. Some large games that contain messaging services might also fall within the definition (a possibility that is also recognized in the European Electronic Communications Code).

The position where an operator is providing the platform for others to use—for example services like Blogger and Wordpress (which in principle could be included because the comment functionality allows interaction) or a decentralized social network like Mastodon—is more complex because there are two possible levels which could take responsibility. One approach would be to suggest that both the software designer and the person deploying the platform have responsibility, though that responsibility would differ. The designer of the software would be responsible for the design of the platform; the deployer for moderation (to the extent that that did not constitute preinstalled automated functions) and complaints.

While search engines do play a constitutive role in creating a user's online information environment, and can clearly take steps to affect the flow of content, our proposal for Carnegie excludes them from the regime; by contrast, the UK Government's Full Government Response expressly includes them. In our view, the level of engagement and interactivity is less; moreover, the discoverability of information may raise a whole set of issues around the right to receive information, public service, and impartiality that may not be best dealt with through the lens of a duty of care, or any duty of care imposed may have distinctive features to take these particular public interest concerns into account. So while there may be a case for imposing regulatory obligations around search, more work needs to be done as to what that would look like.

The proposal limits the regime to those displaying/transmitting user-generated content. It does not apply to operators that are responsible for content that they make available, such as the traditional press or broadcasters. We do not regard ex-post moderation as 'editorial control'.

While there is a case to argue that small companies should lie outside the regime, this is outweighed by the following factors. First, some groups are sufficiently vulnerable (e.g., children) that any business aiming a service at them should take an appropriate level of care, no matter what its size or newness to market. We can see this in other sectors, for example basic hygiene principles apply even to the smallest sandwich shop. Second, design and resourcing errors in a growth stage have caused substantial problems for larger services, especially when growth is rapid. The GDPR emphasis on privacy by design also sets basic design conditions for all services, regardless of size. The impact of the broad scope is mitigated as the regime does not envisage that an operator should take all possible measures, no matter how costly. It may be that the position of SMEs, and their available resources, are a factor a regulator should take into account when assessing the proportionality of a response.

CODES OF PRACTICE

An essential element of the regime is the use of codes to provide more detail as to what good practice looks like; codes are more appropriate for dealing with technical detail than legislation. The process for developing these codes should be set down in statute so as to ensure the regulator acts in a fair and transparent manner. Given the complexity of the issues, the proposal envisaged that the regulator should have two advisory councils, one made up of technical experts (including those with knowledge of behavioural psychology) and the other representing different groups of users.

The codes should not focus on types of content or particular harms, but rather on system issues, including the impact of design on content and information flows. The Carnegie proposal identified the following areas:

- assessment of risk—factors informing suitable, sufficient, up-to-date processes of risk assessment (including risk assessment and product safety before deployment of new features/services);
- transparency of platform, referring to the steps to carry out its statutory duty (including complaints), specifying reporting format;

- access to platforms (age controls; anonymous platforms; user verification techniques);
- communications techniques and tools (e.g., augmented reality, deepfakes, likes; retweets, ease of linking to external content sources);
- considerations relating to terms and conditions of service and information statements about risk and harm;
- training for staff;
- risk factors in service design (e.g., impact of metrics, impact of personalization techniques);
- Discovery and navigation techniques (e.g., autocomplete on searches; default recommender algorithms); and
- How users can protect themselves from harm, including the provision of tools that users can themselves deploy.

The Carnegie proposal also envisaged that reporting on the operation of the complaints and redress mechanisms would form part of a provider's transparency and reporting obligations, so a code should cover this. External review is important not just in terms of effectiveness of harm reduction but in ensuring that the companies are operating fairly, that the meaning of terms of service are clear and consistently applied, that the rights of some groups are not prioritized over those of others and that when take down is in issue, the decision to take content down or not to take it down can be objectively verified.

Some issues are particularly urgent—notably child sexual exploitation and abuse and terrorism—and may need swift response. Specific codes would likely be required in these areas, not necessarily detailing what prohibited content is, but how relevant law enforcement authorities and the platforms should effectively interact (bearing in mind existing rules about investigatory techniques, the gathering of evidence and the prosecution of crime). This is a specific form of interlocking regulation. We envisage a general form (discussed later).

While guidance may be provided by the regulator and such guidance may be of particular use for smaller platforms, it may be that larger firms would want to adopt their own approaches. This should be permissible, subject to the overarching control of the regulator; essentially, this is a 'comply or explain' approach. Similarly, industry associations could develop their own versions of codes, which the regulator could (but would not have to) adopt. We also envisaged that there might be a case to have codes which constitute best practice and those which are mandatory. Such mandatory codes would relate to particularly problematic issues (e.g., child sexual abuse and exploitation material).

INTERLOCKING REGULATORY REGIMES

'In real life' regulatory regimes exist across broad swathes of economic, social, and cultural activity. Those who enforce such sectoral regimes have extensive expertise in their subject area. There is already an online element to harms covered by these regulatory regimes and this is likely to increase. Many sectoral regulators, even ostensibly powerful ones, find that they cannot get an effective reaction from the online platforms in relation to harms within their respective remits. The Financial Conduct Authority for instance was unable to persuade Google to take down advertisements when for illegal 'mini bonds' (Hussain 2020).

It is unreasonable to expect the online harms regulator to become expert in all regulatory fields to deal with these sector-specific issues or, indeed, to expect platforms to develop an appreciation of risks in relation to some highly specialist forms of content. What is required is a mechanism whereby the sectoral regulatory regimes may interlock with the duty of care regime. Not only would this lead to better results for society but this might also simplify cross compliance and reduce a regulatory burden for companies.

To achieve 'regulatory interlock' a sectoral regulator identifying online harms in their field needs to be able to notify the online harms regulator in relation to the duty of care of the problem, and that regulator should have a transparent process to assess whether the harms fall within the duty of care. If appropriate, the online harms regulator could then alert regulated operators to these new harm vectors. The online harms regulator could set guidance in relation to these new subcategories of harm and risk vectors with the aim of reducing the compliance burden for regulated operators. The UK security authorities already have systems for high speed interlock for the most serious harms such as CSEA and counter-terrorism. The UK Government's Full Government Response allows for 'co-designation' of another more specialist regulator to help OFCOM fulfil its online harms duties.

It may also be that social media platforms should be under a duty to cooperate with competent regulators (for example by preserving evidence or identifying users), though safeguards should be built in so that due process is respected (and safeguards in other systems are not undermined or circumvented) and users' rights are not disproportionately infringed. The process should be as transparent as possible. In this context it is important to remember that there is a prohibition on requiring general monitoring in Article 15 of the EU e-Commerce Directive (an approach to be maintained in the UK post-Brexit), a prohibition that aims to protect both freedom of speech and privacy.

ENFORCEMENT AND SANCTIONS

The proposed regime does not create a cause of action whereby users may bring an action against the platform (though their existing rights remain unchanged). Instead the regime leaves enforcement to the regulator. The regulator would therefore need to be granted information gathering/auditing powers, as well as a range of enforcement mechanisms.

Throughout this issue of enforcement runs the question of how to make the world's biggest technology companies comply with the laws of a single country in which they are not based. Our starting point was that companies and the people who work for them want to comply with the law. Many companies simply need a request for information from the regulator to nudge them into compliance. So some 'sanctions' are mechanisms to explain the regime to regulated operators and to get the regime to operate more effectively rather than to specifically sanction the operator—an improvement notice providing advice as to a failure and a way to redress the problem. Other companies though may need strong penalties to drive compliance. In our proposals we set out two primary sanctions: large fines along the lines of the GDPR or competition law or, in the case of the most severe behaviours, requiring UK Internet service providers to block access to some services.

Neither of these are straightforward. The microeconomics of fining broadly require marginal pressure on returns to shareholders to drive them to require management to change behaviour. The microeconomic forces do not work well when companies have a multibillion-dollar cash pile and shareholder voting structures that limit the effect of shareholder pressure on the executive team. In many regulated industries, dominant actors have some sort of licence to operate which becomes the fulcrum for regulatory action the ultimate end point of which could be licence withdrawal. The e-commerce directive, however, prohibits licensing of information society services, which includes social media. One alternative is the blocking of non-compliant services by Internet service providers (as was proposed in relation to porn services in the Digital Economy Act 2017). The technical and practical feasibility of this has not been tested, as the Digital Economy Act provisions were not brought into force; copyright owners, however, have had recourse to blocking injunctions relying on the Copyright Designs and Patents Act. Blocking a service may give rise to questions as to whether the response is proportionate, given the knock-on consequences to the users' rights to express themselves and to receive information via that platform.

The challenges of ensuring compliance from large companies are far from unique to the technology sector. Other commentators, such as the NSPCC, have suggested sanctions based on named-director schemes similar to the financial services sector and even criminal sanctions for named directors. Whilst we would not argue against criminal sanctions for the very worst offences such as child sexual abuse and exploitation, we have to bear in mind that arresting people in charge of media companies does not sit well with European democratic traditions and respect for freedom of expression.

CONCLUSIONS

Our proposal demonstrates that regulating social media platforms—or even the Internet—is not impossible. The key is the systemic approach; that is the shift from a focus on specific items of content and a move to a risk management approach. In using the vehicle of the statutory duty of care, the proposal adopts existing mechanisms that are known to work, balancing the flexibility necessary not to stifle innovation whilst ensuring that the needs of users are not overlooked. While the statutory duty of care is a concept based in English law, the fundamentals of the systemic approach could be adopted to use outside this jurisdiction, as the European Commission's proposal for the Digital Services Act illustrates. In moving away from a focus on content, questions about the acceptability of which are likely to be culturally specific and context dependant, makes agreement on a common approach across states more possible.

Post Script

Since this chapter was written, the Government has published the draft Online Safety Bill for pre-legislative scrutiny. It follows to a large extent the position set out in the Full Government Response (DCMS 2020) but, rather than one overarching statutory duty with obligations filled by specific provisions, it establishes a complex set of duties dependent on categorisation of content and operator. Notably, what has been termed "harmful but legal" now forms part of the "adults' safety duty" which applies only to a subset of platforms (not search)—Category 1 providers. There are specific obligations relating to the protection of free speech and privacy on the face of the draft Bill and Category 1 providers are under further obligations with regard to democratic debate and journalistic content. The Secretary of State under the draft bill is given wide-ranging powers to establish "priority" content which is to receive special attention by the platform operators as well as to ensure that OFCOM, which has a key role in developing guidance and Codes of Practice, remains aligned to the Government's policy objectives. In addition to large fines, the draft bill includes business disruption measures and the possibility for provisions guarding individual directors' responsibility to be brought into force. By contrast to the Full Government Response (DCMS 2020), it does not seem to provide for co-designation, though this point may be dealt with by Ofcom's existing general duties in the Communications Act. The inclusion for the specification of certain technologies (a "use of technology notice"), admittedly in limited circumstances, could potentially include upload filters; if so, this might be seen as an exception to the general no monitoring rule. At the time of writing this post-script, pre-legislative scrutiny had not started; it seems unlikely that an act could come into force before 2022 at the earliest nor the full regime become operational before 2023.

REFERENCES

PRIMARY MATERIALS

Legislation

Directive 2000/31/EC of the European Parliament and of the Council of 8 June 2000 on certain legal aspects of information society services, in particular electronic commerce, in the Internal Market (e-Commerce Directive) OJ [2000] L 178/1.

Directive 2010/13/EU of the European Parliament and of the Council of 10 March 2010 on the coordination of certain provisions laid down by law, regulation or administrative action in Member States concerning the provision of audiovisual media services (Audiovisual Media Services Directive) OJ [2010] L 95/1.

Directive (EU) 2015/1535 laying down a procedure for the provision of information in the field of technical regulations and of rules on Information Society Services OJ [2015] L 241/1.

Directive (EU) 2018/1808 of the European Parliament and of the Council of 14 November 2018 amending Directive 2010/13/EU on the coordination of certain provisions laid down by law, regulation or administrative action in Member States concerning the provision of audiovisual media services (amending Audiovisual Media Services Directive) in view of changing market realities OJ [2018] L 303/69.

Directive (EU) 2018/1972 of the European Parliament and of the Council of 11 December 2018 establishing the European Electronic Communications Code (Recast) OJ [2018] L 321/36.

Malicious Communications (Social Media) Bill 2016-17. accessed March 30, 2020. https://services.parliament.uk/bills/2016-17/maliciouscommunicationssocialmedia.html (.

Case Law

Google France and Google Inc. v Louis Vuitton Malletier SA, Google France SARL v Viaticum SA and Luteciel SARL and Google France SARL v Centre national de recherche en relations humaines (CNRRH) SARL and Others ('Adwords') (Joined Cases C-236/08 to C-238/08), judgment 23 March 2010, ECLI:EU:C:2010:159.

L'Oréal SA, Lancôme parfums et beauté & Cie SNC, Laboratoire Garnier & Cie, L'Oréal (UK) Ltd v. eBay International AG, eBay Europe SARL, eBay (UK) Ltd, Stephen Potts, Tracy Ratchford, Marie Ormsby, James Clarke, Joanna Clarke, Glen Fox, Rukhsana Bi ('L'Oréal v eBay'), (Case C-324/09), judgment 12 July 2011, ECLI:EU:C:2011:474.

Everett v. Comojo [2011] EWCA Civ 11. http://www.bailii.org/ew/cases/EWCA/Civ/2011/13.html.

Heyes v. Pilkington Glass Ltd [1998] PIQR P303, (CA).

Steven Threlfall v. Hull CC [2011] PIQR P3 (CA).

Secondary Materials

Beyer, Jessica. 2014. Expect Us: Online Communities and Political Mobilization. Oxford: Oxford University Press.

Committee on Standards in Public Life. 2017. 'Intimidation in Public Life: A Review by the Committee on Standards in Public Life'. December (Cmnd 9543).

Costa, Elisabeth, and David Halpern. 2019. 'The Behavioural Science of Online Harm and Manipulation, and What to Do about It', April 15. Accessed October 27, 2020. https://www.bi.team/publications/the-behavioural-science-of-online-harm-and-manipulation-and-what-to-do-about-it/.

DCMS. 2019. 'Online Harms White Paper'. April (CP57).

DCMS. 2020. 'Online Harms White Paper: Full Government Response to the Consultation'. December (CP354).

Hartzog, Woodrow. 2018. Privacy's Blueprint: The Battle to Control the Design of New Technologies. Cambridge, MA: Harvard University Press.

House of Commons, Select Committee on Digital, Culture, Media and Sport. 2018. 'Disinformation and 'Fake News': Interim Report'. July (Fifth Report of Session 2017–19) (HC 363).

Hussain, Ali. 2020. 'High-Risk Mini-Bond Ads: Banned, but Still on Google. Sites Offering Near-Impossible Returns Continue to Top Online Searches Despite an FCA Clampdown'. The Times, January 5. https://www.thetimes.co.uk/article/high-risk-mini-bond-ads-banned-but-still-on-google-fcfwmwfck.

Kyd, Sally, Tracey Elliot, and Mark Walters. 2017. Clarkson & Keating Criminal Law: Text and Materials. 9th ed. London: Sweet and Maxwell.

Lanier, Jaron. 2019. Ten Arguments for Deleting Your Social Media Accounts Right Now. Vintage Publishing London.

Law Commission. 2018. 'Abusive and Offensive Online Communications: A Scoping Report'. Law Com No. 381, November 1 (HC 1682).

Law Commission. 2020. 'Harmful Online Communications: The Criminal Offences—A Consultation paper'. Consultation Paper 248, September 11.

Law Commission. 2021. 'Intimate Image Abuse'. Consultation Paper 23, February 26.

Leiser, Mark. 2016. 'The Problem with 'Dots': Questioning the Role of Rationality in the Online Environment'. International Review of Law, Computers and Technology 30: 191–210.

Lessig, Lawrence. 1999. 'The Law of the Horse: What Cyberlaw Might Teach'. Harvard Law Review 113: 501.

Lessig, Lawrence. 1999. Code and Other Laws of Cyberspace. Basic Books.

Lessig, Lawrence. 2006. Code: Version 2.0. Basic Books.

Lord Young of Graffham. 2010. 'Common Sense, Common Safety'. Accessed May 12, 2020. https://assets.publishing.service.gov.uk/government/uploads/system/uploads/attachment_data/file/60905/402906_CommonSense_acc.pdf.

Moore, Martin. 2018. Democracy Hacked: How Technology Is Destabilizing Global Politics. Oneworld Publications.

Murray, Andrew. 2007. Regulation of Cyberspace. Oxford University Press.

Norwegian Consumer Council. 2018. 'Deceived by Design: How Tech Companies Use Dark Patterns to Discourage Us from Protecting Our Rights to Privacy', June 27. Accessed March 30, 2020. https://fil.forbrukerradet.no/wp-content/uploads/2018/06/2018-06-27-deceived-by-design-final.pdf.

Ofcom. 2018 'Addressing Harmful Content Online: A Perspective from Broadcasting and On-Demand Standards Regulation', September 18.

Reed, Chris, and Andrew Murray. 2018. Rethinking the Jurisprudence of Cyberspace. Cheltenham: Edward Elgar.

Reidenberg, Joel R. 1997–1998. 'Lex Informatica: The Formulation of Information Policy Rules through Technology'. Texas Law Review 76: 553–593.https://ir.lawnet.fordham.edu/faculty_scholarship/42.

Sacha Desmaris, Pierre Dubreuil, Benoît Loutrel. 2019. 'Creating a French Framework to Make Social Media Platforms More Accountable: Acting in France with a European Vision'. Interim mission report 'Regulation of social networks—Facebook experiment'. Submitted to the French Secretary of State for Digital Affairs. May 2019.

Thaler, R., and C. Sunstein. 2008. Nudge: Improving Decisions about Health, Wealth, and Happiness. London: Penguin Books .

Turow, Joseph. 2012. The Daily You: How the New Advertising Industry Is Defining Your Identity and Your Worth. Yale University Press.

Woods, Lorna. 2012. 'Extension of Journalistic Ethics to Content produced by Private Individuals'. In Freedom of Expression and the Media, edited by MerrisAmos, Jackie Harrison, and Lorna Woods, 141–168. Martinus Nijhoff Publishers.

Zuboff, Shosana. 2015. 'Big Other: Surveillance Capitalism and the Prospects of an Information Civilization'. Journal of Information Technology *30*: 75–89.

6

Minimizing Data-Driven Targeting and Providing a Public Search Alternative

ANGELA PHILLIPS AND ELEONORA MARIA MAZZOLI ■

INTRODUCTION

This chapter argues that radical, systemic change, at a European and even global level, is required if the Internet is to be reclaimed so that it enhances democracy rather than undermining it. The structural problems that we aim to address with this work concern the commercial imperatives and data exploitation that drives search, ranking, and sorting systems of social media and search engines. Even though we are aware that search engines' and social media's systems present different technicalities and business models, we argue that in both systems the criteria and principles used to distribute and organize the overabundance of content online are primarily driven by commercial interests and a need to maximize advertising revenues. This becomes particularly problematic when it comes to the distribution of news, where popularity, virality, and search optimization techniques are increasingly impacting the way in which information is produced and circulated. As we will argue in what follows, these mechanisms have systemic, negative effects on the kind of information that is published, its distribution, and the access to high-quality material.

We therefore believe that there is an urgent need to de-link such commercial imperatives and popularity-driven systems from the distribution of news online. Even though this underlying issue is common of both social media and search engines, for the purpose of this chapter, we will primarily focus on the latter. To tackle this, we propose a two-fold action. First, we need to reduce the commercialization and exploitation of personal data (Zuboff 2015). While the use of data to refine search for an individual has benefits, when that data is used to allow third parties to target individuals with unrequested information, its use must be more closely questioned. Second, we envisage the development of a public service search engine providing an alternative to the market logic of the existing services. Such a service would be based on public service principles rather than commercial ones. A public service search engine would not replace the commercial services, it would however challenge them, by introducing competition over quality of information, rather than profit. Large structural interventions as opposed to minor changes, we argue, are the only way of countering those harms associated with digital dominance, as outlined by Martin Moore and Damian Tambini (2018), and enhancing its benefits.

PROBLEM DEFINITION: THE DOMINANCE OF OPAQUE RANKING SYSTEMS

In an intensely competitive online environment, with an overabundance of content, the 'battle for eyeballs' is subject to complex logics of search and prominence that affect what content can be found, or what instead might end in oblivion. The task of algorithmic news search and recommenders is to filter, organize, and rank the growing abundance of online information, playing a crucial role in nudging audiences' attention. While this impacts all information accessed online, we are particularly concerned with access to news—both passive and active. Scholars have increasingly expressed their concerns about the implications of the circulation of news on those online services where it is no longer the editor who decides what is newsworthy, having been replaced by automated systems and recommenders informed by the quantified interests and preferences of the audience (Helberger 2019, 996). An important factor in this context is the degree of internal and external commercial pressures from advertisers and from other sources of commercial optimization that drive services like search engines and social media platforms (Helberger 2019; Newman 2018; Turow 2005). Depending on the outlet and the metrics used for optimization, these systems can be used not only to increase time spent, advertising revenues, and user satisfaction, but also to actively guide readers and match individual readers with the news they will receive on different services (Helberger 2019, 994).

As further argued by Helberger, the power to actively guide and shape individuals' news exposure also brings fundamental questions about the values and guiding principles of these systems as they impact on the media's democratic mission (Helberger 2019, 994). When popularity, advertising interests, and commercial agreements become primary drivers for prominence online, rather than integrity and diversity of news information, the implications for users and for our news media ecosystem are far-reaching. This indeed leads to an increase in the circulation of extreme material on social media by those who have a vested interest in increasing their following (Bradshaw and Howard 2018), which is in turn, picked up by the search engines that prioritize the most popular material on the basis of factors like recency, click-through rate, current keywords, and trends (Pinsky 2018), and serve it on the basis of users' prior preferences and interactions.

This logic can trap users in a feedback loop in which certain behaviour is measured and then stimulated again and again. Advertisers then batten onto the audience members who are viewing the most popular posts, providing very small payments, per view or click, to publishers (Elvestad and Phillips 2018; McNamee 2019; Wu 2017). This means that very large audiences are required in order to cover the costs of news production. News organizations, attracting smaller audiences, such as local news providers, or those who are actively engaged in research, or who employ high production values, will struggle to cover their costs on advertising income alone (Cairncross 2019; Pickard 2019). It is those who display the greatest expertise in arousing emotion (which then encourages sharing and promotes material in search rankings) who are the most likely to profit from these low margins (Berger and Milkman 2014).

While the aforementioned issues are structurally engrained in the way information circulates through a number of online services, for the purposes of this chapter, we will focus mainly on search engines. Search engines are an ever-changing landscape, and their linked advertising systems are becoming ever more sophisticated through the use of data analytics (Van Couvering 2009). We intend to question the functioning and driving criteria of search and ranking systems of search engines, with a particular focus on the use of data to drive automated targeted advertising. By automated targeted advertising, we refer to those customized techniques that capitalize on consumer's data (such as demographic, psychographic, geographic, and behavioural data) to predict behaviour, interests, and opinions, and influence that behaviour with the help of hypertargeted advertising strategies.

The use of this type of advertising has been widely criticized in recent years, especially with regard to political microtargeting and propaganda (e.g., Bodó et al. 2017; Borgesius et al. 2018). However, the problem goes beyond the direct use of advertising by political organizations. Ranking and prominence of content in search results, combined with news recommender and personalization techniques, which optimize advertising revenues, has infected the way in which news is distributed, marketed, and produced. In order to increase readers' traffic, news organizations are encouraged to supply the kind of content that will be popular on search engines and social media, creating perverse incentives for the development of quickly produced, highly shareable content, often including unresearched opinion, fake or partisan news, and propaganda (Effron and Raj 2020). Criticizing this type of targeting and investigating its political, societal, and economic implications is not new. Attention has been drawn to the impacts of data targeting and profiling for users' privacy and surveillance (e.g., Zuboff 2015), for political campaigning and elections (e.g., Borgesius et al. 2018; Epstein 2018; Moore and Tambini 2018), for misinformation (e.g., Del Vicario et al. 2019), and for diversity of source, content and exposure as opposed to filter bubbles or echo chambers (e.g., Bail et al. 2018; Flaxman et al. 2016; Fletcher 2020; Helberger et al. 2018).

Concerns have also been raised among policymakers. While there are differences between countries, European policy interventions that could have had an impact on targeted advertising, such as the General Data Protection Regulation (GDPR 2016),[1] the revision of the Regulation on Privacy and Electronic Communications (2017),[2] or self-regulatory Code of Practices on Disinformation (2018),[3] have not done so. These proposed solutions often shift the burden of responsibility onto individual users to set filters and manage information, on the one hand, or to the self-regulation of platform organizations, on the other. We know that, faced with an interruption to their reading or information needs, most people when confronted with a pop-up asking for their consent to data use will click 'enable all' even though the vast majority are concerned about privacy (Mager 2017). We also know that relying on self-regulation when profit is at stake is unlikely to be successful (Angelopoulos et al. 2016), as shown for example by the Leveson Inquiry into the behaviour of the British press in 2012, which amply demonstrated the ineffectiveness of self-regulation for improving ethical standards in the print media (Leveson 2012).

Appeals for more systemic interventions addressing search and ranking systems are slowly growing, ranging from media and communication policy proposals, to antitrust and competition law (Bose and Bartz 2020; Competition & Markets Authority 2020). More comprehensive rules on advertising, including targeted advertising, have also been proposed as part of the recent European Digital Services Act Package (European Commission 2020).[4] However, regulatory frameworks still work on the assumption, probably encouraged by industry lobbies, that the advertising models by which the platform organizations raise money cannot themselves be challenged, thus, they often consider transparency as some sort of panacea and they are in danger of legitimizing current industry practices rather than challenging them. There seems to be a general acceptance that the means by which the duopoly of Google and Facebook have cornered the international advertising market is simply the price we have to pay for the use of this technology.

FINDING SOCIAL DEMOCRATIC SOLUTIONS: DE-LINKING SEARCH FROM COMMERCIAL IMPERATIVES

Within this context, this chapter argues for a systemic approach, which recognizes that the reliance on private data collection, coupled with automated third-party targeted advertising, is in itself problematic. Search engine optimization techniques and ranking algorithms do not need to be designed to maximize advertising revenues or popularity in order to function adequately for the purposes of information retrieval. Further, the power to actively guide and shape an individual's news searches and exposure should not be held by a handful of US-based organizations, such as Google and Microsoft, nor should it come without questions and responsibilities (Helberger 2019, 994). In order to achieve systemic change, two key operations need to be addressed: the use of data for targeting, and the organization of search. Thus, within this chapter, we intend first to critically reflect on possible solutions that could improve the implementation of current regulatory frameworks on data targeting; and second, to propose alternative industry models, such as a public interest search engine. We believe that both are needed to achieve more structural changes.

Regulating Data Targeting

Personalization is valuable to users when it is used to refine search and speed up the retrieval of information, especially if it is user-driven. However, there needs to be a clear line drawn between the use of personalization for search (active) and for targeting (passive). Research demonstrates that when data is initially in-put by users (active personalization) it tends to produce a greater diversity of information, whereas personalization that is selected by systems (passive personalization) tends to have 'a negative effect on knowledge' (Beam 2014, 1036). Nevertheless, we have seen the widespread adoption of passive personalization across platforms as a means of targeting material and advertising in order to maximize profit. Passive personalization gives Google Search (or other platforms) the power both to decide what news and information is displayed at the top of the search box and also which advertisements will come with that material when we click on it. Provocative material usually gets the most clicks and earns the advertisers (and Google Search) the highest revenues.

It was only when the use of microtargeting for advertising spread to political campaigning that it triggered international concern (not least from advertisers themselves) (Marvin and Meisel 2017) about the way in which such systems are manipulating public opinion and harming democracy (Bradshaw and Howard 2018; Dobber et al. 2019; Persily 2017). In response to concerns about political misinformation, Google announced that microtargeting of political advertising would be banned on its ad platforms (Spencer 2019), and YouTube announced a series of initiatives for the US 2020 elections, to prevent the spread of videos that have been manipulated with malicious intent (Alba 2020). Similarly, efforts have been made by other platform organizations, notably Twitter, which has introduced new restrictions and bans on microtargeting for political advertising, with the sole exception of news publishers (Wong 2019). Facebook declined to follow these examples on the not unreasonable grounds that it cannot always identify what is, and is not, political speech.

Even though it is now recognized that content curation and moderation are intrinsically part of the service offered by platforms (Gillespie 2010, 2018), we should be cautious in demanding that the major monopoly platforms take an even stronger role in the censorship of content. A better way to address the proliferation of toxic material is to de-link the purely commercial imperatives of search engines from the circulation and production of news. To do so we would argue that it is necessary to stop the use of granular personal data, covertly gathered from individuals, being used to passively target them with advertising or propaganda based on previous preferences and patterns of behaviour. This would not affect opt-in (active) personalization of news, nor would it affect contextual advertising based on search terms, or embedded in publications, but the use of more detailed behavioural data, for the benefit of third parties, would be curbed.

The GDPR (2018) has started the task of regulating the harvesting of data by demanding that it should no longer be taken from our computers and browsers without our permission. It has imposed clauses for explicit consent and positive opt-in requirements, combined with the imposition of a Fair Imposition Principles (Article 5), which include a 'data minimization' principle aimed to reduce the unwanted and unnecessary collection of users' data. In doing so, it has created a two-tier system for data management, which gives far-reaching power to data controllers (mostly the platform organizations), who are regarded as the owners of their client data, while curbing the power of advertising intermediaries, who now need explicit permission to use tracking cookies for the extraction of personal data used for targeting. There are however shortcomings to these approaches. First, the GDPR is an omnibus law, applying to almost all usage of personal data in the private and the public sector, with strict provisions for many types of sensitive data, but it does not contain specific rules for automated targeting advertising nor microtargeting (Dobber et al. 2019, 7). Thus, because of the GDPR applies in many different situations, many of its rules are rather vague and abstract. Second, the practical implementation of the GDPR is complicated for users, publishers, and advertisers. The placing of permission notices is often distracting and confusing. The majority of users are inclined simply to enable cookies because they are concerned (wrongly) that access permission will be denied if they do not (Utz, et al. 2019). Thus, the GPDR has (to date) been too easy to evade by the production of confusing and overelaborate permissions, and hard to enforce simply because of the sheer number of likely targets.

However, the greater problem lies in the failure to curb the way in which platform organizations can make use of the data they are deemed to own and the ability of the tech companies to innovate in order to side-step controls. The major browsers like Mozilla from Firefox (Davies 2019) and Safari from Apple, pre-empted some of these changes by themselves rejecting third-party cookies because of privacy concerns and the creation of 'friction' in the browsing experience. In January 2020, Google announced that it would end support for third-party cookies on Chrome, now the leading web browser (Bohn 2020; Cuthbertson 2020). This looked like good news for users, but in fact third-party cookies will be replaced with 'browser-based and privacy-preserving' mechanisms that could sustain personalization and a 'healthy, ad-supported web' (Cavill 2020). In other words, different means for the same objectives. These new mechanisms are based on the application of 'federated learning', where the goal is to create a high-quality decentralized model trained to analyse aggregated data gathered from a federation of participating systems (Konečný et al. 2016; Southern 2019; Torfi 2020). With this type of decentralized model, the data controller does not have direct access to an individual's personal data. The information is therefore anonymized, it is not stored in a way that connects it to an individual, and it assures a higher level of security and privacy. Thus, a first-party controller like Google would have sweeping powers to use data, while getting around the privacy concerns of GDPR.

It is here that some of the problems with the GDPR become apparent. The law is predicated on the assumption that this is a problem relating to specific individuals, rather than a broader social problem. However, as Hildebrandt points out, what really matters is not the data collection, per se, but the profiling, targeting, and microtargeting that is made possible through it (Hildebrandt 2006). The use of profiling via machine learning would still allow advertisers and campaigners to serve unsolicited and finely targeted information to individuals via the platforms. It makes little difference to an individual if they are being targeted by political propaganda because of embedded cookies, or via machine learning or federated search. In a nutshell, even though the main browsers will change the means of identifying people, the outcomes will not change, with worrying implications that are of great concern for users, civil society, scholars, and policy makers (European Commission 2012, 250). Furthermore, companies like Google would also gain a stronger position vis-à-vis publishers and advertisers. Indeed, control and power over data collection and storage is being concentrated in the hands of even fewer intermediaries (Competition & Markets Authority 2020).

Using machine learning for federated search is therefore just a means of appearing privacy-compliant while strengthening the control over users' data and increasing bargaining power towards publishers. We therefore need a more stringent application of regulation to avoid stripping the GDPR of its purpose. To this end it may be possible to use the data minimization principle of Article 5 of the GDPR. This principle states that personal information processed by companies shall be 'adequate, relevant and limited to what is necessary in relation to the purposes for which they are processed' (Article 5 (c), GDPR). Under this principle, companies need to be able to prove that they only collect personal data they actually need for specified purposes (*relevant*), and such data should be sufficient to fulfil those purposes (*adequate*) without holding more than they need (*limited to what is necessary*) (Information Commissioner's Office 2019, 29). This principle is of pivotal importance for consumers' rights and protection, however, the GDPR does not define these terms, leaving it up to the interpretation and guidelines of the national Data Protection Authorities.

In the specific case of search engines, we would argue that the *relevance, adequacy,* and *necessity* of collecting, storing, and processing granular user-data for the purpose of targeted advertising, can be questioned, not only from a users' perspective, but even from the news publishers' point of view. From a user's perspective, advertisers would find it hard to prove that automated targeted and microtargeted advertising has any intrinsic value for consumers. On the contrary, as we have previously argued in the problem-setting section of this chapter, the manipulation of information that it enables can impact on citizens' rights to receive quality and diverse information (Eskens et al. 2017). Furthermore, a recent commercial report by Digiday and subsequent studies have found that, for the majority of serious publishers, targeted advertising had little value either (Fischer 2020; Lomas 2019b; Marotta et al. 2019; Weiss 2019). A minority found that switching off personalized targeting had actually improved their results. The economic incentives to use microtargeted advertising are clearer for those publishers that exist to push commercial products (Weiss 2019) and for those who are paid per click by advertisers for the 'customers' they attract to their sites.

If collection of data to enable individuals to be targeted by third parties does not seem to be needed for users and publishers, nor for the purposes of information circulation and retrieval, we should question whether these practices are actually necessary for the proper functioning of a search engine. We would argue that they do not actually comply with the data minimization principle and that it might be possible to restrict the use of data for these purposes, by explicitly including data collection for the purpose of third-party automated targeting in the practices that are in breach of the data minimization principle. A list of industry practices' examples that breach this principle is already provided for instance by the Information Commissioner's Office (ICO), the United Kingdom's independent authority set up to uphold information rights in the public interest and promote openness by public bodies and data privacy for individuals (Information Commissioner's Office 2019). Thus, by providing further guidance at European level and through the national Data Protection Authorities, and by including a more elaborated list of criteria, the GDPR could contribute to more structural change and prevent practices like automated targeting, rather than legitimizing them.

Even though data collection is useful for individuals engaging in active searching, when it is used to increase interaction and clicks, or to target unsolicited information, it should not be permitted. This would not end advertising online, but it would reduce passive targeting in which the advertising follows the client, and increase the reliance on more contextual advertising, in which advertisements are attached to publications, or to search terms or key words, providing users with access to the goods and services for which they are actively looking. The advertising industry has undergone a seismic change in a period of less than twenty years. It can equally quickly adapt to a new regime. A return to contextual advertising might also encourage companies to advertise directly with publishers, based on their audience profiles and quality, rather than advertising on platforms and allowing the data to do the work for them. This might have the collateral benefit of improving the income flowing to serious journalism and removing the major incentive for the use of 'click bait' news (Hammond 2015).

Why We Need an Alternative Public Service Search Engine

As we argued in our introduction, the intervention that we propose is two-fold. Complementary to more stringent regulation of data and microtargeting, we recommend the creation of alternative search engines run in the public interest, rather than purely as commercial interests. We will first discuss why we need an alternative public service engine, and what are the shortcomings and strengths of the existing alternatives.

European unease about the growing power of Google Search has so far manifested as a desire to control the power of US-based technology through scattered regulatory initiatives, rather than a desire to produce alternatives to it. This approach does not change the monopoly position of the major search engines. Google Search is responsible for over 92% of searches in the world (2020).[5] The sheer cost of indexing,[6] combined with the network effects achieved with scale, means that it is difficult for rival engines to be established. Further, the difficulty of applying antitrust law to search engines, and the shortcomings of the dominant approach of the Chicago School of Law in the competition analysis of digital platforms, have led to an underestimate of the societal impacts of platform dominance contributing to the establishment of a near monopoly over the delivery of the world's information (Coyle 2018; Moore and Tambini 2018; Wu 2018).

There are two different operations that are required for the retrieval of information online: indexing and search. First, computer systems (web-crawlers) scrutinize pages of content and create an index, that constitutes the infrastructure on top of which a search engine can function. Indexes are stored for future retrieval by search engines. Both these operations are achieved using computer algorithms. Indexing is a long-term process that requires storage systems and massive computing power. The very high cost, effort, and storage required to index a large percentage of the information which is uploaded every day online, means that smaller search engines 'piggy-back' off other indexes such as Google's one, which provides a list of links that are then presented to the user via a browser in response to a search question.

The way in which indexing and search works is a trade secret. Broadly we know that Google Search algorithms look at many factors, including users' previous search history, words of the queries, relevance and timeliness of pages, recency, location, and settings, attributing different weight to each factor (Competition & Markets Authority 2020; Google Search 2019). While it seems that human curation is complementary to automated and federated search, it is unclear how the two systems are combined, and how responsibilities are shared between the company, black-box algorithms and thousands of 'Search Quality Raters' around the world. Finally, there is no transparency around the different technical levers and commercial agreements that organizations use to influence and manipulate rankings in order to achieve a prominent position on the search results.[7]

Alongside Google Search, there are some other successful national search engines that also do their own indexing so that they have control of both the information which is stored and its retrieval. Yandex with roughly 39% of the Russian market (2020);[8] Naver, that dominates the South Korean market; and the Chinese Baidu all do their own indexing independently of US companies. Microsoft-owned Bing and the European Qwant also do their own indexing, but most other search engines pull results from the dominant players. For example Yahoo uses Bing (Lewandowski 2019), and DuckDuckGo takes its results from over 100 other specialist search engines. Some of these search engines have developed as alternative models to the mainstream commercial ones, focusing on improving some of the aforementioned issues around targeting, profiling, and diversity. For instance, DuckDuckGo is the US privacy first search engine, and it distinguishes itself by not profiling its users, not exploiting users' data for targeted advertising and monetization, and by showing all users the same search results for a given search term (Competition & Markets Authority 2020). This search engine also proves that it can be financially sustainable via contextual advertising, even though these revenues are also supported by donations and an initial fundraising for its launch. However, we do not have information on how the system determines ranking, relevance, and quality and it is not clear whether considerations of public interest objectives, diversity, and pluralism of information are taken into account in its search algorithm.

The European-French Qwant search engine, launched in 2013, demonstrates that it is possible to break away from Google's indexing and do things differently. Quant doesn't record users' searches, nor use personal data for advertising or other purposes. Its mission statement emphasizes the importance of neutrality and impartiality, claiming that its 'sorting algorithms are applied equally everywhere and for every user, without trying to put websites forward or to hide others based on commercial, political or moral interests' (Qwant 2019). Underlying what is presented as 'an alternative way of searching information', there seem to be considerations of diversity and public interest over commercial profit. Qwant's selection and prioritization of content is driven by Iceberg, an artificial intelligence system whose algorithms take into account a diverse range of criteria, from the technical and editorial quality of the text or image, to links to the page, comments and mentions on social networks, and the user's online behaviour (Eudes 2016). This search engine still has a standard pay-per-click advertising model developed in cooperation with the Microsoft Bing ad network, but it uses contextual ads rather than targeted ones (Lomas 2019a), and it also relies heavily on funding from institutions like the European Investment Bank and Axel Springer Digital Venture, which has a 20% stake in the company. With the objective of reclaiming 'online independence', the French Government declared that all their digital devices would stop using Google Search as their default search engines, and opt for Qwant (Goujard 2018). However, despite its increasing reach and uptake, it had less than 1% of market share in France in early 2020, while Google Search had 92%.

Towards a Public Service Search Engine in Europe

Quant shows that an alternative is possible, but the time has come for an initiative on a truly European level and at the scale of public broadcasting, that lies between the state and the commercial sector. Public broadcasting has managed to retain a far higher level of public trust than the commercial alternatives (European Broadcasting Union 2020). A public service search engine would also need to be demonstrably free of state interference in order to stand a chance of earning a similar level of trust from citizens, who are increasingly (though unevenly), suspicious of state interventions (Van Der Meer and Hakhverdian 2017), and it should be equally free of the commercial imperatives that drive the major search engines. In order to earn such trust, a search engine should be organized in a way that is transparent to its users, and it should be at least as efficient as commercial alternatives. This might mean using user data in order to improve the individual search experience, but it should not provide data to third parties for the purpose of targeting or personalization.

This endeavour would be best initiated, on a European or global scale, by bodies independent of the state and commerce. Independence is intended as editorial, managerial, and functional independence, which would allow the search engine and the organization or consortium that runs it to be independent from political, state, and private interference. To achieve this, we would propose a governing body composed of interested universities, independent research institutes, and public service media organizations. Together, they would have the necessary spread of expertise and experience to establish and drive such a venture. The consortium would also be relatively free of influence by national interests and be able to establish guidelines for the ranking of search, which would ensure not only the relevance but also the integrity and quality of the information. The venture would however require initial funding that could potentially come from the European Union and its Research and Innovation Framework Programme, Horizon Europe.[9] Additional revenues could then come from the use of contextual advertising. DuckDuckGo has indeed proven that a business model based on initial funding and contextual advertising revenues could be sustainable in the long run even with a relatively small percentage of the market.

To differentiate the search functions offered by this alternative model from the current commercial ones, it would be crucial to establish a ranking and prioritization system that takes into account principles of news diversity and integrity of information. Being exposed to diverse sources and types of content, while ensuring the integrity and trustworthiness of the providers, is pivotal to improving the flow of content and information online. Such criteria could be established by the aforementioned independent board and could build on existing initiatives, such as the Journalism Trust Initiative, which has proposed a collaborative standards-setting process to establish a shared industry code of practice (2019). These criteria should then be explained and made transparent in a user-friendly way to ensure that users understand how content is being prioritized in their search results. Further, as we have previously argued, active personalization that is driven by users, also tends to produce greater diversity of information and news consumption. Thus, while providing transparent ranking parameters, the settings of this public service search engine should also allow users to further personalize their results.[10]

The aspiration of this system is not to challenge current dominant search engines like Google Search, or to replace their services, but rather to provide a viable alternative with higher take-up than the existing ones, which is not commercially and privately run and from which citizens and institutions could benefit. Given the abundance of content and information, and the limited spaces of our devices and their user interfaces, it is important to reflect critically on the principles that would guide the ranking, search, and discovery functions of this alternative model. Those organizations and centres participating in the consortium, should also promote the use of this engine as the default search engine for their digital services just as the French government has done with Qwant, this would allow a faster take-up of the service, which in turn would improve its performance and increase its scale.

SUMMARY AND CONCLUSIONS

Most of the world's information is now available online, but we have ceded responsibility for accessing it to a small group of private companies, and authoritarian governments, who have established themselves as gatekeepers. The control of access by governments is not the focus of this chapter. Our concern is that, with minor exceptions, the private companies that now control access to information, have prioritized the requirements of income generation over public accountability and have tied the vital functions of indexing and search to personalization for the purpose of unsolicited third-party targeting. As we argued, the crossover between search and commerce has distorted the basic functioning of the web, encouraging click-bait and exacerbating polarization, and any attempt at correction needs to address it directly.

One way to de-link the commercial imperatives of search and ranking systems from the distribution and circulation of news online, would require a more stringent implementation of the GDPR regulation, and specifically its data minimization principle. Including data collection for the purpose of third-party automated targeting, in the list of industry practice examples that are in breach of the data minimization principle, would indeed restrict these practices, increase the use of contextual advertising for search, and ultimately break up the vicious cycle that has infected news circulation online. Thus, with a more stringent and clearer implementation of this principle, the GDPR could also contribute to more structural changes. Further, to truly ensure that that the Internet is taken back into public hands, we also suggest the establishment of an alternative model of search engine which would sit independently between the state and the commercial sector. It will require collaboration at European or global level to ensure that access in future cannot become the property of a handful of private companies nor fall under the influence of any individual state.

One of the likely criticisms of these proposals is that the they would harm the new economy that has flourished online. As with any change to the industry and economy, there would be losers. Those companies who flourish by creating products and then targeting advertising on the groups most likely to buy, may well have to work harder to get noticed, but these losses need to be balanced against the likely improvements to public debate and knowledge that would ensue if the mechanisms by which citizens find information and relate to one another were organized to improve debate rather than to boost sales of products and ideas.

NOTES

1. Regulation (EU) 2016/679 of the European Parliament and of the Council of 17 April 2016 on the protection of natural persons with regard to the processing of personal data and on the free movement of such data, repealing Directive 95/46/EC (General Data Protection Regulation) https://eur-lex.europa.eu/legal-content/EN/TXT/PDF/?uri=CELEX:32016R0679.

2. Regulation (EU) 2017/0003 of the European Parliament and of the Council concerning the respect for private life and the protection of personal data in electronic communications and repealing Directive 2002/58/EC (Regulation on Privacy and Electronic Communications) https://eur-lex.europa.eu/legal-content/EN/TXT/?uri=CELEX:52017PC0010.

3. European Code of Practice on Disinformation, 2018. https://ec.europa.eu/digital-single-market/en/news/code-practice-disinformation.

4. The European Digital Services Act Package includes two interlinked proposals, respectively for a Regulation on a Single Market for Digital Services, called as the Digital Services Act (https://eur-lex.europa.eu/legal-content/en/TXT/?qid=1608117147218&uri=COM%3A2020%3A825%3AFIN), and for a Regulation on contestable and fair markets in the digital sector, known as the Digital Markets Act (https://eur-lex.europa.eu/legal-content/en/TXT/?qid=1608117147218&uri=COM%3A2020%3A825%3AFIN). In the former one, the European Commission has proposed new provisions on online advertising, including targeting advertising, including transparency obligations and auditing systems (Articles 24, 28, 29, and 30). At the moment of writing though, both proposals are being discussed according to the ordinary legislative procedure.

5. Source: StatCounter, Global Stats. Search Engine market share worldwide, from September 2019 to September 2020. See: https://gs.statcounter.com/search-engine-market-share.

6. An index in this context is the database of Web pages underlying a search engine.

7. Strategic meta-tagging, indexing, and search engine optimization techniques are often used by creators, publishers, and organizations to game the system and gain a prominent position on search results. Information on marketing, advertising, or sponsorship agreements are also beyond the scope of the Search Quality Raters.

8. Source: StatCounter, Global Stats. Search Engine market share Russian Federation, from September 2019 to September 2020. See: https://gs.statcounter.com/search-engine-market-share/all/russian-federation.

9. For more information on the Horizon Europe framework programme, see: https://ec.europa.eu/info/horizon-europe-next-research-and-innovation-framework-programme_en.

10. https://play.google.com/store/apps/details?id=com.thomsonreuters.reuters&hl=it.

REFERENCES

Alba, D. 2020. 'You Tube Says It Will Ban Misleading Election-Related Content'. *New York Times*, February 3. https://www.nytimes.com/2020/02/03/technology/youtube-misinformation-election.html.

Angelopoulos, C., A. Brody, A. W. Hins, et al. 2016. 'Study of Fundamental Rights Limitations for Online Enforcement through Self-Regulation'. *Institute for Information Law* 37. https://openaccess.leidenuniv.nl/handle/1887/45869.

Bail, C. A., L. P. Argyle, T. W. Brown, et al. 2018. 'Exposure to Opposing Views on Social Media Can Increase Political Polarization'. *Proceedings of the National Academy of Sciences of the United States of America* 115(37): 9216–21. doi: 10.1073/pnas.1804840115.

Beam, M. A. 2014. 'Automating the News: How Personalized News Recommender System Design Choices Impact News Reception'. *Communication Research* 41(8): 1019–41. doi: 10.1177/0093650213497979.

Berger, J., and K. L. Milkman. 2014. 'Emotion and Virality: What Makes Online Content Go Viral?' *Marketing Intelligence Review* 5(1): 18–23. doi: https://doi.org/10.2478/gfkmir-2014-0022.

Bodó, B., N. Helberger, and C. H. de Vreese. 2017. 'Political Micro-Targeting: A Manchurian Candidate or Just a Dark Horse?' *Internet Policy Review* 6(4): 1–13. doi: 10.14763/2017.4.776.

Bohn, D. 2020. 'Google to 'Phase Out' Third-Party Cookies in Chrome, but Not for Two Years. The Browser Battles Are about Privacy More Than Marketshare'. *The Verge*. https://www.theverge.com/2020/1/14/21064698/google-third-party-cookies-chrome-two-years-privacy-safari-firefox.

Borgesius, F. J. Z., J. Möller, S. Kruikemeier, et al. 2018. 'Online Political Microtargeting: Promises and Threats for Democracy'. *Utrecht Law Review* 14(1): 82–96. doi: 10.18352/ulr.420.

Bose, N., and D. Bartz. 2020. 'U.S. House Antitrust Findings on Big Tech Likely in Three Reports—Sources'. *Reuters*, October 6. Accessed October 26, 2020. https://www.reuters.com/article/us-usa-tech-antitrust-idUSKBN26R2V6 .

Bradshaw, S., and P. N. Howard. 2018. *Challenging Truth and Trust: A Global Inventory of Organized Social Media Manipulation. Computational Propaganda Research Project, Oxford Internet Institute*. Oxford. *https://demtech.oii.ox.ac.uk/wp-content/uploads/sites/93/2018/07/ct2018.pdf*

Cairncross, D. F. 2019. 'The Cairncross Review. A Sustainable Future for Journalism'. London. www.gov.uk/government/publications.

Carrie Wong, J. 2019. 'Twitter's Political Ad Ban to Limit Micro-Targeting, Putting Pressure on Facebook'. *The Guardian*, November 15. https://www.theguardian.com/technology/2019/nov/15/twitter-facebook-ad-ban-micro-targeting.

Cavill, S. 2020. 'Google Chrome to Phase Out Third-Party Cookies: Just the Facts'. *Digital Media Solutions*, January 23. https://insights.digitalmediasolutions.com/articles/chrome-phasing-out-third-party-cookies.

Competition & Markets Authority. 2020. 'Online Platforms and Digital Advertising. Market Study Final Report'. London. www.nationalarchives.gov.uk/doc/open-government-.

Coyle, D. 2018. 'Platform Dominance: The Shortcomings of Antitrust Policy'. In *Digital Dominance: The Power of Google, Amazon, Facebook and Apple*, edited by Damian Tambini and Martin Moore, 50–70. Oxford, UK: Oxford University Press.

Cuthbertson, A. 2020. 'Google Finally Getting Rid of Third-Party Cookies in Chrome'. *Independent*, January 15. https://www.independent.co.uk/life-style/gadgets-and-tech/news/google-chrome-cookies-privacy-firefox-safari-a9285021.html.

Davies, J. 2019. 'German Publishers Wrestle with Firefox's Latest Anti-Tracking Changes'. *Digiday*, September 25. https://digiday.com/media/theyre-hurting-german-publishers-wrestle-with-firefoxs-latest-anti-tracking-changes/.

Del Vicario, M., A. Scala, W. Quattrociocchi, et al. 2019. 'Polarization and Fake News: Early Warning of Potential Misinformation Targets'. *ACM Transactions on the Web* 13(10): 10. doi: 10.1145/3316809.

Dobber, T., R. Fathaigh, and F. J. Zuiderveen Borgesius. 2019. 'The Regulation of Online Political Micro-Targeting in Europe'. *Internet Policy Review* 8(4): 1–20. doi: 10.14763/2019.4.1440.

Effron, D. A., and M. Raj. 2020. 'Misinformation and Morality: Encountering Fake-News Headlines Makes Them Seem Less Unethical to Publish and Share'. *Psychological Science* 31(1): 75–87. doi: 10.1177/0956797619887896.

Elvestad, E., and A. Phillips. 2018. *Misunderstanding News Audiences: Seven Myths of the Social Media Era*. 1st ed. London and New York: Routledge.

Epstein, R. 2018. 'Manipulating Minds: The Power of Search Engines to Influence Votes and Opinions'. In *Digital Dominance: The Power of Google, Amazon, Facebook and Apple*, edited by Damian Tambini and Martin Moore, 294–319. Oxford, UK: Oxford University Press.

Eskens, S., N. Helberger, and J. Moeller. 2017. 'Challenged by News Personalisation: Five Perspectives on the Right to Receive Information'. *Journal of Media Law* 9(2): 259–84. doi: 10.1080/17577632.2017.1387353.

Eudes, Y. 2016. 'Qwant: The Encrypted Search Engine That Really Could Challenge Google'. *The World Weekly*, July 11. https://www.theworldweekly.com/reader/view/3001/qwant-the-encrypted-search-engine-that-really-could-challenge-google.

European Broadcasting Union. 2020. 'Trust in Media 2020 Report'. Geneva. Accessed May 14, 2020. https://www.ebu.ch/publications/research/login_only/report/trust-in-media.

European Commission. 2012. 'Safeguarding Privacy in a Connected World. A European Data Protection Framework for the 21st Century'. Brussels. https://eur-lex.europa.eu/legal-content/EN/TXT/PDF/?uri=CELEX:52012DC0009&from=en.

European Commission. 2020. 'The Digital Services Act Package'. Accessed July 16, 2020. https://ec.europa.eu/digital-single-market/en/digital-services-act-package.

Fischer, S. 2020. 'Exclusive: New York Times Phasing Out All 3rd-Party Advertising Data'. *Axios*, May 19. Accessed June 26, 2020. https://www.axios.com/new-york-times-advertising-792b3cd6-4bdb-47c3-9817-36601211a79d.html.

Flaxman, S., S. Goel, J. M. Rao, et al. 2016. 'Filter Bubbles, Echo Chambers, and Online News Consumption'. *Public Opinion Quarterly* 80: 298–320. doi: 10.1093/poq/nfw006.

Fletcher, R. 2020. 'The Truth behind Filter Bubbles: Bursting Some Myths'. Accessed February 22, 2020. https://reutersinstitute.politics.ox.ac.uk/risj-review/truth-behind-filter-bubbles-bursting-some-myths.

Gillespie, T. 2010. 'The Politics of "Platforms"'. *New Media and Society* 12(3): 347–64. doi: 10.1177/1461444809342738.

Gillespie, T. 2018. *Custodians of the Internet: Platforms, Content Moderation*, and *the Hidden Decisions That Shape Social Media*. New Haven and London: Yale University Press.

Google Search. 2019. 'How Search Algorithms Work'. Accessed February 21, 2020. https://www.google.com/intl/en_uk/search/howsearchworks/algorithms/.

Goujard, C. 2018. 'France Is Ditching Google to Reclaim Its Online Independence'. *Wired*, September 20. https://www.wired.co.uk/article/google-france-silicon-valley.

Hammond, P. 2015. 'From Computer-Assisted to Data-Driven: Journalism and Big Data'. *Journalism* 18(4): 408–24. doi: 10.1177/1464884915620205.

Helberger, N. 2019. 'On the Democratic Role of News Recommenders'. *Digital Journalism* 7(8): 993–1012. doi: 10.1080/21670811.2019.1623700.

Helberger, N., K. Karppinen, and L. D'Acunto. 2018. 'Exposure Diversity as a Design Principle for Recommender Systems'. *Information Communication and Society* 21(2): 91–207. doi: 10.1080/1369118X.2016.1271900.

Hildebrandt, M. 2006. 'Profiling: From Data to Knowledge: The Challenges of a Crucial Technology'. *Datenschutz und Datensicherheit—DuD* 30(9): 548–52. doi: 10.1007/s11623-006-0140-3.

Information Commissioner's Office. 2019. 'Guide to Data Protection'. ICO.org.uk. London. https://ico.org.uk/for-organisations/guide-to-data-protection/guide-to-the-general-data-protection-regulation-gdpr/.

Journalism Trust Initiative. 2019. CWA 17493. 'CEN Workshop Agreement'. CWA 17493:2019 E. Brussels, Belgium: CEN-CENELEC Management Centre. https://www.cen.eu/News/Workshops/Pages/WS-2019-018.aspx.

Konečný, J., H. B. McMahan, F. X. Yu, et al. 2016. 'Federated Learning: Strategies for Improving Communication Efficiency'. 1–10. http://arxiv.org/abs/1610.05492.

Leveson, J. 2012. 'An Inquiry into the Culture, Practices and Ethics of the Press'. London. November. Accessed March 6, 2020. www.official-documents.gov.uk.

Lewandowski, D. 2019. 'The Web Is Missing an Essential Part of Infrastructure: An Open Web Index'. *Communications of the ACM* 62(4): 24–27. doi: 10.1145/3312479.

Lomas, N. 2019a. 'Private Search Engine Qwant's New CEO Is Mozilla Europe Veteran Tristan Nitot'. *TechCrunch*, September 19. Accessed June 26, 2020. https://techcrunch.com/2019/09/18/private-search-engine-qwants-new-ceo-is-mozilla-europe-veteran-tristan-nitot/.

Lomas, N. 2019b. 'Targeted Ads Offer Little Extra Value for Online Publishers, Study Suggests'. *Tech Crunch*. https://techcrunch.com/2019/05/31/targeted-ads-offer-little-extra-value-for-online-publishers-study-suggests/.

Mager, A. 2017. 'Search Engine Imaginary: Visions and Values in the Co-Production of Search Technology and Europe'. *Social Studies of Science* 47(2): 240–62. doi: 10.1177/0306312716671433.

Marotta, V., V. Abhishek, and A. Acquisti. 2019. 'Online Tracking and Publishers Revenues: An Empirical Analysis'. 1–35. Paper presented at The Workshop on the Economics of Information Security (WEIS) 2019, Boston, MA. https://weis2017.econinfosec.org/wp-content/uploads/sites/6/2019/05/WEIS_2019_paper_38.pdf

Marvin, G., and S. Meisel. 2017. 'Protecting the Brand in the Era of Fake News: Why Brands Need Advertisement Verification Tools'. *Journal of Digital and Social Media*

Marketing 5(4): 322–31. accessed May 14, 2020. https://hstalks.com/article/3939/protecting-the-brand-in-the-era-of-fake-news-why-b/.

McNamee, R. 2019. *Zucked: Waking Up to the Facebook Catastrophe*. New York: Penguin Press.

Moore, M., and D. Tambini, eds. 2018. *Digital Dominance: The Power of Google, Amazon, Facebook*, and *Apple*. New York: Oxford University Press.

Newman, N. 2018. *Digital News Projec: Journalism, Media*, and *Technology Trends and Predictions 2018*. Oxford: Reuters Institute. Accessed June 26, 2020. https://reutersinstitute.politics.ox.ac.uk/sites/default/files/2018-01/RISJ   Trends   and   Predictions 2018 NN.pdf.

Persily, N. 2017. 'The 2016 U.S. Election: Can Democracy Survive the Internet?' *Journal of Democracy* 28(2): 63–76. doi: 10.1353/jod.2017.0025.

Pickard, V. 2019. *Democracy without Journalism*. New York: Oxford University Press.

Pinsky, D. 2018. '11 Google News Tips to Increase Ranking, Visibility and Traffic'. Accessed June 26, 2020. https://www.forbes.com/sites/denispinsky/2018/01/11/google-news/.

Qwant 2019. 'Qwant, the European Search Engine That Respects Your Privacy'. Accessed February 22, 2020. https://about.qwant.com/.

Southern, L. 2019. 'WTF Is Federated Learning'. *Digiday*, September 14. https://digiday.com/media/what-is-federated-learning/.

Spencer, S. 2019. 'An Update on Our Political Ads Policy'. *Google*. Accessed February 22, 2020. https://blog.google/technology/ads/update-our-political-ads-policy/#click=https://t.co/ByNr2dhfGl.

Torfi, S. 2020. 'Federated Learning: A Remarkable Privacy-Preserving Approach'. Machine Learning Mindset. https://www.machinelearningmindset.com/federated-learning/.

Turow, J. 2005. 'Audience Construction and Culture Production: Marketing Surveillance in the Digital Age'. *Annals of the American Academy of Political and Social Science* 597(January): 103–21. doi: 10.1177/0002716204270469.

Utz, C., M. Degeling, S. Fahl, et al. 2019. '(Un)informed Consent: Studying GDPR Consent Notices in the Field'. *Proceedings of the ACM Conference on Computer and Communications Security*: 973–90. doi: 10.1145/3319535.3354212.

Van Couvering, E. 2009. 'Search Engine Bias: The Structuration of Traffic on the World-Wide Web. London School of Economics and Political Science'. London School of Economics and Political Science. Ahttp://etheses.lse.ac.uk/41/.

Van Der Meer, T., and A. Hakhverdian. 2017. 'Political Trust as the Evaluation of Process and Performance: A Cross-National Study of 42 European Countries'. *Political Studies* 65(1): 81–102. doi: 10.1177/0032321715607514.

Weiss, M. 2019. 'Digiday Research: Most Publishers Don't Benefit from Behavioral Ad Targeting'. https://digiday.com/media/digiday-research-most-publishers-dont-benefit-from-behavioral-ad-targeting/.

Wu, T. 2017. 'The Attention Merchants: The Epic Struggle to Get Inside Our Heads'. London: Atlantic Books. Accessed October 23, 2020. https://ebookcentral.proquest.com/lib/londonschoolecons/detail.action?docID=5114743.

Wu, T. 2018. 'The Curse of Bigness: Antitrust in the New Gilded Age'. Columbia Global Reports.

Zuboff, S. 2015. 'Big Other: Surveillance Capitalism and the Prospects of an Information Civilization'. *Journal of Information Technology* 30(1): 75–89. doi: 10.1057/jit.2015.5.

7

Accelerating Adoption of a Digital Intermediary Tax

ELDA BROGI AND ROBERTA MARIA CARLINI ■

Everywhere today men are conscious that somehow they must deal with questions more intricate than any that church or school had prepared them to understand. Increasingly they know that they cannot understand them if facts are not quickly and steadily available. Increasingly they are baffled because the facts are not available; and they are wondering whether government by consent can survive in a time when the manufacture of consent is an unregulated private enterprise. For in an exact sense the present crisis of western democracy is a crisis in journalism.

—LIPPMAN (1920)

Unlike the times when Walter Lippman wrote his famous 'Liberty and the News', facts are quickly and steadily available in the digital era, but the concentration of 'manufacture of consent' remains in the hands of 'unregulated private enterprise'. A century later, democratic risks related to the concentration of ownership in news media production have not faded; at the same time, new risks have arisen, related to the concentration of ownership in the market of the intermediaries to the news and to the disruption of the old news media business model. In this chapter we will focus on the economic threats to media pluralism in a digital environment dominated by digital platforms as gateways to the news; and on the potential role of fiscal policy in supporting news media viability and media pluralism,[1] arguing for the rationale of a digital tax and proposing mechanisms at the EU level to distribute part of the tech dividend.

DIGITALIZATION AND MEDIA PLURALISM

The Great Disruption

Digitalization has hugely impacted the media environment, both from the consumption and from the production side. At the beginning of the digital revolution, a vast field of opportunities seemed to pave the way to a new era for media pluralism, curbing the market power of the media industry's big players. Opportunities could be found in the abundance and speed of information, in the availability of sources, in the possibility to access—and verify—news without physical and geographical borders, in the reduction of costs and entry barriers, in the democratization of the media. These opportunities are still available; but so are significant new risks: exposure to misinformation, lack of choice and of transparency in the algorithmic selection of content, opaqueness of sources, abuse of personal data, hate speech, reduction of the quality and diversity of information, economic threats to the traditional news media model. A growing concern about the digital threats to media pluralism arose, related to the dominance of a few online platforms that have reshaped the whole ecosystem of the media, even if the new players operate in a different market, not directly in the production of information (Evans 2009; Martens et al. 2018; ACCC 2019; Ofcom 2019; Parcu 2019; The Cairncross Review 2019).

Social media, search engines, news aggregators and messaging apps may not be considered as 'media', as they neither produce—or produce to a very limited extent—original informative content nor have editorial responsibility for the third-party content they disseminate. In this sense, they do not compete directly in the market of news media providers. Nonetheless, they are now the main players in the media market. Platformization has changed the ways people access news, increasingly mediated by the algorithms of a digital platform. This has led to major changes on the users side: in the availability of news often for free, in the unbundling of news content from newsrooms, in the possibility to be at the same time *users* and *producers* of news, and in the overload of the limited amount of personal attention. On the producers' side, the role of digital platforms disrupted the legacy media business model: a two-sided market, in which the traditional media matched readers/audience, on one side, with advertisers, on the other. The news media provider was at the centre of this exchange, the distribution of news being a secondary, and derivative, business. In the digital environment, the distribution becomes the core: it is the place in which the attention market's resources are allocated (Wu 2017). Acting as intermediaries, the digital platforms collect consumer data and in so doing harvest market resources through targeted advertisement. This leads to 'a vertical disintegration between news production on the one hand and distribution and advertising on the other hand' (Martens et al. 2018); and provides information for free, reducing the consumers' willingness to pay for the news.

The role of digital platforms as gatekeepers goes far beyond the media; recently, the European Union put forward new European regulation with the Digital Service Act and the Digital Market Act, both identifying the 'digital gatekeepers' or the 'very large online platforms' as players that need specific regulation, the traditional competition and regulation frameworks being unfit to tackle the consequences of the scale of their business across the whole digital ecosystem. Although the DSA and DMA will affect the media environment, we argue that specific policies may be needed for the media sector, to preserve the fundamental principle of media pluralism and media freedom. The role of digital platforms as gatekeepers to news leads to two major economic threats to media pluralism:

1. The market power of the intermediaries. While ownership concentration in the media sector has historically been seen as a major threat to pluralism, and media-specific rules have sometimes been provided in competition and regulation laws, the dominance of the digital gatekeepers to news is not covered by the old media-specific regulation, even if it is a challenge to media diversity affecting the way in which people 'encounter and engage with information' (Helberger 2019).

2. The sustainability of news media production, due to the effects of digital competition on the business model of traditional media (the old gatekeepers), based on market revenues from advertising and sales. The extent of the disruption may vary depending on the different media system, and tends to increase the more it is based on market advertisement. However, a look at recent trends in the United States and Europe shows that the tendency is generalized and, so far, not substantially counteracted by the emergence of alternative models in the news media industry.

These effects are evident in the graphs that follow, showing the market trends for the newspaper industry in the United States and European Union.

As shown in the graphs (Tables 7.1–7.3), in the United States newspaper advertising revenue fell by 70.5% between 2000 and 2018; in the same period, journalistic employment fell by 47%. In the European Union, between 2011 and 2017, newspapers' value added at factor cost fell by 13.7% (almost 2 billion euros), and journalistic employment in the sector decreased by 27.6% (minus 86,000 journalists). More recent surveys confirm the trend. According to the results of the Media Pluralism Monitor 2020, the decline of market revenues for newspapers continued in 2018 and 2019 in twenty-two EU countries, while the revenues remained stationary in three countries and slightly increased in three other countries (Brogi et al. 2020).

The newspaper sector is only one part of the media industry, the one that historically was the core of investigative journalism and what has been called public interest news. The other traditional media are not protected by the general downturn, even if at a minor extent. Considering all the sectors related to news

Table 7.1 US—ESTIMATED ADVERTISING AND CIRCULATION REVENUE
OF THE NEWSPAPER INDUSTRY (US DOLLARS)

	Advertising Revenue	Circulation Revenue
2004	48,244,000,000	10,988,651,000
2005	49,435,000,000	10,746,901,000
2006	49,275,402,572	10,548,344,000
2007	45,375,000,000	10,294,920,096
2008	37,848,257,630	10,086,956,940
2009	27,564,000,000	10,066,783,026
2010	25,837,698,822	10,049,360,689
2011	27,078,473,864	9,989,064,525
2012	25,316,461,215	10,448,561,493
2013	23,587,097,435	10,641,662,892
2014	22,077,809,951	10,744,324,061
2015	20,362,238,293	10,870,292,720
2016	18,274,943,567	10,910,460,499
2017	16,476,453,084	11,211,011,020
2018	14,346,024,182	10,995,341,920

Pew Research Center, Journalism and Media (https://www.journalism.org/
fact-sheet/newspapers/).

Table 7.2 US—TOTAL NUMBER OF NEWSROOM EMPLOYEES
IN THE NEWSPAPER SECTOR AND TOTAL CIRCULATION OF DAILY
NEWSPAPERS

	Employees	Circulation *
2004	71,640	54,626
2005	72,600	53,345
2006	74,410	52,329
2007	73,810	50,742
2008	71,070	48,597
2009	60,770	45,653
2010	55,260	
2011	54,050	44,421
2012	51,430	43,433
2013	48,920	40,712
2014	46,310	40,420
2015	44,120	37,711
2016	42,450	34,657
2017	39,210	30,948
2018	37,900	28,554

Pew Research Center, Journalism and Media (https://
www.journalism.org/fact-sheet/newspapers/).

Table 7.3 PUBLISHING OF NEWSPAPERS

Value added at factor cost—million euro

GEO/TIME	2011	2012	2013	2014	2015	2016	2017
European Union— 28 countries (2013–2020)	15,929.1	14,903.1	14,554.3	14,526.0	14,496.1	14,022.5	13,748.5

Persons employed—number

GEO/TIME	2011	2012	2013	2014	2015	2016	2017
European Union— 28 countries (2013–2020)	3,11,406	3,02,373	2,83,906	2,64,369	2,49,788	2,34,912	2,25,381

Source: Eurostat—Annual detailed enterprise statistics for services (NACE Rev. 2 H-N and S95).

production (newspapers, radio and TV broadcasting, and agency news), Eurostat data show a decrease between 2011 and 2017 by 11.7% in the value added at factor cost; and by 14.9% in employment.[2]

The Covid-19 Effect

The 2020 pandemic crisis has accelerated and exacerbated these trends by spurring a huge shift in consumer behaviour which, according to Microsoft CEO Satya Nadella,[3] brought about two years' worth of digital transformation in only two months.

One prominent phenomenon, related to the Covid-19 and the media, is reflected in the term 'infodemic':[4] as the first pandemic in the social media era, the crisis has meant not only a health emergency, but also a rapid spread of disinformation, sometimes boosted by politicians themselves. The 'infodemic' has put big social media platforms in the spotlight once more, as they found themselves in a position to contribute to the diffusion of disinformation, as well as to fight it; also, they offered their technological capabilities to help track the spread of the virus. In doing so, the social media networks and (more generally) the digital platforms acquired a growing public role that poses new and unprecedented challenges, both in terms of their relationship with users (a huge collection of sensitive personal data is at stake) and with the institutions.

Risks also arise with regard to the news media economy.[5] The short-term impact of the lockdown on market sales and advertising, as well as the foreseeable medium-term impact of the economic crisis, threatens the sustainability of news media production. Evidence from the Media Pluralism Monitor shows that media viability indicators noticeably worsened all over the European Union in 2020; the decrease being led by advertising expenditure for media, that, despite the huge increase in attention and demand for news, decreased in most countries far more than the GDP.[6]

The digital platforms appear to have been the winners from the pandemic, even the ones whose business model is essentially based on advertising and consequently could have been damaged by the 'big lockdown' of the economy. Data of market capitalization of the so-called GAFAM show, together with the predictable huge boost of Amazon's value (plus 68% from January to November 2020), a significant increase for Apple (+ 51%, the first US company to surpass $2 trillion in market value), Microsoft (+ 35%), and also for the players whose revenues are mostly originated by digital advertising (Facebook + 32%, Google-Alphabet + 26%). According to GroupM, in 2021 digital advertising on the platforms was set to overtake spending on all the traditional media for the first time, with a share of 52%.[7]

If these trends are confirmed, we could be near to the moment in which the traditional model of the 'old' media platforms, in which advertisement financed journalism, will no longer be sustainable. The search for alternative market models, which was proceeding slowly, in times of recession will be more difficult still. In this respect, the news media industry is not different from other industries disrupted by the disintermediation which characterizes the digital platform's model. What is different is its role in democracy as a watchdog of the powerful and as a tool for public debate and civic participation. As Parcu (2019) points out,

> the threat coming from the spread of self-generated content, and the impoverishment of traditional media, may directly jeopardize the existence of a journalistic profession, thus becoming another example of the progressive disappearance of the middleman, as is happening in many other areas of the economy. The difference is that, in other areas, the middleman was often a factor of inefficiency and rent exploitation, while, in producing news, the mediation of a specific and neutral professional category has a specific role in creating or preserving quality, especially by keeping a distance between immediate and partisan interests and the news.

From this perspective, the disruption of the traditional business model of news media should be considered as the crisis of a public interest sector. If media pluralism and quality information are to be considered undersupplied public goods in the digital age (Parcu 2019), a role for public intervention is at stake. Addressing the digital challenges to the 'old' competition and regulation framework will not restore a vanished business model; the competition and regulation tools might not be sufficient to tackle the market failure in providing the public good of pluralistic and independent information in the digital world. The European model, with its tradition in public service media and public support to private media, has some potential to face this challenge; at the same time, this model has to face the risks of political capture of the media and the scarcity of public resources.

In parallel, the public response to the crisis led to widespread fiscal stimulus. In some cases, national rescue packages provided public help to the media sector. What is more relevant for the scope of this chapter, the long-standing debate on the digital corporations' taxation came to a turning point, because the EU Commission announced its intention to go ahead with its own proposal in case the multilateral negotiations inside the Organisation for Economic Cooperation and Development (OECD) fail. A digital levy is mentioned among the new own resources to be introduced by the European Union to finance the post-coronavirus recovery effort.[8] Within the European model, the pandemic itself and the search for resources could increase pressure for the adoption of a digital tax. Whereas in the current debate the call for digital taxation is motivated by fairness in the distribution of the fiscal burden and by the public budget needs, we argue that the tax can be seen as a tool that can contribute to face the platforms' dominance in digital markets and to foster resilience of the disrupted traditional industries. As we will see in the next section, some of the designed tax schemes are shaped on the very characteristic of the platforms' business model, in which the value is generated by the users' data and by their interconnection. In extracting this value, digital platforms monetize the free good of people's attention; and at the same time disrupt the business model of the 'old' players on the attention markets, the legacy media, whose content becomes a commodity to be offered on the platforms to engage 'eyeballs'. A digital tax may have an indirect effect on the attention markets, helping to restore an even playing field. A more direct effect might be pursued finalizing part of its revenue to support the production of a pluralistic information; in other words, to address the failure of the market in providing the public good of media pluralism. Following this approach, after describing the features of the digital tax proposals, and the (so far) unrelated attempts to make the platforms pay for the news, we will propose that part of the digital tax's revenue should be allocated to support the news media, basing this argument on the rationale in the economic literature and in some historical precedents.

MAKE PLATFORMS PAY (TAXES) FOR THE NEWS

The Digital Tax Schemes

Proposals for tax reform are occurring at multiple levels: individual jurisdictions are pursuing a variety of tax reforms designed to ensure that digital platforms pay their fair share through a variety of Digital Services Taxes (DSTs). By the end of 2020, around half of European countries have adopted proposals for DSTs.[9]

Despite attempts to coordinate at the EU level, the patchwork of approaches enables large platforms to profit shift to reduce taxation.

Tax challenges arising from digitalization are the object of a widespread debate and an international reform process, which has not reached, so far, a consensus-based proposal. The intergovernmental economic think tank the OECD is coordinating a global attempt to develop an international approach to reduce tax losses due to tax avoidance of major multinationals, including the platform companies. This was prompted by the disruption of the international fiscal system of profits taxation. The main aim of such a reform, in the OECD's process[10] as in the European debate and in several initiatives at national level, would be to restore equity in the distribution of the fiscal burden. Whilst the issue of tax avoidance by multinational enterprises is older than digitalization,[11] it is exacerbated by the very characteristics of the digital economy: lack of physical presence (scale without mass), predominance of intangible assets, and the value coming from users' participation (network effects). As a consequence, the digital multinational companies benefit from an average tax rate that can be sensitively lower compared to the traditional Multinational Enterprise (MNE)'s tax rate, and that can become negative in the presence of aggressive tax planning, as estimated in the European Union by the impact assessment accompanying the Commission's proposals for digital taxation (Table 7.4).

In 2020 the OECD process was supposed to come to an end, with a final secretariat proposal for a unified approach based on two pillars: a new profit allocation system, based on the place in which the users of the digital services are located; and a global anti-erosion proposal, a sort of minimum tax at the level of the significant shareholders of a corporation.[12] In June 2020 the OECD process came to an impasse when the US Treasury Secretary declared that the United States was unable to agree on a change to global taxation laws that would affect national digital companies.[13] In April 2021, OECD negotiations resumed with a new impetus, following the proposal by the new US administration for a global minimum tax rate.[14]

Table 7.4 Effective Average Tax Rates of Different Model Companies

	Domestic Company	Multinational Group	Multinational Group Engaged in Aggressive Tax Planning Using Most Beneficial IP Box Regime
Traditional business model	20.9	23.2	16.2
Digital business model	8.5	9.5	-2.3

Source: European Commission, Annex 2 of the Impact Assessment accompanying the proposals for digital taxation (SWD (2018) 81 final) https://ec.europa.eu/transparency/regdoc/rep/10102/2018/EN/SWD-2018-81-F1-EN-MAIN-PART-1.PDF.

In the wait for an international consensus-based solution, the EU Commission had launched in 2017 its own strategy, which led to two proposals for a Council Directive for a 'Fair Taxation of Digital Economy':[15] a long-term proposal, aimed to identify a significant digital presence to update the principle of 'permanent establishment', and an interim tax on revenue of certain digital transactions, levied on companies above fixed thresholds of gross revenue (DST).[16]. In spite of growing pressure from public opinion and the commitment of the majority of EU member states, the EU Council was unable to approve the DST proposal. Therefore, it failed to achieve its main aim—to avoid fragmented unilateral initiatives at the national level, which would undermine the digital single market and the very effectiveness of the tax. These national initiatives went on, and a form of taxation on digital services was scheduled or approved between 2019 and 2020 in six EU countries (France, Italy, Austria, the Czech Republic, Slovenia, and Spain) and in the United Kingdom. The coronavirus outbreak gave new impetus to a coordinated effort at European level, inside or outside the OECD process. In the new scenario created by an unprecedented health and economic emergency, which pushed the EU Commission to revise the traditional tools in public finance, a form of digital tax, together with a carbon tax, was proposed to finance the interest payment to repay the debt contracted to face the crisis.

At the time of writing, the international process on global corporate taxation is still open and it is not clear how such a taxation will be shaped. The key issues are the level of the levy, and the allocation of tax rights between national governments, that should be based on the local sales and users' location. In the current debate, less attention has been given to the use of the revenue levied by the reformed digital taxation.

An EU Digital Tax to Support Journalism

There are several reasons to shape the digital tax not as a 'dumb tax' which aims to be neutral in social policy terms but rather to earmark (part of) its revenue to support public goods. The first is that the digital platforms benefit from news media content without paying for it. The second is that an enforceable obligation can address the imbalance of power between the different players in the attention market. The third reason is that such a provision would give back to the public, in terms of quality and reliable information, the value that they massively transfer to the digital platforms for free—their data and the users' generated content. The main characteristics of the DST schemes are aligned with these reasons, as they apply the new tax only above certain threshold of gross revenue, cover the main players in the new media ecosystem (social media, search engines, algorithmic aggregators), and anchor the levy to the users' value location, regardless of the fact that there is a payment by the users themselves.

As mentioned previously, some European countries adopted or are adopting legislation on DST. A project on a brand new DST should nonetheless be implemented at the EU level, as 'uncoordinated measures taken by Member States individually risk further fragmenting the Single Market and distort competition, hampering the development of new digital solutions and the Union's competitiveness as a whole'.[17] According to the estimates in the EU directive proposal, a tax rate of 3% would levy EUR 5 billion each fiscal year (at the EU level). Even a minor part of this potential revenue would be sufficient to base a new European policy to support media pluralism in the digital age, with a mechanism that would be in continuity with the European media model, historically characterized by the presence of public service media, commercial media, and public support to private media. On top of the establishment of the tax, the institution of an European Fund for Media Pluralism could create the conditions for fair and objective funding of initiatives aimed at supporting pluralism in member states. The aim of this Fund should be to finance investigative and quality journalism, promoting diversity, competition, and innovation.

The allocation criteria of this Fund should be designed carefully to guarantee fair, objective, and non-discriminatory distribution of the resources across all EU member states, to avoid media's capture by political interests. The distribution of the resources by the EU should be carried out in a fair and transparent way. While there is an ongoing debate on whether, in general, the allocation of EU funds to member states should be conditional upon the respect of the rule of law, the European Fund for Media Pluralism should follow a different logic and directly benefit the media environment, contributing to boost plurality in a given country. While avoiding a direct management of the money of the Fund by the member states, the European Union should play a role in directly 'injecting' resources to support media initiatives through a different set of measures including not only those that directly support the media industry but also a set of initiatives that aim at creating new business models less reliant on advertising and more on paid subscriptions. This could include, for instance, vouchers to the citizens, in order to support users with incentives, including subsidies or tax credits for digital subscriptions; other types of vouchers intended to be used for media literacy initiatives;[18] financing directly journalistic projects that meet quality criteria using grants; privileging startups and product innovation. An EU Fund for Pluralism could be also used to support EU-wide and independent news networks relying on transparent and 'plural-by-design' algorithms, and transnational investigative journalism projects.

To summarize, the main objective of the proposed scheme should be to reinvent and finance independent journalism, not to transfer funds from the new digital conglomerates to the old legacy media conglomerates; and to do this with transparent and accountable criteria, avoiding the political capture—in so doing, it would differ from the solutions that have so far emerged from the long-term confrontation between platforms and content producers.

The weak link in the chain is the political willingness of EU member states to approve measures that may result in intruding on and limiting their fiscal and media policies: this comes along with the potentially difficult definition of 'public interest journalism' or 'quality journalism' when deciding the allocation of the funds. Therefore, an objective and non-discriminatory distribution of the Fund should prefer all those measures that have a limited margin of discretion and are aimed at empowering citizens and their possibility to pay for news, and media literacy initiatives. Favouring high professional standards of the journalistic profession could be another interesting segment of funding: 'Offering journalists specific competencies to contrast disinformation et similia, and to improve the quality of information online through fact checking tools and the automation of the news rooms, may become a long-term public policy goal' (Parcu and Rossi, forthcoming).

This type of measure aimed at injecting resources in the media market in a way that is not potentially conducive to media capture should also be preferred when designing a fund for pluralism at the national level. It must be stressed that in markets characterized by high ownership concentration, by national institutional contexts often marked by political dependency of PSM and lack of transparency in the state support to the media sector,[19] risks may arise from a closer economic relationship between the news media oligopolies and the governments, and direct involvement of governments themselves in the distribution of the digital dividend could result in unfair allocation of resources. Such a scenario would boost political capture of media and would menace competition, journalists' editorial autonomy and frustrate the very goal of any financial support to media viability.[20] The draft Recommendation of the Council of Europe Committee of Ministers on promoting a favourable environment for quality journalism in the digital age[21] recommends, for example, allocating public resources for so-called quality journalism and to boost new business models.[22] These policy measures range from state direct support schemes, suggesting the involvement of 'media stakeholders and civil society organisations that represent the whole diversity of society' in the elaboration of such measures, in order to establish equitable and fair criteria of allocation and protect media independence, to incentives for users: member states 'could consider complementing any policies aimed at promoting and facilitating the production and dissemination of quality news and other media content by encouraging its consumption through tax-based or other incentives for users, including through subsidies for (digital) news subscribers'.

The Audiovisual Precedent and the Copyright Debate

A logical precedent of a Fund for Media Pluralism, even if implemented at the national level, can be seen in the European AVMS directive to protect the European audiovisual industry threatened by the new big players of global competition.[23] Following several initiatives at national level, the directive stated that

> In order to ensure adequate levels of investment in European works, Member States should be able to impose financial obligations on media service providers established on their territory. Those obligations can take the form of direct contributions to the production of and acquisition of rights in European works. The Member States could also impose levies payable to

a fund, on the basis of the revenues generated by audiovisual media services that are provided in and targeted towards their territory.

This provision gives to the member states the choice to impose such an obligation, and does not cover all the digital intermediaries, being limited to 'media service providers' (the video-sharing platforms are not included). Its aim appears to be the safeguarding of European cultural identity through economic support coming from emergent businesses. The funding arrives via direct contribution more often than via taxation. Nevertheless, the AVMS directive set a path, calling the emergent businesses in the sector to support, in some form, the legacy ones.

New proposals for digital taxes and subsidies should be evaluated alongside other regulatory benefits, for example in relation to copyright reform, which might be an alternative to tax policy. The EU directive on copyright and related risks imposes an obligation on digital platforms to negotiate with publishers (who now enjoy a neighbouring right, the 'publisher's right' on press publications) remuneration schemes for sharing original content. The directive has been strongly opposed by the digital platforms, who are not willing to pay for the content shared.[24] Being directed to redistribute wealth in favour of content producers by the digital platforms, the copyright directive scheme might help to rebalance the market power in the media environment. But its benefit (if fully implemented, which is not the case so far) would go mostly to the big players in the media market, not necessarily boosting media pluralism with the entrance of new and diverse players. While it is too early to assess the effectiveness of the implementation of the Directive in EU member states, the fact that the publishers are the main intended recipients of the revenues of the implementation of the directive has already provoked criticism. The Directive provides a support mechanism to journalism that is not straightforward, but conditional upon the implementation by Member States of the last paragraph of Article 15 of the Directive, according to which they 'shall provide that authors of works incorporated in a press publication receive an appropriate share of the revenues that press publishers receive for the use of their press publications by information society service providers'.

On top of this, the negotiating mechanism envisaged by the copyright directive may also fall short in creating a virtuous circle and could backfire. The big digital players may refuse to reach an agreement with publishers and stop sharing their editorial content, causing a drop of Internet traffic and online advertising revenues to publishers and journalists. Google has already used this negative approach in Germany and Spain,[25] before the EU Directive was passed, and used it in France, where the copyright directive is already transposed into the national legal order. According to the Decision of April 9, 2020, of the French Competition Authority,[26] this behaviour may amount to an anticompetitive practice: Google has a dominant position on search services and may have abused it, by imposing on the publishers unfair negotiation conditions, by circumventing the law forcing a general standard of non-remuneration, and by refusing any negotiation and remuneration to the publishers, treating the same way economic actors placed in

different situations beyond any objective justification, and therefore having implemented a discriminatory practice. Therefore, the French Authority ordered
Google to negotiate the remuneration in good faith with the publishers who requested it. Google appealed this decision, but soon after a negotiation occurred,
the platform reached an agreement with the main publishers in France.[27] Facing
growing pressure from governments and regulators, the digital platforms started
to negotiate voluntary agreements with the more prominent publishers in several
countries in Europe. In what it described as a 'licensing programme to support the
news industry', Google reached agreements for publishers to contribute to a 'news
experience', due to launch in 2021 in Germany, Australia, and Brazil.[28]

Forms of voluntary negotiations, or mandatory bargaining,[29] can be seen as
a way to shift resources from platforms to publishers and contribute to finance
the disrupted news media industry. But the recent experiences prove that their
outcome may reward just a few market players in just a few countries, and in so
doing fall short in guaranteeing an effective support to media pluralism. This is
why taxation will provide a more effective policy solution.

Voluntary Funding

It may be argued that news subsidies or new taxes are not necessary because of
other funding models such as membership and philanthropy. Donorship initiatives are very common in the big-tech realm, and big companies are using
their resources to support causes of public interest. During the Covid-19 crisis,
in April 2020, Google announced a journalism emergency relief fund for local
newsrooms; and the Facebook Journalism Project launched in May 2020 to
support local newsrooms hit by Covid-19. Lacking regulation in the sector,
voluntary funding by the platforms to journalistic initiatives and startups, to
media literacy projects and to NGOs is often supported by policymakers. For
instance, the aforementioned Recommendation of the Committee of Ministers
of the Council of Europe on quality journalism in the digital age calls on online platforms to accept their responsibilities, supporting the practice as a sort
of self-taxation. 'Online platforms, other relevant internet intermediaries and
advertisers that engage in large-scale dissemination and monetisation of third-
party content should recognise their responsibility to make meaningful contributions to media publishers or public entities, financially and through other
means'.[30] The digital platforms in some way acknowledge the problem of media
sustainability and the need for journalistic original content, and try to address
it in their own way, out of a self-regulated and unilateral initiative.[31] These contributions could not, however be seen as an alternative to a fiscal policy, as they
are voluntary and, therefore, guarantee neither a stable revenue, nor fair and
objective distribution criteria. There is no guarantee they will provide the scale
of resources necessary and will be subject to criticisms that they compromise
media independence.

Free Goods and Public Goods

So far, we argued that the proposal of a digital tax earmarked to support the public good of media pluralism could be more effective and straightforward in comparison with other attempts to make the big platforms pay for the content that they use, and to curb their market power. In this section, we will argue the rationale of the proposal, framing it in the economic theories of digital markets; and comparing it with similar or alternative proposals to face the crisis of the legacy media business model.

In their 'The Hidden Cost of Free Goods: Implications for Antitrust Enforcement', Gal and Rubinfeld (2016) analyse the welfare effects of the provision of most free goods by the platforms, in which personal data is the real currency, and the benefits for the consumers are direct while the costs are indirect, not perceived by the consumer, and often related to market other than the one in which the free good is distributed. 'For example, accepting a free newspaper saves the cost of buying another one, or makes for a good pastime. Yet this may imply that other, more critical and fact-based sources of information are not accessed due to monetary or time limitations, indirectly affecting the democratic process in which public opinion serves as an important check on the use of political power. The consumer might therefore not be aware of such costs'. Their existence, the authors argue, highlights the limits of the antitrust enforcements and the need for regulation.

The role of externalities—in a neoclassical approach to the digital markets analysis—is also underlined by Newman (2019), using the category of the 'attention markets'. Among the hidden costs not perceived by the consumers, there is the 'attention cost', namely the cost in terms of time spent on, apparently free, consumption. 'Attention markets exhibit a number of features that render them likely to fail'; considering that 'Competition alone cannot be expected to cure all ills in attention markets'. To face them, the author calls for the neoclassical remedies to market failures: 'price caps' on the level of attention costs and, additionally or alternatively, 'pigouvian taxes on attention consumption'. Pigouvian taxes are currently proposed as a remedy to externalities, to internalize into the consumers' or firm's costs the hidden cost of actions that are not evaluated by market forces. These are often found in the environmental field, e.g., pollution, congestion, and so on. In the consumer welfare perspective, a digital tax targeted on the consumers' value can be seen as a Pigouvian tax, aiming to compensate for a market failure.

From a different perspective, Romer (2019) proposes a form of digital tax 'to prevent a tragedy of commons', in other words, the undersupply of a public good in the presence of market failures. In the Nobel laureate's proposal, this tax should be levied on the sales of targeted digital advertising, or designed as a surcharge to the corporate income tax. Such a tax would impact the platforms' business model, and force them to change it: 'the goal is make the market work, not to collect revenue'.

Disinformation, Misinformation, and Public Service Journalism

According to these approaches, taxing the digital platform would help the news media plurality in itself by restoring an even market, monetising the negative externalities of the platforms' model and (in Romer's perspective) even transforming the very characteristics of this model. It should be noticed that, according to this approach, a tax translation on final prices would not be an unwanted or problematic effect: monetizing the 'free good' of attention, it would rather reach the goal.[32] On the other hand, the international reform process's debate, being focused on the taxation's fairness, has a more general and basic goal: the redistribution of the tech dividend. In this perspective, the DST is a tool to counteract tax avoidance on digital multinationals' profits, calling the winners of digitalization to contribute to the public treasury, from which they benefited since their very origin (monetizing the Internet's invention). In this case the tax translation would be an unwanted effect, depending on the exercise of the monopolistic power in defending the actual level of profits.

In this framework a rationale may be found for earmarking the digital tax revenue to the support of the news media sector: not only trying to fix the market—restoring an even play field, internalizing negative externalities—but also financing the policies in supplying the public good that the market cannot provide to a sufficient extent.

Several proposals in the current debate of journalism's crisis require a more active and direct public support, calling on the platforms to contribute to journalism financing. This is the case of the proposal of a 'public media tax'. In his *Democracy without Journalism? Confronting the Misinformation Society*, Pickard (2020) summarizes the scope and functions of such a tax: 'Redistributing revenue as part of a new regulatory approach could address the twin problems of unaccountable monopoly power and the loss of public service journalism. Facebook and Google (which owns YouTube) should help fund the very industry that they simultaneously profit from and eviscerate. These firms could pay a nominal 'public media tax' of 1 percent on their earnings, which would generate significant revenue for a journalism trust fund'. A similar, but more ambitious, plan proposed by the media reform organization Free Press calls for a broader tax on digital advertising, potentially yielding $2 billion dollars per year for public service journalism' (Karr and Aaaron 2019). Other proposals tend to systemise the voluntary and self-managed philanthropic initiatives set by the digital platforms to help journalism (Bell 2017).

CONCLUSION

This chapter has proposed the establishment of an EU DST, to support a media pluralism fund. A fiscal policy at EU level on digital platforms will be possible to implement only as a common effort, to avoid platforms abusing their negotiating power and to avoid fragmenting the EU response and, consequently, fair competition. Time could be ripe to push for such measures at a more international level, according to the OECD, considering also that the COVID-19 crisis has boosted the role of digital players (OECD 2020). In the wait for an international consensus-based solution, within the European Union the pandemic itself and the search for resources to fund the economic crisis could act as an accelerator of the adoption of a digital tax. Even if finalized not to support the media sector but rather to maintain fair taxation and fair competition within the EU single market.

At the moment this chapter is written, the European Union approved an EU Recovery fund, financed by all EU member states to face the Covid-19 crisis at the EU level: the path for a new financial policy of the European Union is set and it is likely that the European Union will try to find its own resources and develop its own fiscal policy. According to Closa et al.: 'European leaders can use this opportunity to agree on new own resources for the EU, if necessary by enhanced cooperation. Currently, there are two obvious sources. . . . The first is a tax on digital, one of the few sectors benefiting from the crisis. The second is a carbon emissions tax' (Poiares Maduro et al. 2020). Each of these sources deals with strategic choices on the future of our societies. We have argued for using part of the 'digital dividend' to reinforce independent journalism and restoring the role of media freedom in our democracies. Such a provision would shift resources from the digital gatekeepers (the winners of digitalization) to professional journalism (the losers) out of a transparent mechanism, based on the updated rules of a fair taxation, rather than depending on the benevolence of the winners. The European Union has the chance define a new mechanism that may help set standards for democratic renewal at international level.

NOTES

1. As noted by Helberger (2019), there is a general conceptual disagreement about the notion of 'media pluralism' and 'media diversity'. For the purpose of this chapter, the authors consider the holistic definition adopted by the Media Pluralism Monitor as developed and implemented by the Centre for Media Pluralism and Media Freedom (Brogi et al. 2020) and will focus on the economic dimension of media pluralism.

2. Eurostat—Annual detailed enterprise statistics for services (NACE Rev. 2 H-N and S95) (data extracted on March 2020, years 2011–2017, referred to EU28—with UK). For the years 2018–2019 the MPM2020 assessment shows a 'medium risk' in the indicator which measures media viability, which includes all sectors of the media industry.

3. Reported in Waters (2020).

4. See WHO (2020): 'The 2019-nCoV outbreak and response has been accompanied by a massive 'infodemic'—an over-abundance of information—some accurate and

some not—that makes it hard for people to find trustworthy sources and reliable guidance when they need it'.

5. See Nicolaou and Barker (2020), Nielsen (2020), Ponsford (2020), Luo (2020).

6. See Bleyer-Simon and Carlini (2021).

7. In this estimate, digital extension of traditional media (newspapers, TV, cinema, audio, magazines) is considered.

8. See point A29 in the Conclusions of the Special Meeting of the European Council, held in July 2020: 'As a basis for additional own resources, the Commission will put forward in the first semester of 2021 proposals on a carbon border adjustment mechanism and on a digital levy, with a view to their introduction at the latest by 1 January 2023' (European Council 2020).

9. https://taxfoundation.org/digital-tax-europe-2020/.

10. Since 2015 OECD identified digitalization as one of the main areas of the Base Erosion and Action Plan (BEPS) (OECD 2015). For a summary of the international process on the profits taxation, see Carlini (2020).

11. Tørsløv et al. (2018) estimates that close to 40% of multinationals' profits are shifted to tax havens every year. Crivelli et al. (2015) quantify revenue losses of base erosion and profit shifting by multinationals around 400 billion USD for OECD countries.

12. OECD (2019).

13. https://www.ft.com/content/1ac26225-c5dc-48fa-84bd-b61e1f4a3d94.

14. See Financial Times, https://www.ft.com/content/847c5f77-f0af-4787-8c8e-070ac6a7c74f.

15. See European Commission (2018a, 2018b, 2018c). The first proposal was to update the principle of permanent establishment to identify a 'significant digital presence' from which profits originate; the second directive proposal shifts the taxation from profits to gross revenues from digital services.

16. In the Commission's proposal, the interim DST has the following characteristics: (1) it would be levied on companies generating more than 750 million EUR worldwide and more than 50 million in the European Union; (2) it is meant to be temporary, in the wait for an international solution; (3) it is not a tax on profits, but on gross revenues; (4) the tax base refers to specific digital services characterized by users' value creation (thus covering online advertising, social networks, transmission of data collected about and from users); (5) the place of taxation is the State where the users are located; (6) the tax base is calculated according to the quantity of the digital users; (7) it has threshold criteria; the tax rate is 3%, net of value added tax and other similar taxes.

17. Proposal for a Council Directive on the common system of a digital services tax on revenues resulting from the provision of certain digital services, European Commission (2018c).

18. See Stigler Committee on Digital Platforms (2019) and ACCC (2019). For an overview of the proposals, see also Parcu and Rossi (forthcoming).

19. The Media Pluralism Monitor (Brogi et al. 2020) highlights high risks in the media ownership concentration, which are growing as the media industry resorts to defensive mergers to face the crisis; and worrying levels of risk related to the indicators of political independence of the media, transparency in the state regulation of resources, and the independence of PSM governance and funding.

20. This is also why the recommendation stresses the importance in involving an independent body in the allocation of funds. 'Any subsidies or other forms of financial support should be granted on the basis of objective, equitable and viewpoint neutral legal criteria, within the framework of non-discriminatory and transparent procedures, and should be administered by a body enjoying functional and operational autonomy, such as an independent media regulatory authority'.

21. Council of Europe (2019). This draft recommendation is pending approval.

22. Appendix to the Recommendation, Guidelines on promoting quality journalism in the digital age: 1.4.3. 'States could also consider redistributive measures aimed at equitable sharing of marketing and advertising revenue among media organisations that produce such content, and major online platforms and other relevant internet intermediaries that benefit significantly from its distribution. Such measures could be developed independently of the payment of any fees applicable under copyright laws, as far as the latter are insufficient to achieve a balanced distribution, and should seek to benefit media publishers of different sizes and profiles, consistent with their specific contributions to public interest journalism'.

23. Directive (EU) 2018/1808.

24. On top of this, the Directive clearly states that an online platform is not shielded by the e.Commerce directive when it comes to copyright protection, as it is not considered a mere network intermediary, but performing an 'act of communication to the public or an act of making available to the public for the purposes of this Directive when it gives the public access to copyright-protected works or other protected subject matter uploaded by its users'. Article 17 of Directive (EU) 2019/790 on copyright and related rights in the Digital Single Market and amending Directives 96/9/EC and 2001/29/EC. This means that online platforms are considered active actors in distributing information.

25. See Rosati (2013, 2014).

26. Autorité de la Concurrence (2020).

27. See Rosemain (2021).

28. Reported in Barker (2020).

29. In the Australian case, the News Media Mandatory Code obliged the platform to negotiate with the publishers. After being fiercely opposed by Google and Facebook, the law was amended to recognize bilateral agreements in order to suspend the enforcement of the Code. Critics of this solution pointed out that the law may end up favouring big media over small publishers (see ACMA 2021; Lomas 2021).

30. 'They should thereby contribute to the preservation of quality journalism in markets in which they have a significant business presence and where they generate important revenue from online news. Such contributions should be independent from the choice of tools and platforms of the beneficiaries and there should be strong guarantees for the editorial autonomy of the benefiting media. These contributions should also extend to the development and promotion of MIL initiatives that empower individuals to recognise and value quality journalism. Online platforms are encouraged to partner with civil society, governments, educational institutions, and other stakeholders to support efforts aimed at improving critical thinking and digital media literacy'. https://rm.coe.int/msi-joq-2018-rev7-e-draft-recommendation-on-quality-journalism-finalis/168098ab76 (the Recommendation was approved by the CDMSI and is forthcoming).

31. A similar aim may be traced in Facebook's decision, on June 2020, to update the algorithm to prioritize original reporting in its News Feed. https://www.axios.com/newsletters/axios-media-trends-40d2f971-c434-4359-8a0f-7fa4155626bc.html?utm_source=newsletter&utm_medium=email&utm_campaign=newsletter_axiosmediatrends&stream=top.
32. The tax translation on consumers was menaced by Amazon in response to France's DST, and considered by the government as a retaliation.

REFERENCES

ACCC. 2019. 'Digital Platform Inquiry—Final Report'. Accessed November 10, 2020. https://www.accc.gov.au/publications/digital-platforms-inquiry-final-report.

Autorité de la concurrence. 2020. 'Décision n° 20-MC-01 du 9 avril 2020 relative à des demandes de mesures conservatoires présentées par le Syndicat des éditeurs de la presse magazine, l'Alliance de la presse d'information générale e.a. et l'Agence France-Presse', April 9. Accessed November 10, 2020. https://www.autoritedelaconcurrence.fr/fr/decision/relative-des-demandes-de-mesures-conservatoires-presentees-par-le-syndicat-des-editeurs-de.

Barker, Alex. 2020. 'Google Strikes Deals to Pay for News in Three Countries'. Financial Times, June 25. Accessed November 10, 2020. https://www.ft.com/content/28fbefd3-e5e3-4968-b265-6b530e752516.

Bell, Emily. 2017. 'How Mark Zuckerberg Could Really Fix Journalism'. Columbia Journalism Review, February 21. Accessed November 10, 2020. https://www.cjr.org/tow_center/mark-zuckerberg-facebook-fix-journalism.php.

Bleyer-Simon and Carlini. 2021. Media Economy in the Pandemic: A European Perspective, forthcoming

Brogi, Elda, et al. 2020. 'Monitoring Media Pluralism in the Digital Era: Application of the Media Pluralism Monitor 2020 in the European Union, Albania and Turkey in the years 2018–2019'. 2020 Policy Report. Accessed November 10, 2020. https://cadmus.eui.eu/bitstream/handle/1814/67828/MPM2020-Policy Report.pdf?sequence=5&isAllowed=y.

Carlini, Roberta. 2020. 'Digital Taxation and Media Policy'. In Research Handook on EU Media Law and Policy, edited by P. L. Parcu and E. Brogi. Elgar Publishing, forthcoming.

Council of Europe. 2019. 'Draft Recommendation CM/Rec(20XX)XX of the Committee of Ministers to Member States on Promoting a Favourable Environment for Quality Journalism in the Digital Age'. Strasbourg: Council of Europe. Accessed November 10, 2020. https://rm.coe.int/msi-joq-2018-rev7-e-draft-recommendation-on-quality-journalism-finalis/168098ab76.

Crivelli, Ernesto, Ruud De Mooij, and Michael Keen. 2015. 'Base Erosion, Profit Shifting and Developing Countries'. International Monetary Fund Working Papers, no. 15/118. Accessed November 10, 2020. https://www.imf.org/external/pubs/ft/wp/2015/wp15118.pdf.

Directive (EU) 2018/1808 of the European Parliament and of the Council of 14 November 2018 amending Directive 2010/13/EU on the coordination of certain provisions laid down by law, regulation or administrative action in Member States concerning

the provision of audiovisual media services (Audiovisual Media Services Directive)
in view of changing market realities. Accessed November 10, 2020. https://
data.consilium.europa.eu/doc/document/PE-33-2018-INIT/en/pdf.

Directive (EU) 2019/790 of the European Parliament and of the Council of 17 April 2019
on copyright and related rights in the Digital Single Market and amending Directives
96/9/EC and 2001/29/EC. Accessed November 10, 2020. https://eur-lex.europa.eu/
eli/dir/2019/790/oj.

European Commission. 2018a. 'Communication from the Commission to the European
Parliament and the Council. Time to Establish a Modern, Fair and Efficient Taxation
Standard for the Digital Economy', 146 final. Brussels: European Commission.
Accessed November 10, 2020. https://ec.europa.eu/transparency/regdoc/rep/1/
2018/EN/COM-2018-146-F1-EN-MAIN-PART-1.PDF.

European Commission. 2018b. 'Proposal for a Council Directive Laying Down
Rules Relating to the Corporate Taxation of a Significant Digital Presence', 147
final. Brussels: European Commission. Accessed November 10, 2020. https://
ec.europa.eu/taxation_customs/sites/taxation/files/proposal_significant_digital_
presence_21032018_en.pdf.

European Commission. 2018c. 'Proposal for a Council Directive on the Common System
of a Digital Service Tax on Revenues Resulting from the Provision of Certain Digital
Services', 148 final. Brussels: European Commission. Accessed November 10, 2020.
https://ec.europa.eu/taxation_customs/sites/taxation/files/proposal_common_
system_digital_services_tax_21032018_en.pdf.

European Council. 2020. 'Conclusions—Special Meeting of the European Council
(17, 18, 19, 20 and 21 July 2020)'. Accessed November 10, 2020. https://
www.consilium.europa.eu/media/45109/210720-euco-final-conclusions-en.pdf.

Evans, David, S. 2009. 'The Online Advertising Industry: Economics, Evolution, and
Privacy'. Journal of Economic Perspectives 23(3): 37–60.

Gal, Michal, and Daniel Rubinfeld. 2016. 'The Hidden Cost of Free Goods: Implications
for Antitrust Enforcement'. 80 Antitrust L.J. 521 (2015–2016): 539.

GroupM. 2020. 'The Global Mid-Year Report'. Accessed November 10, 2020.
https://dmx9040v9xyo8.cloudfront.net/uploads/2020/06/groupmg
lobaladvertisingforecast.pdf.

Helberger, Natali. 2019. 'Challenging Diversity—Social Media Platforms and a New
Conception of Media Diversity'. In Digital Dominance, edited by Martin Moore and
Damian Tambini, 154–56. Oxford: Oxford University Press.

Karr, Timothy, and Craig Aaron. 2019. 'Beyond Fixing Facebook'. Free Press. Accessed
November 10, 2020. https://www.freepress.net/sites/default/files/2019-02/Beyond-
Fixing-Facebook-Final_0.pdf.

Lippman, Walter. 1920. Liberty and the News. New York: Harcourt, Brace and Howe.

Lips, Wouter. 2019. 'The EU Commission's Digital Tax Proposals and Its Cross-Platform
Impact in the EU and the OECD'. Journal of European Integration 42(7): 975–90,
doi: 10.1080/07036337.2019.1705800.

Luo, Michael. 2020. 'The Fate of the News in the Age of Coronavirus'. New Yorker,
March 29. Accessed November 10, 2020. https://www.newyorker.com/news/annals-
of-communications/the-fate-of-the-news-in-the-age-of-the-coronavirus?utm_
source=twitter&utm_medium=social&utm_campaign=onsite-share&utm_
brand=the-new-yorker&utm_social-type=earned.

Martens, Bertin, Luis Aguiar, Estrella Gomez-Herrera, and Frank Mueller-Langer. 2018. 'The Digital Transformation of News Media and the Rise of Disinformation and Fake News—An Economic Perspective'. Digital Economy Working Paper 2018-02; JRC Technical Reports: 23. Accessed November 10, 2020. https://ec.europa.eu/jrc/communities/sites/jrccties/files/dewp_201802_digital_transformation_of_news_media_and_the_rise_of_fake_news_final_180418.pdf.

Newman, John M. 2019. 'Regulating Attention Markets'. University of Miami Legal Studies Research Paper. https://ssrn.com/abstract=3423487 or http://dx.doi.org/10.2139/ssrn.3423487:14, 45.

Nicolaou, Anna, and Alex Barker. 2020. 'Coronavirus Rips a Hole in Newspapers Business Models'. Financial Times, June 25. Accessed November 10, 2020. https://www.ft.com/content/b6fdec4c-e3e7-43b9-a804-03c435de65bb.

Nielsen, Rasmus K. 2020. 'What Will the Coronavirus Pandemic Mean for the Business of News?' Reuters Institute for the Study of Journalism, Accessed November 10, 2020. https://reutersinstitute.politics.ox.ac.uk/risj-review/what-will-coronavirus-pandemic-mean-business-news.

OECD. 2015. 'Addressing the Tax Challenges of the Digital Economy, Action 1—2015 Final Report'. *OECD/G20 Base Erosion and Shifting Project*. Paris: OECD Publishing. Accessed November 10, 2020. https://www.oecd.org/ctp/addressing-the-tax-challenges-of-the-digital-economy-action-1-2015-final-report-9789264241046-en.htm.

OECD. 2019. *'Secretariat Proposal for a "Unified Approach" under Pillar One'*. Public consultation document, 9 October/12 November 2019. Paris: OECD Publishing. Accessed November 10, 2020. https://www.oecd.org/tax/beps/public-consultation-document-secretariat-proposal-unified-approach-pillar-one.pdf.

OECD. 2020. *'Tax and Fiscal Policy in Response to the Coronavirus Crisis: Strengthening Confidence and Resilience'*. Paris: OECD Publishing. Accessed November 10, 2020. https://read.oecd-ilibrary.org/view/?ref=128_128575-o6raktc0aa&title=Tax-and-Fiscal-Policy-in-Response-to-the-Coronavirus-Crisis.

Ofcom. 2019. *'Online Nation Report'*. London: OFCOM: 41–64. Accessed November 10, 2020. https://www.ofcom.org.uk/research-and-data/internet-and-on-demand-research/online-nation/narrative.

Parcu, Pier Luigi. 2019. 'New Digital Threats to Media Pluralism in the Information Age'. EUI Working Papers RSCAS 2019/19. Accessed November 10, 2020. https://cadmus.eui.eu/bitstream/handle/1814/61890/RSCAS%202019_19.pdf?sequence=1&isAllowed.

Parcu, Pier Luigi and Maria Alessandra Rossi. 'Policy Changes to Strengthen the Protection of Media Freedom and Media Pluralism in the EU'. In Research Handook on EU Media Law and Policy, edited by P. L. Parcu and E. Brogi. Elgar Publishing, forthcoming.

Pickard, Victor. 2020. Democracy without Journalism? Confronting the Misinformation Society. Oxford: Oxford University Press.

Poiares Maduro, Miguel, George Papaconstantinou, and Carlos Closa. 2020. *'EU and Covid-19: Time to Think Outside the Box'*. Florence: EUIdeas. Accessed November 10, 2020. *https://euideas.eui.eu/2020/04/21/eu-and-covid-19-time-to-think-outside-the-box/*.

Ponsford, Dominic. 2020. 'Coronavirus and the News Industry: What We've Learned so Far and How We Can Weather the Storm'. Pressgazette, March 24. Accessed

November 10, 2020. https://www.pressgazette.co.uk/coronavirus-and-the-news-industry-what-we-have-learned-so-far-and-how-we-can-beat-it/.

Romer, Paul. 2019. 'A Tax That Could Fix Big Tech'. New York Times, May 6. Accessed November 10, 2020. https://www.nytimes.com/2019/05/06/opinion/tax-facebook-google.html.

Rosati, Eleonora. 2013. 'What Happened after the German Lex Google? Google News Became Opt-In'. The IPKat, June 23. Accessed November 10, 2020. https://ipkitten.blogspot.com/2013/06/what-happened-after-german-lex-google.html.

Rosati, Eleonora. 2014. 'Google Announces End of News in Spain'. The IPKat, December 11. Accessed November 10, 2020. https://ipkitten.blogspot.com/2014/12/google-announces-end-of-news-in-spain.html.

Seely, Anthony. 2020. 'Digital Services Tax'. Briefing Paper, Number 8719, April 3. London: House of Commons Library. Accessed November 10, 2020 https://commonslibrary.parliament.uk/research-briefings/cbp-8719/.

The Cairncross Review. 2019. 'A Sustainable Future for Journalism'. Policy paper. London: UK Gov, Department for Digital Culture, Media and Sport. Accessed November 10, 2020. https://www.gov.uk/government/publications/the-cairncross-review-a-sustainable-future-for-journalism.

Tørsløv, Thomas R., Ludvig S. Wier, and Gabriel Zucman. 2018. 'The Missing Profits of the Nations'. Working Paper 24701, Cambridge (MA): NBER. Accessed November 10, 2020. https://gabriel-zucman.eu/files/TWZ2018.pdf.

Waters, Richard. 2020. 'Microsoft Growth Accelerates as Pandemic Boosts Cloud Business'. Financial Times, April 30. Accessed November 10, 2020. https://www.ft.com/content/ac054397-eb9a-4198-a050-18961f39feb9.

WHO. 2020. 'Situation Report n. 13'. February 2. Accessed November 10, 2020. https://www.who.int/docs/default-source/coronaviruse/situation-reports/20200202-sitrep-13-ncov-v3.pdf?sfvrsn=195f4010_6.

Wu, Tim. 2017. The Attention Merchants. New York: Penguin Random House.

PART III

Safeguarding Privacy

8

Treating Dominant Digital Platforms as Public Trustees

PHILIP M. NAPOLI[1] ■

INTRODUCTION

As policymakers across the globe confront the question of if, or how, to intervene in the structure and operation of large digital platforms such as Facebook and Google, policy deliberations often turn to the massive aggregations of user data that fuel the business models of these platforms. As Graef (2018, 71) has stated, 'When exploring the topic of digital dominance, a discussion of the role of data is inevitable'.

These data aggregations are beginning to be recognized as a source of market power that may justify structural interventions such as antitrust enforcement (Graef 2018); though antitrust authorities continue to grapple with the atypical characteristics of markets and firms that are structured around the provision of free services in order to gather and monetize massive aggregations of user data (Newman 2020). In addition, policymakers have begun to embrace the notion that platforms that accumulate user data must be subject to explicit obligations related to how they gather, share, and utilize those data (see, e.g., Lynskey 2018). The European General Data Protection Regulations represent a prominent case in point.

One idea that has gained particular traction is treating these digital platforms as *information fiduciaries*. As explained by Jack Balkin and Jonathan Zittrain (2016, 3–4), 'In law, a *fiduciary* is a person or business with an obligation to act in a trustworthy manner in the interest of another. . . . An *information fiduciary* is a person or business that deals not in money but in information', such as doctors, lawyers, and accountants. The three basic duties of information fiduciaries are: (1) a duty of care (to act competently and diligently so as not to harm the principal, beneficiary, or client); (2) a duty of confidentiality (i.e., to not disclose users' data to untrustworthy third parties); and (3) a duty of loyalty (that is, to keep their clients' interests in mind and act in their clients' interests (Balkin 2016, 2018).

Treating digital platforms as information fiduciaries would facilitate regulatory interventions related to the privacy and security of user data. A key point regarding information fiduciaries is that, 'because of their different position, the First Amendment permits somewhat greater regulation of information fiduciaries than it does for other people and entities' (Balkin 2016, 1186). However, under the information fiduciary model, regulation would be confined to the privacy and security of user data (issues that do, in some instances, raise free speech concerns).

And so, as Balkin (2018, 15) notes, 'the fiduciary approach leaves social media companies free to decide how they want to curate and organize public discussion, focusing instead on protecting privacy and preventing incentives for betrayal and manipulation'. More specifically, the information fiduciary approach does not lead us to 'expect that Facebook has a duty to keep us from receiving links from our Facebook friends that are misleading or emotionally disturbing' (Balkin 2016, 1228–29).

This information fiduciary proposal has resonated broadly in the United States. It has been widely covered by journalists and embraced by many lawmakers (see Khan and Pozen 2019). However, policy concerns about large digital platforms extend well beyond issues of how user data are aggregated, shared, and handled, encompassing content-related concerns such as disinformation, hate speech, and violence. In the current environment, in which coronavirus-related misinformation has become such a significant public health challenge; in which protests against racial injustice have highlighted long-standing concerns about hate speech; and in which political campaigns and government actors continue to exploit social media platforms in order to distribute polarizing and frequently inaccurate messaging (contributing to events such as the January 6, 2021, attack on the US Capitol), policy responses that go no further than protecting the privacy and security of user data seem inadequate. Indeed, some critics of the information fiduciary proposal have contended that such an approach does not go far enough in terms of providing policymakers with the scope of authority needed to address the full range of policy concerns raised by digital platforms and their role in various aspects of contemporary political, economic, and cultural life (Khan and Pozen 2019).

Building upon this information fiduciary framework, in the United States some policy advocates have argued that the failure of social media platforms to meet specific fiduciary duty of care criteria should trigger the elimination of the immunity from liability granted under Section 230 of the Communications Decency Act (Citron 2019; Fried 2020). Such arguments take on added significance given the flurry of recent actions from policymakers directed at possible revisions to Section 230 (Executive Order on Preventing Online Censorship 2020; Limiting Section 230 to Good Samaritans Act 2020; US Department of Justice 2020). As currently constructed, Section 230 makes platforms largely immune from civil liability for the content posted to their platforms by third parties. As legal scholar Danielle Citron (2019, 8) has proposed, Section 230 should be amended to limit immunity only to those platforms that take 'reasonable steps to address known unlawful uses of its services that create serious harm to others'.

However, as public interest advocate Harold Feld (2019, 141) has noted, any targeted or complete elimination of Section 230 'would do little to get at the kinds of harmful content increasingly targeted by advocates'. So, for instance, even absent Section 230, large swaths of disinformation that do not injure individual or organizational reputations through the violation of libel and defamation laws would remain unaffected (Hwang 2017). For this reason, it may be necessary to consider, as this chapter does, a more proactive regulatory framework that operates beyond both Section 230's focus on civil liability and the duties related to the treatment of user data that might be incumbent upon information fiduciaries.

In the United Kingdom the notion of formalizing a government-enforced duty of care for social media platforms is a centrepiece of the Secretary of State for Digital, Culture, Media, and Sport's (2019) online harms white paper. However, within the context of the UK framework, the scope of relevant harms is much broader than what falls within the parameters of the United States' evolving model, and explicitly includes areas such as disinformation and voter manipulation.

The difference between where the United States and the United Kingdom are in this regard can be explained, in part, by what Franks (2019, 106) describes as 'First Amendment fundamentalism', which is the tendency for US policymakers and the courts to take an absolutist approach to the principle of freedom of speech. Recent free speech cases in the United States have granted virtually absolute First Amendment protection to even acknowledged and intentional political disinformation (Spicer 2018).

Thinking then about the US context, could we imagine a regulatory framework in which—in contrast to the information fiduciary model—we *could* expect that a platform such as Facebook has an affirmative duty to keep users from receiving disinformation and other categories of harmful content along the lines of those outlined in the United Kingdom's online harms white paper? Answering this question takes us into the admittedly treacherous realm of devising a compelling rationale for a regulatory framework that addresses the nature of the content distributed by social media platforms in a way that could withstand First Amendment scrutiny. Towards these ends, the focus of this chapter considers treating these platforms as *public trustees.*

Treating digital platforms as public trustees is not a new idea. It has been suggested elsewhere, though has not been explored in much detail (see, e.g., Regan 2017; Whitne 2020; Wu 2020). Indeed, what has been missing thus far from these discussions is a detailed exploration of the established characteristics and criteria of the public trust model, and how those might apply in developing a regulatory framework for digital platforms. In the approach outlined here, I propose treating the massive aggregations of user data as a *public resource.* Within the context of the public trust framework, this means treating aggregate user data as the *trust property* which effectively triggers the classification of the digital platforms as public trustees.

In developing this argument, the first section of this chapter provides an overview of the public trustee concept and its application in policymaking—with a particular emphasis on its application within media-related contexts such as the one being considered here. The second section argues for the applicability of the public trustee concept to large aggregators of user data such as social media platforms and search engines. The crux of this argument is that the large aggregations of user data that undergird the business models of these platforms represent a contemporary version of the type of public resource that has triggered the application of the public trustee regulatory framework in the past—a framework in which limitations on trustees' First Amendment freedoms have been acknowledged as constitutional. The third section delineates key limitations and boundaries in terms of how this public trustee framework would be applied. This section also considers the specific criteria and applicational thresholds that could be brought to bear. The concluding section offers some preliminary thoughts on possible public interest obligations for dominant digital platforms.

PUBLIC TRUSTS AND PUBLIC TRUSTEES

As a starting point for this analysis, it is important to flesh out the public trustee concept and the broader public trust doctrine in which it is embedded (see Sax 1970), since the public trustee terminology has a tendency to be used somewhat loosely and indiscriminately. The public trust doctrine has its origins in English common law, but with roots dating back to ancient Rome, where concepts such as res publica (a common asset) and res communis (property that is open to all) were first developed (Epstein 2016).

The doctrine has gone largely dormant in its country of origin (Willers 2017), but has become well-established in the United States and many other countries, typically in relation to environmental resources (Blumm and Guthrie 2012). The public trust doctrine has its origins in the governance of natural resources such as waterways (and the preservation of public access to these waterways as transportation channels), but has expanded over time to include wildlife, parklands, and the atmosphere (Quirke 2016).

The public trust doctrine 'requires that certain property be used for public benefit, because of either its unique characteristics or its essentially public nature' (Corbett 1996, 615). A public trust involves three elements: (1) a *trustee*, who holds the trust property and is subject to *fiduciary duties* to deal with it for the benefit of another; (2) a *beneficiary*, to whom the trustee owes *fiduciary duties* to deal with the trust property for his or her benefit; and (3) a *trust property*, which is held by the trustee for the beneficiary (Quirke 2016, 2).

Typically, the government is the trustee of these natural resources and must manage them subject to fiduciary duties (Quirke 2016; Sax 1970). However, in some instances, the government essentially delegates trustee responsibilities to private actors. This is the case, for instance, with the system of broadcast regulation in the United States, in which broadcast licensees receive access to the broadcast spectrum (but do not own it); and in exchange for such access are designated as public trustees of the airwaves (Red Lion Broadcasting v. FCC 1969). As public trustees, these broadcasters have historically been subject to a wide range of fiduciary duties in the form of an ever-evolving set of public interest obligations, some of which represent intrusions upon their speech rights (see Napoli 2019b).

In the framework being proposed here, user data aggregators such as Facebook and Google are the trustees. The public whose personal data are being aggregated and monetized are the beneficiaries. The trust property, in this case, is the aggregate user data.

It is important to note that the nature of the resources that fall within the public trust framework 'will necessarily change over time, as scientific knowledge and societal awareness advance' (Quirke 2016, 8; see also Sax 1980). It has also been noted that the application of the public trust doctrine has steadily expanded over time (Babcock 2015). These observations are particularly important as we consider the expansion of the public trustee doctrine here to a new context— aggregate user data—as these observations help to justify the expansion of the public trustee model to the dominant digital platforms.

APPLYING THE PUBLIC TRUSTEE MODEL TO DOMINANT DIGITAL PLATFORMS: AGGREGATE USER DATA AS PUBLIC RESOURCE

As was noted in the Introduction, the notion of treating large digital platforms as public trustees is not new. Regan (2013), for instance, argues for a number of specific reasons why treating these platforms as public trustees would make sense. As she notes:

> First, the large online players are operating at the scope and scale where 'public interest, convenience, and necessity' demand that they be more regulated. Second, a public trustee approach avoids the somewhat messy issues of proving 'concentration' and anti-competitive behavior entailed in antitrust regulation. Third, the public trustee approach draws upon the link between privacy and trust that has emerged from public opinion surveys and the academic literature on privacy. (Regan 2013, 1037)

A key point in this passage is that categorizing these platforms as public trustees could represent the most logical and effective point of entry for any regulatory interventions. Another key point is that the public trustee framework would only apply to those platforms operating at a scope and scale that trigger broader concerns about the public interest implications of how they operate and are being used. Reflecting this perspective, the proposal being put forth here is similarly oriented, applying only to the most dominant platforms, while leaving smaller, upstart platforms free from public trustee burdens.

What's missing from Regan's (2013) analysis, and from the other inquiries into the possibility of applying the public trustee doctrine to large digital platforms, is a clear articulation of the nature of the trust property at issue, and how it meets the public resource criteria that are traditionally associated with type of resources that are treated as a public trust.

Accomplishing this task requires that we delve into the nature of user data, and the ambiguous and contested realm of the appropriate property status of such data. As a starting point, it is important to note that wide-ranging debate persists over whether individuals should have property rights over their user data (for an overview, see Napoli 2019b). Arguments for granting individuals property rights in their user data and arguments for denying individuals property rights in their user data both make compelling cases (Napoli 2020b).

The persistence of these debates can be attributed to the distinctive, ambiguous, and complex characteristics of user data as a resource. While there seems to be general agreement that user data represent a valuable resource, exactly what kind of resource they are remains difficult to pin down. The well-known 'data is the new oil' metaphor has been widely debated (see, e.g., Hasty 2015; Hirsch 2014; Marr 2018; 'The World's Most Valuable' 2018), raising questions over if, or how, policy-makers should treat user data as a natural, depletable resource like oil. The lack of a fully satisfactory analogy is highlighted by the fact that the World Economic Forum (2011, 5) has described personal data as a 'new asset class'.

Given the novel, ambiguous character of user data, perhaps it is not surprising that 'no jurisdiction either in the U.S. or Europe has adopted or comprehensively considered the option to legally introduce property rights in personal data' (Purtova 2015, 85). In the United States, while some lawmakers have embraced the notion that 'you own your data', no legislation formalizing this perspective has yet to make it out of Congress (McNamee 2019).

In Europe, the General Data Protection Regulation (GDPR) is perhaps the most comprehensive effort to date to impose a concrete regulatory framework on the aggregation and usage of user data; yet it falls short of establishing users' explicit property rights in their data. As Daniel Chase (2018) describes the GDPR, 'While the EU's dignity-approach might cringe at the idea of personal data as property, their regulatory approach practically embodies property rights law. Though property is not mentioned once in the EU's GDPR, its protections. . . . are all crucial elements of American property law. (5; see also Pearce 2018). Yet, the GDPR's provisions 'stop short of confirming that personal data can definitively be considered property' (Pearce 2018, 201). In fact, the term 'property' is almost completely absent from the text of the GDPR, appearing only twice in relation to tangential issues.[2] Thus, there may be some form of 'quasi-property rights' inherent in personal data (for a more detailed discussion, see Pearce 2018), which suggests that 'there are perhaps additional dimensions to the ongoing . . . debate that are yet to be fully explored' (Pearce 2018, 208).

The debates and policy initiatives centred on the question of property rights in user data would seem to indicate that, while some form of property rights are appropriate, traditional notions of individual property rights don't quite fit. Instead, the flawed system persists, in which users grant platforms wide-ranging rights to their user data, clicking through byzantine terms and conditions documents that typically go unread; and even if read, are most likely poorly understood. In sum, the situation described thus far seems to indicate that we need 'A new paradigm for understanding what data is—and what rights pertain to it' (Tisne 2018).

The proposal being put forth here is an effort to flesh out such a new paradigm. The recommendation here is that we approach property rights in user data not from an individual property rights perspective, but rather from a collective property rights perspective. That is, we think about aggregate user data as a collectively owned resource—'owned by the people' in a manner similar to how policymakers in the United States approach the broadcast spectrum (see Berresford 2005). Such an approach would not only capture some of the distinguishing characteristics of user data described earlier but would also reflect where the value in user data resides.

Whatever the exact nature of one's individual property rights in one's user data may be, when these data are aggregated across millions of users, their fundamental character changes in such a way that they are best conceptualized as a public resource. Certainly, it is in this massive aggregation that the economic value of user data emerges. As Zuboff (2015, 79) notes, 'Individual users' meanings are of no interest to Google or other firms. . . . In this way, the methods of production of 'big data' from small data and the ways in which 'big data' are valued reflect the formal indifference that characterizes the firms relationship to its population of 'users'. Populations are the sources from which data extraction proceeds. Also, collective benefits arise when individual-level data are aggregated, as this allows for the observation of broader patterns that might otherwise go unnoticed, or the formulation of generalizable insights (Tisne 2018). This is why Tisne (2018) notes that 'cumulatively, [data] is a *collective good*' (emphasis added). Thus, in this collective formulation of a valuable resource, we should consider a form of collective ownership.

Reflecting this position, some privacy advocates have suggested that recent legislative proposals to require platforms to determine and disclose to individual users the value of their data (e.g., the Designing Accounting Safeguards to Help Broaden Oversight and Regulations on Data Act 2019) are fundamentally problematic. Instead, they propose a collective negotiation model, in which individuals band together to form a 'privacy union' to collectively negotiate the value of their aggregate data and the terms and conditions for its use (Barber 2019). As Zuboff (2019) has argued, 'Data ownership is an individual solution when collective solutions are required'.

This proposal obviously involves a substantial reorientation in terms of how policymakers and platforms approach user data, which has generally involved a continuum ranging from individual ownership to platform ownership. Collective ownership obviously represents something very different, particularly in terms of the regulatory interventions it facilitates.

To illustrate this point, it's worth delving a bit more deeply into the analogy with the broadcast spectrum. From a property standpoint, spectrum has been characterized as a common asset, or what the Romans termed res publica (Calabrese 2001). This concept serves as the foundation for the public trust doctrine. This characterization seems particularly well-suited to aggregate user data as well, given the unique resource characteristics of user data described above. It is worth noting that treating spectrum as a natural resource has been prominent not only in the US context, but in a variety of European policymaking contexts as well (for more details, see Ryan 2005, 10622–23).

In both the spectrum and user data cases, there is a public character to the resource. Also in both cases, there is no expectation that this resource is legitimately accessible by the entirety of the public. Rather, the access limitations inherent in the resource compel the imposition of public service obligations upon those who do obtain access, in order to assure that the public accrue benefits from their collectively held resource. In the broadcast spectrum context, these access limitations are a by-product of the inherent 'scarcity' of the broadcast spectrum (i.e., that there is not enough space within the spectrum to accommodate all who might like to broadcast, without encountering debilitating signal interference). One could certainly argue that the spectrum-user data analogy breaks down here, given that user data are not a finite resource, are constantly being generated, and can be shared and duplicated in ways that the spectrum cannot. That being said, it is also the case that massive user data *aggregations* of the size and scope of those accumulated by platforms such as Facebook and Google are quite scarce in that they are limited to a select few dominant firms. And certainly we don't want or expect these platforms to grant widespread public access to these user data aggregations, for a variety of privacy and security reasons.

In this way, both the broadcast spectrum and aggregate user data are somewhat different from traditional public resources, where the guiding logic of the public trustee model is typically to assure public access. This is not the goal in the spectrum and user data contexts. In these contexts, access to a collectively owned resource is inherently limited to a privileged few, which is what requires these privileged few to operate as public trustees.

Finally, perhaps most important in drawing this analogy between the broadcast spectrum and aggregate user data is recognizing that, within the context of broadcast regulation, this public trustee framework has been deemed sufficiently expansive by policymakers and the courts to justify a limited degree of content-based regulation (see, e.g., Red Lion Broadcasting v. Federal Communications Commission 1969). That is, once an entity has been granted access to the public resource (the broadcast spectrum, in this case), this triggers a quid pro quo, in which that entity relinquishes some degree of freedom of speech in order to abide by a set of public interest obligations associated with access to that resource.

Transferring this model to the digital platforms context would facilitate extending beyond Balkin's information fiduciary regulatory framework and its focus on data privacy and security issues and into high-priority content-related contexts such as disinformation, violence, and hate speech. Specifically, those platforms with privileged access to sufficiently large aggregations of user data to be considered a public resource would enter into a similar quid pro quo relationship, involving adherence to a set of public interest obligations. These obligations could involve affirmative obligations related to policing/filtering certain types of content and/or amplifying other types of content. The key point here is that, through treating aggregate user data as a public resource such content-related public interest obligations would be premised on a rational basis that has proven capable of withstanding First Amendment scrutiny.

APPLICATION AND LIMITATIONS

Given the significant implications of this proposal (in terms of providing a justification for content-based regulation of social media platforms), it is important to consider how the application of this public trustee framework to digital platforms might work. As a first step in this regard, it is important to explicitly lay out the fairly limited scope of what is being proposed here.

Scope

First, as much as the broadcast spectrum model has been drawn upon as an analogy, the proposal being put forth here is not intended to—and need not—generate any kind of comparable government-licensing model for digital platforms. Rather, the argument here is that once a firm becomes a user data aggregator of sufficient size/ scope, the public interest obligations associated with being a public trustee of the aggregate user data public resource kick in. Thus, digital platforms would be subject to a set of public interest obligations, but not any kind of associated licensing scheme. From an implementation standpoint, the ideal approach here may be to draft legislation that establishes the public character of the resource at issue and creates a new agency with regulatory oversight of this resource, similar to how the Radio Act of 1927 established the public resource character of the broadcast spectrum and created the Federal Radio Commission to oversee this resource and to assure that licensees served the public interest. Former Democratic presidential candidate Andrew Yang (2019) proposed the creation of a Department of the Attention Economy that would focus on harms and social responsibility related to digital platforms. The regulatory authority for such an agency would be premised upon the public resource character of aggregate user data. However, as is discussed in more detail in the Conclusion, a model in which content-related obligations are overseen by a more independent, co-regulatory body is preferable, particularly in light of how political pressures were placed on social media platforms in the run-up to the 2020 US presidential election (Napoli in press).

Along related lines, the argument being put forth here is not intended to establish a point of entry for any notion of government ownership of—or access to—the aggregations of user data that fall within the public resource framework being advocated here. Admittedly, there is a very real danger of a slippery slope in this regard, given that government ownership/control of a resource is typically central to the public trustee model. For this proposal to work, then, the 'owned by the people' philosophy, espoused in relation to the broadcast spectrum, needs to become much more literal in the aggregate user data context than it has been in the broadcast spectrum context. As much as it is 'owned by the people', the broadcast spectrum is, for all intents and purposes, owned and allocated by the federal government on behalf of the people. This clear delineation would need to be part of any legislation drafted along the lines described previously.

Within the context of aggregate user data, 'owned by the people' should be more closely connected to true collective ownership and decision-making. This is because the process of granting access to the public resource in question is genuinely a collective decision, made each time an individual agrees to engage with a digital platform. When enough of these individual decisions are made, and the platform's user base reaches a certain size, the aggregation of these individual decisions to grant a platform access to a user's data means that the public trustee governance framework becomes effective—without the government obtaining any kind of privileged position in relation to the data.

From an implementation standpoint, this could be achieved through the crafting of formalized terms of access to users' data that would become part of the user agreements that users enter into with digital platforms. And so, while the governance framework that guides the behavior of the user data aggregators would come from the government (in the form of public interest obligations), access to the underlying public resource would stay outside the scope of governmental authority.

In this regard, it is also important to emphasize that the application of the public trustee model to digital platforms does not represent carte blanche for government regulation of these platforms, just as the public trustee model in US broadcasting has not meant carte blanche for government regulation of broadcasting. Instead, what developed in broadcasting was a regulatory framework that, while more extensive than what is applied to other media, still represents fairly limited intrusions into the speech rights of broadcasters; and, according to some interpretations, provides a logical and constitutionally sound counterweight to the unregulated media sector (see Bollinger 1991). We could similarly consider the application of the public resource rationale to the data aggregations of social media platforms, and the public interest obligations associated with these aggregations, as a counterweight to the largely unregulated space of the broader Internet, where the regulatory rationale being proposed here would not apply (Napoli 2019a).

In order to thoroughly delineate the limitations of what is being proposed here, it is also important to make clear why the notion of aggregate user data as a public resource applies only to large digital platforms and not to advertiser-supported media in general (which all involve the monetization of some form of user data). In general, this is because the model under which traditional ad-supported media have operated and the model under which large digital platforms operate are different in a number of fundamental ways.

First, traditional ad-supported media have monetized audience data derived from relatively small samples of media users, who have knowingly volunteered to take part in the measurement process and typically receive compensation for doing so (Napoli 2003). This is very different from the digital platform model, in which all users must agree to the terms of data extraction in exchange for access to an increasingly necessary communications platform, and certainly nobody is receiving financial compensation in exchange for having their data aggregated.

Second, even when the audience measurement systems for other media involve a census rather than a sample (think, for instance, of traffic audits for websites), the scope of the user data that can be gathered through such an approach is infinitesimal compared to what can be gathered through large digital platforms, given that this approach involves measuring activity through the prism of the site, rather than through the monitoring of actual users (Napoli et al. 2014). Monitoring individual sites, and how users engage with them, provides dramatically less data about the users than monitoring users and their behaviour directly as they move across the Internet and engage with platforms such as social media sites and search engines.

Third, the data aggregation for other ad-supported media has traditionally been conducted not by the media outlets themselves, but rather by third-party measurement firms (Nielsen, comScore, etc.), in a long-standing 'separation of powers' model (Napoli 2003) that seems to have been dismantled in the digital platform context. This model is largely missing from the data aggregation and monetization conducted by social media platforms, for instance.

Fourth, and most obviously, the scale and scope of data gathering that can be undertaken by large digital platforms dwarfs what can be achieved in almost any other mediated communication context, given the size of user bases and the breadth and depth of information users provide through the various means of interacting with the platforms. On this front, it is important to mention the additional data points that can be reliably imputed from these data when they are being extracted from such a large user base (Purtova 2015). Other digital media entities, such as Internet Service Providers (ISPs) and websites cannot come close to matching the breadth and depth of user data that large social media platforms are able to accumulate. Facebook is reported to have over 29 thousand data points on the average user (McNamee, 2019). Only Google, through its cross-platform data gathering (search, email, YouTube, maps, etc.) extracts comparable amounts of user data (McNamee 2019).

Finally, it is important to emphasize that the application of the public trustee model to digital platforms being proposed here is targeted at a select few platforms, and not at aggregators of user data in general. The logic here is that only when platforms reach a certain size/scope in their user data gathering do they cross the threshold into the realm of public trustee. Essentially, only user data aggregations of a to-be-determined size meet the threshold of a public resource. This approach is consistent with calls for a regulatory framework that is targeted at only the largest, most dominant platforms, and that allows smaller and upstart firms to operate without comparable regulatory burdens. In addition, this proposal is directed primarily at those user data aggregators who simultaneously operate as content distributors, given that the proposal's core motivation is to address how content-related platform regulation could operate within the confines of the First Amendment. That being said, one could certainly argue that the notion of user data as a public resource may have broader applicability, such as to the massive aggregations of user data accumulated by large consumer analytics firms.

Thresholds

All of this raises the question of exactly what it should take for a digital platform to qualify as a public trustee of aggregate user data. How many users must a platform have before their user data aggregation triggers the public trustee framework? At what scale does the aggregation of user data meet the criteria of a public resource? As a starting point for thinking about these questions, we can look to current examples in which user-base thresholds have been used as a trigger for the application of a particular regulatory framework. Germany's Network Enforcement Act, for example, applies once a social networking platform reaches a threshold of 2 million users. As another example, recent legislation introduced in the United States to scale back Section 230 liability immunity is limited to platforms with either 30 million US users or 300 million global users; and more than $1.5 billion in global revenue (Limiting Section 230 Immunity to Good Samaritans Act 2020). Ultimately, answering this question likely ends up being more of a political process than an empirical process, but certainly more work needs to be done to determine the exact applicational parameters that are appropriate for this proposal.

A user-base threshold alone may be insufficient, given that some platforms may develop large user bases, but in theory might not gather and monetize user data as a core element of their business model—in which case, classifying them as a public trustee would not be consistent with the logic being put forth here. So, perhaps in addition to a user-base threshold, there would need to be an accompanying threshold that takes into consideration the scope of data gathering being undertaken (in terms of, for example, the number of data points gathered per user); and/or in terms of the extent to which the monetization of user data is central to the platform's revenue model.

CONCLUSION

The primary goal of this chapter has been to lay out some of the key parameters associated with conceptualizing dominant digital platforms as public trustees. The main task that this chapter has undertaken in this regard is to delineate aggregate user data as the public resource that triggers the public trustee regulatory framework. While the public trustee concept operates in many different countries around the world, and could thus be brought to bear in numerous digital platform regulatory contexts, within the US context that is the primary focus of this analysis, the key implication is that designating dominant digital platforms as public trustees can provide a justification for imposing content-related regulations that could withstand First Amendment scrutiny. In this way, this proposal can facilitate the kind of more expansive regulatory reach that critics have identified as a key shortcoming of the information fiduciary model, by providing the necessary regulatory rationale for potentially addressing content-related concerns such as disinformation and hate speech. In this way, the proposal put forth here uses the characteristics of user data, and the widely acknowledged need for a regulatory regime that better reflects the distinctive characteristics of user data, as the entry point for constructing a more comprehensive regulatory framework.

In moving from theory to reality, the reality is that, at the time of this writing (April, 2021), we are in the early stages of recovering from an administration that demonstrated a tendency to pursue regulatory interventions of digital platforms for transparently politically self-serving reasons (see Napoli 2020a), which has served as a powerful reminder of the dangers of advocating for more expansive governmental authority. From this standpoint, the proposal being put forth here has the acknowledged potential to be co-opted and abused in the ways that those who oppose any form of government intervention in the media sector fear the most. But, in so many ways, the Trump administration did not (and hopefully will not, going forward) represent the norm in American politics and policymaking. In addition, the platforms have recently adopted more socially responsible stances in relation to their roles as content moderators and gatekeepers—an evolution that is being driven by a combination of political events and advertiser pressures (Ortutay and Arbel 2020; Shieber 2020). This trend to some extent counteracts the necessity for policymakers to move in the direction proposed here; though whether these platforms are doing all that they should remains open to debate (Aten 2020), as does whether these platforms should possess unchecked content moderation and gatekeeping authority on such a massive scale (Fisher 2020).

With these considerations in mind, perhaps the best approach for building upon the ideas presented here would be for the new regulatory agency along the lines of the one described above (or for Congress) to mandate the creation of an independent, multi-stakeholder governance body that oversees and audits the content filtering and moderation procedures of dominant digital platforms, and that develops and enforces explicit criteria and performance benchmarks related to the algorithmic treatment and policing of different categories of harmful content such as violence, hate speech, and disinformation. To some extent, the platforms are already taking their own limited steps in this direction, with actions such as Facebook's creation of its Oversight Board (Clegg 2020). This proposal is similar to Wheeler et al.'s (2020) proposal for a Digital Platform Agency and an associated Code Council.

One possible model involves adapting the congressionally mandated self-regulatory apparatus that oversees the audience measurement industry in the United States to the oversight of social media platforms (Napoli and Napoli 2020). Such an approach puts the design and enforcement of both data- and content-related public interest obligations at arm's length from both government regulators and the platforms themselves. Even this type of co-regulatory model would likely be subjected to court challenge and First Amendment scrutiny, which is where this chapter's proposal to treat massive aggregations of user data as a public resource, and dominant digital platforms as public trustees, would remain useful in providing the necessary constitutionally defensible rationale for countering such challenges.

NOTES

1. This research was made possible in part by grants from the Carnegie Corporation of New York and the Knight Foundation. The statements made and views expressed are solely the responsibility of the author.
2. Specifically, in relation to the use of user data in the workplace to protect employee or customer property; and in relation to provision requiring data aggregators to provide users with remote access to their personal data, but not in a way that would facilitate access to the aggregators' intellectual property (which is being treated as something separate from the aggregate user data).

REFERENCES

Babcock, Hope M. 2015. 'What Can Be Done, if Anything, about the Dangerous Penchant of Public Trust Scholars to Overextend Joseph Sax's Original Conception: Have We Produced a Bridge Too Far?' *New York University Environmental Law Journal* 23(3): 390–433.

Balkin, Jack M. 2018. 'Fixing Social Media's Grand Bargain'. *Hoover Institution*. October. https://www.hoover.org/research/fixing-social-medias-grand-bargain.

Balkin, Jack M. 2016. 'Information Fiduciaries and the First Amendment'. *UC Davis Law Review* 49(4): 1183–234.

Balkin, Jack M., and Jonathan Zittrain. 2016. 'A Grand Bargain to Make Tech Companies Trustworthy'. *The Atlantic*, October 3. https://www.theatlantic.com/technology/archive/2016/10/information-fiduciary/502346/.

Barber, Gregory. 2019. 'Senators Want Facebook to Put a Price on Your Data. Is That Possible?' *Wired*, June 26. https://www.wired.com/story/senators-want-facebook-price-data-possible/.

Barr, William P. 2020. 'Remarks before the Department of Justice Workshop on Section 230: Nurturing Innovation or Fostering Unaccountability?', February 19. https://www.justice.gov/opa/speech/attorney-general-william-p-barr-delivers-opening-remarks-doj-workshop-section-230.

Berresford, John W. 2005. 'The Scarcity Rationale for Regulating Broadcasting: An Idea Whose Time Has Passed'. Federal Communications Commission Media Bureau Staff Research Paper. https://transition.fcc.gov/ownership/materials/already-released/scarcity030005.pdf.

Bollinger, Lee C. 1991. *Images of a Free Press*. Chicago: University of Chicago Press.

Blumm, Michael C., and Rachel D. Guthrie. 2012. 'Internationalizing the Public Trust Doctrine: Natural Law and Constitutional Statutory Approaches to Fulfilling the Saxion Vision'. *U.C. Davis Law Review* 45: 741–808.

Calabrese, Michael. 2001. 'Battle over the Airwaves: Principles for Spectrum Policy Reform'. Working Paper, New American Foundation.

Chase, Daniel. 2018. 'Who Owns the Data? An Argument for a Property Rights Approach to Transatlantic Data Protection'. *Medium.* https://medium.com/@Daniel_ Chase_/who-owns-the-data-an-argument-for-a-property-rights-approach-to-transatlantic-data-protection-ddc5cc8fc212.

Citron, Danielle K. 2019. 'Testimony before the House Committee on Energy & Commerce, Hearing on "Fostering a Healthier Internet to Protect Consumers"', October 16. https://energycommerce.house.gov/sites/democrats.energycommerce.house.gov/ files/documents/Testimony_Citron.pdf.

Clegg, Nick. 2020. 'Welcoming the Oversight Board'. *Facebook Newsroom*, May 6. https:// about.fb.com/news/2020/05/welcoming-the-oversight-board/.

Corbett, Krystilyn. 1996. 'The Rise of Private Property Rights in the Broadcast Spectrum'. *Duke Law Journal* 46: 611–50.

Designing Accounting Safeguards to Help Broaden Oversight and Regulations on Data Act. 2019. 116th Congress, 1st Session.

Executive Order on Preventing Online Censorship. 2020. May 28. https:// www.whitehouse.gov/presidential-actions/executive-order-preventing-online-censorship/.

Feld, Harold. 2019. *The Case for the Digital Platform Act: Breakups, Starfish Problems, and Tech Regulation.* Washington, DC: Roosevelt Institute.

Fisher, Anthony L. 2020. 'Don't Make Social Media Tech Bro Billionaires Arbiters of Truth'. *Business Insider*, May 20. https://www.businessinsider.com/ dont-make-social-media-tech-bro-twitter-facebook-arbiters-truth-2020-5.

Franks, Mary A. 2019. *The Cult of the Constitution: Our Deadly Devotion to Guns and Free Speech.* Stanford, CA: Stanford University Press.

Friel, Neil. 2020. 'Testimony before the U.S. House of Representatives Committee on Energy and Commerce, Joint Subcommittee Hearing on "Disinformation Online and a Country in Crisis"', June 24. https://docs.house.gov/meetings/IF/IF17/ 20200624/110832/HHRG-116-IF17-Wstate-FriedN-20200624.pdf.

Graef, Inge. 2018. 'When Data Evolves into Market Power—Data Concentration and Data Abuse under Competition Law'. In *Digital Dominance: The Power of Google, Amazon, Facebook and Apple*, edited by Damian Tambini and Martin Moore, 71–97. Oxford, UK: Oxford University Press.

Hasty, Andrew. 2015. 'Treating Consumer Data Like Oil: How Re-Framing Digital Interactions Might Bolster the Federal Trade Commission's Privacy Framework'. *Federal Communications Law Journal* 67: 293–323.

Hirsch, Dennis. 2014. 'The Glass House Effect: Big Data, the New Oil, and the Power of Analogy'. *Maine Law Review* 66: 374–95.

Hwang, Tim. 2017. 'Dealing with Disinformation: Evaluating the Case for CDA 230 Amendment'. http://dx.doi.org/10.2139/ssrn.3089442.

Khan, L. M., and David E. Pozen. 2019. 'A Skeptical View of Information Fiduciaries'. *Harvard Law Review* 133: 497–541.

Kosseff, Jeff. 2019. *The Twenty-Six Words That Created the Internet*. Ithaca, NY: Cornell University Press.

Limiting Section 230 Immunity to Good Samaritans Act. 2020. 116th Congress, 2nd Session, https://www.hawley.senate.gov/sites/default/files/2020-06/Limiting-Section-230-Immunity-to-Good-Samaritans-Act.pdf.

Lynskey, Orla 2018. 'The Power of Providence: The Role of Platforms in Leveraging the Legibility of Users to Accentuate Inequality'. In *Digital Dominance: The Power of Google, Amazon, Facebook and Apple*, edited by Damian Tambini and Martin Moore, 176–201. Oxford, UK: Oxford University Press.

Marr, Bernard. 2018. 'Here's Why Data Is Not the New Oil'. *Forbes*, March 5. https://www.forbes.com/sites/bernardmarr/2018/03/05/heres-why-data-is-not-the-new-oil/#6ab9b0623aa9.

McNamee, Roger. 2019. *Zucked: Waking Up to the Facebook Catastrophe*. New York: Penguin Press.

Napoli, Philip M. 2003. *Audience Economics: Media Institutions and the Audience Marketplace*. New York: Columbia University Press.

Napoli, Philip M. 2019a. *Social Media and the Public Interest: Media Regulation in the Disinformation Age*. New York: Columbia University Press.

Napoli, Philip M. 2019b. 'User Data as Public Resource: Implications for Social Media Regulation'. *Policy and Internet* 11(4): 439–59.

Napoli, Philip M. 2020a. 'Social Media Platforms Genuinely Need Some Form of Regulation'. *The Hill*, March 5. https://thehill.com/opinion/technology/501705-social-media-platforms-genuinely-need-some-form-of-government-regulation.

Napoli, Philip M. 2020b. 'Defining Data'. *InterMedia* 47(4): 36–40.

Napoli, Philip M. in press. 'The Symbolic Uses of Platforms: The Politics of Platform Governance in the U.S.'. *Journal of Digital Media and Policy*.

Napoli, Philip M., Paul J. Lavrakas, and Mario Callegaro. 2014. 'Internet and Mobile Audience Ratings Panels'. In *Online Panel Research: A Data Quality Perspective*, edited by M. Callegaro, R. Baker, J. Bethlehem, A. S. Goritz, J. A. Krosnick, and P. J. Lavrakas, 387–407. West Sussex, UK: Wiley.

Napoli, Philip M., and Anne B. Napoli. 2019. 'What Social Media Platforms Can Learn from Audience Measurement: Lessons in the Self-Regulation of Black Boxes'. *First Monday* 24(12). http://dx.doi.org/10.5210/fm.v24i12.10124.

Newman, John M. 2020. 'Antitrust in Attention Markets: Objections and Responses'. *Santa Clara Law Review* 59: 743–69.

Ortutay, Barbara, and Tali Arbel. 2020. 'Social Media Platforms Face Reckoning over Hate Speech'. Associated Press, June 29. https://apnews.com/6d0b3359ee5379bd5624c9f1024a0eaf.

Pearce, Henry. 2018. 'Personality, Property and Other Provocations: Exploring the Conceptual Muddle of Data Protection Rights Under EU Law'. *European Data Protection Law Review* 4: 190–208.

Purtova, Nadezhda. 2015. 'The Illusion of Personal Data as No One's Property'. *Law, Innovation and Technology* 7(1): 83–111.

Quirke, Douglas. 2016. 'The Public Trustee Doctrine: A Primer'. White paper, University of Oregon School of Law Environmental and Natural Resources Law Center. https://law.uoregon.edu/sites/law1.uoregon.edu/files/mary-wood_0/mary-wood/PTD_primer_7-27-15_EK_revision.pdf.

Regan, Priscilla M. 2017. 'Reviving the Public Trustee Concept and Applying It to Information Privacy Policy'. *Maryland Law Review* 76: 1025–43.

Ryan, Patrick S. 2004. 'Application of the Public Trust Doctrine and Principles of Natural Resource Management to Electromagnetic Spectrum'. *Michigan Telecommunications and Technology Law Review* 10: 285–372.

Ryan, Patrick S. 2005. 'Treating the Wireless Spectrum as a Natural Resource'. *Environmental Law Reporter* 35: 10620–29.

Sax, Joseph L. 1970. 'The Public Trust Doctrine in Natural Resources Law: Effective Judicial Intervention'. *Michigan Law Review* 68(3): 471–566.

Sax, Joseph L. 1980. 'Liberating the Public Trust Doctrine from Its Shackles'. *UC Davis Law Review* 14: 185–94.

Secretary of State for Digital, Culture, Media & Sport. 2019. 'Online Harms'. White Paper, April. https://assets.publishing.service.gov.uk/government/uploads/system/uploads/attachment_data/file/793360/Online_Harms_White_Paper.pdf.

Shieber, Jonathan. 2020. 'As Advertisers Revolt, Facebook Commits to Flagging "Newsworthy" Political Speech That Violates Policy'. *TechCrunch*, June 26. https://techcrunch.com/2020/06/26/as-advertisers-revolt-facebook-commits-to-flagging-newsworthy-political-speech-that-violates-policy/.

Spicer, Robert. 2018. *Free Speech and False Speech: Political Deception and Its Legal Limits (or Lack Thereof)*. Cham, Switzerland: Palgrave Macmillan.

Stewart, Concetta M., Gisela Gil-Egui, and Mary S. Pileggi. 2004. 'Applying the Public Trust Doctrine to the Governance of Content-Related Internet Resources'. *Gazzette: The International Journal for Communication Studies* 66(6): 497–515.

'The World's Most Valuable Resource Is No Longer Oil, but Data'. 2017. *The Economist*, May 6. https://www.economist.com/leaders/2017/05/06/the-worlds-most-valuable-resource-is-no-longer-oil-but-data.

Tisne, Martin. 2018. 'It's Time for a Bill of Data Rights'. *MIT Technology Review*, December 14. https://www.technologyreview.com/s/612588/its-time-for-a-bill-of-data-rights/.

US Department of Justice. 2020. 'Section 230—Nurturing Innovation or Fostering Unaccountability?' https://www.justice.gov/file/1286331/download.

Wheeler, Tom, Phil Verveer, Gene Kimmelman. 2020. 'New Digital Realities, New Oversight Solutions in the U.S.: The Case for a Digital Platform Agency and a New Approach to Regulatory Oversight'. Shorenstein Center, August. https://shorensteincenter.org/wp-content/uploads/2020/08/New-Digital-Realities_August-2020.pdf.

Whitney, Heather. 2020. 'Search Engines, Social Media, and the Editorial Analogy'. In *The Perilous Public Square: Structural Threats to Free Expression Today*, edited by D. E. Pozen, 115–45. New York: Columbia University Press.

Willers, Marc. 2017. 'The Public Trust Doctrine's Role in Post-Brexit Britain'. *Garden Court Chambers*, March 31. https://www.gardencourtchambers.co.uk/news/the-public-trust-doctrines-role-in-post-brexit-britain.

Wu, Tim. 2020. 'Is the First Amendment Obsolete?' In *The Perilous Public Square: Structural Threats to Free Expression Today*, edited by D. E. Pozen, 15–43. New York: Columbia University Press.

Yang, Andrew. 2019. 'Andrew Yang: As President, I Will Establish a Department of the Attention Economy'. *CNN*, November 20. https://www.cnn.com/2019/11/18/perspectives/andrew-yang-technology/index.html.

Zuboff, Shoshana. 2019. 'It's Not That We've Failed to Rein in Facebook and Google. We've Not Even Tried'. *The Guardian*, July 2. https://www.theguardian.com/commentisfree/2019/jul/02/facebook-google-data-change-our-behaviour-democracy.

Zuboff, Shoshana. 2015. 'Big Other: Surveillance Capitalism and the Prospects of an Information Civilization'. *Journal of Information Technology* 30: 75–89.

9

Establishing Auditing Intermediaries to Verify Platform Data

BEN WAGNER AND LUBOS KUKLIS ■

INTRODUCTION

What you don't know can't hurt you: this seems to be the current approach for re-sponding to disinformation by public regulators across the world. Nobody is able to say with any degree of certainty what is actually going on. This is in no small part because, at present, public regulators don't have the slightest idea how disin-formation actually works in practice. We believe that there are very good reasons for the current state of affairs, which stem from a lack of verifiable data available to public institutions. If an election board or a media regulator wants to know what types of digital content are being shared in their jurisdiction, they have no effective mechanisms for finding this data or ensuring its veracity. While there are many other reasons why governments would want access to this kind of data, the phenomenon of disinformation provides a particularly salient example of the consequences of a lack of access to this data for ensuring free and fair elections and informed democratic participation.

This chapter will provide an overview of the main aspects of the problems asso-ciated with basing public regulatory decisions on unverified data, before sketching out some ideas of what a solution might look like. In order to do this, the chapter develops the concept of auditing intermediaries. After discussing which problems the concept of auditing intermediaries is designed to solve, it then discusses some of the main challenges associated with access to data, potential misuse of inter-mediaries, and the general lack of standards for the provision of data by large on-line platforms. In conclusion, the chapter suggests that there is an urgent need for an auditing mechanism to ensure the accuracy of transparency data provided by large online platform providers about the content on their services. Transparency data that have been audited would be considered verified data in this context. Without such a transparency verification mechanism, existing public debate is based merely on a whim, and digital dominance is likely to only become more pronounced.

WHAT IS THE PROBLEM?

At present, public policy debates about online content are highly dependent on data provided by private sector organizations, almost always from a country outside their own jurisdiction. This problem is not just restricted to policy challenges associated with disinformation. It is clear that the need for accurate data transcends one particular regulatory area—be it media regulation, data protection, or telecommunications regulation.

For all of these areas, policymakers not only do not know how to resolve the policy issues at hand but also are unable to gain even a basic understanding of what the core problems associated with it might be. Private companies' voluntary provision of data in transparency reports is problematic not just because that data is unverified but also because their own presentation of categories and standards for transparency data allow them to shape the dimensions of the debate extensively. The way in which private sector platforms like Google or Facebook provide transparency reports under public disclosure requirements such as the German Network enforcement law or the EU General Data Protection Regulation is as a mechanism to manage the visibility of certain categories and obscure visibility from other categories (Flyverbom 2016; Albu and Flyverbom 2019).

Even in cases where transparency is mandated by law such as the German Network Enforcement Act (NetzDG), researchers and regulators alike have found the transparency data provided by Facebook to be highly problematic, with Facebook fined 2 million Euros for miscategorizing and misreporting data required in its government reporting requirements under the NetzDG (Wagner et al. 2020). This is due in part to Facebook prioritizing its own internal content moderation policy over external legal constraints systematically, but also to a lack of a joint industry standard by which data about content moderation is published. There is neither a standardized format provided by NetzDG that the resulting transparency data provided by either Facebook or any other online platform could be considered comparable. This lack of standardized reporting cannot just be blamed on states alone. It is equally due to the failure of large online platforms to standardize the manner in which they report their content moderation practices.[1]

Regulators and the general public are thus unable to make accurate determinations about what is happening in online platforms because they are currently unable to access accurate data about them. This limits both effective decision-making about the nature of existing policy problems policymakers are aware of, as well as the ability to be able to respond to policy challenges they are not yet aware of.

In all of these contexts, the dominance of large transnational online platforms exacerbates this problem. Large platforms are more easily able to 'play' existing national jurisdictions against each other, for example, by threatening to switch the locations of their head offices if tangible regulatory burdens are increased. This was one of the key reasons why Tesla built their first European office in the Netherlands, and it seems a plausible way to explain the weak implementation of the EU data protection law GDPR by the Irish data protection authority. As one leading international election observer noted, 'we're running after the tech companies, they have enormous resources, and they're playing us' (Wagner 2020). The dominance of large online platforms also contributes to limiting the ability of any one regulatory jurisdiction to gain access to relevant data.

WHAT COULD BE THE SOLUTION?

From the perspective of the authors, the most helpful response would be to develop an institutionalized mechanism for the verification of platform data. This would ensure that the data public regulators receive is accurate and verified. At the same time, if all regulators were given competences and capacities to verify data important for the exercise of their duties individually, it would create considerable redundancies. These redundancies may not only be inefficient economically but could also cause complicated situations potentially leading to mishandling of the data itself. As such, a separate institutionalized mechanism which provides a verification function for data provided by platforms to regulators would be the most effective response to this problem. In this context, verified data is understood as verified data provided as part of transparency reports by platforms or similar public disclosures. Independent auditors have checked this data to ensure it is an accurate representation of the state of the platform.

Importantly, gaining access to relevant data does not mean access to all data at all times by all regulators. This article should not be misunderstood as an argument for the creation of NSA-Style 'direct access' to online platforms by any regulator who wishes to respond to a policy problem. Rather, there is a clear need for verified data that answers specific policy questions that regulators have, as well as for existing regular reporting requirements. Providing any government regulatory agency with unlimited access to a dominant online platform is highly problematic and only serves to increase existing challenges around digital dominance. Giving public sector actors unfettered access to dominant online platforms does not reduce the problem of digital dominance.

There are some notable exceptions to this, in particular in the context of platforms hosted by more authoritarian governments. It seems plausible that the government of China has direct access to relevant data on large online platforms such as Sina Weibo, TikTok, or WeChat (Wagner 2012; Jiang and Fu 2018; Jiang 2019; Kloet et al. 2019; Hong and Harwit 2020). Indeed, the Chinese government's ability to correct what they consider disinformation on these platforms in near real-time and heavily influence platform developments in the area of content moderation suggest a great deal of access to data and a close relationship between government regulators and large online platforms. It seems unlikely that government regulators in a situation like this would have concerns with being provided inaccurate or incomplete data. However this highly authoritarian solution is not a plausible solution for democratic governments, it is not possible to safeguard key human rights such as freedom of expression or privacy while also enabled unfettered access to what the citizens of democratic governments do online.

It can even be argued in this context that the existing lack of access and accountability in the area of online platforms makes authoritarian approaches to the governance of the Internet more likely. National regulators unable to access accurate data from dominant online platforms are left with few good policy options. This is particularly the case when the unchecked power of these platforms has the ability to influence elections or other key democratic goods. Rather than strengthen the authoritarian impulses of states across the world, there is an urgent need for models of government that enable an approach that allows for greater accountability of the power of dominant online platforms. The first step in order to achieve this is providing access to accurate and verified data.

Auditing Intermediaries

Within this context, the appropriate institutional accountability mechanism (Bovens 2010) to ensure the accuracy of data provided by online platforms is to create an auditing intermediary—public or private sector entity, that audits data provided by large online platforms upon request. Doing so would resolve a variety of problems associated with privacy, scope, security, redundancy, capacity, and institutional capture within the auditing process.

First, by bundling the auditing process through centralized auditing intermediaries, it limits the exposure of sensitive private data to as few actors as possible. Privacy and data protection are central concerns for organizations that wish to provide transparency, with existing privacy laws such as the GDPR limiting mechanisms disclosure (Bankston 2018; Keller 2018). Using auditing intermediaries limits challenges associated with privacy and data protection, as it can ensure that a more limited subset of verified data is provided to both regulators and the general public. It also follows the principle of data minimization, which is enshrined in Article 5 of the GDPR.

Second, by distancing the audit process from the regulator that is asking for data, it ensures that regulatory action does not overstep its bounds (Viscusi 1996; Hodge 2015). Particularly given the diversity of regulators with an interest in regulating online platforms and the considerable power which can be drawn from access to their data, ensuring that regulators remain within the scope of their mandate is particularly important (Becker 2013; Yan 2018).

Third, by limiting the number of points through which the online platforms need to interact with outside intermediaries, it limits potential security risks that could arise from providing a broad set of different regulators access to a wide variety of systems. It is to be assumed that any kind of access provided to data by large online platforms is highly likely to constitute a considerable security risk. As a result, limiting the number of individuals with access limits the potential exposure to this specific risk.

Fourth, having numerous regulators involved in auditing is likely to create numerous unnecessary and redundant processes in which similar regulators ask similar questions which need to be answered separately over and over again. This challenge is not dissimilar to regulating government surveillance practices (Korff et al. 2017), where ensuring effective oversight depends heavily on ensuring that online platforms are not able to provide conflicting answers to a set of broadly similar questions. At the same time, centralizing the answers provided through a central point avoids redundancy and strengthens the coherence of the overall argument being made.

Fifth, organizing auditing of transparency data through an external auditing intermediary ensures that even regulators without the capacity to organize audits themselves still may have access to such a system through auditing intermediaries. Even existing European regulation like the GPDR is posing considerable challenges in regard to enforcement, with key regulators like the Irish Data protection authority seen as lacking the capacity to do so effectively (Scally 2020). This challenge is even more the case in jurisdictions which are less developed and have fewer resources to invest in regulation as a result. However, it is precisely these jurisdictions where regulatory support is most needed. The ability to regulate a large online platform should not be limited to the largest and most powerful regulators.

Sixth, there is an ongoing interchange of staff between media regulators and those being regulated, which brings with it the risk of institutional capture of the regulators (Nielsen et al. 2019; Short 2019). This risk is even more pronounced in regard to auditing intermediaries, as a result of their potential access to particularly sensitive material. A staff member of an auditing intermediary could not audit Facebook and then work for Google six months or even several years later. As these kinds of restrictions are particularly onerous and limit the recruitment of staff, they should be limited to a small group of auditors rather than a wider regulatory body, although they are of course desirable for regulators as well. As such, the creation of an auditing intermediary brings considerable benefits with it, but what would it look like in practice?

Public or Private Auditing Intermediaries?

The most important question about an auditing intermediary is the question of whether such an intermediary would be public, private or somewhere in between. While both are legitimate approaches to the challenge of auditing intermediaries, due to limited space this chapter only develops the approach of a public intermediary further here. What could such an independent public intermediary look like?

The first and most important is that any such public intermediary would need to be highly independent. This has been a challenge in previous iterations of public sector platform regulation, which is part of why an independent agency—preferably at a European level—would be of such high importance. For example, the German 'Bundesamt für Justiz' (BfJ) is entrusted with enforcing the German Network Enforcement Act (NetzDG) which is, in turn, one of the key current elements of platform regulation in Europe. However, the BfJ is not an independent regulator, rather it is directly attached to the German Ministry of Justice and has to follow the instructions of the Ministry and the politically appointed Minister of Justice (Wagner et al. 2020). As such, a public agency similar to the BfJ would not be in a position to conduct this kind of verification.

We thus believe that it is important to create a new institution that draws on auditing expertise in the private and public sectors to verify the claims made by social media providers. One stage removed are media and other regulators, who are themselves independent agencies within the national context. The extent of their independence, however, varies to a considerable degree. And even those that can be considered sufficiently independent are usually not equipped with the capacities or competencies for auditing data. Although not inconceivable, it would require a substantial restructuring of these institutions in every member state to allow for such an activity.

Finally, there is the case of data protection authorities (DPAs), which are also independent agencies. Through their experience and expertise with data protection impact assessments under the GDPR and their in-house technical skills, they would be well-equipped to conduct these kinds of audits. However, they are already significantly understaffed and underfunded to respond to the GDPR, without having additional burdens for additional tasks placed upon them. Importantly, their role as DPAs in ensuring the compliance with data protection rules and regulations is very different than auditing the accuracy of transparency reports.

Such an institution could be created within the context of the proposed European Digital Services Act (DSA). It should, however, be a distinct legal entity to safeguard its independence from other institutional actors working in this area. The ability to draw on expertise from the European Court of Auditors, from the European Data Protection Supervisor (EDPS), as well as from the private sector would be essential to enable the effective functioning of this institution.

This institution would be responsible for collecting verified data and making them available only to authorities endowed with the legal competence to use them, to a legally specified extent for a legally-specified purpose. The collection and verification of the data on the one hand, and their use for regulatory purposes on the other, would, therefore, be distinct processes, which would further enhance the independence of the institutions involved, and the security of the data in question.

WHAT CHALLENGES DOES THE CREATION OF AN AUDITING INTERMEDIARY CREATE?

The proposal of auditing intermediaries brings with it its own set of challenges. The following section briefly provides an overview of what these difficulties are and how some of these difficulties might be overcome.

How Much Access Do Auditing Intermediaries Need?

One of the key challenges raised by the proposal of auditing intermediaries is how much access to data these intermediaries would actually need. It is, of course, easy to raise privacy concerns in this context. After all, who wouldn't be concerned about a government regulator having access to all the digital content they are sharing? Public regulators do not need access to all digital content to combat disinformation or to respond to problematic online content or hate speech. Nor do they—as some policy proposals have suggested—need to 'break encryption' or mandate unencrypted communications on key platforms in order to be able to conduct it effectively.

Instead, like any other similar auditor from the financial sector, they would need access to some relevant data about the platform, the infrastructure behind it, and the existing policies in place. This is similar to the way in which the compliance with anti–money laundering (AML) rules is monitored in the financial sector. Banks in the United States are required under existing US AML legislation to monitor certain types of transactions and submit suspicious activity reports to the Financial Crimes Enforcement Network (Naheem 2015). When compliance with money laundering legislation is audited, auditors are not interested in looking at each individual transaction or document received by the bank, but rather at the procedures and mechanisms that have been put in place to produce these results (Naheem 2016). The analogy can thus be drawn that auditing the processes and procedures in place to produce reporting is likely to be much more effective than providing access to all pieces of data. Thus, auditing mechanisms do not have to include personal data of any individuals. An understanding of the procedures around how personal data is processed, managed, and governed is likely to be far more important. Being able to reproduce and spot check that the transparency reports are being produced accurately represent the data governance practices of the individual platform is critical to any meaningful audit.

Misuse of Auditing Intermediaries for Strategic National Interests

Even without any kind of direct access, auditing intermediaries remain an important locus of power. Given their ability to gain some degree of access to the dominant online platforms they are auditing, they will quickly become the focus of struggles for power. While this is evidently already the case within powerful online platforms themselves (Moore and Tambini 2018), auditing intermediaries are likely to be in a similar situation. Thus, they need to be adequately shielded from these power struggles by guaranteeing their institutional independence and ensuring their staff selection and maintenance procedure is beyond reproach. Without meaningful protection, auditing intermediaries would quickly lose their credibility as impartial auditors (Funnell et al. 2016; Gipper et al. 2019). This is why it is so important to safeguard their independence and ensure effective staff selection and maintenance procedures.

Standard Setting for Online Platform Transparency Reports

Finally, one of the most significant challenges is that common standards for the provision of data in transparency reports or indeed for different types of regulatory requests currently do not exist. Each company publishes its own data and each regulator makes requests in its own format. This lack of standardization and structure in reporting requirements makes it highly challenging for regulators, the general public, academics, and dominant online platforms alike. As each platform has developed an 'organic structure' for responses to regulatory compliance, the meaning of platform responses to these requests is far from clear, let alone comparable.

At the same time, standard setting for transparency reports takes place primarily through individual legislative acts for specific sectors or policy domains. There is no linkage for the reporting standards for privacy under the GDPR and for German the Network Enforcement Law (NetzDG), nor any attempt to coordinate or structure them in a systematic way. This leads to challenges as the systems of the platforms are not providing comparable data because the infrastructure that they have in place was not designed to collect it in such a manner. This challenge of structuring access to data is similar to government requests for additional passenger data from airlines (Hasbrouck 2020). Typically, the ways in which data is requested from online platforms and airlines alike assume common system and reporting mechanisms that allow for a systematic and standardized response. In doing so, they ignore the considerable time and investment required to ensure reporting is possible in a systematic and standardized manner.

Of course, all of this energy would not have to be expended if large online platforms had already, through an industry group, trade body, or similar structure, come up with their own joint standards for managing and governing content on their platforms. For the airline industry, three airlines associations WCO/IATA/ICAO got together, and in their joint 'API Contact Committee' developed a standardized format and protocol called PNRGOV.[2] As such standards are lacking, there is a need for public sector actors to step in and define these standards themselves. Ideally, by standardizing compliance requirements systematically, this would enable a common regulatory framework that allows regulators to make requests of online platforms without constantly reinventing the wheel.

CONCLUSION

Current transparency data provided by online platforms does not stand up to rigorous scrutiny, either by independent academics, media regulators, or civil society. In the same way that the financial services regulator relies on 'auditing intermediaries' to ensure the accuracy and veracity of the annual reports of companies, so too should media regulators and election boards be able to rely on auditing intermediaries to ensure that the data they receive is accurate. In which other industry would it be considered reasonable to take the claims of a private company about key financial aspects of its business on face value without independent verification? If we can expect this level of audited scrutiny for financial transactions, why not also for digital content?

This chapter has shown several other examples from other areas, most notably the financial services and aviation, where elements of relevant mechanisms exist. Although there is no need to reinvent the wheel, the extraordinarily dominant power of large online platforms requires even higher standards of transparency, accountability, and good governance, if auditing intermediaries are to be successful. We believe that this chapter has shown that it is possible to develop auditing intermediaries and that there are many strong reasons to do so.

Importantly, a regulator of this kind can strengthen freedom of expression rather than impeding it. Freedom of expression is the right to seek, receive, and impart information, even if it is frequently reduced to being able to say whatever you want without facing any consequences for doing so. Auditing intermediaries can strengthen the right to seek and receive information, by making sure that users are completely and accurately aware of how the content on large platforms is governed. Ensuring greater transparency of online platforms means users will know why some content was removed, why other content stayed up, or why platform algorithms show certain types of content and not others. This contextual information is crucial to being able to exercise freedom of expression rights. Without it, users have to rely on statements made by the large online platform without any verification or validation of the underlying data. By doing so, auditing intermediaries can contribute to stopping the spiral of privatization of the governance of freedom of expression, making it more transparent and accountable towards users and the public at large (Wagner 2011, 2018).

What is not possible, at this point, is to continue public debates or regulatory policy about the actions of large online platforms based on unverified data. Only if regulators have an accurate picture of what is actually happening on large online platforms, whether regarding disinformation or numerous other public policy issues, can they make accurate determinations of what steps to take. Neither regulators nor the general public should have to rely on the benevolence of online platforms to know what is going on in their own media environments.

NOTES

1. See, for example, https://rankingdigitalrights.org/.
2. See https://media.iata.org/iata/passenger-data-toolkit/library.html for further details.

REFERENCES

Albu, O. B., and M. Flyverbom. 2019. 'Organizational Transparency: Conceptualizations, Conditions, and Consequences'. *Business & Society* 58: 268–97.

Bankston, K. 2018. 'How We Can "Free" Our Facebook Friends'. *New America Foundation.*

Becker, L. 2013. 'Accountability Gets Personal'. *Risk* 26: 28–29.

Bovens, M. 2010. 'Two Concepts of Accountability: Accountability as a Virtue and as a Mechanism'. *West European Politics* 33: 946–67.

Flyverbom, M. 2016. 'Digital Age Transparency: Mediation and the Management of Visibilities'. *International Journal of Communication* 10: 13.

Funnell, W., M. Wade, and R. Jupe. 2016. 'Stakeholder Perceptions of Performance Audit Credibility'. *Accounting and Business Research* 46: 601–19.

Gipper, B., C. Leuz, and M. Maffett. 2019. 'Public Oversight and Reporting Credibility: Evidence from the PCAOB Audit Inspection Regime'. The Review of Financial Studies, 1–148.

Hasbrouck, E. 2020. 'Airline Passenger Data and COVID-19'. https://papersplease.org/wp/2020/04/06/airline-passenger-data-and-covid-19/

Hodge, N. 2015. 'Overstepping Their Authority: As Regulatory Actions Increase, Organizations Are Finding That Regulators Can Be Overzealous in Their Pursuit of Justice'. *Risk Management* 62: 28–33.

Hong, Y., and E. Harwit. 2020. 'China's Globalizing Internet: History, Power, and Governance'. *Chinese Journal of Communication* 13: 1–7.

Jiang, M. 'Cybersecurity Policies in China'. CyberBRICS: Mapping Cybersecurity Frameworks in the BRICS. 2019.

Jiang, M., and K.-W. Fu. 2018. 'Chinese Social Media and Big Data: Big Data, Big Brother, Big Profit?' *Policy & Internet* 10: 372–92.

Keller, D. 2018. 'Comments on the Guidelines on Transparency under Regulation 2016/679'. Rochester, NY: Social Science Research Network.

Kloet, J. de, T. Poell, Z. Guohua, et al. 2019. 'The Platformization of Chinese Society: Infrastructure, Governance, and Practice'. *Chinese Journal of Communication* 12: 249–56.

Korff, D., B. Wagner, J. Powles, et al. 2017. 'Boundaries of Law: Exploring Transparency, Accountability, and Oversight of Government Surveillance Regimes'. Rochester, NY: Social Science Research Network.

Moore, M., and D. Tambini. 2018. *Digital Dominance: The Power of Google, Amazon, Facebook, and Apple.* New York, USA: Oxford University Press.

Naheem, M. A. 2015. 'HSBC Swiss Bank Accounts—AML Compliance and Money Laundering Implications'. *Journal of Financial Regulation and Compliance* 23: 285–97.

Naheem, M. A. 2016. 'Money Laundering: A Primer for Banking Staff'. *International Journal of Disclosure and Governance* 13: 135–56.

Nielsen, R. K., R. Gorwa, and M. de Cock Buning. 2019. 'What Can Be Done? Digital Media Policy Options for Europe (and Beyond)'. Reuters Institute for the Study of Journalism, Oxford.

Scally, D. 2020. 'German Regulator Says Irish Data Protection Commission is Being "Overwhelmed"'. *Irish Times*, Feb 3, 2020.

Short, J. L. 2019. 'The Politics of Regulatory Enforcement and Compliance: Theorizing and Operationalizing Political Influences'. *Regulation & Governance*, 1–33. https://onlinelibrary.wiley.com/doi/abs/10.1111/rego.12291

Viscusi, W. K. 1996. 'Regulating the Regulators'. *The University of Chicago Law Review*: 63(4): 1423–61.

Wagner, B. 2011. 'Freedom of Expression on the Internet: Implications for Foreign Policy'. *Global Information Society Watch* : 18–20.

Wagner, B. 2012. *After the Arab Spring: New Paths for Human Rights and the Internet in European Foreign Policy*. Brussels, Belgium: European Union.

Wagner, B. 2018. 'Free Expression?—Dominant Information Intermediaries as Arbiters of Internet Speech'. In *Digital Dominance: The Power of Google, Amazon, Facebook and Apple*, edited by M. Moore and D. Tambini. Oxford: Oxford University Press. Pp. 219–240.

Wagner, B. 2020. 'Digital Election Observation: Regulatory Challenges around Legal Online Content'. *Political Quarterly 91*: 1–6.

Wagner, B., K. Rozgonyi, M.-T. Sekwenz, et al. 2020. 'Regulating Transparency? Facebook, Twitter and the German Network Enforcement Act'. Barcelona, Spain: ACM Conference on Fairness Accountability and Transparency (FAT* 2020).

Yan, X. 2018. 'The Jurisdictional Delimitation in the Chinese Anti-Monopoly Law Public Enforcement Regime: The Inevitable Overstepping of Authority and the Implications'. *Journal of Antitrust Enforcement* 6: 123–49.

10

Promoting Data for Well-Being While Minimizing Stigma

FRANK PASQUALE ■

The data protection landscape is rapidly shifting. More data is being collected about individuals. Data points from disparate sources are increasingly intermingled. The 'big data' imperative—increasing the volume, variety, and velocity of information—has become a byword of business, driving digital dominance as leading firms centripetally attract more data with the promise that they have an insuperable edge at storing and analysing it. The resulting frenzy of surveillance and predictive analytics has provoked widespread concern. Despite rising activity and employment in the data protection field, there is widespread belief that the privacy, security, and confidentiality of consumer data is increasingly compromised.

Growing distrust in the data economy is also undermining crucial public health initiatives. For example, sizeable numbers of citizens in the United States would not download exposure notification and contact tracing apps in the wake of the COVID-19 pandemic, despite the personal and public value of widespread usage of such apps (particularly when outbreaks are at the earliest stages, or when they have been brought under some control by physical distancing). For many, trust was undermined by the role of massive tech firms in some app infrastructure, or that of the government. A general suspicion of the data economy may not be far behind, challenging the trust necessary for research projects that will be of great use to individuals and society as a whole.[1]

Policymakers in the United States and Europe are presently grappling with the proper interpretation of legal authorities in order to address these challenges. There are also numerous concrete proposals for new legislation designed to deter misuse of data. These will continue to play a role in restoring trust. However, there is also a need to critically articulate a long-term vision for a rapidly developing data infrastructure. Whom does it serve? What knowledge does it seek to create? What entities should be trusted to make particularly sensitive inferences about persons, and how can authorities properly identify, certify, and monitor such entities?

We can begin to answer such questions by addressing certain concrete dilemmas that have emerged from the frontiers of big data inference. This chapter will focus on medical inferences and predictions made with data taken either wholly, or in part, from non-health-sector entities.[2] This chapter develops some simple principles to guide future discussions in the field, to explore the proper mix of consent-based and regulatory interventions.[3]

These inferences are diverse. For example, consider all the ways in which an Internet platform user's cancer diagnosis could be inferred by Internet platforms without any access to the user's medical records. The user may repeatedly search for information about her treatment plan on Google, or simply use Gmail to communicate the diagnosis to a friend, or use a non-Google account to email the same information to someone who does use Gmail. Either Apple or Google could geolocate the user's repeated visits to an oncology office. The user may announce her condition on Facebook, or may click on ads or stories of particular interest to those with cancer on any site being tracked by Facebook or Google. A large online retailer like Amazon may be able to deduce that a class of users have both purchased books on cancer, and wigs (which are often desired by those who have lost hair due to chemotherapy). Nor are industries traditionally considered 'data-intensive' the only places such inferences can be made. One of the earliest, celebrated examples in this area came from Target, a US brick-and-mortar retailer which used massive purchasing records to predict which of its customers was likely to be pregnant.

Sometimes these inferences may permit firms to serve customers better. However, there are many ways in which they can be used against consumers. As Nathan S. Newman argued in 'How Big Data Enables Economic Harm', the 'increasing loss of control of private data by individuals seems to be leaving them vulnerable to economic exploitation by a range of corporate actors'.[4] For example, for a certain retailer, those living in 'higher-income locations were offered better deals than low-income communities, because those poorer areas had fewer local retail outlets competing with the online stores'.[5] The same logic of disadvantage could compound the misfortune of illness. Indeed, virtually everyone has had, or will have, a health problem or disability that could lead future employers, insurers, landlords, or business partners to discount their abilities, or find ways to take advantage of them. Such discrimination may be illegal, but is very difficult to detect, since there are so many alternative grounds on which to rationalize a decision that was in fact discriminatory.

Given the diversity of these examples, a classification of medical inferences and predictions made with data taken either wholly, or in part, from non-health-sector entities may be useful. The following categories, while not exhaustive, map much of the relevant conceptual territory:

1. **Simple declaration:** When shopping at a grocery store, a person may buy a drug containing pseudoephedrine, like Sudafed. When they do so, they may sign a declaration or otherwise indicate that they have sinus

congestion, to reassure authorities that they are not going to use the drug as a precursor to making methamphetamines. COVID-19 declarations regarding quarantine and symptoms have also proliferated.

2. **Basic and multifactor inference:** A clothing shop may keep track of customers' waistlines and other measurements. The shop may predict that a portly customer is more likely to have diabetes than a petite one. More factors may come into play, particularly for larger players. Their dominance of a field (say, for example's Amazon's in retail) may allow them to put together data sources that are ordinarily unavailable to a more specialized business. Thus, as Australian, German, Italian, and now US antitrust authorities have recognized, there is an intimate connection between domination of an online market and troubling collection, analysis, and use of data.

3. **Somatic tells:** A person may move their mouse or type in ways that disclose 'microtremors', or tiny levels of motion that are usually undetectable by humans. These microtremors may help predict neurodegenerative illness occurring within weeks, months, or years.[6] Note that once again, dominance in a field enables such tells to be detected more quickly, since they can usually only be made on the basis of a massive number of observations. As COVID-19 infections continue, firms with access to large stores of surveillance data may try to identify precursors of an infection—ranging from proximity to known cases or clusters, to somatic indicia of infection.[7] 'Thermal cameras' are supposedly capable of identifying fevers, and might feed into facial recognition or gait recognition databases to identify particular persons as likely to be infected with COVID. The US Pentagon has even experimented with long-range imaging equipment that can allegedly detect a person's heartrate (and potentially personally identifying patterns of biological data) from over a mile away.

This wealth of data will have many consequences, both heartening and troubling. In general, we should shape the datasphere to ensure that it is used to promote public ends, while avoiding discrimination and other data misuse. We may want our doctors and public health authorities to access each of the four categories of information mentioned earlier, but we need not let banks, employers, or others use it.

Restricting data collection, use, and processing properly will itself require a 'meta-surveillance' above the levels of surveillance described in the situations sketched earlier. By registering some initial ethical evaluations of each situation, we can begin to build an ethical framework for other examples of medical inferences from non-medical data that will become common over coming decades.

In any of the situations described earlier, several types of action may be occurring. The first is (a) collection, where the data controller observes and records some information about the data subject, or attributes a characteristic to them. The second is (b) analysis or processing, where two or more pieces of information are combined to make an inference. The third is (c) transfer, which can either be for some consideration (sale) or *gratis*. The fourth is (d) use, when the information defined in a, b, or c is actually applied in a decision-making process to impose some burden or grant some benefit or opportunity.[8] These four categories of data collection, analysis, transfer, and use help clarify the stakes of the earlier scenarios, indicating some 'regulatory footholds' where policymakers can help shape the data society and data economy.

SIMPLE DECLARATION

In the first situation, one of simple declaration, the collection of the data is often mandated by law, in response to public health concerns. For example, with respect to decongestants, the basic purpose of the data collection is to ensure a single person does not buy 20 or 100 times the amount of the drug they need, to make methamphetamines. The situation *simpliciter* does not implicate analysis, but does already raise some important issues of transfer and use. When the state forces this kind of declaration upon citizens, it should also take steps to ensure that the resulting data is not used against them. While nasal congestion may not seem like a serious medical condition, even a single data point could be one of the hundreds or thousands of parameters in a big data model assessing health or other characteristics. Permitting such health data to inform such categorizations by private entities without a public health purpose is not part of the social contract between citizens and states that empowers public health authorities.

Data collectors of basic illness information should not be permitted to share such information in marketing, or to do their own marketing, without specific consent. They should also be required to respect blanket refusals of consent, with some difficult-to-accomplish overrides. And consent should be as easy to withdraw as it was to grant.

Where already established, rules of consent also need better enforcement, with routine audits to ensure compliance. While 'blanket consents' should be permitted to avoid repeated requests for permission from an entity, they should only last for a set period of time (say, a year), and requests for renewals should link to (or indicate a URL for) descriptions of what has happened to the data. Consent must also be as easy to withdraw as it is to give. Ideally, all business associates, contractors, and subcontractors who have received identifiable data should be able to report to the data subject as to what was done with the data.

None of these entities should be able to sell the relevant data to financial scoring, employee evaluation, or insurance firms, even with consent. Persons deserve an inalienable right not to be judged by finance firms on the basis of their health data, *and* not to be pressured into consenting to granting such data. Such principles are based on a 'containment of misfortune' principle, whereby societies should try, to the extent possible, not to permit bad fortune in one area (such as health) to cascade and compound in other areas (such as financial stability). A cancer diagnosis is often devastating. Big data methods should not be permitted to ensure that it also translates into reduced employability, insurability, or creditworthiness.

It may seem unfair to prevent a particularly healthy person from obtaining better insurance premium rates, by selling health data, or wearing a device which continually reports on their optimal heart rate and blood pressure. However, the discounts obtained from such competition to prove oneself healthier than others, derive from the derogation of others based on their relative sickness. Thus progressive jurisdictions may even decide not to allow persons to provide such dossiers themselves, wary of the 'unraveling' dynamics that may emerge when persons compete to be seen as the healthiest.[9] Discounts have to be paid for by someone. 'Wellness programs' in the United States are a classic example of this type of transfer from the sick or disabled to the healthy.[10] The programs give discounts to those who engage in certain 'wellness activities', but these discounts do not necessarily come out of the insurer's bottom line. Rather, premiums overall may be raised on everyone, in order to provide discounts to the persons assumed to be healthier, who perform the wellness activities.

The unraveling dynamic demonstrates the social value of privacy. Once a critical mass of persons decides to provide a dossier to demonstrate their health in order to qualify for a lower rate for insurance, they effectively force everyone else to do so under penalty of a higher rate, since the insurer will wonder 'what have they got to hide'. Such a prohibition may be styled as a restriction on the use of data by insurers, rather than a restriction on the ability of persons to communicate their health data to insurers. Nevertheless, leaving open the ability to communicate such data (even with a denial of its use) is a dangerous strategy, since monitoring the insurer's use of data is something rarely done well by present authorities.

BASIC AND MULTIFACTOR INFERENCE

Despite its simplicity, the clothing measurements scenario poses some normative complexities. As Helen Nissenbaum has eloquently argued, privacy is often a matter of contextual integrity.[11] The closer the data is to the transaction (or type of transaction), the more appropriate its use will be. Waist size, for example, is obviously necessary to tailor trousers; it may also help the store to develop marketing campaigns personalized to different customers. Some pharmaceutical manufacturers or 'reducing services' (like health spas) may be seeking the information in order to assist the customer to manage his or her condition. Each of these modes of inference is likely unobjectionable. However, if the data or inference of obesity is sold beyond such 'assistive services', to enable stigma and suspicion, more serious concerns arise, including the risk of the data being used to sort and rank persons to grant advantages or disadvantages.

Multifactor inferences raise another level of complexity. There is controversy over whether they tend to be more or less accurate than simple inferences. On the one hand, making a prediction based on more parameters may seem obviously superior to one based on only a few. However, some of the inferences now being made seem particularly tenuous or troubling. For example, the *Wall Street Journal* has reported that a clinical trial recruitment firm found that factors like having a large car and an extensive cable TV package were correlated with obesity. The 'just so story' here is that the persons are 'couch potatoes' who watch TV instead of exercising, and who can only fit into a large automobile. But of course another counter-story is possible: some of these persons may be watching the television while on a treadmill or stationary bike, and may be using their large automobile to transport sporting equipment. As Dan McQuillan warns, machine learning often makes powerful predictions, 'prompting comparisons with science. But rather than being universal and objective, it produces knowledge that is irrevocably entangled with specific computational mechanisms & the data used for training'.[12]

This raises the question of whether multifactor inferences are particularly worrisome and in need of review by the person they classify. In some particularly sensitive areas, the answer is yes. However, we must be wary of forcing on to persons the 'work of watchdogging' implicit in an expectation of such reviews.[13] There are thousands of entities that make such predictions about individuals. Instead of putting the burden on individuals to engage in 'cyberhygiene', regulators need to ensure that health data and inferences are only used for permissible purposes.

This will become increasingly important as sensitive inferences proliferate. A music streaming service may keep track of every song a customer plays. The service may predict that customers who listen to certain kinds of music are likely to be depressed—either because of an intuitive association of certain music with sadness or despair, or via cross-correlated data (such as a survey of depressed persons finding what music they most often listen to), or via data trades with other firms (which may, for example, sell to the music streaming service a list of the sites that a person has visited, allowing the music streaming service to correlate listening activity with visits to sites that offer assistance to the depressed).[14] Intuitive associations about mental health may also lead to classifications of persons simply based on music they listen to.

There are also multisite correlations and assumptions based on metadata. For example, a social media service may keep track of when and how often a user is on the site (for example, intermittently or obsessively; at the same afternoon time each day, or at varied times in the middle of the night). The service may also complete studies of the words they post (or write out but refrain from posting). These ways of using the site, or words written or posted, may be correlated with the habits and words of others reliably identified as violent or suicidal, or successful and cheerful. Large Internet firms also may also make use of monitoring via sites around the Internet, allowing them to aggregate information about users' interests and behaviour patterns across the Internet. Internet users cannot keep track of this on their own. Even data trusts would find that task daunting, especially given the amount of proprietary and trade secret protected information involved.[15] The critical policy step now is to lay down clear and auditable 'rules of the road', particularly for dominant firms, to prevent such digital traces and inferences from being used in stigmatic and discrediting ways.

SOMATIC TELLS

There are many ways in which our bodily interactions with computers may 'speak' aspects of our health conditions to them, without even notifying us of the communication. Consider the example of a website tracking users' mouse movements (including microtremors undetectable by the human eye) in order to predict if particular users would be likely to develop certain disease states in the future. Such 'somatic tells' may merit a Copernican shift in the governance of data. Rather than assuming that data collection, processing, and use is in general permitted, and that regulators must struggle to catch up and outlaw particular bad acts, we may flip the presumption. In that case, data collectors and brokers would need to obtain the permission of the state before they engage in certain kinds of data collection, analysis, use, and transfer.

This 'licensing' alternative becomes increasingly compelling as other data sources further refine the predictive ability of algorithms here—particularly that gathered by in-home robotics systems. A device like Amazon's Alexa, Microsoft's Project Evo, or Google Home, may be set to record everything persons say in their home. Indeed, some dolls have already recorded children's conversations.[16] Privacy advocates are deeply—and rightly—concerned about transforming the 'connected home' into a 24/7 monitoring apparatus.[17]

Several harms may arise out of the development of mental and physical health inferences by firms which are not directly authorized by data subjects, or the state, to engage in such data collection and analysis. When readings of emotions result in differential attention or other social sorting, the vulnerable may be harmed. In the case of classifications of mental illness, even deeper problems arise from the forms of 'distant diagnosis' now beginning to be embedded in AI. Machines that may secretly categorize thousands or millions of individuals as 'mentally ill', for example, offend basic notions of human dignity and due process.

A historical analogy helps dramatize the normative issues here. During the 1964 United States presidential election, *Fact* magazine published a long story, complete with an informal poll of over one thousand psychiatrists, concluding that the Republican nominee (Barry Goldwater) was 'psychologically unfit to be president'. Goldwater later successfully sued the magazine for libel.[18] In the wake of the scandal, the American Psychiatric Association revised its principles of medical ethics to warn members not to try to diagnose public figures from afar, even if enormous amounts of data were known about them. This is now known as the Goldwater Rule. Even in the wake of the presidency of Donald Trump— a figure with far more obvious infirmities than Goldwater—the rule has largely been respected. Perhaps it is time for the mavens of AI-driven emotion parsing to take a similarly modest approach with respect to their own abilities. Certainly any AI-driven conclusion that a person is mentally ill, unstable, or likely to be a criminal should be made with extreme caution, with ample opportunity for contestation, and with tight restrictions on its transfer and use. Sadly, Silicon Valley firms appear to be patenting systems that are capable of doing just this, and without strict regulation, such methods they will likely spread to other forms of customer, tenant, and worker evaluation.[19]

Mere notification or transparency about such digital diagnoses is not an adequate response to the dangers of manipulation and misrecognition they raise. In some cases, the mere suggestion of a mental health problem may spark the anxiety or compulsion it is merely meant to identify. The pressure to make one's voice legible to an automated agent or bot on the phone is already annoying and, for many, anxiety-generating. Now imagine crafting the right combination of respect and nonchalance for automated customs services, nonthreatening movements for police robots, and the countless other situations where we might suddenly be called upon to code and recode demeanour, carriage, and body language to be acceptable to machines. The scope and reach of affective computing is long overdue for regulation.

CONCLUSION

Policymakers must work to reduce the risks of sharing mental health data. Its stigmatizing potential continues to grow. For example, there is increasing pressure on schools and governments to identify 'problem kids' at a younger and younger age. According to a recent study, about 20% of citizens account for 81% of criminal convictions, 78% of prescriptions, 66% of welfare benefits —and this group 'can be predicted when as young as three years old from an assessment of their brain health'.[20] What if certain tones of voice or patterns of interaction are deemed to be hallmarks of behavioural problems to come? Who has access to such data? And how can they act on it? The New Zealand Social Development Minister has given a bracing explanation for stopping the risk scoring of children: 'God knows, do we really want people with clipboards knocking on people's doors and saying 'hello, I'm from the Government, I'm here to help because your children are going to end up in prison?"[21] Absent strong safeguards against misuse of medical inferences, however, the use of such predictive scoring may well grow.

The problem will not only affect children. Health systems around the world are increasingly emphasizing 'data liquidity'—that is, the ability of patients to view, download, and share their own health data via apps or other intermediating storage and analysis services. The push for data liquidity is particularly dangerous in the United States, because once a patient downloads her data and stores it on her own account, federal HIPAA protections no longer apply to this downloaded data. The protections apply to health care institutions (covered entities), not to health data itself. Even where consent is given, there may be unexpected, untoward, and discriminatory analyses and uses of data that should be the concern of law.

As large-scale data collection and its potential uses proliferate, consent-focused models of privacy will become less realistic. Nor will ex post enforcement of substantive limitations on data collection, analysis, and use be workable, given the rapidity of many firms' data analysis, the limitations of regulators, the range of harms now enabled by large-scale collection, analysis, and use of personal data, and the impenetrable trade secrecy shielding so much data processing from serious scrutiny.

Instead of these increasingly outmoded models, ex ante regulation of large-scale data collection, analysis, use, and sharing should become common in jurisdictions committed to enabling democratic governance of personal data. Defining permissible purposes for the licensure of large-scale personal data collection, analysis, use, and sharing will take up an increasing amount of time for regulators, while law enforcers will need new tools to ensure that regulations are actually being followed. While posing great challenges to governments, the articulation and enforcement of these specifications will prove an essential part of the foundation of a truly emancipatory data policy.

Key Recommendations for Interventions

1. Large data controllers which maintain health information should not be permitted to use that information, nor share it with others, without specific consent from the data subject or governmental authorization.
2. Policymakers should audit large data controllers in order to ensure compliance.
3. Data subjects should be empowered to specifically choose to opt in or, at least, opt out of marketing based on health inferences.
4. When there is a risk of health data being used for specifically stigmatizing purposes, governments are justified in banning the transfer and use of such inferences.
5. If the roles of doctors, administrators, and AI experts are to blur in future collection, analysis, and use of health data, policymakers should ensure that the ethical and fiduciary standards of medical professionals govern these roles.
6. As machines' ability to infer health states via human-computer interaction grows, new safeguards should assure such inferences are only used to assist data subjects, and not to discriminate against them.

NOTES

1. For excellent analysis of the role of trust in privacy regulation generally, see Waldman (2018).
2. To clarify terms here: 'medical inferences and predictions made with data taken either wholly, or in part, from non-health-sector entities' merits two specifications. First, 'medical inferences and predictions' are either inferences about the current (or predictions about the future) mental and physical state of an individual. Second, 'data taken either wholly, or in part, from non-health-sector entities' refers to any data set that includes data collected by entities that are not covered by specific health privacy laws. Such laws (such as the Health Insurance Portability and Accountability Act (HIPAA) and Health Information Technology for Economic

and Clinical Health Act (HITECH) in the United States, or relevant portions of the GDPR in Europe) set forth specific protections for data subjects given the sensitivity of health information. My concern in this piece is that, as AI and machine learning methods better develop inferences and predictions, a whole new class of sensitive data is being created that merits the type of protections specifically directed at the collection, analysis, sharing, sale, and use of data specifically targeted by law, but which escapes such coverage thanks to regulatory arbitrage or the poor fit of old legal approaches to new realities. Analysis of data within the health sector includes Pasquale (2013) and Mulder (2019).

3. This chapter addresses the policy implications of the proliferation of this type of health data. For a legal analysis of the current landscape, see Marks (2021).

4. Newman (2014).

5. Newman (2014).

6. A study gesturing in this direction already occurred with data from the search engine Bing. It identified persons who extensively searched for information about Parkinson's disease on Bing. White et al. (2018). Some in this group—which is far more likely to have Parkinson's than the population as a whole—tended to have certain tremors in their mouse movements. Such tremor data, and similar physical activities like speed of typing and mouse movements, are not the kind of performance we expect to be judged on. As more databases are combined and analyzed, other, even more subtle signals about our likely future health conditions will emerge. The more data about precursors to troubling fates is available, the better AI will get at predicting them.

7. Golden (2020). ('One of the tools the NBA will use with players is a "smart ring" that players will wear during their time at Disney World. The ring can measure body temperature, respiratory functions and heart rate, which are all things that can signal whether or not someone is sick. All players and essential staff members will be given the option to participate in health monitoring using the ring. The titanium rings . . . are capable of predicting COVID-19 symptoms up to three days in advance with 90% accuracy, according to the company.')

8. I loosely follow here a typology deployed by Jack Balkin (2016).

9. Peppet (2011).

10. Hull and Pasquale (2018).

11. Nissenbaum (2004).

12. McQuillan (2018). See also Suresh and Guttag (2020), identifying historical bias, representation bias, measurement bias, aggregation bias, and evaluation bias in algorithmic decision-making.

13. Dewandre (2015).

14. Of course, merely visiting a site about depression is not proof that a person is depressed. However, big data processes are not predicated on perfect accuracy for all persons they profile. They instead promote profitable categorizations over large groups of persons, increasing the value of estimated or statistical data. Even if a person is merely visiting a given site out of concern for a friend, they may well end up as 'regarded as' depressed, or 'depression-concerned'. Whereas categories of mental illness diagnosis by physicians fulfilled both an individually clinical and social need, these new categories like 'depression-concerned' elide the therapeutic to focus purely on commercial imperatives.

15. Pasquale (2015).
16. Gibbs (2015); Carman (2016); FTC (2016).
17. Peppet (2014).
18. Goldwater v. Ginzburg, 414 F.2d 324 (2d Cir. 1969).
19. Holmes (2020). For an example of a challenge to workplace personality tests as a prelude to discrimination against those with mental illness, see Weber and Dwoskin (2014).
20. Davis (2016); Caspi et al. (2016).
21. Ballantyne (2019).

REFERENCES

Balkin, Jack. 2016. 'Information Fiduciaries'. *University of California at Davis Law Review* 49: 1183.

Ballantyne, Neil. 2019. 'The Ethics and Politics of Human Service Technology: The Case of Predictive Risk Modeling in New Zealand's Child Protection System'. Draft. https://www.researchgate.net/publication/341319494_THE_ETHICS_AND_POLITICS_OF_HUMAN_SERVICE_TECHNOLOGY_THE_CASE_OF_PREDICTIVE_RISK_MODELING_IN_NEW_ZEALAND'S_CHILD_PROTECTION_SYSTEM.

Brown, Sherrod, US Senator for Ohio. 2020. 'Brown Releases New Proposal That Would Protect Consumers' Privacy from Bad Actors'.

Brynjolffson, Eric, and Andrew McAfee. 2018. *Machine, Platform, and Crowd*. New York: W. W. Norton.

Carman, Ashley. 2016. 'This Doll Recorded Kids' Conversations without Parental Consent'. *The Verge*, December 8. http://www.theverge.com/circuitbreaker/2016/12/8/13868826/my-friend-cayla-ique-intelligent-robot-privacy-policy.

Caspi, A., Houts, R., Belsky, D. et al. 2017. 'Childhood Forecasting of a Small Segment of the Population with Large Economic Burden'. *Nature Human Behaviour* 1(5). https://doi.org/10.1038/s41562-016-0005

Data Accountability and Transparency Act (DATA Act), S. 20719, 116th Cong. § 102(b)(4) (as proposed to the Senate, 2020).

Davis, Nicola. 2016. '"High Social Cost" Adults Can Be Predicted from as Young as Three, Says Study'. *The Guardian*, Medical Research, December 12. https://www.theguardian.com/science/2016/dec/12/high-social-cost-adults-can-be-identified-from-as-young-as-three-says-study.

Dewandre, Nicole. 2015. 'The Human Condition and the Black Box Society'. *Boundary2*, December 16. https://www.boundary2.org/2015/12/dewandre-on-pascal/.

Dulleck, Uwe, and Rudolf Kerschbamer. 2006. 'On Doctors, Mechanics and Computer Specialists—The Economics of Credence Goods'. *Journal of Economic Literature* 44(1): 5–42. https://ssrn.com/abstract=870788.

Feldman Barrett, Lisa, Ralph Adolphs, Stacy Marsella, Aleix M. Martinez, and Seth D. Pollak. 2019. 'Emotional Expressions Reconsidered: Challenges to Inferring Emotion from Human Facial Movements'. *Psychological Science in the Public Interest* 20(1): 1–68. https://journals.sagepub.com/stoken/default+domain/10.1177%2F1529100619832930-FREE/pdf.

FTC. 2016. 'Complaint of Electronic Privacy Information Center ("EPIC"), In re: Genesis Toys and Nuance Communications'.

Gibbs, Samuel. 2015. 'Privacy Fears over "Smart" Barbie That Can Listen to Your Kids'. *The Guardian*, March 13. https://www.theguardian.com/technology/2015/mar/13/smart-barbie-that-can-listen-to-your-kids-privacy-fears-mattel.

Golden, Jessica. 2020. 'Inside the NBA's Plan to Use Smart Technology and Big Data to Keep Players Safe from Coronavirus'. *CNBC*, June 17. https://www.cnbc.com/2020/06/17/nba-coronavirus-plan-smart-technology-to-keep-players-safe.html.

Goldwater v. Ginzburg, 414 F.2d 324 (2d Cir. 1969).

Holmes, Aaron. 2020. 'Airbnb Has Patented Software That Digs through Social Media to Root Out People Who Display "Narcissism or Psychopathy"'. *Business Insider*, January 6.

Hull, Gordon, and Frank Pasquale. 2018. 'Toward a Critical Theory of Corporate Wellness'. *BioSocieties* 13(1): 190–212.

de Jaegher, Kris, and Marc Jegers. 2001. 'The Physician-Patient Relationship as a Game of Strategic Information Transmission'. *Health Economics* 10(2001): 651–68.

Maring, Nicole. 2019. 'Facebook Using AI to Stop Insensitive Notifications after Someone Dies'. *Forbes*, April 10. https://www.forbes.com/sites/nicolemartin1/2019/04/10/facebook-using-ai-to-stop-insensitive-notifications-after-someone-dies/#37a0282d7074.

Marks, Mason. 2021. 'Emergent Medical Data: Health Information Inferred by Artificial Intelligence'. *U.C. Irvine Law Review* (forthcoming).

McQuillan, Dan. 2018. 'People's Councils for Ethical Machine Learning'. *Social Media + Society* 4(2): 1–10. https://doi.org/10.1177/2056305118768303.

Mulder, Trix. 2019. 'The Protection of Data Concerning Health in Europe'. *European Data Protection Law Review,* University of Groningen Faculty of Law Research Paper No.17/2020, Available at SSRN: https://ssrn.com/abstract=3506795.

Newman, Nathan. 2014. 'How Big Data Enables Economic Harm to Consumers, Especially to Low-Income and Other Vulnerable Sectors of the Population'. *Journal of Internet Law* 18: 11.

Nissenbaum, Helen. 2004. 'Privacy as Contextual Integrity'. *Washington Law Review* 79: 119.

Pasquale, Frank, 2013. 'Grand Bargains for Big Data'. *Maryland Law Review* 72: 682.

Pasquale, Frank. 2015. *The Black Box Society: The Secret Algorithms That Control Money and Information.* Cambridge, MA: Harvard University Press.

Pasquale, Frank. 2020. *New Laws of Robotics: Defending Human Expertise in the Age of AI,* Cambridge, MA: Harvard University Press.

Peppet, Scott R. 2011. 'Unraveling Privacy: The Personal Prospectus and the Threat of a Full-Disclosure Future'. *Northwestern University Law Review* 105: 1153.

Peppet, Scott R. 2014. 'Regulating the Internet of Things: First Steps toward Managing Discrimination, Privacy, Security, and Consent'. *Texas Law Review* 93: 85–176.

Suresh, Harini, and John V. Guttag, 'A Framework for Understanding Unintended Consequences of Machine Learning'. arXiv 1901.10002 (2020).

United States National Committee on Vital and Health Statistics. 2019. 'Report—Health Information Privacy Beyond HIPAA: A Framework for Use and Protection', June 18. https://ncvhs.hhs.gov/wp-content/uploads/2019/07/Report-Framework-for-Health-Information-Privacy.pdf.

Waldman, Ari Ezra. 2018. *Privacy as Trust*. Cambridge: Cambridge University Press.

Weber, Lauren, and Elizabeth Dwoskin. 2014. 'Are Workplace Personality Tests Fair? Growing Use of Tests Sparks Scrutiny amid Questions of Effectiveness and Workplace Discrimination'. *Wall Street Journal*, September 29. https://www.wsj.com/articles/are-workplace-personality-tests-fair-1412044257.

White, Ryen W., P. Murali Doraiswamy, and Eric Horvitz. 2018. 'Detecting Neurogenerative Disorders from Web Search Signals'. *NPJ Digital Medicine* 1: 9. doi:10.1038/s41746-018-0016-6.

PART IV

Protecting Democracy

11

Responding to Disinformation

*Ten Recommendations for Regulatory Action
and Forbearance*

CHRIS MARSDEN, IAN BROWN, AND MICHAEL VEALE ■

INTRODUCTION

This chapter elaborates on challenges and emerging best practices for state regulation of electoral disinformation throughout the electoral cycle. It is based on research for three studies during 2018–2020: into election cybersecurity for the Commonwealth (Brown et al. 2020); on the use of artificial intelligence (AI) to regulate disinformation for the European Parliament (Marsden and Meyer 2019a; Meyer et al. 2020); and for UNESCO, the United Nations body responsible for education (Kalina et al. 2020). The research covers more than half the world's nations, and substantially more than half that population, and in 2019 the two largest democratic elections in history: India's general election and the European Parliamentary elections.

We found the claim of Tambini (2018, 270) still holds true, that there is 'surprisingly little analysis of the messages themselves, or of the validity of some of the more worrying claims about new forms of propaganda'. We do not know, and cannot measure, the individual or combined effect of the digitally dominant platforms on elections. We here refer to dominance in both the competition law definition (including Facebook/WhatsApp/Instagram, Apple, Google/Alphabet, Amazon, Microsoft—the so-called GAFAM platforms) (Competitions and Markets Authority 2020, particularly Appendix W), and also more broadly the more vernacular notion of large platforms (including Twitter, TikTok, and others) (Barwise and Watkins 2018).

We use the EU High Level Group's definition of disinformation as 'false, inaccurate, or misleading information designed, presented and promoted to intentionally cause public harm or for profit' (High level Group on Fake News and

Online Disinformation 2018, 10), as distinguished from misinformation, which refers to unintentionally false or inaccurate information (Wardle and Derakhshan 2017).[1] We include accurate information presented with deceptive provenance or authorship—for example, emails stolen from Hillary Clinton's 2016 presidential campaign and the Democratic National Committee leaked via WikiLeaks and a fake hacker persona, 'Guccifer 2.0', which turned out to be a front for the Russian military intelligence agency GRU (Rid 2020, 377–86). The topic of disinformation became even more high-profile during the World Health Organization-diagnosed 'infodemic' relating to the COVID19 pandemic of 2020 (Silverman 2014), but we do not analyse that specific phenomenon here, since '[t]actics that work against dangerous health misinformation are likely to be less effective and more harmful when applied to political speech' (Kreps and Nyhan 2020).

Regulating digital dominance in electoral disinformation presents specific challenges in three very distinctive fields: election law, media law, and mass communications regulation, and targeted online advertising (including data protection law). International human rights law places strict limits on state actions restricting freedom of opinion and expression, summarized recently by UN Special Rapporteur David Kaye:

> In accordance with Article 19 (1) [of the International Covenant on Civil and Political Rights (ICCPR)], freedom of opinion may not be subject to any interference. Article 19 (2) robustly defines freedom of expression as one that is multidirectional ('seek, receive and impart'), unlimited by viewpoint ('information and ideas of all kinds'), without boundaries ('regardless of frontiers'), and open-ended in form ('or through any other media'). Article 19 (3) provides narrow grounds on which Governments may restrict the freedom of expression, requiring that any limitation be provided by law and be necessary for respect of the rights or reputations of others, or for the protection of national security or public order, or of public health or morals. That is, such limitations must meet the tests of necessity and proportionality and be aimed only towards a legitimate objective. (Special Rapporteur on the promotion and protection of the right to freedom of opinion and expression 2020 para. 11)

The ICCPR also states, 'all peoples have the right of self-determination' (Article 1) and the opportunity to 'take part in the conduct of public affairs, directly or through freely chosen representatives', and to 'vote and to be elected at genuine periodic elections . . . guaranteeing the free expression of the will of the electors' (Article 25 ICCPR).

Russian state interference in the 2016 US presidential elections, via false information shared on social media (Corera 2020 chap. 26; Special Counsel Robert S. Mueller III 2019), has been a high-profile global media story ever since it was first revealed. But these tactics go back at least to 2011, when Russia was accused of deliberately faking news of political corruption in Ukraine (Sanovich 2018), and since when Iran's national broadcaster has used fake accounts to post on Facebook about 'a wide range of themes, from perennial Iranian concerns, such as the country's enmity with Israel and Saudi Arabia, to more surprising and momentary topics, such as the Occupy Movement of 2012 and the Scottish independence referendum of 2014' (Nimmo et al. 2020, 1). The interference by foreign state actors in digital platforms continued through the 2020 US election season. Organized disinformation tactics were used pre-Internet throughout the Cold War by the Soviet Union, United States, and their allies, and date back to the Bolshevik Revolution itself (Rid 2020). There have been (fiercely disputed) allegations of similar tactics by other states, such as China in Taiwan's 2020 elections (Aspinwall 2020). They are increasingly used by domestic political actors during election campaigns—which can be difficult to differentiate from foreign state influence operations (Aspinwall 2020). Group messaging tools owned by digitally dominant platforms, such as WhatsApp and Instagram, have also been used to spread electoral disinformation in countries including Brazil and India (see, e.g., Machado et al. 2018).

Since 2015, targeting of voters with disinformation worldwide has significantly increased (Communications Security Establishment of Canada 2019)—although the impact on electoral outcomes is still unclear. As Karpf noted: 'Generating social media interactions is easy; mobilizing activists and persuading voters is hard' (Karpf 2019). For instance, much of the disinformation shared by Russia before and during the 2016 elections focussed on stoking general partisan tensions, including building group identities. Rid (2020) found that

> [t]he [St Petersburg Internet Research Agency's] most engaged content, perhaps counterintuitively, was not designed to polarize but to build communities. The IRA's overall outreach on Facebook achieved approximately 12 million shares in the United States before Election Day in 2016, just under 15 million 'likes,' and just over 1 million comments. The majority of these interactions, however, happened with benign crowd-pleasing posts, not with the most polarizing and vile content.

Political parties and campaigning organizations make heavy use of voter data and social media to reach voters via direct marketing and targeted adverts (Select Committee on Democracy and Digital Technologies 2020). There has been a corresponding drive in parties and campaigns for detailed information about voters beyond that in electoral rolls. In some cases, such data been obtained or processed illegally (see, e.g., Information Commissioner's Office 2020a, 2020b), or used in the context of high levels of microtargeting online, resulting in illegal electoral overspend (BBC 2019).

Claims of disinformation must be expected from partisans at all stages of the electoral lifecycle, from voter registration to voting processes, to training of poll workers and observers, the location and timing of polling station opening, to vote tallying, to announcement of winners, to accounting for party and third-party finances, and even to post-election evaluation and proposals for reform. The losing party may call the integrity of the electoral management body (EMB) into doubt,

and in sophisticated information campaigns, is met by similar calls from the win-
ning party, to 'even the score'. The EMB is thus traduced on all sides. Without a
robust independent media, public broadcast ethos, and political support, EMBs
struggle under this onslaught.

Implementing best practices against electoral disinformation will require action by EMBs, data protection agencies, communications and media regulators,
parliamentary authorities, and ministries of justice and equivalent (Brown et al.
2020). However, neither effective implementation nor a disinterested assessment
of best practice can be guaranteed. Electoral laws are—like much history—written
by the winners, often immediately after their victory. The UN Special Rapporteur
also noted: 'disinformation is an extraordinarily elusive concept to define in law,
susceptible to providing executive authorities with excessive discretion to determine what is disinformation, what is a mistake, what is truth' (Special Rapporteur
on the promotion and protection of the right to freedom of opinion and expression
2020 para. 42). Legal frameworks need to be updated as a response to disinformation challenges discovered during electoral processes, as well as encompassing
international best practice (European Commission 2020).

ELECTORAL CAMPAIGNS, INTERFERENCE, AND DISINFORMATION

Digital political campaigning began in the 1990s as the World Wide Web
popularized the Internet outside universities, with Canada and Singapore two
of the first countries to deploy broadband on a large scale to the general public.
High- and middle-income countries have since seen a huge growth in broadband Internet coverage, with the deployment of high-speed mobile networks
and smartphone ownership in the past decade further impacting political
and electoral information. Low-income countries have also seen significant
increases in national communications infrastructure, international connectivity, and mobile phone penetration (ITU Telecommunication Development
Bureau 2019).

For states, electoral disinformation is a complex multi-agency issue to regulate. Existing political coverage rules (for instance, requirements of impartiality and declarations of spending and origin of advertising) often only apply
to political parties and the use of broadcast media, not print (newspaper),
online or outdoor posters. Broadcast rules can apply to all broadcasting political coverage, with a 'fairness rule' and hate speech laws, with specific regulation of electoral periods for public service broadcasters. The sheer volume of
social media posts has led many governments to adopt rules (such as Codes
of Conduct; see Brown et al. 2009; Tambini et al. 2007) for the social media
platforms on which posts, videos, and other content is shared, rather than
quixotically pursuing the numerous and often anonymous posters of disinformation themselves.

The increase in advertising and content production both inside and outside electoral periods in online media is capable of causing disruption to existing electoral campaign rules, with so-called troll factories producing large volumes of often distorted or untrue posts which cannot be easily traced to any single source in domestic politics, and state actors even using unwitting local activists to promote them (Corera 2020; Special Counsel Robert S. Mueller III 2019). However, the impact of the notorious St. Petersburg 'Internet Research Agency' (IRA) may have been overstated, according to Rid (2020):

> It is unlikely that the trolls convinced many, if any, American voters to change their minds. . . . On Twitter, the IRA's impact practically vanished in the staggering number of election-related tweets. . . . The St. Petersburg troll den generated less than 0.05 percent of all election-related posts. The IRA, according to the data released by Twitter, boosted candidate Donald Trump's retweet count with only 860 direct retweets over the entire campaign.

Disinformation consumption in the United States (where most large-scale studies have so far taken place) appears to vary by political viewpoint, with one study finding '63% of all page-level traffic to untrustworthy websites observed in our data during the study period came from the 20% of news consumers with the most conservative information diets' (Guess et al. 2020). A second study examining American Twitter users in 2016 concluded: 'Only 1% of individuals accounted for 80% of fake news source exposures, and 0.1% accounted for nearly 80% of fake news sources shared. Individuals most likely to engage with fake news sources were conservative leaning, older, and highly engaged with political news' (Grinberg et al. 2019). Benkler (2019) summarized his research findings: 'Even where we did find traces of Russian origins in campaigns that did make it into the mainstream, the propaganda pipeline ran through Infowars, Drudge, and Fox News. That is, the primary vectors of influence were willing amplification of the information operations by the mainstays of the domestic American outrage industry'. He concluded: 'The crisis of democratic societies may be helped along by disinformation and propaganda, and certainly is fanned and harnessed by political opportunists, but it is fuelled by a decades-long extractive and distorted political economy'.

Given this ideological distribution, regulatory responses to disinformation have unsurprisingly became an intensely partisan affair in the United States, with the head of Facebook's Washington, DC, office reportedly telling colleagues: 'We can't remove all [false news] because it will disproportionately affect conservatives' (Timberg 2020). Another former Facebook employee (and current member of the UK legislature) has written that 'suppression of speech that is predominantly being made by one party in a contested space is an unavoidably partisan action', which social media companies are understandably eager to avoid (Allan 2020). But much of the short-term impact of

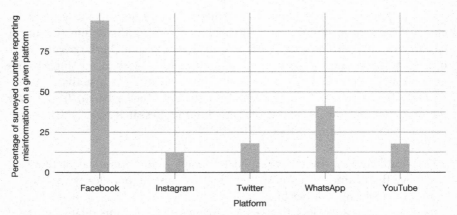

Figure 11.1 Reported cases of misinformation on social media platforms in surveyed Commonwealth countries.

disinformation comes when it is repeated by traditional media outlets and politicians, 'who are the primary sources of political news and commentary' (Weintraub 2020).

One broad challenge to regulating the intersection of modern campaigning, electoral integrity, and disinformation is the varying abilities of EMBs to monitor the online and platform environment, as 'there are many unfounded claims and opportunities for misinformation about the process of our elections' (Department of Homeland Security 2020). All the Commonwealth countries responding to our survey in mid-2019 have experienced the dissemination of misinformation in relation to their elections processes. Figure 11.1 shows a breakdown of the amount of reported cases per social media platform, showing the dominance of the Facebook properties in permissive misinformation.

The straightforward EMB response for high-profile false information relating to elections is to rapidly publicize corrections, using EMB websites and social media channels, as well as interviews on broadcast media and briefings for journalists. EMBs can also report clear instances of disinformation relating to elections— such as false information about the polling date or location of polling stations—to social media platforms, which will remove it where it breaches their terms and conditions.

Less clear-cut examples of electoral disinformation can be much more controversial to deal with. US President Donald Trump reacted furiously (Figure 11.2) when Twitter added a fact-checking link to his tweet claiming (with no evidence) that greater use of postal votes during the Covid-19 pandemic would lead to higher levels of electoral fraud: '@Twitter is now interfering in the 2020 Presidential Election'.[2] The tweets also contained a specific falsehood: that California was sending postal ballots to all residents 'no matter who they are or how they got there' (in reality, only to registered voters):

Donald J. Trump @realDonaldTrump · May 26
There is NO WAY (ZERO!) that Mail-In Ballots will be anything less than substantially fraudulent. Mail boxes will be robbed, ballots will be forged & even illegally printed out & fraudulently signed. The Governor of California is sending Ballots to millions of people, anyone.....
Get the facts about mail-in ballots
44.4K
39K
133.9K
Donald J. Trump @realDonaldTrump · May 26
....living in the state, no matter who they are or how they got there, will get one. That will be followed up with professionals telling all of these people, many of whom have never even thought of voting before, how, and for whom, to vote. This will be a Rigged Election. No way!
Get the facts about mail-in ballots
15.6K
21.7K
81.1K

Figure 11.2 President's election Twitter: mail-in ballots

By producing its own 'fact-check' (which heavily quoted journalists' tweets), rather than relying on independent third-party fact-checkers citing more in-depth analysis (as Facebook policy held, while exempting posts from politicians), Twitter and its staff became targets for highly critical responses from President Trump and his supporters. This continued when a Trump tweet was labelled by Twitter as containing 'manipulated media' for containing video falsely edited to look as if it had been broadcast by CNN (Figure 11.3):

Donald J. Trump @realDonaldTrump · 6h
BREAKING NEWS
TERRIFIED TODLER RUNS FROM RACIST BABY
CNN
1:00 10.6M views
Manipulated media
60.2K
142.4K
295.6K

Figure 11.3 President's election Twitter: false news
Source: Conger, Kate. 2020. 'Twitter Labels Trump Tweet about "Racist Baby" as Manipulated Media'. *New York Times*.

Trump also had his tweets doubting the integrity of the vote count in the 2020 presidential election flagged by Twitter (Figure 11.4), despite which it attracted over a million 'Likes':

Donald J. Trump ✔
@realDonaldTrump

I WON THIS ELECTION, BY A LOT!

⚠ Official sources may not have called the race when this was Tweeted

3:36 pm · 7 Nov 2020 · Twitter for iPhone

192.4K Retweets   **693.6K** Quote Tweets   **1.1M** Likes

Figure 11.4 President's election Twitter: election integrity

More broadly than disputed tweets or social media in a hotly disputed election, Edelman explained that: 'political truth is a difficult thing to pin down, because politics is fundamentally about convincing other people to accept your interpretation of reality' (Edelman 2020). Candidates are likely to always challenge the media's framing of news as the first rough draft of history.

An emerging legal battleground in this area is whether there should be obligations on social media firms to carry certain speech. In Poland, a recent bill published by the Ministry of Justice would lead to moderation decisions by platforms being overseen by a 'Freedom of Speech Council'. However the appointment and oversight processes of this council do not guarantee independence and lend themselves to being populated by the ruling party of the day, and while its decisions can be appealed, they can only be appealed to administrative courts who do not typically deal with, or understand, the complex area of governing freedom of expression (Panoptkyon Foundation 2021). Over the pond, in a recent opinion, US Supreme Court Justice Clarence Thomas has suggested that social media firms should have common carry obligations and restricted First Amendment rights, indicating the potential for future flashpoints of this type there too.[3]

INTERNET 'SWITCH-OFF' AND DISINFORMATION LAWS

Internet shutdowns (general removal of transit so that all services are restricted by telecoms companies on order of the government) have been resorted to by governments in the immediate election and vote counting period (see, e.g., RSF 2019). There were 213 documented incidents of full and partial closure in 2019 alone (Access Now 2020). The African Commission on Human and Peoples' Rights in 2016 noted 'the emerging practice of State Parties of interrupting or limiting access to telecommunications services such as the Internet, social media and messaging services, increasingly during elections' (African Commission on Human and Peoples' Rights 2016). Fuller reported: '[i]n Zimbabwe, following sporadic internet blackouts in the midst of civilian protests in January 2019, the country's High Court issued a ruling in which it declared the shutdown illegal and ordered telecom operators to restore access' (Fuller 2019). Purdon et al. (2015) found 'Pakistan has often instructed telecommunication operators to suspend mobile and/or Internet networks where intelligence indicates a threat to national security'.

General Internet shutdowns are contrary to international standards. The UN Human Rights Council (2016) stated that it

> condemns unequivocally measures to intentionally prevent or disrupt access to or dissemination of information online in violation of international human rights law and calls on all States to refrain from and cease such measures.

A 2015 Joint Declaration by global and regional human rights bodies stated Internet 'kill switches' can never be justified under international human rights law, even in times of conflict (United Nations (UN) Special Rapporteur on Freedom of Opinion and Expression et al. 2015 para. 4(c)).

Colonial-era criminal defamation laws were used in the period before the Commonwealth in response to claimed hate speech and to prevent opposition to colonial government. These have continued in many Commonwealth jurisdictions. However, in 2019, several countries passed antidisinformation and hate speech laws for online media, extending controls into the Internet environment. Singapore in May 2019 passed the Protection from Online Falsehoods and Manipulation Act 2019 (POFMA). It gives ministers powers to require online actors to remove disinformation, and regulators to stop access to Internet providers in Singapore that continue to carry such messages. Part 2 of POFMA criminalizes the communication of false statements of fact in Singapore in certain circumstances, and acts which enable or facilitate the communication. Section 7 provides that a person must not do any act in or outside Singapore in order to communicate in Singapore a statement knowing or having reason to believe that it is a false statement of fact that may affect political stability. Individuals who contravene section 7(1) face a fine of up to $50,000 and/or imprisonment for up to 5 years. Organizations face a fine of up to $500,000. The punishment is enhanced if an unauthentic online account or a bot is used to communicate the statement and for the purpose of accelerating the communication. Under Part 3, 'the Minister may direct the Infocomm Media Development Authority of Singapore (IMDA) to order an internet access service provider (ISP) to take reasonable steps to disable local access to the online location where the false statement of fact is communicated' (Chng 2019).

In the context of recent laws, it is important to consider their impacts in a framework of freedom of expression and human rights more generally. A joint declaration from the freedom of expression rapporteurs of several intergovernmental organizations, in collaboration with international civil society groups, called for the abolition of criminal defamation laws and the wholesale avoidance of general prohibitions on disinformation.[4] The UN Human Rights Committee, established by the International Covenant on Civil and Political Rights, emphasizes in General Comment No. 34 that restrictions on speech online must be strictly necessary and proportionate to achieve a legitimate purpose. The 2017 Joint Declaration by global and regional human rights bodies notes the existence of attempts by some governments to suppress dissent and to control public communications through such measures as:

- repressive rules regarding the establishment and operation of media outlets and/or websites;
- interference in the operations of public and private media outlets, including by denying accreditation to their journalists and politically motivated prosecutions of journalists;
- unduly restrictive laws on what content may not be disseminated;
- the arbitrary imposition of states of emergency;
- technical controls over digital technologies such as blocking, filtering, jamming and closing down digital spaces; and
- efforts to 'privatise' control measures by pressuring intermediaries to take action to restrict content. (UN Special Rapporteur on Freedom of Opinion and Expression et al. 2017)

Responses that seek to generally censor the Internet or even shut it down during elections may be disproportionate as well as illegal under international law. The Commonwealth, for example, has already concluded that direct government regulation is seen as censorship, and is not the best practice to respond to potential social media disinformation (Commonwealth Electoral Network 2016, 2). Suspending social media platforms during elections can potentially impact large numbers of voters, whose wider communication could be jeopardized by such a restriction (for instance, suspending WhatsApp or Skype, which are vital communications tools for users).

More proportional practices in democratic elections are ensuring that EMBs can liaise with social media platforms to remove and counter deliberate disinformation regarding electoral registration and voting, and ensuring that claims about disinformation that form hate speech, defamation, or fraud are promptly dealt with by the independent judiciary. Political name-calling can be classified by political opponents as disinformation or hate speech, which is one reason for the continued role of the independent judiciary as the arbiter of such decisions.

REGULATING THE USE OF SOCIAL MEDIA FOR ELECTORAL DISINFORMATION

We now detail state responses to those—typically GAFAM—self-regulatory processes for disseminating and/or controlling disinformation that we explained in the previous section. Many proposed approaches to tackling disinformation issues would extend broadcast rules to non-broadcast content, whether text-based or in any case at the user's individual choice. Yet care must be taken here, as this would, in all likelihood, increase the concentration of online communication in the hands of the largest platforms that can employ economies of scale in deploying proprietary filters to remove harmful content.

Digitally dominant platforms are essential actors in regulation of disinformation (GAFAM is the acronym used to denote Google/Apple/Facebook/Amazon/Microsoft-owned platforms and other entities). Google, Facebook ,and Twitter have deployed AI tools at large scale to combat disinformation, claiming this is the only cost-effective response to the billions of messages passed across their platforms daily (Marsden and Meyer 2019a)—particularly when their content moderation staff cannot easily work remotely during the 2020 Covid-19 pandemic, due to the general insecurity of home offices. Opinions are divided over whether regulating such platforms is a legitimate point of intervention, in particular because this could lead to two types of content moderation 'arms race':

- in reporting disinformation, where trolls are as likely to overwhelm well-meaning citizens when each reports against the other;
- in coding debates, so that fact checkers and other self-regulatory enforcers cannot control the amount of disinformation as it emerges in images and videos as well as text.

Examples of these content moderation arms races from the Internet's regulatory history include the attempts to prevent child abuse image and terrorist video distribution, as well as unauthorized sharing of copyrighted files. In each case, the use of technologies (such as comparing hash values) in theory permitted removal before publication by the platforms deploying the technology, specifically YouTube and Facebook. In practice, the proliferation of content was restricted but by no means prevented by such technological intervention.

The use of AI and machine learning to detect content has seen success in some areas, but struggles heavily in areas which are as value-laden, subjective, and complex as disinformation (Marsden and Meyer 2019b). Social media platforms have claimed that AI will be able to spot disinformation. It is broadly the case that disinformation cannot be effectively automatically detected by new techniques such as machine learning, as it is highly context-specific, and there is no clear canonical reality against which to judge.

Automated filtering is a heavy-handed tool, and will result in a large number of 'false positives', where bona fide statements are confused with 'fake news'. These open up new cybersecurity threats, as machine learning systems are capable of being fooled and 'poisoned', for example by political actors wishing to suppress the speech of specific opponents' voices (Biggio and Roli 2018).

Canada has focussed on traceability of political advertising, to ensure transparency in the advertising spend by major parties and to prevent violations of campaign finance laws by 'shadow' advertising by groups closely associated with political causes or parties. In Canada in 2019, 'online platforms that accept political advertising in Canada will be required to show more transparency than they have in the past' (Thompson 2019). While Facebook and Twitter complied with these rules, Google chose instead to prohibit Canadian political advertising (Boutilier 2019).

The most detailed state regulation of political advertising on social media platforms found in our survey was in India, where political parties must get approval for ads from a committee organized by the EMB. The committee provides a QR code that must be included in an approved ad, and which is checked by online platforms. The committee checks the ad content, and that the publisher is certified, and also logs the price paid for the ad, which is made publicly available.

Politicians must follow a code of conduct, and the EMB maintains a public website listing actions taken against violators. A 150-person Electronic Media Monitoring Committee monitors media articles during elections, and transmit specific articles to districts to check. An EMB app also allows citizens to report code of conduct violations, with a photo and location; districts must deal with these reports within 100 minutes. Platforms are required to take down illegal content notified to them within 15 minutes.

The Election Commission of India (ECI) convened a meeting with representatives of social media platforms and the Internet and Mobile Association of India (IAMAI) preceding the May 2019 general elections. Social media platforms submitted a 'Voluntary Code of Ethics for the 2019 General Election' (Press Information Bureau 2019). Platforms voluntarily undertook to create a dedicated reporting mechanism for the ECI, create fast response teams to take action on reported violations, and facilitate political advertisement transparency. The mechanism allows ECI to notify platforms of violations under s. 126, Representation of the People Act 1951. In the event of conflict between the Voluntary Code of Ethics and the legal framework, the latter prevails. Platforms must take down reported content within three hours, during the two-day non-campaigning 'silence period' before polling. Platforms provide reports to IAMAI and ECI on their actions.

Disinformation during elections in South Africa is regulated by Section 89(2) (c) of the Electoral Act and Item 9(1)(b) of the Electoral Code of Conduct, which prohibits a false statement of fact, and not the expression of comments and ideas. These issues were tested in the Constitutional Court in a case concerning a text message sent by a political party to 1.5 million citizens in 2014, concerning allegations of corruption about then-President Zuma.[5] The text was found to be permitted electoral communication, and not prohibited by Section 89(2). There is also a defamation offence, which has led to recent jurisprudence requiring removal of false online content.[6]

South Africa's EMB noted in 2016 the growth of online disinformation. The Directorate of Electoral Offences was established ahead of the 2016 Municipal Elections to investigate alleged breaches of the Code of Conduct and prohibited conduct. To help distinguish between official and fake adverts, political parties contesting the May 2019 elections were asked to upload all official advertising material used by the party to an online political advert repository (http://www.padre.org. za). Complaints relating to alleged breaches of the Code of Conduct must be submitted to the Electoral Court or the Directorate for Electoral Offences. In August 2019, the number of complaints and the success rate in examination were not evaluated. In addition, the Electoral Commission launched an innovative online reporting platform for citizens to report instances of alleged digital disinformation, the 411 Campaign (Electoral Commission of South Africa n.d.). '411' is Internet slang in southern Africa for disinformation. Developed in conjunction with Media Monitoring South Africa, the platform provided for the online submission and tracking of complaints relating to disinformation encountered on social media platforms, hosted on www.real411.org. The digital platform was intended for complaints related only to social media and not to replace existing channels and processes for investigating alleged breaches of the Code of Conduct. 156 complaints were logged by election day, to be considered by a panel of relevant experts including those with expertise in media law and social and digital media.[7] They will make recommendations for possible further action, which could include:

- Referring the matter for criminal or civil legal action;
- Requesting social media platforms to remove the offensive material;
- Issuing media statements to alert the public and correct the disinformation.

The UN Special Rapporteur has specifically argued that:

a. General prohibitions on the dissemination of information based on vague and ambiguous ideas, including 'false news' or 'non-objective information', are incompatible with international standards for restrictions on freedom of expression, and should be abolished.
b. Criminal defamation laws are unduly restrictive and should be abolished. Civil law rules on liability for false and defamatory statements are legitimate only if defendants are given a full opportunity and fail to prove the truth of those statements and also benefit from other defences, such as fair comment.
c. State actors should not make, sponsor, encourage or further disseminate statements which they know or reasonably should know to be false (disinformation) or which demonstrate a reckless disregard for verifiable information (propaganda).
d. State actors should, in accordance with their domestic and international legal obligations and their public duties, take care to ensure that they disseminate reliable and trustworthy information, including about matters of public interest, such as the economy, public health, security and the environment. (UN Special Rapporteur on Freedom of Opinion and Expression et al. 2017)

There is scope for standardizing (the basics of) notice and appeal procedures and reporting, and creating a self-regulatory multi-stakeholder body, such as the UN Special Rapporteur's suggested 'social media council' (Special Rapporteur on the promotion and protection of the right to freedom of opinion and expression 2018 paras 58, 59, 63, 72). Such a multi-stakeholder body could, on the one hand, have competence to deal with industry-wide appeals and, on the other hand, work towards a better understanding and minimization of the effects of AI on freedom of expression and media pluralism.

ONLINE BEHAVIOURAL ADVERTISING AND DISINFORMATION

Targeted online behavioural advertising (OBA)—shown to Internet users based on profiles of their previous online and increasingly offline behaviour and characteristics—may use both legitimate and illegally obtained data sources. Disinformation threats may seek to suppress or increase voter motivation in specific targeted segments of the population by geography or expressed political motivation—so-called microtargeting to 'fire up the base' (motivate) or to suppress voter turnout via demotivational messages. The algorithms used to select which adverts are shown to social media users often promote adverts that users are more likely to click on—favouring emotional and partisan appeals even at a lower bidding price by advertisers.[8]

The European Union and the major global social media platforms have co-operated to create a new Code of Conduct to combat electoral disinformation via this route. The European Union was the first multilateral organization to develop a response to disinformation, investing very substantially in research and then regulation in the period since 2014 (Meyer et al. 2020). The EU-orchestrated multi-stakeholder forum industry self-regulatory 'Code of Practice on Online Disinformation' was intended to demonstrate the voluntary commitments of the major social media platforms to achieve greater transparency in political advertising, prior to the European Parliament elections of May 2019 (European Commission 2018). This was the world's second-largest democratic election after India's 2019 parliamentary election.

The Code of Practice includes commitments relating to scrutiny of ad placements, political and 'issue-based' advertising, integrity of services, empowering users, and empowering the research community. Part of the industry response to the Code of Practice concerned rectifying the limited access platforms provide to political advertisements using their systems. In April 2021, the European Union committed to a revision of the Code, demonstrating the extent to which it is heavily guided and sponsored self-regulation: '[our] assessment found: inconsistences in application; gaps in the scope; lack of common definitions; lack of key indicators and independent oversight. This initiative issues guidance on how to better apply the code' (European Commission 2021). Explicitly paid for political advertisements are increasingly placed in online 'ad archives', such as those provided by Facebook and by Google (Facebook n.d.; Google n.d.). The main intention of these systems is to allow civil society actors and regulators to identify and audit the political advertising spend by actors deemed political by the platform. Users themselves can access such an archive, but the information in the archive is not currently presented to them when, for example, they browse a site and view an ad.

The Mozilla Foundation has proposed, along with over seventy researchers, standards for effective political advertising archives that should be enforced upon platforms (Mozilla 2017). Their recommendations include that the ad archive should be comprehensive, including 'direct electioneering content, candidates or holders of political office, matters of legislation or decisions of a court, functions of government'. They also argue that the ad archive should 'provide information about targeting criteria and information about impressions, content, payment, and microtargeting features' and 'support research, by allowing bulk access and download and persistent, well-documented meta-data . . . both up-to-date and historical data'. The advertising archive should be accessible to the public. A consistent challenge is ensuring that companies deliver workable advertising archives, such as those in line with the above guidelines. In the European Union, Facebook's attempt to create such a system has been described as 'inadequate', pointing to challenges in enforcement more broadly (Mozilla 2019).

NATO has reported the continued need for EMB and wider government readiness against disinformation threats (NATO StratCom COE 2018). In a cybersecurity context, it points to the large and changing 'scale of the black-market infrastructure for developing and maintaining social metric manipulation software, generating fictitious accounts, and providing mobile proxies and solutions for SMS activation' (NATO StratCom COE 2019, 16). These systems rely on security loopholes, data breaches, and the use of bots at scale in order to influence disinformation on a large scale.

The European Commission, announcing its European Democracy Action Plan in December 2020, stated it: "will steer efforts to overhaul the Code of Practice on Disinformation into a co-regulatory framework of obligations and accountability of online platforms, in line with the upcoming Digital Services Act. To that end, the Commission will issue guidance to enhance the Code of Practice in spring 2021 and set up a more robust framework for monitoring its implementation." (European Commission, 2020, point 3)

DISINFORMATION AND DATA PROTECTION
POLITICAL EXEMPTIONS

Privacy and data protection legislation is a key component of electoral integrity in the complex ecosystem of behavioural advertising data sharing and brokerage that has developed over the last two decades. Significant damage to perceived electoral integrity can be done if a party, campaign, or candidate misuses data to manipulate voters via targeted disinformation. The European-style data protection laws implemented in at least 142 countries usually require a regulator which is truly independent from government, and which has powers and resources effective for and commensurate with its role (Greenleaf and Cottier 2020).

Data protection laws commonly provide higher protection for 'sensitive' or 'special category' data commonly used in electoral processes, such as *data revealing political opinions or affiliations.*[9] Such restrictions tend to have exemptions for electoral processes, but these exemptions must be balanced against the need for high protection, risk assessment, and scrutiny. A report commissioned by the UK data protection regulator concluded:

> To the extent that contemporary elections are 'data-driven', their worst effects have been apparent in countries whose data protection laws do not cover political parties. In most democratic countries where parties are covered by data protection law, and have been for decades, there is little evidence that these restrictions have impeded their ability to perform their basic

democratic roles of political mobilization, elite recruitment and policy development. (Bennett and Oduro Marfo 2019)

Depending on the local data protection or privacy regime, some organizations involved in elections may be allowed to process these specific categories of data with lower restrictions than other actors, or even be out of scope of the law entirely. In the United Kingdom, for example, political parties are bound by the requirements of the Data Protection Act 2018, although registered parties benefit from being able to process data on political opinions without relying on consent (with voters allowed to opt out in writing from processing by specific parties and campaigns).[10] A similar framework can be seen in South Africa's Protection of Personal Information Act 2013.[11] South Africa's Electoral Commission is in discussions with the national Information Commissioner about protection of electoral data, with public concerns expressed about commercial marketers and debt collectors accessing voter records. Political parties want access to the full voter list to verify voters.

In Malta, the Office of the Data Protection Commissioner has stated that political parties must get consent before processing political opinions (Pace 2018). In Australia, political parties are not considered as organisations for the purposes of privacy law,[12] and other organizations undertaking political activities, such as parties' (sub-)contractors and volunteers, are also exempted.[13] In Canada, the political parties 'fall between the cracks' of the national privacy regime (Bennett and Bayley 2012), as they are not governmental institutions for the purposes of public sector privacy law,[14] and are exempted from federal private sector privacy legislation by virtue of not meeting the definition of 'federal work, undertaking or business'.[15] Some issues around the use of the electoral roll are regulated by electoral law, but the application and scope of this is inconsistent and patchy (Bennett and Bayley 2012).

In addition to data protection law, many countries have related provisions that focus on unsolicited and direct marketing. These fall in different types of law depending on the jurisdiction. In the Commonwealth's EU members (Cyprus and Malta and, until/unless it modifies its EU-based law, the United Kingdom), these follow the e-Privacy Directive,[16] which in large part focusses on implementing the fundamental right to confidentiality of communication (Zuiderveen Borgesius and Steenbruggen 2019). In Canada, this issue became controversial with the illegal impersonation of the EMB, in the 2011 elections, by a campaigner for a major party using automated calling (Brown et al. 2020, 31–32).

While much of the EU policy debate relating to platform regulation takes place in narrow competition economics terms, it could have a much broader impact on European societies, given the increasing use of major Internet platforms as essential 'social infrastructure'—used by families to share news and photos; schools to communicate with parents; sports teams to arrange games; politicians to communicate with constituents; campaign groups to organize protests; and many other aspects of modern-day life (Brown and Marsden 2013). It is no longer easy for many individuals to 'opt out' of using such platforms.

Many issues around elections, such as the use of data on social media platforms or in the advertising technology domain, span borders and jurisdictions. They cannot be tackled on the domestic level alone. Regulators must therefore be part of global and regional groupings to share information and build a coherent strategy for international challenges.

TEN RECOMMENDATIONS FOR FURTHER REGULATORY ACTION AND FORBEARANCE

The starting point for democratic governments in dealing with electoral disinformation must always be the importance of freedom of expression, especially for political speech, and compliance with international human rights law. Special rapporteurs of the United Nations (UN), Organization for Security and Co-operation in Europe (OSCE), and Organization of American States(OAS) highlighted in a joint statement in 2020 'the essential role that freedom of expression and information, free, independent and diverse media and a free and accessible Internet play in ensuring free and fair elections, including referenda, in particular by informing the public about parties and candidates and their platforms'. They also expressed their alarm at 'the misuse of social media by both state and private actors to subvert election processes, including through various forms of inauthentic behaviour and the use of "computational propaganda"' (UN Special Rapporteur on Freedom of Opinion and Expression et al. 2020).

At this relatively early stage of large-scale use of online tools of political persuasion, there is significant uncertainty about the overall impact of disinformation on election outcomes. Karpf notes: 'There is no evidence that psychographic targeting actually works at the scale of the American electorate, and there is also no evidence that Cambridge Analytica in fact deployed psychographic models while working for the Trump campaign. The company clearly broke Facebook's terms of service in acquiring its massive Facebook dataset. But it is not clear that the massive dataset made much of a difference' (Karpf 2019). Rid (2020) concluded:

> On Twitter, the IRA's impact practically vanished in the staggering number of election-related tweets. Approximately 1 billion tweets related to the campaigns were posted during the fifteen months leading up to the election. The St. Petersburg troll den generated less than 0.05% of all election-related posts. The IRA, according to the data released by Twitter, boosted candidate Donald Trump's retweet count with only 860 direct retweets over the entire campaign.

Researchers will need much greater access to data held by social media platforms to assess (with any level of confidence) the impact of disinformation on users' political opinions, activities, and voting processes, including failure to vote.

Given human rights imperatives, and uncertainties about the overall effect of electoral disinformation, policymakers must be extremely cautious in legislative and other responses, recognising also the unpredictable outcomes of regulation on other areas of freedom of expression, from broadcasting and newspaper publishing, to advertising regulation, and to disinformation in less overtly political arenas, including (topically in 2020) public health pandemics. Our ten recommendations for policymakers take account of these imperatives and uncertainties:

1. Electoral management boards (EMBs) should not request the operation of Internet shutdowns during election periods, or at any other point not objectively assessed a national emergency and sanctioned by a superior court. Such an injunction may be achieved with great speed, and the need for procedural legitimacy before such an extreme response is in our view essential.
2. Governments should avoid Internet shutdowns as a response to disinformation concerns, while ensuring false announcements are responded to where defamatory, fraudulent, or unjustifiably casting doubt on official EMB results and guidance. We acknowledge that heads of state may seek faster executive redress, but also that such action may not appear disinterested or legitimate prior to a court decision.
3. Disinformation is best tackled by governments through media pluralism and literacy initiatives, as these allow diversity of expression and choice. Governments should encourage social media platforms to consider the use of source transparency indicators, and highlighting and deprioritization of disinformation identified by independent fact-checkers. Users need to be given the opportunity to understand how their search results or social media feeds are built, and edit their search results/feeds where desirable.
4. Freedom of expression as a fundamental right should be protected from automated private censorship by dominant social media platforms, and thus disinformation should be regulated by legislation with independent appeal to courts of law. Options to ensure independent appeal and audit of platforms' regulation of their users should be introduced. When technical intermediaries need to moderate content and accounts, detailed and transparent policies, notice and appeal procedures, and regular reports are crucial (see, further, Meyer et al. 2020).
5. Governments should consider legislating to ensure that platforms and advertising networks are obliged to make political ads public, in line with best practices in the area which allow public research and scrutiny. They should also consider requiring major platforms to develop privacy-protective mechanisms by which independent researchers can investigate the societal impact of disinformation (and other phenomena).
6. Governments may be aided by a template agreement with social media companies for memoranda of understanding relating to disinformation, potentially based on the EU Code of Practice or India's example; and should make public such agreements.

7. Governments should strengthen reporting and publication of political spending online as well as offline, with independent electoral authorities monitoring all donations and uses of 'dark money' to try to influence campaigns.

8. Governments should ensure privacy and data protection laws are in place to protect voter data wherever it is held, including in the private sector. These laws should allow political parties and candidates to engage with voters; but any exemptions that affect voters' trust or data protection and security should be carefully limited. States without a data protection or privacy law should look to establish one in line with existing international standards and institutional practices.

9. Personal data and privacy issues around elections should be overseen by a regulator which is truly independent from government, and which has powers and resources effective for and commensurate with its role.

10. Governments should support accurate, independent identification and attribution of disinformation, working with neutral fact-checking organizations.

Our first three recommendations may be seen as an expression of the obvious, but media literacy and preventing Internet switch-offs are not yet accepted best practices in all parts of the world. The UN/OSCE/OAS special rapporteurs have expressed concern that 'many States are passing laws which . . . unduly limit freedom of expression, expand State control over the media, restrict Internet freedom and/or further the ability of various actors to collect personal data'. They deplore 'restrictions on the ability of the public to access the Internet, including complete or partial shutdowns, which seriously limit the ability of media, parties, candidates and others to communicate with the public, as well as the ability of members of the public to access information' (United Nations (UN) Special Rapporteur on Freedom of Opinion and Expression et al. 2020, 2).

Note the reference to false announcements, far too common a claim on results day and thereafter in many nations. Both could be abused by governments and candidates lacking integrity, as seen in the Trump tweet. The UN/OSCE/OAS special rapporteurs recommend 'States should adopt appropriately clear and proportionate laws that prohibit the dissemination of statements which are specifically designed to obstruct individuals' right to vote, such as by intentionally spreading incorrect information about where or when to vote' (United Nations (UN) Special Rapporteur on Freedom of Opinion and Expression et al. 2020, para. 1(c)(ii)).

Recommendation 5 has the regulatory aim of forcing social media platforms to display sources of all advertising, as third-party advertising may influence voters significantly even on single issues that later define their voting behaviour (as in the 2018 Irish abortion referendum), while recommendation 7 will ensure further transparency of the funders of political advertising. The UN/OSCE/OAS special rapporteurs have stressed 'the need for robust rules and systems requiring transparency of parties and candidates in relation to media spending on elections' (United Nations (UN) Special Rapporteur on Freedom of Opinion and Expression et al. 2020, 2).

Recommendation 10 emphasizes the importance of independent assessment of the accuracy or otherwise of alleged disinformation, and identification of its origins. Claims and counterclaims about the accuracy of political statements can quickly become highly partisan in electoral contents, while the secrecy of (some) state information operations can make them difficult to identify. An inaccurate claim of disinformation by Taiwan's government in 2019 'gave the [opposition] KMT and its supporters the opportunity to question the [governing] DPP's credibility when it discusses Beijing's desire to meddle in Taiwanese politics'. The chair of Taiwan's National Communications Commission (NCC) resigned in April 2019, complaining: 'If there is any website, any TV station they report to be untrue or disinformation, [the governing party] want the NCC to punish them or block the website. For me, it is impossible to do that. That is not the responsibility of the NCC' (Aspinwall 2020).

Recommendation 5 also emphasizes the need for much better-quality data— currently held by the platforms—to be available to independent researchers, so that societies can gain a deeper understanding of how disinformation affects democracy, and what would therefore be proportionate responses. As Rid states: 'At-scale disinformation campaigns are attacks against a liberal epistemic order, or a political system that places its trust in essential custodians of factual authority'. Benkler concludes: 'No specific electoral outcome better serves Russia's standard propaganda agenda—disorientation and loss of trust in institutions generally—than the generalization of disorientation and de-legitimation of institutions represented by the present pitch of the debate over election interference' (Benkler 2019). This delegitimation effect has already been seen in Taiwan, where a 2019 'anti-infiltration law' was boycotted by the opposition in parliament but passed unanimously by the governing party.

Our recommendations are framed with a view to the different regulatory traditions inside national electoral frameworks—crudely Anglo-American (Westminster system) self-regulation, European co-regulation, and state regulation (Marsden et al. 2020). Recommendation 6 calls for explicit terms of engagement between social media platforms and governments, not necessarily for legislation such as that found in Singapore, Germany, and France.

It is in the enforcement of disinformation laws that we are most likely to see the regulatory outcomes diverge between different regulatory and electoral-political traditions, and research into the institutional models for regulating disinformation is urgently required. Researchers need to anchor disinformation research in national responses to digitally dominant platforms across electoral, media and communications and data protection laws. Moreover, disinformation regulation must be responsive to the international human rights law standards of legality, necessity, and proportionality.

The United Nations Special Rapporteur quotes Hannah Arendt on the totalitarian dangers of disinformation: 'If everybody always lies . . . nobody believes anything any longer' (Arendt 1978; Special Rapporteur on the promotion and protection of the right to freedom of opinion and expression 2020, paras 58–59). The need to accurately analyse responses to disinformation will remain pressing in this increasingly GAFAM-dominated age.

NOTES

1. The EU's interinstitutional terminology database IATE (Inter-Active Terminology for Europe) specifically notes that disinformation should not be confused with misinformation, defined in IATE as 'information which is wrong or misleading but not deliberately so' (Bentzen 2015).

2. The president posted the Tweet at 1240 am at https://twitter.com/realdonaldtrump/status/1265427538140188676; it provoked 81,000 retweets and 223,000 "likes" (archived at https://web.archive.org/web/20200528040606/https://twitter.com/realdonaldtrump/status/1265427538140188676).

3. *Biden v. Knight First Amend. Inst. at Columbia Univ.*, No. 20-197, 2021 WL 1240931 (U.S. Apr. 5, 2021).

4. In very narrow specific circumstances pertaining to judicial reputation, criminal defamation with a financial penalty rather than imprisonment has been considered appropriate in the European Court of Human Rights—see *Peruzzi v. Italy* (App no 39294/09) judgment of June 30, 2015.

5. *Democratic Alliance v. African National Congress and Another* (CCT 76/14) [2015] ZACC 1.

6. *Trevor Manuel v Economic Freedom Fighters and Others* ([2019] ZAGPJHC 157) Johannesburg High Court, May 30.

7. Retrieved from data at https://www.real411.org/complaints.

8. Facebook disputed claims from the Trump 2016 presidential campaign their advertising costs were consequently much lower than Hillary Clinton's. See Breland (2018).

9. See, e.g., Regulation (EU) 2016/679 of the European Parliament and of the Council of April 27, 2016, on the protection of natural persons with regard to the processing of personal data and on the free movement of such data, and repealing Directive 95/46/EC (General Data Protection Regulation), OJ 2016 L 119/1, art 9.

10. Data Protection Act 2018 (United Kingdom), sch 1 para 22.

11. Protection of Personal Information Act 2013 (South Africa) s 31.

12. Privacy Act 1988 (Australia), s 6C(1).

13. Privacy Act 1988 (Australia), s 7C.

14. Privacy Act 1982 (Canada), s 3.

15. Personal Information Protection and Electronic Documents Act S.C. 2000, c. 5 (Canada), s 4(1).

16. Directive 2009/136/EC of the European Parliament and of the Council of November 25, 2009 amending Directive 2002/22/EC on universal service and users' rights relating to electronic communications networks and services, Directive 2002/58/EC concerning the processing of personal data and the protection of privacy in the electronic communications sector and Regulation (EC) No 2006/2004 on cooperation between national authorities responsible for the enforcement of consumer protection laws, OJ L 337, 18.12.2009, 11–36.

REFERENCES

Access Now. 2020. 'Targeted, Cut Off, and Left in the Dark: The #KeepItOn Report on Internet Shutdowns in 2019'. *The #KeepItOn Coalition*. https://perma.cc/S7EL-37LE.

African Commission on Human and Peoples' Rights. 2016. 'Resolution on the Right to Freedom of Information and Expression on the Internet in Africa—ACHPR/ Res.362(LIX)2016'. Retrieved October 18, 2020. https://www.achpr.org/sessions/ resolutions?id=374.

Allan, Richard. 2020. 'Partisan—The Missing Word'. regulate.tech Blog26 April. Retrieved October 18, 2020. https://www.regulate.tech/partisan-the-missing-word-26th-april-2020/.

Arendt, Hannah. 1978. 'Hannah Arendt: From an Interview 26 October'. *New York Review of Books*.

Aspinwall, Nick. 2020. 'Taiwan's War on Fake News Is Hitting the Wrong Targets'. *Foreign Policy*, 10 January.

Barwise, T. P., and L. Watkins. 2018. 'The Evolution of Digital Dominance: How and Why We Got to GAFA' pp. 21–49 in Digital Dominance: The Power of Google, Amazon, Facebook, and Apple. Oxford University Press, New York, NY. Edited by Moore Martin and Tambini Damian. doi: 10.35065/PUB.00000914.

BBC. 2019. 'Brexit: Vote Leave Drops Appeal against Referendum Spending Fine'. *BBC News*. Retrieved October 18, 2020. https://www.bbc.co.uk/news/ uk-politics-47755611.

Benkler, Yochai. 2019. 'Cautionary Notes on Disinformation and the Origins of Distrust'. *MediaWell (Social Science Research Council)*. https://mediawell.ssrc.org/expert-reflections/cautionary-notes-on-disinformation-benkler/.

Bennett, Colin, and Robin M. Bayley. 2012. 'Canadian Federal Political Parties and Personal Privacy Protection: A Comparative Analysis'. *Office of the Privacy Commissioner of Canada*. Retrieved May 12, 2019. https://www.priv.gc.ca/ en/opc-actions-and-decisions/research/explore-privacy-research/2012/pp_ 201203/#toc5.

Bennett, Colin, and Smith Oduro Marfo. 2019. 'Privacy, Voter Surveillance and Democratic Engagement: Challenges for Data Protection Authorities'. Wilmslow: Information Commissioner's Office. doi: 10.2139/ssrn.3517889.

Biggio, Battista, and Fabio Roli. 2018. 'Wild Patterns: Ten Years after the Rise of Adversarial Machine Learning'. *Pattern Recognition* 84: 317–31. doi: 10.1016/ j.patcog.2018.07.023.

Boutilier, Alex. 2019. 'Twitter Announces Rules for Canadian Political Advertising'. *The Star*. Retrieved October 18, 2020. https://www.thestar.com/politics/federal/2019/ 08/29/twitter-announces-rules-for-canadian-political-advertising.html.

Breland, Ali. 2018. 'Facebook Says Trump Paid More Than Clinton for Digital Advertising'. *The Hill*. Retrieved October 18, 2020. https://thehill.com/policy/technology/ 375915-facebook-says-trump-paid-more-than-clinton-for-digital-advertising.

Brown, Ian, Lilian Edwards, and Christopher T. Marsden. 2009. 'Information Security and Cybercrime'. In *Law and the Internet*, edited by Edwards Lilian and Waelde Charlotte. Hart: Oxford.

Brown, Ian, and Christopher T. Marsden. 2013. *Regulating Code: Good Governance and Better Regulation in the Information Age*. Cambridge, MA: MIT Press.

Brown, Ian, Christopher T. Marsden, James Lee, and Michael Veale. 2020. *Cybersecurity for Elections: A Commonwealth Guide on Best Practice*. London: Commonwealth Secretariat. doi: 10.14217/e56e4289-en.

Chng, Darren Grayson. 2019. 'POFMA: Singapore's Anti-Fake News Law'. *Society for Computers and Law*. Retrieved October 18, 2020. https://www.scl.org/articles/10541-pofma-singapore-s-anti-fake-news-law.

Commonwealth Electoral Network. 2016. *New Media and the Conduct of Elections*. London: Commonwealth Secretariat.

Communications Security Establishment of Canada. 2019. '2019 Update: Cyber Threats to Canada's Democratic Process'. Government of Canada. https://perma.cc/RU5S-9G77.

Competitions and Markets Authority. 2020. *Online Platforms and Digital Advertising: Market Study Final Report*. London: HM Government.

Conger, Kate. 2020. 'Twitter Labels Trump Tweet about "Racist Baby" as Manipulated Media'. *New York Times,* 16 September.

Corera, Gordon. 2020. *Russians among Us: Sleeper Cells, Ghost Stories and the Hunt for Putin's Agents*. London: Williams Collins.

Edelman, Gilad. 2020. 'Twitter Finally Fact-Checked Trump. It's a Bit of a Mess'. *Wired* 27 May, Retrieved October 18, 2020 https://www.wired.com/story/twitter-fact-checked-trump-tweets-mail-in-ballots/ .

Electoral Commission of South Africa. n.d. 'Report Digital Disinformation'. Retrieved October 18, 2020. https://www.elections.org.za/content/Elections/2019-National-and-provincial-elections/Report-digital-disinformation/.

European Commission. 2018. *Code of Practice on Disinformation*. Brussels: European Commission.

European Commisison (2020) European Democracy Action Plan: making EU democracies stronger, Press release,3 December 2020: Brussels, Retrieved June 28, 2021 https://ec.europa.eu/commission/presscorner/detail/en/IP_20_2250

Facebook. n.d. 'Ad Library'. Facebook. Retrieved October 18, 2020. https://www.facebook.com/ads/library/?active_status=all&ad_type=political_and_issue_ads&country=CN.

Fuller, Simon. 2019. 'Our Digital Future'. International Bar Association. Retrieved October 18, 2020. https://www.ibanet.org/Article/NewDetail.aspx?ArticleUid=60554B04-C95A-494B-845B-60BAFC7CA4C6.

Google. n.d. 'Political Advertising on Google'. Google Transparency Report. Retrieved October 18, 2020. https://transparencyreport.google.com/political-ads/home.

Greenleaf, Graham, and Bertil Cottier. 2020. '2020 Ends a Decade of 62 New Data Privacy Laws'. *Privacy Laws and Business International Report* 163: 24–26.

Grinberg, Nir, Kenneth Joseph, Lisa Friedland, Briony Swire-Thompson, and David Lazer. 2019. 'Fake News on Twitter during the 2016 U.S. Presidential Election'. *Science* 363(6425): 374–78. doi: 10/gf3gmt.

Guess, Andrew M., Brendan Nyhan, and Jason Reifler. 2020. 'Exposure to Untrustworthy Websites in the 2016 US Election'. *Nature Human Behaviour* 4(5): 472–80. doi: 10/dpcn.

High Level Group on Fake News and Online Disinformation. 2018. *A Multi-Dimensional Approach to Disinformation*. Luxembourg: Publications Office of the European Union. doi: 10.2759/739290.

Information Commissioner's Office. 2020a. 'Bounty UK Fined £400,000 for Sharing Personal Data Unlawfully'. ICO. Retrieved October 18, 2020. https://ico.org.uk/about-the-ico/news-and-events/news-and-blogs/2019/04/bounty-uk-fined-400-000-for-sharing-personal-data-unlawfully/.

Information Commissioner's Office. 2020b. 'ICO Issues Maximum £500,000 Fine to Facebook for Failing to Protect Users' Personal Information'. ICO. Retrieved October 18, 2020. https://ico.org.uk/about-the-ico/news-and-events/news-and-blogs/2018/10/facebook-issued-with-maximum-500-000-fine/.

ITU Telecommunication Development Bureau. 2019. *Measuring Digital Development: Facts and Figures 2019*. Geneva: ITU.

Kalina, Bontcheva, Julie Posetti, Denis Teyssou, Trisha Meyer, Sam Gregory, Clara Hanot, and Diana Maynard. 2020. 'Balancing Act: Countering Digital Disinformation While Respecting Freedom of Expression: Broadband Commission Research Report on "Freedom of Expression and Addressing Disinformation on the Internet"'. Paris: UNESCO.

Karpf, David. 2019. 'On Digital Disinformation and Democratic Myths'. *MediaWell (Social Science Research Council)*. https://mediawell.ssrc.org/expert-reflections/on-digital-disinformation-and-democratic-myths/.

Kreps, Sarah, and Brendan Nyhan. 2020. 'Coronavirus Fake News Isn't Like Other Fake News'. *Foreign Affairs*, 30 March.

Machado, Caio, Beatriz Kira, Gustavo Hirsch, Nahema Marchal, Bence Kollanyi, Philip N. Howard, Thomas Lederer, et al. 2018. 'News and Political Information Consumption in Brazil: Mapping the First Round of the 2018 Brazilian Presidential Election on Twitter'. Oxford Internet Institute Blogs. http://blogs.oii.ox.ac.uk/comprop/wp-content/uploads/sites/93/2018/10/machado_et_al.pdf.

Marsden, Chris, and Trisha Meyer. 2019a. *Regulating Disinformation with Artificial Intelligence: Effects of Disinformation Initiatives on Freedom of Expression and Media Pluralism*. Brussels: European Parliament. doi: 10.2861/003689.

Marsden, Chris, and Trisha Meyer. 2019b. 'How Can the Law Regulate Removal of Fake News?' *Society for Computers and Law*. Retrieved October 18, 2020. https://www.scl.org/articles/10425-how-can-the-law-regulate-removal-of-fake-news.

Marsden, Chris, Trisha Meyer, and Ian Brown. 2020. 'Platform Values and Democratic Elections: How Can the Law Regulate Digital Disinformation?' *Computer Law and Security Review* 36: 105373. doi: 10/ggjt4w.

Meyer, Trisha, Christopher T. Marsden, and Ian Brown. 2020. 'Regulating Internet Content with Technology: Analysis of Policy Initiatives Relevant to Illegal Content and Disinformation Online in the European Union'. Chapter 16, pp. 309–327. In *Disinformation and Digital Media as a Challenge for Democracy*, edited by E. Kużelewska, G. Terzis, D. Trottier, and D. Kloza. Cambridge: Intersentia.

Mozilla. 2017. 'Facebook and Google: This Is What an Effective Ad Archive API Looks Like'. *The Mozilla Blog*. Retrieved June 21, 2019/https://blog.mozilla.org/blog/2019/03/27/facebook-and-google-this-is-what-an-effective-ad-archive-api-looks-like.

Mozilla. 2019. 'Facebook's Ad Archive API Is Inadequate'. *The Mozilla Blog*. Retrieved July 9, 2019. https://blog.mozilla.org/blog/2019/04/29/facebooks-ad-archive-api-is-inadequate.

NATO StratCom COE. 2018. *The Black Market for Social Media Manipulation*. Riga: NATO StratCom COE.

NATO StratCom COE. 2019. *Protecting Elections: A Strategic Communications Approach*. Riga: NATO StratCom COE.

Nimmo, Ben, C. Shawn Eib, Léa Ronzaud, Rodrigo Ferreira, Thomas Lederer, and Melanie Smith. 2020. 'Iran's Broadcaster: Inauthentic Behavior: Facebook Takes Down Covert Assets Linked to State Broadcaster'. *Graphika*. https://perma.cc/8ACK-R7S2.

Pace, Yannick. 2018. 'Parties Face Hefty Fines over Electoral Profiling without Consent'. *Malta Today*. Retrieved October 18, 2020. http://www.maltatoday.com.mt/news/national/87128/gdpr__parties_face_hefty_fines_over_electoral_profiling_without_consent.

Panoptkyon Foundation. 2021. 'Ustawa o wolności słowa? Raczej ustawa inwigilacyjna 2.0!'. *Fundacja Panoptykon*. Retrieved April 12, 2021. https://panoptykon.org/inwigilacja-2-0.

Press Information Bureau. 2019. '"Voluntary Code of Ethics" by Social Media Platforms to Be Observed in the General Election to the Haryana and Maharashtra Legislative Assemblies and All Future Elections'. *Government of India*. Retrieved October 18, 2020. pib.gov.in/Pressreleaseshare.aspx?PRID=1586297.

Purdon, Lucy, Arsalan Ashraf, and Ben Wagner. 2015. 'Security v Access: The Impact of Mobile Network Shutdowns, Case Study Telenor Pakistan'. Internet Policy Observatory Retrieved October 18, 2020 at https://repository.upenn.edu/internet-policyobservatory/13/ .

Rid, Thomas. 2020. *Active Measures: The Secret History of Disinformation and Political Warfare*. London: Profile Books.

RSF. 2019. 'Benin's Citizens Deprived of Internet on Election Day | Reporters without Borders'. *Reporters without Borders*. Retrieved October 18, 2020. https://rsf.org/en/news/benins-citizens-deprived-internet-election-day.

Sanovich, Sergey. 2018. 'Russia: The Origins of Digital Misinformation'. Pp. 21–40 in *Computational Propaganda: Political Parties, Politicians, and Political Manipulation on Social Media*, edited by Samuel C. Wooley and Philip N. Howard. Oxford: Oxford University Press. doi: 10.1093/oso/9780190931407.003.0002.

Select Committee on Democracy and Digital Technologies. 2020. *Digital Technology and the Resurrection of Trust (HL Paper 77)*. London: House of Lords.

Silverman, Craig, ed. 2014. *Verification Handbook: An Ultimate Guideline on Digital Age Sourcing for Emergency Coverage*. Maastricht: European Journalism Centre.

Special Counsel Robert S. Mueller III. 2019. 'Report on the Investigation into Russian Interference in the 2016 Presidential Election'. Washington DC. Retrieved from https://perma.cc/9R75-FSBR.

Special Rapporteur on the promotion and protection of the right to freedom of opinion and expression. 2018. 'Report of the Special Rapporteur to the Human Rights Council on online content regulation (A/HRC/38/35)'. *United Nations*. http://ap.ohchr.org/documents/dpage_e.aspx?si=A/HRC/38/35.

Special Rapporteur on the promotion and protection of the right to freedom of opinion and expression. 2020. 'Report on Disease Pandemics and the Freedom of Opinion and Expression (A/HRC/44/49)'. *United Nations*. Retrieved October 18, 2020. https://www.undocs.org/A/HRC/44/49.

Tambini, Damian, Danilo Leonardi, and Chris Marsden. 2007. *Codifying Cyberspace: Communications Self-Regulation in the Age of Internet Convergence*. London: Routledge.

Thompson, Elizabeth. 2019. 'Most of Canada's Top Websites Won't Post Federal Election Ads This Year | CBC News'. *CBC*. Retrieved October 18, 2020. https://www.cbc.ca/news/politics/online-election-advertising-canada-1.5116753.

Timberg, Craig. 2020. 'How Conservatives Learned to Wield Power inside Facebook'. 20 February *Washington Post*.

UN Human Rights Council. 2016. 'Resolution Adopted by the Human Rights Council on 1 July 2016—32/13. The Promotion, Protection and Enjoyment of Human Rights on the Internet (A/HRC/RES/32/13)'. Office of the High Commissioner for Human Rights. Retrieved October 18, 2020. https://ap.ohchr.org/documents/dpage_e.aspx?si=A/HRC/RES/32/13.

UN Special Rapporteur on Freedom of Opinion and Expression, OSCE Representative on Freedom of the Media, OAS Special Rapporteur on Freedom of Expression, and African Commission on the Human and People's Rights Special Rapporteur on Freedom of Expression and Access to Information. 2017. 'Joint Declaration on Freedom of Expression and "Fake News", Disinformation and Propaganda'. Retrieved July 10, 2019. https://www.osce.org/fom/302796?download=true.

United Nations (UN) Special Rapporteur on Freedom of Opinion and Expression, Organization for Security and Co-operation in Europe (OSCE) Representative on Freedom of the Media, and the Organization of American States (OAS) Special Rapporteur on Freedom of Expression. 2020. 'Joint Declaration on Freedom of Expression and Elections in the Digital Age'. *Office of the High Commissioner for Human Rights*. Retrieved October 18, 2020. https://www.osce.org/representative-on-freedom-of-media/451150.

United Nations (UN) Special Rapporteur on Freedom of Opinion and Expression, Organization for Security and Co-operation in Europe (OSCE) Representative on Freedom of the Media, the Organization of American States (OAS) Special Rapporteur on Freedom of Expression, and the African Commission on Human and Peoples' Rights (ACHPR) Special Rapporteur on Freedom of Expression and Access to Information. 2015. 'Joint Declaration on Freedom of Expression and Responses to Conflict Situations'. Office of the High Commissioner for Human Rights. Retrieved October 18, 2020. https://www.ohchr.org/EN/NewsEvents/Pages/DisplayNews.aspx?NewsID=15921&LangID=E.

Wardle, Claire, and Hossein Derakhshan. 2017. *Information Disorder: Toward an Interdisciplinary Framework for Research and Policymaking*. DGI(2017)09. Strasbourg: Council of Europe Report DGI(2017)09.

Weintraub, Karen. 2020. '"Fake News" Web Sites May Not Have a Major Effect on Elections'. 2 March, *Scientific American*.

Zuiderveen Borgesius, Frederik J., and Wilfred Steenbruggen. 2019. 'The Right to Communications Confidentiality in Europe: Protecting Privacy, Freedom of Expression, and Trust'. *Theoretical Inquiries in Law* 20(1): 291–322. doi: 10/gf2xzk.

12

Creating New Electoral Public Spheres

MARTIN MOORE ■

Democratic governments need to recognize that dominant technology plat-
forms will never adequately perform certain functions of the public sphere—
most notably during election campaigns—and create alternative public
service digital public spheres.

The dominant technology platforms have become our global public sphere. This should not be unduly surprising given the ubiquity, accessibility, and range of their services (in many cases offered free at point-of-use). Indeed, as will be argued in this chapter, the technology platforms in many ways conform more closely to the normative Habermasian public sphere than legacy media. Yet, they are also deficient as a public sphere. Where they are deficient, and in order to avoid public migration to online private spheres, democratic societies should seek to develop and nurture alternative digital public spheres. One such alternative should be for election campaigns, since there is now significant evidence to show the multiple deficiencies of the platforms in performing the communications functions necessary during electoral campaigns. This chapter will provide a rationale for the development of alternative digital public spheres and sketch out what an alternative electoral digital public sphere might look like.

From February 2020 onwards, for periods of weeks or sometimes months, a large proportion of the world's population was required to stay at home or observe curfews in order to slow the spread of COVID-19. During these periods people relied much more heavily than usual on the Internet for their work, their news, and their communication, and particularly on the services of the dominant technology platforms. In the United Kingdom in April 2020, people spent over four hours-a-day online, a record figure (Ofcom, 2020). In the United States, over half the population said the Internet had become essential to them during the crisis (Vogels et al. 2020). The major US technology platforms each saw significant increases in their users. Netflix added about 16 million subscribers in the first three months of 2020 (BBC 2020). News viewership on YouTube rose 75% compared to the previous year (Bergen and Chang 2020). YouTube even reduced its video quality in order to cope with the global surge in demand (Shaw 2020). Facebook's family of services attracted 3 billion people in the first quarter of 2020, 11% higher than in 2018 (Facebook 2020). And 44% of people globally reported spending more time on social media than prior to the onset of the virus (Statista 2020a). For a period in spring 2020 it was reported that 3.9 billion people were told or strongly advised to remain in their homes, meaning that access to public life for half the population of the world became almost entirely mediated, and a vast proportion of this mediation was via a handful of technology platforms (Sandford 2020).

Yet, though accentuated by global coronavirus lockdowns and curfews, the major tech platforms had already taken on many of the roles we associate with a public sphere. By the summer of 2020, a third of the world's population were using one of Facebook's services to share news with one another. One and a half billion people were using Google's gmail as their email service (including over 60% of 18- to 29-year-olds). 1.8 billion were watching YouTube regularly (Statista 2020b). In China, where the services of US information intermediaries are much less accessible, just under half the population uses WeChat. In total, over two-thirds of those with online access across the globe already used these platforms to communicate, to discover news, to do business, and to be distracted and entertained. The novel coronavirus simply consolidated and accelerated this trend.

In certain senses the technology super-platforms meet, or even exceed, the ideal of a public sphere conceptualized by Jurgen Habermas (Habermas, 1989, 2005, 2006). Habermas's original, eighteenth-century, bourgeois public sphere was characterized, he argued, by its rational-critical discourse and by its accessibility. Though, as Habermas's critics have highlighted, it was hardly accessible to most. 'Women of all classes and ethnicities were excluded from official political participation on the basis of gender status', Nancy Fraser writes, 'while plebeian men were formally excluded by property qualifications' (Fraser 1992). The technology platforms do not exclude people on the basis of gender, ethnicity, or class status. Indeed, some of them have made accessibility and connectivity a core part of their mission. Facebook's Mark Zuckerberg's goal is to use his company's services to make the globe more open and connected and 'to bring the world closer together' (Zuckerberg 2017).

Furthermore, the platforms address some of the degeneration of the public sphere that Habermas associated with its evolution in the nineteenth and twentieth centuries. By giving the public access to the tools of production, publication, and distribution, the platforms have undermined A. J. Liebling's mid-twentieth-century dictum that 'Freedom of the press is guaranteed only to those who own one' (Liebling 1960). They have reduced the capacity of the mass media to act as a strong gatekeeper, one which restricted access to certain elites and expressed the public's voices chiefly through opinion polls or heavily mediated vox pops. Similarly, Habermas's hope that a reformed and revived public sphere would open political parties and government bureaucracies to greater public participation has, at least in some instances, been realized (Gerbaudo 2018).

The accessibility of our new digital public sphere led the journalist and television news anchor Jon Snow to claim in 2012 that ours is an 'age in which "we the people" have their greatest opportunity ever to influence the information agenda' (Snow 2012). An age where we achieve that 'illusive [sic] entity "the level playing field"'. The new information intermediaries are central, Snow claimed, to this levelling. 'I see Twitter as a fundamental element, a signpost, and more at the Gateway to the Golden Age', as are, he argued, Facebook and Google. Snow's claims reflected a prevailing post–Arab Spring democratic establishment consensus that the platforms were both a disrupting and democratizing force (Castells 2012; Naim 2013).

Yet, though these information intermediaries may better fulfil one of Habermas's main criteria for a normative public sphere—accessibility, they appear less capable of enabling another—rational-critical discourse. Platforms have been found to be awash with misinformation and disinformation (European Commission 2018; Woolley and Howard 2019; Avaaz 2020). Our information ecosystem, Claire Wardle of First Draft News writes, 'is now dangerously polluted' (Wardle 2019). Over two-thirds of the public are worried about misinformation and disinformation in countries including Brazil, the United States, and the United Kingdom (Reuters Institute 2019). So prolific was the production of misleading information about COVID-19 in early 2020 that the Secretary General of the WHO claimed the world was experiencing an 'infodemic' alongside the coronavirus pandemic (WHO 2020). The platform intermediaries have also empowered strategic—rather than rational-critical—communication, both by political actors seeking election (for example through targeted advertising) and by State and non-state actors deliberately attempting to undermine and corrupt the democratic process (for example, by Russia's Internet Research Agency in the United States in 2016).

Concern about the deficiencies of these information intermediaries in performing the functions of a normative public sphere has sparked multiple initiatives, by the platforms themselves, by national and supranational authorities, by civil society, and by other motivated parties, to reform and regulate the platforms. In a separate chapter in this volume Chris Marsden and his colleagues document new laws (such as Singapore's POFMA), new regulations (such as the preapproval of political advertisements in India), and new Codes of Practice (such as the self-regulatory Code of Practice on Online Disinformation organized by the European Union) to instil greater responsibility in the platforms. In another chapter, Jacob Rowbottom proposes that in addition to this, some of the public service obligations that have applied to broadcasters in the past, like guaranteeing 'regulated media organisations a prominent place in search results and in news feeds', should now be applied to dominant technology platforms.

Some of these reforms ought to address the more damaging ways in which the platforms enable and incentivize the degradation of rational-critical discourse. But however much they reform themselves, or are reformed, it has already become clear that they will never satisfactorily perform all the functions of a normative Habermasian public sphere. This is partly because this is not, nor has it ever been, their primary aim. None of the dominant platforms was set up with the intention of becoming our new public sphere. Each was established to perform a particular function: Google to help people to search the web, Facebook to give people the opportunity to connect, Twitter to tell people what's happening, Amazon to be the 'everything store' (Auletta 2009; Kirkpatrick; Bilton 2013; Stone 2013). Their success in providing these services allowed them to scale, and to extend their activities and services. Google began as a search engine, but its success led it to expand into digital advertising (notably through Adsense and DoubleClick), email, video streaming, Internet browsing, operating systems, maps, online storage, and a panoply of more leftfield 'moonshots' (Mazzucato 2020). Facebook opened to the general public in 2006, and its growth led it to acquire Instagram, WhatsApp, and Oculus. Amazon evolved from an online bookseller to an on-line general store, 'a delivery and logistics network, a payment service, a credit lender, an auction house, a major book publisher, a producer of television and films, a fashion designer, a hardware manufacturer, and a leading provider of cloud server space and computing power' (Khan 2017). Scale also allowed them to take on many of the roles we previously associated with the press and mass media (Moore 2016). Amazon spends an estimated $5–6 billion a year on media content (Sherman 2019). Google claims to have sent $14 billion to support news in 2018. Facebook claimed its video content, Facebook Watch, had 720 million users in 2019. Following the success and phenomenal growth of their original goals therefore, these companies became, in addition to their roles as digital inter-mediaries, media conglomerates. This was a consequence of their communicative and infrastructural dominance, not the cause of it.

They are also unable to fulfil the functions of a normative democratic public sphere because their business models constrain and distort their efforts. The two most important information intermediaries—Google and Facebook—rely for their income on digital advertising. The particular model of digital advertising they each use is distinctive from pre-digital advertising and was essentially in-vented by each company to suit its purposes (Wu 2016; Moore 2018; Zuboff 2019). The models rely on engagement, on behavioural tracking, on popularity, and on growth. This reliance compromises the capacity of the platforms to nur-ture deliberative communication or to promote communicative rationality. Their need to promote user engagement, for example, means they need to prioritize content and advertising that captures attention. Their need to track user behav-iour means they cannot, for commercial reasons, draw a clear line between peo-ple's public and private spheres (Fuchs 2012). Their need to use popularity as a proxy for authority incentivizes the manipulation of social signals, and their con-tinual focus on growth discourages them from increasing the filters on partici-pation or publication. Realistically, we should only expect them to perform the functions of a normative public sphere to the extent that it fits with their corporate objectives and extant business models. To this extent one could argue that the commercialization and centralization of the digital public sphere, a process that Habermas described happening over the course of two centuries in the analogue world, has been concertinaed into the first two decades of the twenty-first century (Habermas 1989; Calhoun 1992).

A third reason why it is unreasonable that democratic societies should expect these platforms to fulfil the functions of a normative public sphere is because of the lack of clarity in their relationship with nation states. These platforms, though mostly based in the United States, do not conform to democratically established political boundaries. On the contrary, they are ideologically, structurally, and commercially transnational. Their relationships with national governments are equivocal, indistinct, and sometimes rivalrous. We saw this, for example, in the Prism surveillance programme as outlined in the papers leaked by Edward Snowden, and increasingly see it in the platforms' provision of public services, including healthcare, education, and transport (Moore 2018). We also see it in their ongoing attempts to avoid paying national taxes. Habermas emphasized the importance of a separation between the public sphere and the State, yet these organizations' relationships with states is much more ambiguous.

For these reasons we should not expect the platforms to perform the roles of a normative public sphere. Nor should we be excessively harsh on their incapacity. Indeed, it would not be possible for any single organization, or a small handful of organizations, simultaneously to perform all the roles we expect of the public sphere. As Peter Dahlgren, Todd Gitlin, Alex Bruns, and others have previously argued, the idea of one single public sphere is misguided. In any complex society there are, and need to be, numerous different public spheres (or 'sphericules' as Gitlin termed them) which conform to different norms, fulfil different functions, and serve a variety of participants (Dahlgren 2005; Gitlin 1998, Bruns 2015). Equally, we need to be cognizant that contemporary criticisms of the deficiencies of the technology platforms echo some of the criticisms levelled at legacy media in the twentieth and early twenty-first century (regarding partiality, for example, and influence on elections). Moreover, in the performance of certain functions the democratic deficiencies of the platforms should not matter overmuch. As Dahlgren, Kruse, and others note, most people, most of the time, use media and communications for entertainment and distraction, not to learn about politics or engage in political discussion. This is as true for the information intermediaries as it was for the legacy media giants of the twentieth century (Dahlgren 2005; Kruse 2018).

There are, however, parts of the public sphere which need to work differently if democratic systems are to function, and where the deficiencies of the platforms can not only distort and obstruct these functions, but actively undermine them. One these is around election campaigns. Although the extent to which use of the platforms has contributed to the loss or victory of any specific candidate in a democratic election is contested, there is clear evidence that the platforms have been used to bypass electoral rules and norms, and—in some cases—to compromise the legitimacy of the process and the outcome (Tambini 2018; Moore 2018). In 2016, the Russian Internet Research Agency pursued a social media campaign deliberately intended 'to undermine the U.S. electoral system' (US DOJ 2019). Supporters of Jair Bolsonaro used WhatsApp during the 2018 election campaign in Brazil to distribute false information (Resende et al. 2019; Machado et al. 2019). Across the world, the Computational Propaganda Project found, there is evidence of State led social media manipulation campaigns in seventy countries (Bradshaw and Howard 2019).

In addition to concerted attempts by States and well-financed individuals to manipulate campaigns online, the major platforms have also found it difficult to maintain civility, forestall abuse, prevent harassment, and constrain the proliferation of false or distorted information. In 2017 the UK's Committee on Standards in Public Life found that 'A significant proportion of candidates at the 2017 general election experienced harassment, abuse and intimidation'. Social media, the Committee reported, was the most significant factor driving this abuse of Parliamentary candidates (Committee on Standards in Public Life 2017). This was backed by subsequent research showing a substantial rise in abuse on Twitter, in absolute and proportional terms, between the 2015 and 2017 UK general elections (Gorrell et al. 2018), and has been echoed during elections in the United States, India, Brazil, and Germany.

Recognizing the ways in which their services and tools have been used to undermine electoral laws and norms, after 2016 the platforms introduced measures intended to prevent this. Facebook set up an 'election war room', set up barriers to stop foreign organizations buying political ads, established a political ad archive, and committed to supporting independent fact-checking organizations worldwide (Zuckerberg 2017b; Frenkel and Isaac 2018). Twitter updated its rules around elections and invested in further detection of manipulation (Harvey and Roth 2018). YouTube strengthened its rules on 'deceptive practices', to reduce the quantity of false or misleading information around elections (YouTube 2020).

Yet, however many reforms these platforms make, they will remain incapable of performing the functions needed from a normative democratic public sphere during election campaigns. There are, in addition to the broader reasons outlined above, three additional reasons for this. The first is that platform participation does not correspond to political representation. In other words, there is no means by which to ensure that, by using the platforms during an election campaign, each citizen will be able to participate in a public sphere that corresponds to their representative democratic unit, in which they can engage with fellow citizens from that same unit (be that a ward, riding, constituency, district, state, or nation), and in which they can find out information about candidates and about the electoral process (such as when, where and how to vote). Right now you can go on Facebook and express your views about a candidate or election, but only your social network will be exposed to those views. If you do the same on Twitter there is a chance it may go beyond your social network, but little likelihood of it being seen by the other voters from your representative political unit. If you do consciously aim your message at a candidate, there is no guarantee they will be exposed to it (assuming they are even active on the social network) or that they will know it comes from one of the voters they are seeking to represent. On the existing technology platforms you are, therefore, being given an opportunity to speak, without any guarantee—or even likelihood—that the relevant voters or candidates will hear you or will have any democratic incentive to respond.

Platforms will also remain incapable of performing the functions of an ideal democratic public sphere during elections because of their inability to insist upon, or enforce, the use of real names. Platforms like Twitter, Reddit, and Tumblr have never compelled users to provide their real name. Facebook has sought to impose a real name policy, with mixed results. Google tried and failed to enforce real names when it introduced Google+. This is not to argue that these platforms should or should not impose strict real name policies. There are strong arguments in favour of online pseudonymity or anonymity, such as protection for the marginalized and abused, insulation against context collapse, and shielding against overly intrusive surveillance (danah boyd 2011; Hogan 2013). However, in certain online contexts, the use of pseudonymity or anonymity can compromise the very purpose of the online space. One such context is a digital public sphere specifically geared to fulfilling certain functions during election campaigns, such as giving actual voters the opportunity to speak to fellow citizens within their voting district and to question candidates for election in that district. In such a space there would be significant value associated with the use of real names, and significant cost to the use of pseudonymity or anonymity. Real names would, for example, allow for a greater replication of face-to-face norms of civility, accountability, and even deliberation. It has been shown that people adapt their behaviour online according to their visibility and their awareness of the potential and actual audience, and that 'continuity of identity within a particular discursive context is a necessary condition for a minimal form of communicative accountability' (A. Moore et al. 2020). Creating such a space would give people an opportunity to speak as a voter, alongside other voters, with genuine and recognized democratic status.

The third reason the platforms will remain deficient as public spheres during elections is due to their inability to incentivize, or obligate, the cooperation and active involvement of candidates. Candidates may choose to be active on Facebook, or Instagram, or Twitter, but they are not obligated to be. Similarly, they may choose to respond to questions from others on social media, but may choose not to (and may see little incentive to respond in many cases). Candidates may also choose to provide certain factual information about themselves and their candidacy online, but they are not obliged to provide such information (nor to be strictly factual). Nor are they obliged to participate in any equivalent of hustings online (such as that pioneered by Reddit's popular Ask Me Anything). Were there to be dedicated online public spaces for election campaigns, spaces that corresponded to electoral representation, and in which voters spoke with real names, then there would be a clear incentive for candidates to participate in those spaces. Moreover, candidates could be obligated, as part of their candidacy, to provide certain factual information that was made available to the relevant voters in these dedicated online spaces, and required to participate in online hustings during which voters could ask questions and expect an answer.

There are numerous additional electoral functions that such digital public spheres could perform. They could aggregate information about candidates such that voters would be able to assess and compare their proposed programmes. They could enable people to check if they are registered to vote and, if not, to register or apply for a postal vote. They could provide basic factual information about the vote itself (such as data, time, and polling locations). They could provide access to archives of relevant election advertising. These archives, where they currently exist, are currently provided by some of the technology platforms themselves, with minimal external guidance or oversight. Were these companies required to submit the ads to a public repository, the ads could then be organized such that voters could access all those that were directly relevant to them (i.e., related to the candidates they have an opportunity to vote for). Such public spheres could go even further in their provision of information. They could provide access to candidate donations and spending. They could even provide the campaigns themselves with access to a shared pool of voter data—if democratic states wanted to ensure a level playing field of digital knowledge for all candidates.

Not only would the dominant technology platforms be unable to provide such public spaces for the reasons outlined previously, it is unlikely they would want to. To run these spaces would mean having constantly to adapt to evolving democratic conventions and norms (as well as electoral laws). It would mean performing functions that would compromise their financial interests, and it would mean taking on roles normally only undertaken by statutory regulators (such as requiring candidates to submit factual information). Equally, democratic societies should not want such public spaces to be run by these transnational commercial corporations. If they are to be sufficiently independent and non-partisan such that they are, and are seen to be, legitimate by the public, they will have to be managed by non-commercial institutions with clearly established remits, powers, and resources.

It might seem strange to many who have grown up with the Internet, that the political information and forums outlined earlier are not already provided in digital form by democratic states. Yet in most cases central governments have left this to local authorities, to the market, or to civil society, and the result has been that the information is inconsistent and piecemeal, and the opportunities for online interaction with fellow voters or candidates fragmented and erratic.

To give one illustration, in the United Kingdom up to 2015 it was peculiarly difficult to find information online about upcoming elections, where you could vote, or even the candidates competing for your local constituency or council. For candidates, each local authority (over 400 in total) would release the names of registered candidates in a Statement of Persons Nominated (SOPN), on a set date before election day, invariably on a pdf posted on the council website. As well as not being machine-readable, these statements included little to no contact information, no information on election promises, and no biographical context. Addresses of polling stations would be published in a similar way (if released

online at all). If democratic authorities make so little effort to communicate electoral information digitally, then it is not surprising that the space is easily occupied
by disinformation and misinformation.

So difficult was it to discover basic information online about candidates and
where and how to vote, that a civic technologist, Sym Roe (who had previously
worked on the Ministry of Justice's digital services) decided to try and appeal for
volunteers to manually upload what information was available from each Council
to a database, such that it could be made discoverable and reusable. Roe was
building on a nascent project that he and a few others at the United Kingdom's My
Society had started prior to the 2010 election, called Democracy Club. In 2015
Roe and his two colleagues managed to enthuse over 8,000 volunteers who collectively captured as much available candidate information as they could, in addition to the addresses of all the polling stations. They then made this data available
in a machine-readable form such that it could be integrated and reused by other
sites (including one they built for the purpose at WhereDoIVote.co.uk). Google
then developed a widget which accessed this data and allowed anyone to search—
via their postcode—for candidates in their area competing in upcoming elections.
Facebook later used the data too, to direct people to their nearest polling station.
Where Do I Vote was used 600,000 times in the 2015 election, having never existed before.

Democracy Club was so successful in 2015, and attracted so many volunteers
(referred to affectionately as 'Wombles') that Sym Roe and his two colleagues,
Joe Mitchell and Chris Shaw, decided to keep it going—unaware, of course, of
the number of electoral contests there would be in the United Kingdom over the
subsequent five years. By the General Election of December 2019 they were gathering data on candidates, voting, and polling stations in every election with the
exception of parish and town councils. Their data was being referred to and reused by the Electoral Commission, local authorities, media outlets, charities and
the UK Parliament. Yet, the three of them were also exhausted and unsure how,
and if, the project would continue (Roe, 2020). They began it as a public service,
supported by a series of small grants, hoping that at some stage its value would
be recognized and a foundation or public body would take it over. To date, that
has not happened. Should they decide not to continue, then much of the valuable
work they have done to provide foundational digital information for elections
could disappear.

The United Kingdom is not alone in its failure to provide such basic information online, or to support digital infrastructure that provides a foundation
for democratic knowledge and participation. Indeed, most democratic states are
similar (Renwick and Palese 2019). In the United States, for example, a not-for-
profit organization called Democracy Works plays a similar role to Democracy
Club in the United Kingdom, developing digital tools to make it easier for people
to vote and providing non-partisan information on candidates. Germany is an
exception to the rule, having a dedicated federal agency for civic education (the
Bundeszentrale für politische Bildung or BpB for short) whose purpose is to
strengthen democracy and promote civil society. Established in its present form

in 1952, the BpB produces significant amounts of printed and broadcast material for schools and the general public, funded by a budget of 64 million euros with a staff of 220 (bpb.de). The BpB has also developed digital tools—such as the Walh-Oh-Mat voting advice app (discontinued in 2019), though it has not yet sought to build digital electoral public spheres.

This moment calls for ambitious positive interventions in the public sphere. For inspiration, countries could look to an intervention the UK government made almost one hundred years ago. In 1922 the UK Post Office decided that rather than grant radio broadcast licences to the many manufacturers who applied, it would persuade them instead to invest together in one broadcast station, to be called the British Broadcasting Company (Curran and Seaton 1997, 112). It was not a decision driven by ideology, or by a conviction that monopoly was the best policy, that was to come later. However, it turned out to be one of the most consequential government interventions in the democratic public sphere. The BBC went on to become the most influential global public broadcaster of the twentieth century. New institutions are now needed, institutions that are suited to the time, the temper, and the technology. The remit of one such institution should be to organize and oversee the development of digital public spheres that correspond to representative political units. Public spheres built with democratic purpose and values embedded within their structures.

Numerous writers and commentators have expressed the hope that the Internet would perform the normative functions of Jurgen Habermas's public sphere since the invention of the web (Rheingold 1993; Fernback and Thompson 1995; Blumler and Coleman 2001). At least as many have noted its failure to do so, including Habermas himself (Habermas 2006; Pappacharissi 2010; Iosifidis 2011). Over the last decade, these hopes—and critiques—have migrated to the dominant technology platforms, as these platforms have become our de facto global public sphere (Shirky 2011; Kruse et al. 2018). Yet, democratic states need to recognize that these tech platforms, while suitable for some functions of the public sphere, will never be suitable for others. One of these is providing a structured forum, and a source of electoral information, for voters during election campaigns. If states believe in the importance of both accessibility and rational-critical discourse, and want digital technology to enhance rather than to undermine the democratic process, then they should acknowledge this and support the development of alternative digital public spheres for election campaigns. These would have to be set up and managed by a body sufficiently independent of government and provided with adequate resources and powers. The alternative is to rely still more on the leading tech platforms who cannot—when it comes to these particular functions—be relied upon.

REFERENCES

Avaaz. 2019. 'US2020: Another Facebook Disinformation Election?' November 5. https://secure.avaaz.org/campaign/en/disinfo_report_us_2020/.

Auletta, Ken. 2009. *Googled: The End of the World as We Know It*. London: Penguin Press.

BBC. 2020. 'Netflix Gets 16 Million New Sign-Ups Thanks to Lockdown'. BBC, April 22. https://www.bbc.co.uk/news/business-52376022.

Bergen, Mark, and Emily Chang. 2020. 'YouTube Sees 75% Jump in News Views on Thirst for Virus Updates'. Bloomberg.com, April 13. https://www.bloomberg.com/news/articles/2020-04-13/youtube-sees-75-jump-in-news-views-on-thirst-for-virus-updates.

Bilton, Nick. 2013. *Hatching Twitter*. London: Sceptre.

Blumler, Jay G., and Stephen Coleman. 2001. 'Realising Democracy Online: A Civic Commons in Cyberspace'. Citizens Online and IPPR, Research Publication No.2, March 2001.

boyd, danah. 2011. '"Real names" policies are an abuse of power'. 4 August 2011. *Apophenia*. http://www.zephoria.org/thoughts/archives/2011/08/04/real-names.html

Bradshaw, Samantha, and Philip N. Howard. 2019. 'The Global Disinformation Order 2019 Global Inventory of Organised Social Media Manipulation'. Computational Propaganda Project, Oxford Internet Institute, Oxford University.

Bruns, Axel, and Tim Highfield. 2015. 'Is Habermas on Twitter? Social Media and the Public Sphere'. In *The Routledge Companion to Social Media and Politics*, edited by Axel Bruns et al. Abingdon: Routledge. Pp. 56–73.

Calhoun, Craig, ed. 1992. *Habermas and the Public Sphere*. Cambridge, MA: MIT Press.

Castells, Manuel. 2012. *Networks of Outrage and Hope: Social Movements in the Internet Age*. Cambridge: Polity Press.

Committee on Standards in Public Life. 2017. 'Intimidation in Public Life A Review by the Committee on Standards in Public Life'. December 2017. CM 9543.

Dahlgren, P. 2005. 'The Internet, Public Spheres, and Political Communication: Dispersion and Deliberation'. *Political Communication* 22: 147–62. doi:10.1080/10584600590933160.

European Commission. 2018. 'A Multi-Dimensional Approach to Disinformation: Report of the Independent High Level Group on Fake News and Online Disinformation'.

Facebook. 2020. 'Facebook Reports First Quarter 2020 Results'. April 29. https://investor.fb.com/investor-news/press-release-details/2020/Facebook-Reports-First-Quarter-2020-Results/default.aspx.

Fernback, Jan, and Brad Thompson. 1995. 'Computer-Mediated Communication and the American Collectivity: The Dimensions of Community within Cyberspace'. Annual Convention of the International Communication Association. Albuquerque, New Mexico, May 1995. https://people.well.com/user/hlr/texts/VCcivil.html.

Fraser, Nancy. 1992. 'Rethinking the Public Sphere: A Contribution to the Critique of Actually Existing Democracy'. In *Habermas and the Public Sphere*, edited by Craig Calhoun. Cambridge, MA: MIT Press. Pp. 109–142.

Frenkel, Sheera, and Mike Isaac. 2018. 'Inside Facebook's Election "War Room"'. NYTimes.com, September 19. https://www.nytimes.com/2018/09/19/technology/facebook-election-war-room.html.

Fuchs, Christian. 2012. 'The Political Economy of Privacy on Facebook'. *Television and New Media* 13(2): 139–59. doi:10.1177/1527476411415699.

Gerbaudo, Paolo. 2018. *The Digital Party: Political Organisation and Online Democracy*. London: Pluto Press.

Gitlin, T. 1998. 'Public Sphere or Public Sphericules?' In *Media, Ritual and Identity*, edited by T. Liebes and J. Curran, 175–202. London: Routledge.

Gorrell, Genevieve, Mark Greenwood, Ian Roberts, Diana Maynard, and Kalina Bontcheva. 2018. 'Online Abuse of UK MPs in 2015 and 2017: Perpetrators, Targets, and Topics'. arXiv:1804.01498.

Habermas, J. 1989. *The Structural Transformation of the Public Sphere*. Cambridge, MA: MIT Press.

Habermas J. 2005. 'Concluding Comments on Empirical Approaches to Deliberative Politics'. *Acta Politica* 40: 384–92.

Habermas, J. 2006. 'Political Communication in Media Society: Does Democracy Still Enjoy an Epistemic Dimension? The Impact of Normative Theory on Empirical Research'. *Communication Theory* 16(4): 411–26. doi: 10.1111/j.1468-2885.2006.00280.x.

Harvey, Del, and Yoel Roth. 2018. 'An Update on Our Elections Integrity Work'. Twitter, October 1. https://blog.twitter.com/en_us/topics/company/2018/an-update-on-our-elections-integrity-work.html.

Hogan, Bernie. 2013. 'Pseudonyms and the rise of the real-name Web'. In: *A companion to new media dynamics*. Edited by John Hartley, Jean Burgess, and Axel Bruns. Chichester: Wiley. Pp. 290–307.

Iosifidis, Petros. 2011. 'The Public Sphere, Social Networks and Public Service Media'. *Information, Communication and Society* 14(5): 619–37. doi: 10.1080/1369118X.2010.514356.

Khan, Lina. 2017. 'Amazon's Antitrust Paradox'. *Yale Law Journal* 126: 3.

Kirkpatrick, David. 2010. *The Facebook Effect: The Real Inside Story of Mark Zuckerberg and the World's Fastest-Growing Company*. London: Virgin Books.

Kruse, Lisa M., Dawn R. Norris, and Jonathan R. Flinchum. 2018. 'Social Media as a Public Sphere? Politics on Social Media'. *Sociological Quarterly* 59(1): 62–84. doi: 10.1080/00380253.2017.1383143.

Liebling, A. J. 1960. 'The Wayward Press'. *New Yorker*, May 14.

Machado, Caio, Beatriz Kira, Vidya Narayanan, Bence Kollanyi, and Philip Howard. 2019. 'A Study of Misinformation in WhatsApp Groups with a Focus on the Brazilian Presidential Elections'. In *Companion Proceedings of the 2019 World Wide Web Conference (WWW '19)*, 1013–19. New York: Association for Computing Machinery. doi:https://doi.org/10.1145/3308560.3316738.

Moore, A., R. Fredheim, D. Wyss, and S. Beste. 2021. 'Deliberation and Identity Rules: The Effect of Anonymity, Pseudonyms and Real-Name Requirements on the Cognitive Complexity of Online News Comments'. *Political Studies*, 69(1), pp. 45–65. https://doi.org/10.1177/0032321719891385.

Moore, Martin. 2016. 'Tech Giants and Civic Power'. King's College London.doi.org/10.18742/pub01-027.

Moore, Martin. 2018. *Democracy Hacked: How Technology Destabilized Global Politics*. London: Oneworld.

Naim, Moses. 2013. *The End of Power*. New York: Basic Books.

Newman, Nic, Richard Fletcher, Antonis Kalogeropoulos, and Rasmus Kleis Nielsen. 2019. 'Reuters Institute Digital News Report 2019'. The Reuters Institute for the Study of Journalism, Oxford University.

Ofcom. 2020. 'Online Nation: 2020'. Summary report, June 24.

Papacharissi, Z. A. 2010. *A Private Sphere: Democracy in a Digital Age*. Cambridge, UK: Polity Press.

Renwick, Alan, and Michela Palese. 2019. 'Doing Democracy Better: How Can Information and Discourse in Election and Referendum Campaigns in the UK Be Improved?' The Constitution Unit, University College London.

Resende, Gustavo, Philipe Melo, Hugo Sousa, Johnnatan Messias, Marisa Vasconcelos, Jussara Almeida, and Fabrício Benevenuto. 2019. '(Mis)Information Dissemination in WhatsApp: Gathering, Analyzing and Countermeasures'. In The World Wide Web Conference (WWW '19), 818–28. New York: Association for Computing Machinery. doi:https://doi.org/10.1145/3308558.3313688.

Rheingold, Howard. 1993. The Virtual Community: Homesteading on the Electronic Frontier. Reading: Addison Wesley.

Roe, Sym. 2020. 'Interview with Sym Roe of Democracy Club'. Conducted by Martin Moore via Microsoft Teams on May 15.

Shaw, Lucas. 2020. 'YouTube to Limit Video Quality around the World for a Month'. Bloomberg.com, March 24. https://www.bloomberg.com/news/articles/2020-03-24/youtube-to-limit-video-quality-around-the-world-for-a-month.

Sherman, Alex. 2019. 'How the Epic "Lord of the Rings" Deal Explains Amazon's Slow-Burning Media Strategy'. CNBC, March 8.https://www.cnbc.com/2019/03/08/amazon-prime-video-feature.html.

Shirky, Clay. 2011. 'The Political Power of Social Media Technology, the Public Sphere, and Political Change'. Foreign Affairs 90(1): 28–41.

Snow, Jon. 2012. 'Hugh Cudlipp Lecture: Poised for Journalism's Golden Age', January 23. https://www.channel4.com/news/by/jon-snow/blogs/hugh-cudlipp-lecture-poised-journalisms-golden-age.

Statista. 2020a. 'In-Home Media Consumption Due to the Coronavirus Outbreak among Internet Users as of March 2020, by Country. "Spending Longer on Social Media"'. https://www.statista.com/statistics/1106498/home-media-consumption-coronavirus-worldwide-by-country/.

Statista. 2020b. 'Number of YouTube Users Worldwide from 2016 to 2012'. https://www.statista.com/statistics/805656/number-youtube-viewers-worldwide/.

Stone, Brad. 2013. The Everything Store: Jeff Bezos and the Age of Amazon. London: Little Brown and Company.

Tambini, Damian. 2018. 'Social Media Power and Electoral Legitimacy'. In Digital Dominance: The Power of Google, Amazon, Facebook and Apple, edited by Martin Moore and Damian Tambini. New York: Oxford University Press. Pp. 265–293.

US Department of Justice. 2019. 'Report on the Investigation into Russian Interference in the 2016 Presidential Election'. Special Counsel Robert S. Mueller. March 2019. https://www.justice.gov/storage/report.pdf.

Vogels, Emily A., Andrew Perrin, Lee Rainie, and Monica Anderson. 2020. '53% of Americans Say the Internet Has Been Essential during the COVID-19 Outbreak'. Pew Research Center, April 30. https://www.pewresearch.org/internet/2020/04/30/53-of-americans-say-the-internet-has-been-essential-during-the-covid-19-outbreak/.

Wardle, Claire. 2019. 'Information Disorder: "The Techniques We Saw in 2016 Have Evolved"', October 21. https://firstdraftnews.org/latest/information-disorder-the-techniques-we-saw-in-2016-have-evolved/.

World Health Organisation (WHO). 2020. 'Director-General Speech at Munich Security Conference', February 15. https://www.who.int/dg/speeches/detail/munich-security-conference.

Woolley, Sam, and Philip N. Howard. 2019. 'Computational Propaganda Worldwide'. In *Computational Propaganda*, edited by Sam Woolley and Philip N. Howard. New York: Oxford University Press. Pp. 3–18.

Wu, Tim. 2016. *The Attention Merchants: The Epic Scramble to Get Inside Our Heads*. New York: Penguin Random House.

YouTube. 2020. 'How YouTube Supports Elections'. YouTube Official Blog, February 3. https://youtube.googleblog.com/2020/02/how-youtube-supports-elections.html.

Zuboff, Shoshana. 2019. *The Age of Surveillance Capitalism, The Fight for a Human Future at the New Frontier of Power*. London: Profile Books.

Zuckerberg, Mark. 2017a. 'Bringing the World Closer Together'. Facebook.com, June 22. https://www.facebook.com/notes/mark-zuckerberg/bringing-the-world-closer-together/10154944663901634/.

Zuckerberg, Mark. 2017b. Facebook post, September 21. https://www.facebook.com/zuck/posts/10104052907253171.

Transposing Public Service Media Obligations to Dominant Platforms

JACOB ROWBOTTOM ▪

In recent years, it has become common to hear claims that electoral systems are vulnerable to a range of ills via activity on the digital media. The common concerns include misinformation, polarization, foreign interference, and a lack of transparency. As a result, changes to election laws and special rules to curb 'fake news' are sometimes demanded. This chapter will argue that the issues facing the electoral system are unlikely to be resolved through any quick legislative fix. The argument will be that any solution is likely to be found in media law as well as election law. The role of media law is important because the problems facing the electoral system are partly rooted in changes in the way campaign messages are communicated.

While the challenges to the integrity of elections have arisen in many countries, this chapter will focus on the experience in the United Kingdom. The United Kingdom provides a useful case study, as media law has played an important role in regulating the conduct of election campaigns. In particular, the broadcast media (and more specifically the public service sector) provides a highly regulated forum. The regulatory framework applied to the broadcast media performs three functions during campaigns. First, the regulations constrain and impose duties on the election coverage on television and radio. Second, the broadcast media play a role in the ecosystem for electoral communications, providing a forum for the claims made by campaigners (and on the digital media) to be subjected to scrutiny. Third, the regulation of broadcasters and the norms of the professional journalists indirectly regulate the conduct of parties, candidates, and other campaigners.

The system of broadcast regulation remains important, but only applies to licensed broadcasters and does not regulate digital media services. As more electoral activity has moved online, the regulatory framework no longer plays such a central role. As a result, there is a risk of losing some of the positive qualities and standards that broadcast coverage can bring to the debate. That concern is reflected in some of the current criticisms of digital campaigning. The discussion will therefore consider various policies to ensure that the goals underpinning election-related broadcast regulations continue to be served in the digital era. The first set of policies looks at ways to maintain the regulatory framework applied to broadcasters and support the public service media. The second looks at ways of regulating the direct messages made by campaigners on the digital media, so that some of the standards that have previously been expected of election commu-nications disseminated via the media cannot be so easily avoided through paid digital advertising. Finally, the discussion will consider whether public service obligations in elections should extend beyond broadcasters and to some of the digital platforms. While the discussion focusses on UK law, the updated regula-tory framework that will be proposed and outlined below provides a model that can be used in other systems facing similar threats to the integrity of elections.

HOW MEDIA LAW REGULATES ELECTIONS

The media ecosystem and channels for communication have a significant im-pact on the way election campaigns are conducted. During the latter part of the twentieth century, coverage on television, and the press provided the main chan-nels for politicians to get their message to a mass audience. The nature of mass media communications imposed some constraints on campaigners. For example, a message on television or in a tabloid newspaper could be viewed by any person. Campaigners had to be wary of making a statement to appeal to one section of the electorate if it could alienate another group of voters. That meant that there was, to some degree, a shared conversation in which people were exposed to similar messages and considered similar issues. The point should not be exaggerated, as different people read newspapers and magazines with distinct political slants. However, there was a limit to how tailored a political message could be. While the nature of the media and the values of journalists and editors constrained the conduct of national election campaigns, so did the regulations applicable to the media. In particular, some broadcasting laws may have played a more significant role than election law in regulating the conduct of campaigners.

Three examples show how broadcasting regulations have had an impact on campaigners in UK elections. First, the prohibition on paid political advertising on the broadcast media meant that parties and campaigners never had the oppor-tunity to engage in the high-spending 'spot' advertising campaigns that charac-terized US campaigns in the late twentieth century. Instead, qualifying political parties have been given some free airtime, known as 'party election broadcasts', which tend to last for several minutes (a longer duration than a commercial ad-vertisement). As election spending in support of political parties was not subject to a limit until 2000, the ban did much to keep the costs of campaigning down. The ban also had an effect on the nature of campaign communications. While the

30-second audiovisual format for television advertisements used in other jurisdictions is sometimes criticized for lacking depth or sophistication, the UK ban
avoided that issue by ruling out such short paid messages.

As paid political advertising on television and radio has always been banned,
political campaigners have relied on the mediated coverage to get their messages
across on the broadcast media. Such mediated coverage is subject to content regulations, which has provided a second control on the conduct of elections. Most
significantly, broadcasters are subject to rules on impartiality and due accuracy in
relation to news and are subject to special rules during elections. Such rules therefore impact on the choices about election coverage, such as which political parties
or representatives to invite onto programmes (Ofcom 2019a). Under the impartiality rules, broadcasters are expected to offer a level of inclusive coverage and
provide access on fair terms to parties and candidates, taking into account levels
of support. Editorial decisions have been subject to legal challenge, for example
where particular parties have not been included in leader's debate programmes (R
[on the application of Liberal Democrats] v. ITV Broadcasting Ltd [2019] EWHC
3282). Such examples show how the distribution of a key communicative resource
is governed by rules in media law.

The impartiality rules also mean that if candidates or party representatives appear on a television programme, they can expect to be challenged and interro-
gated by the journalist or reporter. If the media includes an inaccurate statement
from a politician or party without sufficient scrutiny or challenge, then that could
fall foul of the regulations requiring due accuracy. How well those rules work in
relation to media coverage is debatable, and sometimes the damage will be done
just by reporting a falsity (see Broughton Micova, cited in Ofcom 2017, [3.20]).
However, the regulation at least provides a channel of accountability and a system
in which falsities *should* be corrected. The reliance on the mediated coverage led
political managers to develop aggressive news management strategies (commonly
referred to as 'spin' in the early 2000s), which sought to steer news coverage in as
favourable direction as possible. While such strategies raised genuine concerns
about the quality of political information on the media, it showed how campaign
strategy was conducted with a focus on media coverage and politicians did not
have direct control over the conditions of campaign publicity.

A third type of control provided in the broadcast regulations are the content
standards that have a more direct impact on campaigners. For example, party election broadcasts are subject to certain content regulations, such as those relating to
harm and offence, and fairness and privacy (Broadcasters Liaison Group 2019).
In 2001, ProLife Alliance, a political party, was not permitted to include images
of aborted foetuses in its party election broadcast, as the content violated rules
on offensive material (R [on the application of ProLife Alliance] v. BBC [2003]
UKHL 23). That proved to be a particularly controversial application of the rules,
raising the question of what boundaries, if any, should be imposed on political
speech. Such cases are not isolated, and on other occasions broadcasters have
refused to carry party election messages that could be understood to be racist
(Rowbottom 2009).

To summarize, the policy choices in media law have had a significant impact on the conduct of election campaigns in previous years. Whether those constraints are desirable divides opinion. For example, there are complaints that broadcast regulations restrict free speech, as shown in a number of legal challenges (see R [on the application of Animal Defenders International] v. Secretary of State for Culture, Media and Sport [2008] UKHL 15). The regulatory framework applied to broadcasters, also worked to empower newspapers, which were not subject to equivalent regulations and were exempt from campaign spending rules. While the workings of the broadcast regulations may not have been perfect, the rules provided a framework governing electoral debates in one of the main communicative forums. That framework ensured that campaigns were not a free for all, and not dominated by high-spending, one-sided coverage on television and completely unchallenged falsities.

DIGITAL MEDIA

The digital media is fundamentally changing the way that election campaigns are conducted. In the United Kingdom, campaigners are no longer as dependent on the mediated news coverage to get a message to a mass audience than in previous decades. Political parties and other campaigners can communicate directly with voters through digital advertising, through their own websites and through networks of supporters. That environment may work to give politicians the confidence to bypass the traditional media institutions, where the coverage may be challenging or unfavourable. For example, in the 2019 General Election, Prime Minister Boris Johnson avoided a television interview with Andrew Neil, which would otherwise have been regarded as a key media event during the campaign. Similarly, for a period after the 2019 election, government representatives refused to appear on BBC Radio 4's flagship *Today* programme as a way to signal disapproval of its coverage. While the digital media may empower citizens, it can also weaken some of the media institutions that are expected to hold politicians to account .

The ability for both politicians and citizens to communicate directly with the public on the digital media can be seen as part of a broader transition in the workings of British democracy. For example, John Keane has argued that the dominance of the broadcast media in political communications in the twentieth century went hand in hand with a model of representative democracy, in which political parties were the central institutions for political participation (Keane 2009, 79). By contrast, in the current political environment, people have more opportunities to participate outside of the traditional institutions, for example by forming shorter-term informal campaign groups. Those working outside of the traditional political institutions may also rely on digital channels to disseminate political messages. To some, the development is to be welcomed as a new and open participatory form of democracy. However, in recent years more commentators have focussed on the risks flowing from the use of the digital media, in so far as it has

made elections more open to misinformation, extreme content, and foreign interference (to name just a few concerns).

While the changes in campaign methods are fundamental, the developments
are complex and evolving. The changes take place alongside a degree of continuity
in the system of electoral communication. This means that traditional media
institutions may no longer have dominance as the *only* means to communicate
with a national audience, but still remain of great importance for national election communications. Early studies of the 2019 General Election suggest that the
broadcast media, the BBC in particular, remained the leading source of political
information (Fletcher et al. 2020). The costs of running a comprehensive news organization, along with the 'winner takes all' distribution of attention in the digital
media, means that a relatively small number of institutions are likely to continue
to provide the focal point for campaign news. As long as broadcasters remain in
such a position, the media regulations will continue to play some role in regulating the conduct of the campaign.

The traditional media institutions also interact with the digital media. Online
sources provide stories and leads on information that are reported in the press
and on television. The discussion in the digital media may follow and critique
stories on the traditional media. What happens in the broadcast coverage and
in newspapers affects the other parts of the media ecosystem. In a study of US
political communications, Benkler et al. (2018) found that right-of-centre broadcasters often amplified messages from right-wing blogs and other online sources.
The broadcast sector thereby played a role that helped to explain the success of the
right-of-centre digital media sources in American politics.

Whether a media institution amplifies certain messages or sources is partly a
matter of editorial choice. Media institutions can choose to interact with digital
content by interrogating claims made and, where appropriate, debunking falsities. If the latter approach is taken, then media institutions can provide an
antidote to some of the harms associated with digital electoral communications.
Along such lines, Humprecht et al. (2020) found that in systems with a strong
public service media, the public are less vulnerable to problems of misinformation. The thinking is that by providing high-quality information, the public
will be less susceptible to misleading stories. The framework for regulating the
media provides a tool that can be used to steer media institutions towards performing such functions.

So far, the discussion has argued that media laws remain important in governing the conduct of elections. That does not mean the status quo can be taken for
granted. As will be explained, the regulatory framework is under pressure and
there is no case for complacency. The discussion will consider the ways that the
values underpinning the existing media laws can be advanced in relation to the
digital media. The following sections will look at three areas of policy. The first
section will consider ways that the regulatory framework for broadcasters can
continue to be effective in the digital media ecosystem. The second will consider
ways that paid advertising on the digital platforms can be regulated. The third
will consider whether the technology companies should be subject to certain

public service style obligations, by subjecting those companies to some standards equivalent to those applied to broadcasters.

SUPPORTING THE PROFESSIONAL MEDIA

The first set of policy considerations focusses on ways to support the professional media in performing certain functions in the election campaign. Given the continuing importance of the broadcast media, an obvious starting point is to keep the existing regulatory framework for broadcasters intact. That would mean that broadcast institutions continue to provide a space where the public are exposed to diverse perspectives and where arguments are expected to be challenged.

Maintaining the existing regulatory framework for broadcasters, however, is likely to be a short-term policy solution. There are now many media organizations that provide the equivalent of broadcast content online but without the need for a broadcast licence. Those outside of the regulatory framework include not just niche services, but services in direct competition with mainstream television and radio, such as Netflix and Amazon Prime. At present, those streaming services do not provide news coverage. However, if such companies were to provide broadcast style political coverage, the content would not be subject to impartiality obligations or the special rules on election coverage. Such organizations may choose to be impartial for commercial and professional reasons, but that would be a matter for the company's choice. In such circumstances, licensed broadcasters providing news would complain that they have to compete with unregulated digital media companies for audiences without a level playing field. Demands to deregulate the broadcast sector would be likely to follow. Such a scenario is speculative, but it is not far-fetched to imagine such a development, in which case the broadcast rules would be unlikely to survive in the medium term.

To avoid such a development, one policy option is to extend some broadcast-style media regulations to certain digital media bodies. That would hopefully allow licensed broadcast services to compete with digital news on a roughly level playing field, and would also ensure that some parts of the digital media meet regulatory standards of impartiality and accuracy in the election coverage. That in turn would shape the conduct of the campaign in the ways outlined earlier. The difficult question for such an option is deciding which digital media organizations should be subject to broadcast style regulations. One answer is to apply such standards to those media bodies that are publicly funded or public owned. While that is the least controversial option, it means that a very limited sector would be subject to the regulations. Any large or dominant privately owned video streaming services would still operate outside of the framework and have a competitive advantage over the regulated licensed broadcasters.

An alternative response is to extend some broadcast-style rules to services that are roughly equivalent to those found on television and radio. Such an approach is similar to that taken in the initial version of the video on-demand regulations, which applied special regulations (unrelated to elections) to 'TV-like' services based in the UK.[1] That approach also has limits, insofar as it relies on licensed television services as the main comparator to determine who should be regulated. As more content is consumed online, licensed television services are less distinctive, and do not provide such a useful basis for defining the market to be regulated. Another option is to widen the approach so that some broadcast style regulations are applied to those providing audiovisual content on the digital media (even if not 'TV-like'). Such an approach would be too expansive, if it were to impose election related regulations on small niche media companies, politically attached sites, and amateur content. Moreover, some larger services that disseminate audiovisual content, such as *YouTube*, primarily host content made by users and thereby perform a function distinct from television. While such a service is one of the main competitors with television, it is more appropriately regulated in relation to elections as a digital platform, which will be discussed later. For these reasons, the provision of audiovisual content alone is not a useful way to identify institutions that should be subject to an online equivalent of broadcast regulations.

A final option is to apply the regulations to media organizations with a certain level of dominance over the market. That would be a controversial option. Under this approach, there would be no reason to limit the regulations to those media bodies that are the functional equivalent of a licensed broadcaster. Such an approach could lead to the application of certain (more limited) public service obligations on newspapers that have a level of dominance over the market. Such an option would also pose a number of challenging questions, such as defining the particular market (in which the company has dominance) and in setting the threshold market share to trigger the various obligations. Such questions are not insurmountable and are addressed in other areas of law. While controversial, that approach to some public service obligations (beyond the state funded media) may be the most sustainable long-term.

In addition to regulation, the important functions performed during election campaigns could be supported by granting privileges to certain sections of the media, for example to secure visibility in the media ecosystem. Such privileges have been part of the deal for public service media—to meet certain regulatory standards in return for privileges that maintain prominence. In the past, these goals have been served by giving public service broadcasters prominence on electronic programme guides. That gives those broadcasters greater visibility, and therefore a competitive advantage over other providers. However, as Ofcom has noted, the current rules on prominence in programme guides might have limited effect in future years, as the way people acquire news changes (Ofcom 2019b).

There are various ways to ensure that services subject to public service obligations maintain a prominent position, and Ofcom has already taken steps to update the framework in relation to television (Ofcom 2019b). Looking in the longer term, digital platforms could be subject to an obligation to give regulated media organizations a prominent place in search results and in news feeds. Such a proposal was considered in the Cairncross Report in relation to newspapers, but was not recommended on account of the difficulties in determining which newspapers are sufficiently 'high quality' to benefit from that privilege (Cairncross 2019). While that is a problem with an unregulated newspaper sector, it is less problematic in relation to the public service media where certain identified news organizations are subject to regulation.

A related option, which fits with the proposals considered above, is to impose certain 'must carry' rules on the leading streaming services. The leading streaming services could thereby be required to carry news programmes (or bulletins) by the public service media organizations, particularly at the time of an election. Such an obligation could also include rules on the degree of prominence and in search results in the guides for streaming. The impact of such a policy would need to be carefully assessed, particularly how it affects traffic to the news organizations' own sites and platforms. However, such a policy could help maintain the reach of the public service news as television consumption habits change.

The previous section noted how rules applicable to broadcasters played a significant role in regulating the conduct of elections. In this section, various policy options have been considered, which aim to sustain and extend the life of that regulatory framework. Those options include the extension of certain regulatory burdens, but also the extension of certain privileges to secure a level of visibility for media outlets meeting those professional standards. Such measures alone will not address some of the ethical issues that arise with digital campaigning taking place outside of the regulated media. To address these issues, the following section will look at the digital platforms as a target for regulation.

RESPONSIBILITIES OF THE DIGITAL PLATFORMS

Given that much electoral communication is now unmediated and made directly available to voters via the digital media, another target for election regulations are the large technology companies, such as social media services or search engines. While some digital platforms produce media content, that is not the primary business for most (at least so far). The digital platforms that primarily host or help users to locate content made by others nonetheless perform a set of functions that are equivalent to some of those performed by the traditional media. In particular, the leading technology companies function as gatekeepers, so access to their services is necessary to reach a mass audience. In addition, the decisions of the technology companies, for example in designing systems for search and recommendation, help to determine which campaigners are likely to seen by which audience. As a result, there are demands to regulate those companies in a way that is broadly analogous to certain areas of media regulation. In the following sections, two possible avenues for regulation will be considered. The first focuses on the regulation of political advertising on digital platforms, which will have a direct impact on the messages of campaigners. The second is broader and considers whether the technology companies could be subject to a set of public service obligations.

Digital Advertising

Digital advertising has been a significant area of controversy in recent elections. The areas of concern will be grouped into four broad themes. The first is money, namely that the opportunities to purchase advertising on the digital media potentially increase the cost of election campaigning. The second is the degree to which digital advertising can be targeted with precision. The third theme is the level of transparency in relation to such paid communications. Finally, there are ethical concerns about the content of the purchased advertisements.

As was noted, the cost of elections in previous decades was kept down by the ban on paid political advertising on the broadcast media. The freedom to advertise on the digital media now opens up a new channel for political spending. While Twitter voluntarily prohibited political advertising in 2019, there is no prospect of a general prohibition on digital political advertising across platforms to keep election costs down. Moreover, digital advertising is not limited only to the very wealthy, so any ban could curtail the ability of small groups to get their message out. Any concerns about high spending can, in principle, be met through the general spending limits applied to all electoral activity. That means less emphasis is placed on media law to control election costs, and the election spending laws are the central constraint. Such an emphasis on election laws means that the regulator, the Electoral Commission, will need sufficient resources and powers to acquire the necessary information and impose sanctions to secure compliance.

Short of a ban on political advertisements there are other steps that can address concerns about the use of money in politics. One area for investigation could be to look at the way that online advertising is sold. For example, looking at whether the system of selling online advertising by auction or by ratings points works to privilege certain political campaigners over others in practice, or whether certain audiences are more costly to reach. If significant differences are to be found, then that could be an area for regulation to ensure that advertising is sold in a way that does not undermine a level playing field for different parties and groups.

A related point concerns the practice of technology companies providing staff to political campaigns to give advice on the best digital strategy on a platform (Kreiss et al. 2018). The provision of staff can constitute a donation in kind to a political campaign, which would require disclosure under the current law. Issues of fairness arise if a social media platform makes certain resources available to one candidate or party, but not another. Regulations should require that any such facility must be made available on equal terms to candidates and parties. However, the ethical concerns are not addressed simply by providing staff to all parties. Such arrangements allow the technology company to develop a close relationship with the political parties. Such a relation could give the company leverage in relation to future laws or policy decisions that affect its business

Money is not the only issue in relation to digital advertising in elections. One of the most prominent criticisms focusses on the targeting of messages at specific groups. The use of targeting is a major departure from advertising on the traditional mass media, in which the message is available for everyone to see. On the digital media, messages can be targeted at particular groups of voters, which will not be seen by others. Such targeting allows for levels of duplicity, so that politicians can signal different priorities to different groups. Targeting can also create an environment where misinformation proliferates, as there is a greater chance that false claims in a narrowly targeted advert will not be seen by an opposing campaign and therefore not be rebutted.

Despite the concerns, targeted advertising can perform some useful functions, for example in ensuring that members of the public receive messages that are most relevant to their interests and priorities. For that reason, an outright ban on all forms of targeting would be too restrictive and would raise difficult questions in defining what is meant by a 'non-targeted' advertisement. An alternative option is to restrict targeting based on certain characteristics or to limit the narrowness of the audience that can be targeted. For example, Google voluntarily limits the characteristics on which audiences can be targeted (Google 2019). Similarly, the Digital Culture Media and Sport Committee (2019, [223]) asked the government to consider restricting the use of custom audience advertising, where the message is targeted at those connected to data held by the advertiser (such as an email address that the campaigner has acquired separately).

Closely related to targeting are concerns about the transparency of digital advertising. One transparency issue has already been mentioned, that a narrowly targeted message may not be subject to scrutiny and rebuttal by opposing campaigners. The leading platforms have already taken steps to address this problem by providing publicly accessible archives of political advertisements, which allow the public to see what claims are being made by campaigners. A second transparency problem arises where the public does not know who is responsible for an advertisement or paying for it. Some advertisements in the 2019 General Election were purchased by groups that were previously unknown to the public and whose name gave little indication of any ideological background. Without such information about the source, the public may have little basis on which to assess the credibility of the messages. To address this transparency issue, the leading platforms now require a disclaimer revealing the person behind the message.

The voluntary steps taken by the companies are important, and those measures explain why third-party advertising was more visible in the 2019 UK General Election campaign. However, there are also some limits. For example, during the 2019 campaign, some media reports queried the extent to which the disclaimer requirements were being enforced (Manthorpe and Martin 2019). The different companies also have differing definitions of political content, which makes comparisons between the various platforms' data difficult. There are limits in the data provided. For example, the data provided in 2019 did not give a precise figure as to how much was spent on a particular advertisement, or which constituency it was targeted at. More fundamentally, as Benkler et al. (2019, 372) point out, such transparency requirements are too important to leave to the companies to devise on their own terms. Instead, any regulation of the digital platforms should include requirements to provide a political advertising archive, with details of the advertiser, the amounts spent and details of targeting (see Department of Digital, Culture, Media and Sport and Home Department 2019). The regulator should oversee the definitions of political advertising, ensure that such requirements are being followed, and that the data is accessible and easily searchable.

The final area of concern relates to the content of digital advertisements and messages. Through the digital platforms, the short spot advertisements that were common in the United States have now become a feature in UK elections. The use of such short messages may work to change the tone of election campaigns (for better or worse), with the proliferation of messages that are a far cry from the types of debate envisaged in some idealistic democratic theories. However, short and provocative election messages are not inherently wrong or unethical. The problems emerge when images and films are manipulated and are misleading as a result. Questions of campaign ethics arose in the 2019 general election, when a Conservative Party message shared on social media included footage of a television interview with Keir Starmer that had been edited (Kentish 2019).[2] The effect of the edit was to make Starmer look more hesitant in response to a question. The message prompted a debate about whether selectively edited footage is legitimate campaign speech or an unfair and misleading method. The example shows how, in the era of the digital campaign, the ethical questions about the appropriate use of short video clips (and the alteration of footage) now have to be confronted.

As a result of these developments, some organizations have called for content standards to be applied to political advertising and to certain messages, for example prohibiting inaccurate statements. For obvious reasons, some technology companies may not want to adjudicate on the merits of political claims, and to do so would risk claims of private censorship. Some steps have been taken by the companies to address such issues, for example by employing independent fact-checking organizations to assess the accuracy of claims made, and then taking remedial measures once the falsity is determined (Facebook 2020). That raises a number of risks, as it might lead to the fact-checking organization becoming financially dependent on the digital platform, or give such an organization too much scope to determine the truth of any politically contested matter. Such a strategy is likely to be most effective in relation to the more blatant and demonstrable falsities. A selectively edited video or exaggeration can be misleading without making a factual claim that is demonstrably false. While there is a role for formal fact-checking arrangements, such measures should work alongside the independent media coverage, which has a broader remit to examine and contest the claims made in the campaign messages.

Much of the focus in the debates about social media has been on paid advertising. However, there will be some types of activity that will to be harder to regulate. The regulation of advertisements sold by digital media companies will not cover those occasions where, for example, a campaigner pays an influencer to carry an electoral message. Formal advertising regulations will not catch the so-called troll farms, where people are paid to post political messages on social media posing as ordinary citizens. Such expenditures are, in theory, controlled in law by campaign spending rules, but the payments may be difficult to detect and will not be known to the audience. Similarly, the digital platform hosting such messages is unlikely to know that the speaker has been paid. As a result, the regulation of advertising alone cannot address all the concerns that are raised by the direct communications on the digital media.

Public Service Obligations

The final set of policy options looks beyond advertising regulation and asks whether the largest digital platforms could be subject to a type of public service regulation. The current debates on platform regulation focus on the prevention of harm as an organizing concept. As a result, much of the discussion of regulation looks at content moderation procedures and requirements to remove or de-list content. Using public service as a rationale for regulation in the context of elections would move the focus away from harm and look for ways to promote the valuable functions performed by the digital platforms. Earlier it was argued that some of the public service obligations that are currently applied to broadcasters should be extended to some large digital services that produce professional media content. That strategy is not appropriate for platforms that do not produce content. The proposal advanced in this section is not to extend broadcast regulations to the platforms, but to adapt public service obligations in a way that is appropriate for companies that host and allow people to locate content made by others. Public service goals could be pursued in very different ways from the broadcast sector, but serve similar democratic goals in making the public better informed and well equipped as citizens.

Along such lines, the companies could be regulated in relation to the algorithms that are used to prioritize content and direct the user's attention. A regulator could assess whether an algorithm is working to ensure that users are served with diverse content and hear messages from a range of political parties and campaigners. None of this would amount to an impartiality obligation, but would at least aim to check that a company's system provides a degree of pluralism in political content and prevents overt biases in the promotion of content.

Serving people with a diverse range of content alone is not sufficient to promote robust democratic debate. As important are the ways that people engage with the content and assess the competing arguments that they are exposed to. Regulators should look at the ways the platforms structure and frame the terms on which people interact with content online. For example, Settle argues that by giving people limited choices to express a response to content, such as whether to 'like' a post, the platforms do little to facilitate reasoned or reflective reactions (Settle 2018, 252). Settle also notes that by showing how many people have viewed, shared or liked a post, the companies may lead people to prejudge the content prior to reading (Settle 2018, 252).[3] Such practices may also contribute to a trend which rewards popularity and the more attention grabbing posts. The Digital Culture Media and Sport Committee (2019, [317]) has also suggested that the platforms should introduce levels of 'friction' in communication, so that people pause for reflection before sharing or commenting on a message. Similarly, some services have limited the number of people that a message can be forwarded to, in order to reduce the potential for misinformation to spread.[4] These areas show how the context in which content is received and framed can be a possible area for regulators to examine to improve the quality of democratic debate.

A broader way in which the platforms can perform a public service function analogous to the broadcast media is through hosting debates or other events during election campaigns. Such a function is to some degree already performed by some platforms, which stream election debates.[5] Such arrangements could be formalized, through a commitment to collaborate with an independent body that would determine the terms of the debate and who is invited to participate. Similarly, the platforms could also provide a forum for candidates to hold question and answer sessions with members of the public, but with certain defined rules of engagement. For example, such rules could be used to determine which questions are put to the candidate (or for an independent organization to select the questions), so the politician cannot use social media as a means to control the context of their own publicity and engagement with the public.

Finally, platforms could offer some free communications to the leading political actors to be disseminated to a mass audience. For example, a video hosting website could provide free time to the leading political parties, so that their messages are seen by a cross section of users. That could be a brief message before the user's chosen video is played. A similar model could apply to other forms of advertising. By taking such an approach, the regulations could develop something equivalent to party election broadcasts for the digital media. That would have the effect of ensuring that leading political parties have access to low cost messaging and would ensure the message goes out on a non-targeted basis so that it is publicly visible.

The technology companies are voluntarily adopting a number of these practices. As noted earlier, such practices should not be left to the companies to choose at their own convenience. However, such public service functions will not easily be achieved through concrete regulatory rules. Such functions are secured through detailed practices that will change over time and may vary according to the particular company. Instead, digital platforms should be subject to periodic public service reviews, in which a regulatory body examines how the services of the platform contribute to a fair electoral process and considers what changes should be made. Such a process would examine the algorithms and the systems of recommendation. The public service review would also examine the way the digital platform structures citizen's engagement. The platforms could also be required to engage in a partnership with independent organizations to provide standards for forums for debate, for candidate engagement, and also to allocate any free messages. A review of such matters would raise challenging issues for a regulator, as there are no agreed criteria on what a democracy requires. However, with no regulatory oversight, such decisions are determined by the commercial priorities of the digital platforms. The point is not to put forward any detailed change, but to propose a system of regulation which subjects the platforms to a periodic public service review and which can provide recommendations and develop codes of practice to protect the integrity of elections and promote robust democratic debate.

There is a further question of how such a system of regulation could be implemented and enforced. As with other systems of media regulation, the regulator would have a range of penalties that could be applied depending on the seriousness and scale of a failure to meet a requirement. The central challenge is jurisdictional as many of the largest services have headquarters based outside of the United Kingdom. The video on demand regulations, referred to earlier, are subject to the country of origin principle in EU law, so that the domestic rules only apply to those services based in the United Kingdom. However, an alternative approach is to apply regulations to services that make content available to audiences within jurisdiction, even where the company is based outside the United Kingdom. That is the approach taken in the UK government's proposals to regulate digital media companies in relation to 'harms' and in the (shelved) plans to require adult websites to verify the age of users (Department of Digital, Culture, Media and Sport and Home Department 2019). Under that approach, provision is made for the domestic authorities to disrupt the activities of non-compliant services based outside of the jurisdiction. Such questions of enforcement arise with any model for comprehensive digital media regulation. However, the types of public service obligation envisaged in the previous discussion would apply only to the major platforms, who have existing relationships with some UK authorities and are more likely to engage with regulatory requirements.

CONCLUSION

The chapter started by noting that by regulating the broadcast media, UK law regulated the conduct of election campaigns. Broadcasting laws helped to keep the cost of campaigning down, provided a forum for challenging claims made in the context of the campaign, and to some degree regulated the messages of the political actors. As more media moves online, the regulatory framework targeting licensed broadcasters will come under increasing strain and seem harder to justify. The increase in campaigning on the digital media means that more electoral activity takes places outside of the broadcast media and is not subject to its regulatory framework.

While there is good reason to celebrate the increased freedom to participate on the digital media, a demise or marginalization of the public service media would impoverish the quality of the United Kingdom's democracy. Accordingly, it has been argued that the public service media is a key part of the ecosystem, which can impact on the other parts of the media and systems of communication. As a result, public service media plays an important role in checking and interrogating claims made by political actors on the digital media and elsewhere. A key policy goal is therefore to ensure the continuing support for the regulatory framework applied to broadcasters and the public service media, and extend its application to some parts of the digital news media. In addition, policies should be designed is to ensure the continuing prominence and visibility of the public service media.

Even with such measures, much campaigning takes place outside of the traditional media, and there is more scope for campaigners to communicate directly with the public. As a result, policymakers will need to look beyond broadcasters and their online equivalents to maintain public service functions in election campaigns. In particular, the digital platforms are appropriate targets for regulatory measures. That includes the regulation of political advertising, to promote transparency and to consider the impact of targeting and the costs of campaigning. Aside from advertising, there is also a case for some public service obligations to be imposed on the larger platforms. Such regulations might look at algorithms, to see that diverse and quality content is promoted, and the ways the digital media frame and structure online interactions. Such goals may not lend themselves to concrete rules, and are best be secured through a periodic regulatory review of the leading platforms.

The discussion has focused on the experience in the United Kingdom and the 'public service' function of the media reflected in the broadcast regulations. However, the general lessons are of broader application. In particular, the integrity of elections cannot be secured with a quick fix or tweak to the rules. The problems of misinformation and lack of transparency are not so easily dealt with in specialized election laws, which may prove to be too blunt to deal with many subtle issues. Instead, the chapter has emphasized the need to focus on the whole infrastructure for election communications. Regulations should not simply aim to prohibit harmful content, but should more actively promote an environment where competing arguments are tested and challenged, where politicians and candidates are held to account, and where high-quality content is known and visible.

NOTES

1. The original statutory provisions for video on demand made a direct comparison with television, see Communications Act 2003, s.368A (as inserted in 2009). However, in 2020, the provision was amended to remove that comparison, so the video on demand standards may now apply to a wider range of services. Some of the video on demand rules have also been extended to video sharing websites under Communications Act 2003, Part 4B, as required under Audiovisual Media Services Directive (2018).
2. The message was posted on social media, rather than a paid advertisement. The example nonetheless shows the type of ethical question that can arise when using short video clips in election messages.
3. The statistics displayed on posted content vary depending on the particular social media service.
4. See, for example the limits on forwarding to the number of chats for WhatsApp, https://faq.whatsapp.com/en/general/26000253/.

5.   For example, in the United States, YouTube offers livestreams of candidate debates
     organized by other bodies and has partnered with media organizations to host elec-
     tion debates.

REFERENCES

Benkler, Yochai, Robert Farris, and Hal Roberts. 2018. *Network Propaganda*.
     Oxford: Oxford University Press.
Broadcasters Liaison Group. 2018. 'Guidelines for the Production of Party Broadcasts'.
Cairncross, Frances. 2019. 'The Cairncross Review: A Sustainable Future for Journalism'.
Department of Digital, Culture, Media and Sport and Home Department. 2019. 'Online
     Harms'. White Paper. CP 57.
Facebook. 2020. 'Fact-Checking on Facebook'. Accessed November 16, 2020. https://
     www.facebook.com/help/publisher/182222309230722.
Fletcher, Richard, Nic Newman, and Anne Schultz. 2020. *A Mile Wide, an Inch
     Deep: Online News and Media Use in the 2019 General Election*. Oxford: Reuters
     Institute for the Study of Journalism.
Google. 2019. 'An Update on Our Political Ads Policy', November 20. https://
     www.blog.google/technology/ads/update-our-political-ads-policy/.
House of Commons Digital, Culture, Media and Sport Committee. 2019. 'Disinformation
     and "Fake News": Final Report'. HC 1791. London: The Stationary Office.
Humprecht, Edda, Frank Esser, and Peter Van Aelst. 2020. 'Resilience to Online
     Disinformation: A Framework for Cross-National Comparative Research'.
     International Journal of Press/Politics 25(3): 333–56.
Keane, John. 2013. *Democracy and Media Decadence*. Cambridge: Cambridge
     University Press.
Kentish, Benjamin. 2019. 'Tory Post Uses Doctored Clip of Labour Brexit Secretary'. *The
     Independent*, November 6.
Kreiss, Daniel, and Shannon McGregor. 2018. 'Technology Firms Shape Political
     Communication: The Work of Microsoft, Facebook, Twitter, and Google with
     Campaigns during the 2016 U.S. Presidential Cycle'. *Political Communication*
     35(2): 155–77.
Manthorpe, Rowland, and Alexander Martin. 2019. 'Google Breaches Own Rules with
     Undisclosed Tory Attack Ad'. *Sky News*, November 21. https://news.sky.com/story/
     google-breaches-own-rules-with-undisclosed-tory-attack-ad-11866416.
Ofcom. 2017. 'Ofcom's Rules on Due Impartiality, Due Accuracy, Elections and
     Referendums'.
Ofcom. 2019a. 'Ofcom Broadcasting Code'.
Ofcom. 2019b. 'Review of Prominence for Public Service Broadcasting'. The Ofcom
     Broadcasting Code (2019) https://www.ofcom.org.uk/__data/assets/pdf_file/0016/
     132073/Broadcast-Code-Full.pdf
Review of Prominence for Public Service Broadcasting https://www.ofcom.org.uk/
     __data/assets/pdf_file/0021/154461/recommendations-for-new-legislative-
     framework-for-psb-prominence.pdf
Rowbottom, Jacob. 2009. 'Extreme Speech and the Democratic Functions Mass Media'.
     In *Extreme Speech and Democracy*, edited by Ivan Hare and James Weinstein.

Oxford: Oxford University Press. Oxford Scholarship Online, 2009. doi: 10.1093/acprof:oso/9780199548781.003.0032

Settle, Jaime. 2018. *Frenemies: How Social Media Polarizes America*. Cambridge: Cambridge University Press.

CASE LAW

R (on the application of Animal Defenders International) v. Secretary of State for Culture, Media and Sport [2008] UKHL 15.

R (on the application of Liberal Democrats) v. ITV Broadcasting Ltd [2019] EWHC 3282.

R (on the application of ProLife Alliance) v. BBC [2003] UKHL 23.

PART V

Reforming Governance

14

A Model for Global Governance
of Platforms

ROBERT FAY ■

INTRODUCTION

Covid-19 has revealed the pervasive nature of digital technologies in our everyday lives. Digital platforms such as Google, Facebook, Twitter, Amazon, and a more recent entrant, Zoom, have provided core societal functions that have enabled us to work, shop, educate ourselves and our children, run businesses, maintain social contact, and receive and disseminate information. At the same time, the uses of these technologies have led to elevated concerns in areas such as surveillance, cyber risks, democracy, public health, competition and monopoly power, and economic prosperity.

At the heart of these platforms are big data and advanced analytic techniques such as artificial intelligence technologies (AI) that form a powerful value chain— McKinsey Global Institute (2018) expects that artificial intelligences technologies in this value chain could boost global GDP growth by trillions of dollars. Not surprisingly there is a global competition by firms and nations to acquire this value, but for this value to be realized requires substantial improvements in governance to unlock data and unleash the technologies.

Current governance arrangements of this value chain are incoherent and fragmented nationally and internationally—where they even exist. At the same time, they typically reflect vested state and corporate interests that can be very difficult to challenge. Further, how data are captured and used in artificial intelligence technologies, and those technologies themselves, are not transparent and typically lack coherent rules and certainly no global rules. More generally, governance arrangements are out of date, reflecting old industrial patterns and not those of the digital economy. Indeed, as argued by Medhora and Owen (2020), 'When world leaders came together in Bretton Woods, New Hampshire, in 1944, they laid the foundation for a model of global governance that would last for more than 70 years. To manage the far-reaching implications of digital technology and hyper-globalization, we must now pick up where they left off'.

The way forward is to create a new institution for the digital realm: a Digital Stability Board (DSB). It would follow the example of the Financial Stability Board (FSB) that was established by the G20 to promote reform of international financial regulation and supervision following the lapses in governance that contributed to the Great Financial Crisis (GFC). The FSB is not treaty-based yet has managed, and delivered, the vast global financial regulatory reform process. Its success in part derives from its transparent multi-stakeholder participatory international forums that include policymakers, regulators, standard-setting bodies, and civil society. In a similar fashion, the DSB would also be a multi-stakeholder forum with a remit to create global governance for big data, AI, and the digital platforms, while allowing national variation to reflect different values and cultures, but avoiding a race to the bottom in governance. Like the FSB, at least initially the DSB would not be treaty-based, and it would have a broad mandate and cover a combination of policies, principles, regulations, standards, and legislation. Developing this governance will involve experimentation, iteration, and international coordination, as well as the engagement of a wide variety of stakeholders to have legitimacy.

This chapter follows up on an article by Fay (2019a) that argued for the creation of a DSB. It begins with a brief overview of recent international initiatives that touch upon big data and AI governance, emphasizing the well-intentioned but disparate initiatives underway. This is followed by an assessment of the many issues that arise from this patchwork of initiatives as well as proposals to enhance international cooperation. The structure of a DSB and its functions are then laid out along with justifications on why a new organization is needed. Two concrete areas where the DSB could begin its work—international standard setting around data and AI, and governance of social media platforms—are briefly described before a concluding section.

RECENT INITIATIVES ON INTERNATIONAL COOPERATION

It is an understatement to say that there are numerous initiatives going on around the world related to governance of the big data, AI, and digital platform value chain.[1] They are both plentiful and at the same time typically not grounded in a coherent overriding global framework, and despite burgeoning efforts at international collaboration, fundamental cross-cutting issues related to the governance of data and AI, including privacy and surveillance, competition, and platform content, remain to be addressed.

This situation is not overly surprising. National authorities are themselves grappling with the wide-ranging nature of the digital economy and the many new benefits and challenges that it brings, and international cooperation is not necessarily yet—or high—on their radar. Yet it needs to be given that data and digital technologies do not respect national borders. Further, many countries may not even feel that they would have a voice or the expertise to participate in such discussions.

At the same time, trying to achieve a global framework is made all the more difficult by the splintering of the Internet into data realms (Aaronson and Leblond 2018). In the United States, the focus of policymakers has been on open data flows, de facto national champions, and digital chapters in trade agreements that prioritize data flows back to the de facto champions, thus supporting a continued rise in their dominant monopoly power. In essence the view is to let 'big tech regulate big tech'. In the European Union, where national champions do not exist, there has been a focus on strategic regulations, standards and regulation, data-rights regimes, and competition policy; while China has set itself apart with its 'Great Firewall', national champions, and influence in other countries through its Belt and Road initiative and its strategic push into standard setting. The geopolitical battle is illustrated emphatically with the US administration's 2020 decision to ban the use of TikTok and WeChat under the guise of national security related to perceived concerns over the collection and use of the private data of American citizens by the Chinese authorities.[2] Although the ban has been rescinded, a new executive order is in place on "Protecting Americans' Sensitive Data from Foreign Adversaries" that will examine, among other things, the implications of the unrestricted transfer of sensitive data to foreign adversaries. .

This complicated political and economic background reveals the challenges inherent in trying to achieve global cooperation. The basis for international cooperation would typically start with national regulations and legislation, but there is a patchwork of regulations and policies in place, if anything has been done at all. Aaronson (2018) notes the diversity and perhaps disparity in approaches to data and artificial intelligence governance proposals: as of 2018, only 2 countries had national data strategies, 17 had national AI strategies, and 107 countries had national data laws. Not surprisingly they are least advanced, if they exist at all, in less developed countries, where governance frameworks tend to be weakest (see, for example, an assessment of Africa by Ademuyiwa and Adeniran (2020).

At the regional level, the best-known regulation of data is the European General Data Protection Regulation (GDPR), which was introduced in 2018. Europe notes that it is the 'toughest privacy and security law in the world' and 'it imposes obligations onto organizations anywhere (globally), so long as they target or collect data related to people in the EU'. It relies on reciprocal recognition for firms outside the EU, which is required for them to operate within the union. It thus imposes a de facto GDPR rule on countries who wish to operate in the European Union (Aaronson and Leblond [2019] provide a succinct overview of GDPR). The European Union is now embarking on further enhancements to its digital strategy with the proposed Digital Markets Act and the Digital Services Act. The former sets criteria on when core platform providers may be deemed to be "gatekeepers" and thus in need of additional supervision. The latter proposes a package that 'seeks to ensure the best conditions for the provision of innovative digital services in the internal market, to contribute to online safety and the protection of fundamental rights, and to set a robust and durable governance structure for the effective supervision of providers of intermediary services'.[3] Not surprisingly, given the size of the European Union, the fact that all of its member countries are compelled to follow GDPR as well as its extraterritorial nature, combined with the forthcoming Acts will make the European Union an even more powerful player in global governance. The span of Europe's influence goes beyond these initiatives.[4] The Council of Europe's Convention 108 on the 'Protection of Individuals with regard to Automatic Processing of Personal Data' was first introduced in 1981 with fifty-five signatory countries and is a legally binding document (thus beyond Europe and transnational in scope) on personal data protection.[5] It was updated in 2018 to reflect new technologies and innovations, is consistent with GDPR, and will be used by the European Union in its reciprocity assessments for GDPR compliance.

At the international level, the G7, G20, and international organizations have been active particularly in the area of artificial intelligence. Under the Canadian G7 Presidency, Canada and France agreed to a Joint Partnership on AI to provide recommendations on the use of AI based on shared principles of 'human rights, inclusion, diversity, innovation and economic growth'.[6] This joint partnership has since morphed into the Global Partnership on AI (GPAI) that was formally launched on June 15, 2020, comprising fifteen countries, including all the G7 nations, with secretariat support from the Organization for Economic Co-operation and Development (OECD) and covering responsible AI, data governance, future of work, and innovation and commercialization.[7] This recent initiative is not to be confused with the Partnership on AI that was established in 2016 by the large IT companies.[8] The G7 and G20 have working groups dedicated to the digital economy and a key initiative under the Japanese G20 Presidency was the 'data flow with trust' and while there has been little substance to date for this objective, this initiative has continued into the Italian Presidency in 2021.

The OECD worked with a wide variety of stakeholders to develop its Principles on Artificial Intelligence, to which forty-two countries have signed on—thus beyond the OECD membership—which outline a set of policies in five broad areas related to the use of AI.[9] It also contains an extensive list of policy initiatives that are underway with seventy-six initiatives across the forty-two countries related to AI. The Open Data Charter is a collaboration between over 100 governments and organizations working to open up data based on a shared set of principles via an International Open Data Charter .[10] Meanwhile, the OECD Privacy Framework serves as the base for much of the work in this area nationally and internationally, including the APEC Privacy Framework, and are being revised.[11] The difficulty in achieving international cooperation is amply demonstrated in the ongoing discussions at the OECD with respect to taxation of multinational enterprises (initially aimed at social media platforms) under the Base Erosion and Profit Shifting (BEPS) initiative.[12] On the one hand, 135 countries are involved in the process showing that collaboration on this scale is possible; on the other hand, the United States' 2020 decision to pull out revealed the discord of vested interests in this domain.

Private, civil society, and non-profit groups have also been active. Although too numerous to enumerate, some of the better known initiatives include the Web Foundation Contract for the Web, which outlines nine principles that governments, the private sector, and citizens agree to follow, the Toronto Declaration on Human Rights in Machine Learning Systems, and the Montreal Declaration on the Responsible Development of AI.[13] In late 2020, the Forum on Information and Democracy released 250 recommendations through its Working Group on Infodemics. They focus on four areas: platform transparency, content moderation, promotion of reliable news and information, and private messaging services.[14]

To make this complicated situation even more confusing, provisions in some trade agreements have also set rules over data flows, algorithmic auditing, and social media platform content and are binding international rules to those party to the agreements. For example, the new Canada, US, Mexico trade agreement contains regulations on cross-border data flows that limit data localization, place strict rules related to algorithmic auditing, and limit the liability of social media platforms on content, essentially incorporating Section 230 of the US Federal Communications Decency Act, that 'provides immunity to online platforms from civil liability based on third-party content and for the removal of content in certain circumstances'.[15] The recently signed Digital Economy Partnership Agreement (Chile, New Zealand, and Singapore) contains articles on data innovation, digital identity, artificial intelligence, and digital inclusion that could serve as the building blocks for a broader agreement on digital governance issues.[16] More generally, provisions in trade agreements have implications for domestic policies such as privacy, national security, and industrial development though these implications are not usually considered (Fay 2020).

Given their global reach, the rules set by the large social media platforms for their own actions should be viewed as de facto global rule setters. For example, Facebook uses its Community Standards and more recently introduced an Oversight Board to govern content, Twitter has its Twitter Rules and has proposed its own social media standard that treats governance essentially as an engineering problem (Fay 2019b).[17] Google uses its Privacy Policy as a guide. TikTok announced a Transparency and Accountability Centre for moderation and data practices and it would be the first platform to provide algorithms, moderation policies, and data flows to regulators, though it is not clear who those regulators will be.[18] These platform-specific initiatives can be viewed as self-regulatory approaches, but not in the usual sense that a group of similar organizations in a sector has come together to define common rules. Indeed, these standards, rules, and policies are defined by each specific platform based on its own defined values. There are many instances in which they treat similar situations very differently. Most recently, this can be seen in decisions by Twitter and Facebook to have different treatment in the fact check of statements by politicians, with Twitter adding warnings while Facebook was initially adamant against any form of content moderation by statements from politicians. Although both platforms now post warning labels and have removed content, and in some cases have banned prominent users from the platform, the rules that determine how they moderate such content and remove users are not clear and not consistent across platforms. Furthermore, there is no external validation of how successful the fact checking is in labelling or removing erroneous and harmful content.

Standard setters have also been active. Girard (2020) provides an overview of standard setting in the area of big data and AI and notes that 'Standard-setting activities in the ICT sector can only be described as extraordinarily complex, opaque, evolutionary, bottom up and unpredictable' (p. 10). Nevertheless, there are many noteworthy initiatives underway including OCEANIS— The Open Community for Ethics in Autonomous and Intelligent Systems— which is a global forum to discuss and collaborate on the development and use of standards in autonomous and intelligent systems.[19] The International Telecommunications Union (ITU) has its Global Symposium for Regulators that examines issues related to the ICT sector, and is actively involved in standard setting for facial recognition while the IEEE has launched the Global Initiative on Ethics of Autonomous and Intelligent Systems (The IEEE Global Initiative).[20] The International Organization for Standardization (ISO) and International Electrotechnical Commission (IEC) have begun standards de-velopment activities under the aegis of the Joint Technical Committee Number 1 (JTC1) to set information and communications technology (ICT) standards for business and consumer applications and includes those related to big data, privacy, AI, Internet of things, and smart cities.[21]

THE RISKS OF THE CURRENT REGULATORY SITUATION ON DIGITAL GOVERNANCE

The patchwork of initiatives, regulations, and self-regulation—and indeed lack of regulation—create a host of issues. A thoughtful piece from the United Nations (2019) that undertook consultations with a wide variety of stakeholders noted that 'we heard a great deal of dissatisfaction with existing digital cooperation ar-rangements: a desire for more tangible outcomes, more active participation by governments and the private sector, more inclusive processes and better follow-up. Overall, systems need to become more holistic, multi-disciplinary, multi-stakeholder, agile and able to convert rhetoric into practice'. (p. 30)[22]

The report identified six main gaps:

1. The low priority assigned to digital technology cooperation nationally, regionally, and globally;
2. The lack of inclusivity in work that is underway by technical and standard-setting bodies and even the capacity of many to participate;
3. The overlap and complex digital cooperation architecture that may not be very effective;
4. The horizontal nature of digital technologies against a background of vertical decision-making;
5. The lack of reliable data and evidence upon which to base policy; and

6. The lack of trust among governments, civil society, and the private sector that can make it more difficult to establish the collaborative multi-stakeholder approach needed to develop effective cooperation mechanisms.

In addition to these noteworthy gaps, there are many other risks and concerns:

7. The lack of transparency in how data are captured and used in AI that could lead to rising mistrust and thus a pullback in sharing data. AI requires big data and a pullback would have detrimental impacts along the value chain. Data are the currency of the digital world; and like any currency, to have value there must be trust and trust comes from proper governance. Like capital, data flows easily across borders and thus requires international regulation. The surge in cross-border data flows, the looming implementation of 5G and the Internet of Things, and an acceleration in digitization in the wake of Covid-19 create the conditions for vast data collection and monetization without a coherent underlying governance framework to create trust. This situation will amplify already existing concerns over the lack of transparency in the value chain, including privacy of personal data, ethical use of AI and monetization of data by social media platforms.

8. Confusion over what rules need to be followed, combined with a lack of consistency, coherence, and enforcement, that elevates compliance costs which can be particularly pernicious for micro and small enterprises. Further, the lack of commonality of consent agreements creates consumer confusion and risks, including those related to privacy and cyber security.

9. The extraterritoriality of some measures such as GDPR that may not be suitable for other jurisdictions and which may not be able to influence such regulations and thus a lack of democratic accountability in those jurisdictions.

10. Embedded vested interests and the power to lobby on the direction of regulation risks a race to the lowest common denominator in rules and regulations and contributes to a lack of effective enforcement of rules. This includes trade rules that could potentially impinge on domestic policy setting in important areas related to privacy, national security, and industrial policy.

11. Self-regulation that has led to market structures that are defined by the platforms to benefit the platforms, which combined with rules designed for an industrial age, has profound implications for areas such as competition policy and innovation, the distribution of the value from the technologies and social cohesion nationally and internationally.

12. Finally, the lack of a comprehensive and coherent assessment of the risks, vulnerabilities, and outcomes of the business models of the digital platforms, and in particular social media platforms, against a

background of rising online harms.[23] The misuse of private data can, and has, led to widespread social harms for which there is currently little governance. This is due in part to a lack of access to the data that the platforms gather that could be used to assess such risks. It is also due to the lack of access to the algorithms that are used to amplify information.

The current state of governance ultimately lacks democratic accountability and representation. Governments themselves have taken insufficient actions, and many different groups have little influence on the direction that governance has taken thus risking entrenchment of a digital divide and lack of inclusiveness—the exact opposite of what had been intended with the founding of the Web.

WHAT ARE SOME OF THE PROPOSED SOLUTIONS?

Aaronson and Leblond (2019) argue for a Single Data Area under a proposed International Data Standards Board (IDSB) where data can circulate freely between participating jurisdictions with a common regulatory environment for governing data that would be based on a common set of standards around data collection, processing, purchase and sale, and so on, as defined by the IDSB. As such, the authors argue that the envisaged single data area would go much further than digital/data rights-based conventions and declarations or trade agreements with digital or e-commerce chapters, which are all limited to general principles. Further, they argue that the development of a common set of standards would help to minimize restrictions on data flows that might arise due to differences in data protection. Any country that met these standards could be welcomed to join. They note that this only applies to data and not to trade in digital goods and services though presumably it could help facilitate the development of them.

The UN report mentioned above proposes three different types of models: an 'Internet Governance Forum Plus', a 'Distributed Co-Governance Architecture' or a 'Digital Commons Architecture' model, each of which would be run by the UN. It notes that 'There was broad agreement that improved cooperation is needed, that such cooperation will need to take multiple diverse forms, and that governments, the private sector and civil society will need to find new ways to work together to steer an effective path between extremes of over-regulation and complete laissez-faire'. (p. 31)

- **An enhanced and empowered Internet Governance Forum (IGF)**, an existing multi-stakeholder platform organized by the UN, to better reflect and incorporate the views of the private sector, civil society, and smaller countries that are typically underrepresented in forum discussions.
- **A distributed 'network of networks'** that would build on existing multi-stakeholder international cooperation mechanisms to offer a fast and

flexible platform to develop and test voluntary norms and principles intended to serve as guardrails at 'Internet speed'.

- **A new 'Digital Commons' architecture** that draws from approaches to how we manage collective action in space, climate, and oceans to develop similar digital common goods—resources upon which digital technologies rely and which require global stewardship, such as Internet protocols.

The UN and stakeholders have indicated that no matter which model is ultimately chosen, they would like to see the IGF enhanced thus it is useful to provide more background about the IGF.[24] It was established in 2006, and the Under Secretary General of UNDESA (United Nations Department of Economic and Social Affairs) oversees the IGF Secretariat. It is funded on a voluntary basis via a separate trust overseen by the UN. It is designed to collect multi-stakeholder views and share policies and practices relating to the Internet and technologies. The issues discussed at the IGF are broad and cover anything from fake news to AI policy. It is led by a Multi-Stakeholder Advisory Group (MAG) appointed by the UN Secretary General—a group of roughly fifty experts and practitioners representing all stakeholder groups and each UN region that are nominated by stakeholder communities. An annual meeting sets out the major program for the IGF, which then is followed up through various subgroups that report in each year. A key feature of the IGF is that it has no decision-making power. This situation was intended with an overriding goal to highlight issues where international attention is needed and use discussion, sharing of best practices and likely peer pressure and influence to deal with them. In the end, however, a criticism was that this situation led to a lack of a focus on concrete outcomes, something that the IGF plus seeks to change.

In a wide-ranging report, the Pathway for Prosperity Commission Digital Roadmap (2019) reiterates many of the same points as those by the United Nations (2019). Two of its recommendations are particularly pertinent:

- Recommendation 8 that 'All governments need to establish a data governance regime'. These should reflect their society's norms and expectations. Though there is no single blueprint, a common standard should be that citizens can trust that their personal information is collected and used in ways that are secure, transparent, and accountable, and that the governance regime demonstrates respect for fundamental human rights and
- Recommendation 26 which calls for 'developing country governments to coordinate on technology governance at the regional and international levels where their values and interests align, and for multilateral organizations to be responsive to the needs of developing countries when creating global standards'.

A DIGITAL STABILITY BOARD

One important achievement of the G20 early in the GFC was the creation of the FSB, formalizing the Financial Stability Forum that had previously existed to discuss financial stability issues, to overhaul global and national regulation in the financial sector. The parallel between the FSB and its genesis, and the state of regulation in the digital sphere, is instructive.

Fuelled by light-touch regulation, banks and insurers grew tremendously in size and power, leading to the creation of some exceptionally large global financial institutions. In many instances this was either encouraged—or at least not discouraged—with the prevailing notion that their expansion was a global good, creating and delivering new financial services to customers with greater efficiency via financial wizardry that turned out to be opaque in terms of network effects, risks, and consequences. And the prevailing view at the time was that self-interest and reputation would constrain bad behaviour. Instead it contributed to one of the worst crises in the past 100 years.

The current regulatory framework for big data, AI, and the social media platforms is reminiscent of the rapid development of financial services globally in the 1990s and 2000s. It is in essence light touch regulation. Like the few global banks that had dominated financial services, there are a few global giants that dominate platforms, but how they operate—capture and combine data with advanced technologies to monetize the data—is opaque. Yet at the same time, regulation remains light touch. Perhaps this is based on the view that the platforms globally are simply too complicated to regulate. Not only do they operate across many jurisdictions but also they span many different areas that touch all aspects of people's lives. Perhaps it is related to the fact that they have provided undeniable benefits to the global community, from social connections to the delivery of financial services. And perhaps it is related to the vested interests that do not want to see reform. This situation is similar to that faced in the financial sector, which led to the crisis and the eventual creation of the FSB.

Reforming international financial regulation and supervision was a daunting task—indeed one that continues to this day—given that mandates and cultures vary tremendously across financial institutions and countries that are involved in regulating and delivering financial services such as central banks, private banks, securities and insurance regulators, standard setters, policymakers, and so on. And there was tremendous resistance, including complaints about rising regulatory burdens and costs. But ultimately it was clear that regulation had been too lax and needed to be addressed urgently and that global banks and insurers needed a more consistent regulatory approach given the risks that they created. It was also essential to rebuild trust in financial institutions. This led to the creation of the FSB.

The FSB reports directly to the G20, and its main decision-making body is the Plenary, which consists of representatives of all Members with fifty-nine representatives from twenty-five jurisdictions, six representatives from four international financial institutions, and eight representatives from six international standard-setting, regulatory, supervisory, and central bank bodies.[25]

In carrying out its work the FSB promotes global financial stability by 'coordinating the development of regulatory, supervisory and other financial sector policies and conducts outreach to non-member countries. It achieves cooperation and consistency through a three-stage process'. [26] The latter includes a vulnerabilities assessment, policy development, and implementation monitoring. Each of these areas has a number of working groups which comprise individuals from countries that are part of the FSB and international standard-setting bodies such as IOSCO and IASB, and engages with a variety of countries and organizations that are outside FSB membership, for example, regional groups—but who may also be affected.[27] The FSB's innovative multi-stakeholder processes have been essential to carrying out its responsibilities, and these processes are a model that can be adapted for digital governance. It reports its actions to and receives orders from the G20, assuring that there is accountability.

Despite the daunting task that the FSB faced, the significant progress in financial sector reform is proof that these processes can achieve real and substantive global reforms and that it does not require treaties to achieve success.[28] So how do we translate this model into one for digital governance?

An analogous DSB would oversee the complex global reform of the digital system. The overarching objective would be to bring coherence and transparency to digital policymaking and regulation, enhance transparency in how data are collected and used in algorithms and by digital platforms, and ultimately bolster the trust in this value chain that is essential for the digital economy to achieve its full potential.

A DSB Plenary body (DSBP) would meet annually (perhaps more often during the setup phase) to set objectives, prioritize and oversee work of the DSB, and set outcomes that are to be achieved. The DSB would consist of officials from countries and existing international organizations that initially join. Each Plenary meeting would include discussions with standard setting bodies, governments and policymakers, regulators, civil society, and the platforms themselves that would also be included in relevant working groups with clear mandates that would report back to the Plenary. More specifically, the broad objectives and structure for the DSB would be the following:

1. *Coordinate* **the development of international governance in standards, regulations, principles, and policies across the big data value chain.** A Digital Governance Group (DGG) would focus on coordinated international governance of the big data and AI value chain, including areas such as privacy, ethics, data quality and portability, algorithmic accountability; social media content, including fake news and mis/disinformation; competition policy; and electoral integrity. The objective would be to develop a set of principles, standards, and policies that can be applied globally, but allow for domestic variation to reflect

national values and customs. Each area could have its own working group that would be approved by the DGG, which would give mandates, accountabilities, and outcome objectives while also ensuring that working groups coordinate.

2. *Monitor* **implementation of DGG initiatives and advise on best practices:** A Digital Monitoring Group (DMG) would monitor the implementation of principles, standards, and policies that had been developed by the DPG and approved by the DSBP. This monitoring could take place in the context of joint work with other organizations: it could feed into OECD peer reviews, IMF and World Bank (WB) country assessments and the WTO as it works on global digital trade rules. The social media platforms themselves would also be peer reviewed to see how they meet rules and regulations.

3. *Assess* **vulnerabilities and governance innovation opportunities.** A Digital Vulnerabilities Group (DVG) would assess new vulnerabilities and risks arising in the digital economy and where international coordination is required. The digital economy is very dynamic, and the global digital ecosystem is evolving rapidly. Further, regulations will change it—in intended and likely unintended ways—and it will be important to assess their impact, and the regulatory and policy actions needed to address any vulnerabilities or gaps on a timely basis. For example, regulatory sandboxes have been widely used in the financial sector and could be used to assess risk around new regulation and governance models and help to promote participatory governance innovations. Importantly, to do the vulnerabilities assessments will require access to platform data and algorithms. Although this would likely be vigilantly opposed by the platforms, in principle giving access to regulators in these areas is no different than what has been done in financial regulatory reform (or indeed in other areas such as the regulation of pharmaceuticals).

4. *Ensure* **that this work feeds into other organizations.** A Digital Outreach Group (DOG) would disseminate best practices that could be implemented at the national level, and also ensure that relevant bodies and civil society are part of the DSB discussions. It could also inform national level efforts particularly in countries and regions where capacity may be limited. And it would ensure coordination with other organizations involved in this area.

WHY A NEW ORGANIZATION?

In this age of populism, antiglobalization, and now the competing vested interests associated with the capture of rents from the use of these technologies, it may seem not only surprising but also self-defeating to propose a new international body. Yet all of these factors make it more essential than ever to embark on a new path for digital governance. A re-enforcement of the data realms or a splintering into multiple spheres would make a chaotic situation even more confusing and substantially diminish the value that can accrue from these technologies in addition to creating the space for substantial harms related to privacy, cyber, and so on.

The creation of the DSB would be a statement, and acknowledgement, that the digital realm needs its own institution and integrated international governance. It is also explicitly outcome focussed—for example derive voluntary standards; implement, assess, and evaluate changes—in a multi-stakeholder setting to avoid the capture of vested interests. It would not be treaty-based at least initially, given that the requirements to create such an institution would be high and could in fact deter its creation. Rather it would be a forum for discussion, with peer pressure as a powerful mechanism via a coalition of the willing that would get its legitimacy via broad and transparent engagement.

The DSB shares characteristics of other proposed models including the IGF plus model, including a focus on multi-stakeholder participation and flexibility to deal with a wide range of digital technology issues. Yet the IGF's association with the UN is both a blessing and a curse. The UN is global in nature and has extensive linkages at the institutional and civic levels. But it is saddled with substantial baggage and suspicions over how some of its bodies operate, such as Chinese and Russian involvement in standard setting in the ITU related to facial recognition and new emerging technologies such as 5G.[29] Moreover, the UN already has very large responsibilities and mandates as do other Bretton Woods institutions such as the IMF and WB. Allowing them to formulate the reforms would likely leave the process piecemeal—its current state. The WTO, which has broad representation and creates global rules, is also not suitable. Even without the paralysis in which the organization finds itself, it does not have the expertise to set digital policy. In fact, there are substantial dangers, as outlined earlier, in having trade negotiators decide rules that go beyond trade. Rather, the WTO would take digital policies, rules, and standards and interpret them for trade.

The OECD, which is arguably leading the international work on digital policy and governance, has shown that it is capable of getting agreement that goes beyond its members with its AI Principles, but it is still seen as representing developed countries. It remains to be seen whether the newly founded GPAI and its Secretariat could serve as a nascent DSB, and it will be important to watch how representation in this newly formed body evolves. The OECD has expertise in many areas including regulation and digital policy though less so in standard setting.

Finally, there are three other issues that might also be raised. First, given the disjointed state of national rule-making, how could one hope to achieve any international consensus on rules? Second, given the data realms, wouldn't those jurisdictions with the most advanced regulation, those where the platforms reside or those with the greatest power dominate decision-making and policy development? And third, how does one reconcile freedom of speech alongside greater regulation of platform content?

The fact that some countries, and regions, do not have laws or regulations in place likely reflects capacity as well as a lack of voice. An international effort could therefore help to build this capacity while giving these countries and regions a voice at the table. The key would be an open and inclusive multi-stakeholder structure with transparent decision-making that would allow their voices to be heard. At the same time, while the data realms exist, it is clear that countries outside of these realms—and indeed some within—are starting to question the dominance of both the platforms and the realms. There are also questions about how certain state actors are coopting these technologies to undermine democratic principles, which has led to the G7 Rapid Response Mechanism, and where a broader coordinated response is necessary.[30]

Finally, different countries have very distinct views on what constitutes freedom of speech and thus how social media content should be regulated. There are two separate issues here. First, as discussed earlier, the platforms are de facto defining and enforcing, based on their own set of rules, what constitutes free speech and imposing these rules globally. Their opaque algorithms make decisions on content dissemination, and its amplification, that are unclear and unregulated. In essence, they have become the arbiters of free speech. The DSB by contrast is designed to have multiple stakeholders with diverse views to discuss and define a global set of rules that reflect national interests and values. Structures such as social media councils are one proposal that could achieve this outcome (Tworek 2019).

Second, a separate related issue is the amplification of content, which is driven by the underlying business model to maximize user engagement and thus advertising revenues of social media platforms Maréchal and Roberts Biddle (2020). Regulations on amplification and microtargeting are clearly needed given the opacity on data collection and use in algorithms and this distinction was likely behind the recent recommendation for a moratorium by several countries, discussed later, on microtargeting false political ads that contain false or misleading information.[31] The DSB would be well suited to deal with regulations on amplification arising from the business model itself.

A collective voice will be much more powerful than an individual voice and could create the momentum necessary to force even the currently entrenched regimes to change especially since the issues span the realms.

A POLITICAL MANDATE WOULD HELP

The collective voice would be enhanced with a political mandate though a collective voice may also sway political direction. The G20 would be a natural body to support the creation of a DSB just as it did with the FSB. One important reason is that the G20 incorporates the data realms outlined earlier and indeed goes beyond them that would lead to more inclusive—even if contentious—discussions. Further, it would be a natural body to outline digital priorities given the meetings of the G20 Digital Ministers and G20 Leaders. Though the vested interests as outlined above may prove difficult for discussions, in fact the G20 is exactly the venue for these difficult discussions that need to occur.

If the G20 is not yet a possibility, another option is the International Grand Committee on Disinformation (IGC)—which comprises a diverse set of countries and over 400 million citizens—that could serve as a natural springboard to launch the DSB.[32] The Committee's focus has been on governance of social media platforms, including their role in disseminating fake news and mis- and disinformation. The existence of the IGC is evidence of the desire to create global rules for the digital sphere. The diversity of the IGC membership—small and large countries with differing cultures, values, and institutions—makes it ideal for launching the DSB. Moreover, the United States has also recently engaged with the IGC and appears to be planning to continue to do so, which is important, given that the United States is the home of the major social media platforms. Further, despite the very many differences across these countries, they have shown in their November 2019 meeting in Dublin that they can agree to common principles on platform governance as well as the moratorium of microtargeting false political ads mentioned previously.[33] Finally, the Forum on Information and Democracy presents yet another possible option. It was created in 2019 after thirty states endorsed the International Partnership on Information and Democracy during the meeting of the Alliance for Multilateralism on the margins of the UN General Assembly. It has since been endorsed by thirty-eight countries, representing all regions of the world with the goal 'to promote and implement democratic principles in the global information and communication space'.[34] Ultimately, however, the ideal would be to consolidate these worthwhile, but uncoordinated efforts and discussions under one body like a DSB.

A political mandate would allow the DSB to set overarching principles in its work, for example by creating a Universal Declaration of AI Ethics like that which exists for Human Rights. The declaration could embody the principles for the data value chain and thus be an integrated approach to AI governance.

It is important to note that the DSB does not have to be treaty based to be effective. The FSB is not a treaty-based organization and only became a formal organization under Swiss Law in 2012. Similarly, the General Agreement on Tariffs and Trade (GATT) led to several rounds of negotiations to liberalize global trade and did so with without any autonomous power, independent leverage, or sanction powers and did not become treaty-based until almost fifty years later when it became the WTO and was given additional dispute resolution powers (Irwin 1995).

Finally, funding would come from DSB member countries alongside voluntary donations and in-kind contributions via participation in the DSB working groups. For example, this would include fees assessed to standard-setting bodies as well as the digital platforms.

TWO PRACTICAL EXAMPLES OF WHERE THE DSB COULD BEGIN

Standard Setting for Big Data, AI, and Social Media Platforms

As noted earlier, standard-setting bodies have been active in the area of the big data value chain. As a practical matter, given that laws and regulations typically lag technology, standards and soft law can help to fill the gap, and indeed, standards tend to get embedded in regulations at a later point in time and referred to in international treaties and organizations.

Girard (2020) argues that as the advent of the Internet led to the creation of the Internet Engineering Task Force, standard setting for the digital realm will require the creation of a new body, working groups, and permanent funding to carry out its tasks. Consistent with this notion, the DGG could initially create a Digital Standards Working Group (DSWG).[35] The DGG would oversee the work and would entrust the working group with a mandate to create internationally harmonized technical and governance standards for the data value chains. For example, in the area of data, standards are required to define control/ownership, portability, sharing, removal, tracking, cyber, encryption/anonymization, access, use, quality, storage, security, and so on. There are specific issues related to algorithms, including ethical use, tagging, explainability, safety, risk, and others. The last part of that value chain is the digital platforms that use the algorithms, and there is a wide range of ground where specific standards are required for example content dissemination, competition, privacy, interoperability, transparency, and so on.

As stressed throughout this chapter, an integrated approach is required. For example, some of the arguments over 'biased' algorithms really pertain to the nature of the data that make up training sets. Standards development on data portability such as data sovereignty and residency requirements can facilitate the transfer of data among platforms and across countries, which would ultimately foster consumer choice, competition, and innovation among social media platforms and platforms more generally. Indeed, standards in all of these areas are required to build the trust and transparency necessary to meet the value that McKinsey (2018) has estimated.

The DSWG could also take a sector, such as health care, as an area to begin its focus. Covid-19 has revealed the many data governance gaps, for example with respect to the use of contact exposure tracing apps and data governance. Indeed, as it carries out this work, the DVG could examine specific vulnerabilities that have come to light in areas like privacy, cyber, and data sharing that would help to inform standards development. It would also ensure compliance to relevant human and labour rights regulations/privacy/digital identity requirements. The Digital Outreach Group would assist in communicating standardization activities and outcomes and feeding back into the DVG and DMG. The process of standard setting itself can also help to reveal the many gaps where policies and harder approaches to regulation may be required, and can feed into other areas of the DSB for example governance of social media platforms, discussed later.

Although the DSWG would decide how specifically to engage with stakeholders, because standard setting can reflect vested interests, opening up the standard-setting process under the auspices of the DSB would help to alleviate such concerns and ensure that standards reflect a broad set of values and respect for fundamental human rights, including privacy. The multi-stakeholder approach will be essential to ensure that standards are used to close the data realm divide and allow data to flow across borders, platforms, and applications necessary for the value chain to achieve its full economic potential. Since most of the areas where standards are required for the value chain are in their infancy, since countries across the realms are all struggling to make headway, this is thus an opportune time to create consistent standards. At the same time, as noted in Girard (2020), innovation in standard setting will be required in order for standards to be timely and responsive in this dynamic area. The DSWG would need to innovate on governance to develop standards much more quickly than the two to three years generally required in traditional standard setting.

The DSWG would be expected to draw upon the various international organizations already involved and bring in national efforts. For example, in Canada a Data Governance Standardization Collaborative was established in 2019 to create standardization strategies for data governance that includes 'close collaboration among government, private industry and broader civil society—which includes not-for-profits and non-governmental organizations representing specific, collective interests within society, including those of individual private citizens'.[36]

Once a standard is developed, it would be ratified by the DGG and brought to the DSBP for approval. The DMG would be tasked with monitoring compliance while the DVG would keep an eye on any unintended consequences from the implementation and use of the standards. The DMG and DVG would report at regular intervals to the DGP that would coordinate efforts and report back to the DSBP on progress.

Social Media Platform Governance

In addition to the important role that standards will play in the downstream part of the digital value chain, the upstream social media platforms bring their own specific governance issues that both encompass, and go beyond standard setting. These are explored in the Centre for International Governance Innovation's Models for Platform Governance (CIGI 2019) and include issues related to competition and content moderation. Content moderation has recently been the focus of substantial debate in the United States, as noted earlier. In June 2020, this debate led to the introduction of the Bipartisan Platform Accountability and Consumer Transparency Act (PACT) that proposes new transparency and reporting requirements for social media platforms.[37] The US Department of Justice's subsequently announced in September 2020 its decision to review Section 230 of the Communications Decency Act in four areas:[38]

1. Incentivizing Online Platforms to Address Illicit Content
2. Clarifying Federal Government Enforcement Capabilities to Address Unlawful Content
3. Promoting Competition
4. Promoting Open Discourse and Greater Transparency

To be sure, these proposals have heavy political overtones, and the inconsistency in approaches to fact checking by the platforms, discussed earlier, has in part led to claims of censorship of certain political views. Nevertheless, abstracting from the political debate, it is an opportunity to begin the hard task of global regulation in these areas since these issues have been raised in other jurisdictions. Indeed, the WHO has pointed to the 'Infodemic' associated Covid-19 with 'technology and social media' being used at scale to provide both valuable information, but also being used to amplify false and dangerous information that can 'undermine the global response and jeopardizes measures to control the pandemic'.[39]

Further, any changes to Section 230 themselves will undoubtedly have implications for other countries for example via trade agreements. More generally, the opening of Section 230 allows the opportunity to address the advertising-driven amplification business model of the platforms that underlies some of the content management issues. To be clear the goal would not be to review US legislation per se, but to examine the international implications of the legislation and solutions that are suitable at the global level.

More specifically, under the DGG, working groups could be set up under each of the review areas to discuss the global dimensions of the issues and propose international principles and/or regulations. Standard-setting bodies would get involved in developing standards to tag different types of mis- and disinformation so that this decision does not reside within the ambit of those solely defined by platforms nor solely by governments given concerns over censorship. Indeed, the PACT proposes that the US National Institute of Standards and Technology create a 'voluntary framework, with input from relevant experts, that consists of non-binding standards, guidelines, and best practices to manage risk and shared challenges related to, for the purposes of this Act, good faith moderation practices by interactive computer service providers'. Among others, the standards would include those for sharing of information among providers, for automated detection tools, and for providing data to researchers. It would be highly desirable that such standards were consistent globally, a task that could be undertaken by the DSWG. The DVG could assess the implications of any proposed US legislation for the international community as well as any regulatory gaps that might be created in all jurisdictions. It could also identify issues for US domestic policymakers for example the ability of platforms to skirt US rules in other jurisdictions. The Digital Outreach Group could ensure that all jurisdictions are brought into the discussions.

CONCLUSION

It is important to act now on global governance. The contrast of national/regional efforts against the global nature of the digital economy has created risks to citizens, businesses, and governments. A global regulatory effort is required. The current situation only benefits vested state and corporate interests that are growing more powerful each and every day. At the same time, we need to preserve the benefits that big data, AI, and digital platforms bring to us each and every day.

The many initiatives underway are testament to the desire to change the current fragmented efforts, but these need a globally coordinated effort to ensure that we do not result in a race to bottom, that we minimize confusion and compliance costs, and that inclusivity remains the benchmark of the Internet.

As Tworek (2020) notes, digital platforms stepped up during Covid-19 by sharing more data for research, taking extensive responsibility for content and moving quickly to adopt official institutions such as the WHO as the trusted sources for information.

Taking concerted and coordinated action on global governance under a structure such as a DSB will help to ensure that the benefits of the platforms are magnified and the risks minimized individually and globally.

The ultimate goal is to ensure that trust in the use of digital technologies is built and maintained. Without global governance, trust is likely to erode and with it the substantial benefits that digital platforms can bring. Like reforms of the financial sector, governance changes are required to avoid privatizing the gains of digital technologies and socializing the losses. And the losses are not just monetary in nature; they pertain to fundamental human rights, democracy and public safety.

NOTES

1. See essays in Owen et al. (2019) and references contained therein for some of these initiatives.
2. See https://www.whitehouse.gov/briefing-room/presidential-actions/2021/06/09/executive-order-on-protecting-americans-sensitive-data-from-foreign-adversaries/
3. See European Commission (2020a), page 2.
4. See European Commission (2020b).
5. See Council of Europe (2020).
6. See Government of Canada (2018).
7. See Organization for Economic Co-operation and Development (OECD 2019).
8. See Partnership on AI (2016–2020.).
9. See OECD (2020).
10. See Open Data Charter (ODC 2015).
11. See OECD (2013a). and Asia-Pacific Economic Cooperation (2005).
12. See OECD (2013b)
13. See Contract for the Web (2019); The Toronto Declaration (2018); Montréal Declaration for a Responsible Development of AI Université de Montréal (2017).

14. See Forum on Information and Democracy (2020b).
15. See United States Department of Justice (2020).
16. See New Zealand (2020).
17. See Facebook (2020, n.d.) and Twitter (2020).
18. See Google (2020) and Mayer (2020).
19. See OCEANIS (2021).
20. See ITU (2020) and IEEE (2019).
21. See ISO (2021).
22. See United Nations (2019).
23. Rising online harms are well documented in GOV.UK (2020).
24. See United Nations (2019). A subsequent UN report on digital cooperation also noted that there was support to work with a multi-stakeholder task force to pilot the distributed co-governance model at the national or regional levels. See United Nations (2020).
25. A good review and goals of the FSB can be found in Helleiner (2010).
26. See FSB (2020b).
27. Standard-setting bodies include the Basel Committee on Banking Supervision (BCBS), the International Organization of Securities Commissions (IOSCO), the International Association of Insurance Supervisors (IAIS), the Committee on Payment and Settlement Systems (CPSS), and two private bodies, the International Accounting Standards Board (IASB) and the International Federation of Accountants (IFAC).
28. See FSB (2020a).
29. See Gross et al. (2019).
30. See Government of Canada (2019b).
31. See Houses of the Oireachtas (2019).
32. See The Centre for International Governance Innovation (CIGI 2019) for further details on the history of the IGC.
33. See Houses of the Oireachtas (2019) for details on the principles.
34. See Forum on Information and Democracy (2020a) for information on its goals and mission.
35. This section draws upon a report by CIGI Senior Fellow Michel Girard (2020).
36. See Standards Council of Canada (2020).
37. See https://www.schatz.senate.gov/imo/media/doc/OLL20612.pdf.
38. See United States Department of Justice (2020).
39. See World Health Organization (2020).

REFERENCES

Aaronson, Susan Ariel. 2018. 'Data Is Different: Why the World Needs a New Approach to Governing Cross-Border Data Flows'. The Centre for International Governance Innovation. November 14. https://www.cigionline.org/publications/data-different-why-world-needs-new-approach-governing-cross-border-data-flows.

Aaronson, Susan Ariel, and Patrick Leblond. 2018. 'Another Digital Divide: The Rise of Data Realms and Its Implications for the WTO'. Journal of International Economic Law 21 (2): 245–72.https://doi.org/10.1093/jiel/jgy019.

Ademuyiwa, Idris, and Adeniran Adedeji. 2020. 'Assessing Digitalization and Data Governance Issues in Africa'. The Centre for International Governance Innovation. July 9. https://www.cigionline.org/publications/assessing-digitalization-and-data-governance-issues-africa.

Asia-Pacific Economic Cooperation. 2005. 'APEC Privacy Framework'. https://www.apec.org/Publications/2005/12/APEC-Privacy-Framework.

Bughin, Jacques, Jeongmin Seong, James Manyika, Michael Chui, and Raoul Joshi. 2018. 'Notes from the AI Frontier: Modeling the Impact of AI on the World Economy'. McKinsey Global Institute. https://www.mckinsey.com/~/media/McKinsey/Featured%20Insights/Artificial%20Intelligence/Notes%20from%20the%20frontier%20Modeling%20the%20impact%20of%20AI%20on%20the%20world%20economy/MGI-Notes-from-the-AI-frontier-Modeling-the-impact-of-AI-on-the-world-economy-September-2018.ashx.

Contract for the Web. November 2019. 'A Global Plan of Action to Make Our Online World Safe and Empowering for Everyone'. https://contractfortheweb.org/.

Council of Europe. 2020. 'Modernisation of the Data Protection "Convention 108"'. https://www.coe.int/en/web/portal/28-january-data-protection-day-factsheet.

European Commission. 2020a. 'Proposal for a Regulation of the European Parliament and of the Council on a Single Market For Digital Services (Digital Services Act) and amending Directive 2000/31/EC". December. https://eur-lex.europa.eu/legal-content/en/TXT/?qid=1608117147218&uri=COM%3A2020%3A825%3AFIN .

European Commission. 2020b. 'Proposal for a Regulation of the European Parliament and of the Council on Contestable and Fair Markets in the Digital Sector (Digital Markets Act)'. December. https://eur-lex.europa.eu/legal-content/EN/TXT/PDF/?uri=CELEX:52020PC0842&from=en.

Facebook. 2020. 'COVID-19: Community Standards Updates and Protections'. https://www.facebook.com/communitystandards/.

Facebook. 2020. 'Oversight Board'. https://oversightboard.com/ /.

Fay, Robert. 2019a. 'Digital Platforms Require a Global Governance Framework'. The Centre for International Governance Innovation. October 26. https://www.cigionline.org/articles/digital-platforms-require-global-governance-framework.

Fay, Robert. 2019b. 'Who Should Be Responsible for Decentralized Social Media Standards?' The Centre for International Governance Innovation. December 26. https://www.cigionline.org/articles/who-should-be-responsible-decentralized-social-media-standards.

Fay, Robert. 2020. 'CUSMA's Data and Intellectual Property Commitments Could Inhibit Domestic Policy Flexibility'. The Centre for International Governance Innovation. February 28. https://www.cigionline.org/articles/cusmas-data-and-intellectual-property-commitments-could-inhibit-domestic-policy.

Financial Stability Board (FSB). 2020a. 'Evaluation of the Effects of Too-Big-to-Fail Reforms: Consultation Report'. https://www.fsb.org/2020/06/evaluation-of-the-effects-of-too-big-to-fail-reforms-consultation-report/.

Financial Stability Board (FSB). 2020b. 'Work of the FSB'. https://www.fsb.org/work-of-the-fsb/.

Forum on Information and Democracy. 2020a. 'Principles on Information and Democracy'. https://informationdemocracy.org/principles/

Forum on Information and Democracy. 2020b. 'Working Group on Infodemics Policy Framework'. November. https://informationdemocracy.org/wp-content/uploads/2020/11/ForumID_Report-on-infodemics_101120.pdf.

Girard, Michel. 2020. 'Standards for Digital Cooperation'. The Centre for International Governance Innovation. January 16. https://www.cigionline.org/publications/standards-digital-cooperation.

Google. 2020. 'Google Privacy Policy'. https://policies.google.com/privacy?hl=en-US.

Government of Canada. 2018. 'Canada-France Statement on Artificial Intelligence'. Last modified June 7. https://www.international.gc.ca/world-monde/international_relations-relations_internationales/europe/2018-06-07-france_ai-ia_france.aspx?lang= eng#shr-pg0.

Government of Canada. 2019a. 'Ethical and Methodological Framework for Open Source Data Monitoring and Analysis'. Last modified August 13. https://www.international.gc.ca/gac-amc/publications/rrm-mrr/ethical_framework-cadre_ethique.aspx?lang=eng.

Government of Canada. 2019b. 'G7 Rapid Response Mechanism'. https://www.canada.ca/en/democratic-institutions/news/2019/01/g7-rapid-response-mechanism.html.

Government of Canada. 2020. 'The Governments of Canada and Quebec and the International Community Join Forces to Advance the Responsible Development of Artificial Intelligence'. Last modified June 15. https://www.canada.ca/en/innovation-science-economic-development/news/2020/06/the-governments-of-canada-and-quebec-and-the-international-community-join-forces-to-advance-the-responsible-development-of-artificial-intelligence.html.

GOV.UK. 2020. 'Closed Consultation Online Harms White Paper'. Last modified February 12. https://www.gov.uk/government/consultations/online-harms-white-paper/online-harms-white-paper.

Gross, Anna, Madhumita Murgia, and Yuan Yang. 2019. 'Chinese Tech Groups Shaping UN Facial Recognition Standards'. *Financial Times*, December 1. https://www.ft.com/content/c3555a3c-0d3e-11ea-b2d6-9bf4d1957a67.

Helleiner, Eric. 2010. 'The Financial Stability Board and International Standards'. The Centre for International Governance Innovation. https://www.cigionline.org/sites/default/files/g20_no_1_2.pdf.

High-Level Panel Follow-Up Roundtable 5A/B—Digital Cooperation Architecture. 2019. 'Meeting Note' 1st Session: December 19. https://www.un.org/en/pdfs/HLP%20Followup%20Roundtable%205AB%20Digital%20Cooperation%20Architecture%20-%201st%20Session%20Summary.pdf.

Houses of the Oireachtas. 2019a. 'International Grand Committee Meets in Dublin and Agrees Principles to Advance Global Regulation of Social Media'. Last modified November 7. https://www.oireachtas.ie/en/press-centre/press-releases/20191107-international-grand-committee-meets-in-dublin-and-agrees-principles-to-advance-global-regulation-of-social-media/.

Houses of the Oireachtas. 2019b. 'Update: International Grand Committee on Disinformation and "Fake News" Proposes Moratorium on Misleading Micro-Targeted Political Ads Online'. Last modified November 7. https://www.oireachtas.ie/en/press-centre/press-releases/20191107-update-international-grand-committee-on-disinformation-and-fake-news-proposes-moratorium-on-misleading-micro-targeted-political-ads-online/.

IEEE. 2019. 'The IEEE Global Initiative on Ethics of Autonomous and Intelligent Systems'. Last modified January 19. https://standards.ieee.org/content/dam/ieee-standards/standards/web/documents/other/ec_bios.pdf.

Internet Governance Forum. 'About IGF FAQs'. https://www.intgovforum.org/multilingual/content/about-igf-faqs.

Internet Governance Forum. 'Glossary'. https://www.intgovforum.org/multilingual/lexicon/8#MAG.

Irwin, David. 1995. 'The GATT in Historical Perspective'. *The American Economic Review* 85 (2): 323–328. Papers and Proceedings of the Hundredth and Seventh Annual Meeting of the American Economic Association Washington, DC, January 6–8.

ISO. 2021. 'Who Develops Standards: ISO/IEC JTC 1 Information Technology'. https://www.iso.org/isoiec-jtc-1.html.

ITU. 2020. 'Global Symposium for Regulators'. https://www.itu.int/en/ITU-D/Conferences/GSR/Pages/GSR.aspx.

Leblond, Patrick, and Susan Ariel Aaronson. 2019. 'A Plurilateral "Single Data Area" Is the Solution to Canada's Data Trilemma'. The Centre for International Governance Innovation. September 25. https://www.cigionline.org/publications/plurilateral-single-data-area-solution-canadas-data-trilemma.

Maréchal, Nathalie, and Ellery Roberts Biddle. 2020. 'It's Not Just the Content, It's the Business Model: Democracy's Online Speech Challenge'. New America. Last modified March 16. https://d1y8sb8igg2f8e.cloudfront.net/documents/REAL_FINAL-Its_Not_Just_the_Content_Its_the_Business_Model.pdf.

Mayer, Kevin. 2020. 'Fair Competition and Transparency Benefits Us All'. TikTok. Last modified July 29. https://newsroom.tiktok.com/en-us/fair-competition-and-transparency-benefits-us-all.

Mckinsey Global Institute. 2018. 'Notes from the AI Frontier: Modelling the Impact of on the World Economy'. Discussion paper. September. https://www.mckinsey.com/~/media/McKinsey/Featured%20Insights/Artificial%20Intelligence/Notes%20from%20the%20frontier%20Modeling%20the%20impact%20of%20AI%20on%20the%20world%20economy/MGI-Notes-from-the-AI-frontier-Modeling-the-impact-of-AI-on-the-world-economy-September-2018.ashx.

Medhora, Rohinton P., and Taylor Owen. 2020. 'A Post COVID 19 Digital Bretton Woods'. Project Syndicate. April 17. https://www.project-syndicate.org/onpoint/digital-bretton-woods-new-global-governance-model-by-rohinton-p-medhora-and-taylor-owen-2020-04.

Montréal Declaration for a Responsible Development of AI Université de Montréal. 2017. 'The Declaration'. https://www.montrealdeclaration-responsibleai.com/the-declaration.

New Zealand Foreign Affairs and Trade. 2020. 'Digital Economy Partnership Agreement'. June. https://www.mfat.govt.nz/assets/Uploads/DEPA-Signing-Text-11-June-2020-GMT.pdf

OCEANIS. 2021. 'The Open Community for Ethics in Autonomous and Intelligent Systems (OCEANIS)'. https://ethicsstandards.org/.

Open Data Charter. 2015.'International Open Data Charter'. https://opendatacharter.net/wp-content/uploads/2015/10/opendatacharter-charter_F.pdf.

Organization for Economic Co-operation and Development (OECD). 2013a 'The OECD Privacy Framework'. https://www.oecd.org/sti/ieconomy/oecd_privacy_framework.pdf.

Organization for Economic Co-operation and Development (OECD). 2013b. 'Action Plan on Base Erosion and Profit Shifting'. https://read.oecd-ilibrary.org/taxation/action-plan-on-base-erosion-and-profit-shifting_9789264202719-en#page1

Organization for Economic Co-operation and Development (OECD). 2019. 'Forty-two countries adopt new OECD Principles on Artificial Intelligence'. https://www.oecd.org/going-digital/forty-two-countries-adopt-new-oecd-principles-on-artificial-intelligence.htm.

Organization for Economic Co-operation and Development (OECD). 2020. 'OECD to Host Secretariat of New Global Partnership on Artificial Intelligence'. https://www.oecd.org/going-digital/ai/OECD-to-host-Secretariat-of-new-Global-Partnership-on-Artificial-Intelligence.htm.

Owen, Taylor, Pierre François Docquir, Joan Donovan, Susan Etlinger, Robert Fay, Michel Girard, Robert Gorwa, Gene Kimmelman, Kate Klonick, Sean McDonald, Nanjala Nyabola, Jonathon W. Penney, Karine Perset, Jeremy West, David Winickoff, Andrew Wyckoff, Victor Pickard, Damian Tambini, and Heidi Tworek. 2019. 'Models for Platform Governance'. The Centre for International Governance Innovation. October 29. https://www.cigionline.org/publications/models-platform-governance.

Partnership on AI. 2016–2020 'Our Goals'. https://www.partnershiponai.org/about/.

Pathways for Prosperity Commission. 2019. 'The Digital Roadmap: How Developing Countries Can Get Ahead'. https://pathwayscommission.bsg.ox.ac.uk/digital-roadmap.

Regulation (EU) No. 679/2016 of The European Parliament and of The Council of 27 April 2016 on the Protection of Natural Persons with Regard to the Processing of Personal Data and on the Free Movement of Such Data, and Repealing Directive 95/46/EC. https://gdpr.eu/tag/gdpr/.

Standards Council of Canada. 2020. 'Canadian Data Governance Standardization Collaborative'. https://www.scc.ca/en/flagships/data-governance.

The Centre for International Governance Innovation. 2019. 'Timeline: The International Grand Committee on Disinformation and "Fake News"'. Last modified January 20. https://www.cigionline.org/igc/timeline.

The Toronto Declaration. 2018. 'The Toronto Declaration: Protecting the Right to Equality in Machine Learning'. https://www.torontodeclaration.org/.

The White House. 2021. 'Executive Order on Protecting Americans' Sensitive Data from Foreign Adversaries'. June. https://www.whitehouse.gov/briefing-room/presidential-actions/2021/06/09/executive-order-on-protecting-americans-sensitive-data-from-foreign-adversaries/

Twitter. 2020. 'The Twitter Rules'. https://help.twitter.com/en/rules-and-policies/twitter-rules.

Tworek, Heidi. 2019. 'Social Media Councils'. The Centre for International Governance Innovation. October 28. https://www.cigionline.org/articles/social-media-councils.

Tworek, Heidi. 2020. 'Platforms Adapted Quickly during the Pandemic—Can They Keep It Up?' The Centre for International Governance Innovation. May 14. https://www.cigionline.org/articles/platforms-adapted-quickly-during-pandemic-can-they-keep-it.

United Nations. 2019. 'The Age of Digital Interdependence'. UN Secretary-General's High-Level Panel on Digital Cooperation. https://www.un.org/en/pdfs/Digital Cooperation-report-for%20web.pdf.

United Nations. 2020. 'Report of the Secretary-General Roadmap for Digital Cooperation'. June. https://www.un.org/en/content/digital-cooperation-roadmap/assets/pdf/Roadmap_for_Digital_Cooperation_EN.pdf.

United States Department of Justice. 2020. 'Department of Justice's Review of Section 230 of the Communications Decency Act of 1996'. https://www.justice.gov/ag/department-justice-s-review-section-230-communications-decency-act-1996?utm_medium=email&utm_source=govdelivery.

World Health Organization. 2020. 'Managing the COVID-19 Infodemic: Promoting Healthy Behaviours and Mitigating the Harm from Misinformation and Disinformation'.

Joint statement by WHO, UN, UNICEF, UNDP, UNESCO, UNAIDS, ITU, UN Global Pulse, and IFRC

September 23. https://www.who.int/news/item/23-09-2020-managing-the-covid-19-infodemic-promoting-healthy-behaviours-and-mitigating-the-harm-from-misinformation-and-disinformation.

15

Determining Our Technological and Democratic Future

A Wish List

PAUL NEMITZ AND MATTHIAS PFEFFER ■

The concentration of power in the hands of the GAFAM (Google, Apple, Facebook, Amazon, and Microsoft) as we see it today was possible because the Internet and software remained largely unregulated.[1] The *infant industry* argument, i.e., the classic neo-liberal argument that any legal regulation would stand in the way of innovation and thus the delicate plant of the new Internet economy, was and is a popular argument. It is important to criticize this experience, because with new technological leaps, especially in artificial intelligence and quantum computing, we are faced with similar arguments and could be faced with new and this time irreversible accumulations of power which will make the corporations, which are already powerful today, even more powerful.

Future technologies such as AI and quantum computing must be considered in the context of this concentration of economic and technological power. The analysis of needs for regulating AI requires not only an anticipatory understanding of the potential of this new technology but also a holistic view of the business models of all digital technologies to which it adds and of the power they exercise today.

Hans Jonas's *The Imperative of Responsibility*[2] is the basis of the precautionary principle, which has now become a constitutional principle of European law.[3] It states that if a technology is likely to have long-term, serious consequences for human beings or the environment, we must take tough decisions to avoid these serious negative consequences tomorrow with a probability bordering on certainty. And we have to do it today. To do this, we must invest in the science of technology assessment. And we must put ourselves in the emotional and political position to be able to make the necessary decisions today.

Technological and economic dominance today is more than just a market phenomenon. It pertains to power over democracy. The traditional ex post approach to securing competition and controlling economic power in democracies is not anymore able to deal with the powerful all-purpose platforms and the all-purpose technologies such as AI they are dominating. Incremental market-based solutions and self-regulation will not work. We need positive policy design and new principles of constitutional design which enable a comprehensive, joined up approach of a multitude of instruments.

We want to consciously and deliberately define what world we should live in, i.e., to work with normative demands as to what should be. Those who prefer democracy as a control system to capitalism and technology must substantiate their claim to design. If they do not do so, the combined forces of technology and capitalism will take the shaping of society from citizens and democracy, as they have always tried to do and today try more than ever.

With this deliberate approach in mind, we have drawn up a wish list of seven things we think would help enable us to determine our technological and democratic future.

DECENTRALIZED MOBILE OPERATING SYSTEMS

To decentralize control over data, shift towards edge computing, and enable a quantum Internet.

Under the keyword 'learning at the edge' or 'edge computing', processing will in future be increasingly integrated into networking technology and the devices of the Internet of Things (IoT). Apple's mobile phones will use artificial intelligence on a chip in the phone to process information directly, such as translating speech, which previously could only be processed after transmission to Apple's central data systems. Such technologies may also help address some privacy and data security issues.

Technology can work hand in hand with law to solve problems, indeed law and technology can support or even substitute each other in solving problems. One only has to want this and actively search for such possibilities. And one must keep in mind that the norms must always be determined in the last instance by democracy.

Correctly used edge technology could be one area in which technology companies and democracy can work together, namely when personal data no longer is transferred to central cloud data repositories of the platforms from the mobile phone and other devices under the control of the user. Personal data then in theory cannot be viewed from outside, without permission, because processing is done directly on the phone.

Apple's business model was not previously based on aggregating personal information and advertising. However, if the accumulation of personal data on

Facebook and Google (and other centralizers) could be eliminated through the systematic use of edge technologies, this would be a real step forward, not only for privacy law but also for the data sovereignty of citizens and states. Those who lead in the edge technology may one day be able to play targeted advertising directly with AI from the mobile phone or computer at home, i.e., move the profiling there, and thus avoid the privacy problems of centralization at the operator. With 'edge', Apple could then become the main provider of targeted advertising and steal business from the centralizers of personal data, Facebook and Google.[4]

Let's also not forget that the cards of data processing could be redistributed with 5G. Because of the high transmission speed and capacity, combined learning from decentrally processed data is now possible. It is no longer necessary to bring the data together in a cloud system to learn from Big Data methods. Edge computing will continue to grow and become more attractive with 5G.[5]

The Spanish digital sociologist Manuel Castells points out that 5G could offer the opportunity to advance concepts that challenge the dominance of the GAFAM companies.[6] The SAP professor for digitization, Key Pousttchi from Potsdam, says the same. The current dominance of Apple and Google in mobile phone operating systems will continue into the world of IoT unless Europe invests boldly in its own operating system for the mobile communications of the future, which includes virtual reality and IoT and will operate on 5G and one day the quantum Internet. In the long term, Europe's digital sovereignty is a prerequisite for freedom and democracy and it can only be preserved if Europe itself remains innovative and thus continues to generate its own prosperity. Like other successful European efforts to maintain independence in strategic areas, such as Airbus and Galileo, the mobile communications operating system could be a joint European project for tomorrow. Europe's strength in the field of the IoT and virtual reality would be a starting point for this. Already today, and even more so tomorrow, much of the power to control people and systems lies with those who control the mobile operating system. As a new game is starting with AI, 5G, virtual reality, and IoT, European technology policy should seize these opportunities.[7] In the same way Huawei is developing further an open source version of Android for its own use, to break the dependency on Google and to be able to continue selling hardware with an operating system in case of a US boycott,[8] so Europe should seek to develop an operating system and thus break free of dependencies.

DATA TRUSTEES AND PLATFORMS IN THE PUBLIC INTEREST

To ensure the responsible use of personal data and protect against big tech dominating public services.

In the future, the public interest will have to find greater expression in technical and economic structures. The way to achieve this is not only through financial incentives but also through more strategic regulation. For example, the Data Ethics

Commission of the German Federal Government has suggested that the exercise of data protection rights, and also the benefit from personal data, should be increased by setting up a group of data trustees[9] to professionally manage data in the interest of the individual. These trustees will have a different perspective on important issues. Some could be more oriented towards the monetization of personal data and others more towards the common good, for example by using health data to compare the performance of hospitals. In this way, they can address different preferences of citizens in competition with each other, similar to what happens in the mixed banking system between private banking, savings banks, and cooperative banks.

Just as banks collect the money of savers for lending an investment and thus for the benefit of the economic system as a whole, data custodians could also aggregate and make data anonymous, thus making it available for the development of AI and other data-driven services, in the interest of all. Europe's mixed banking system could even produce data trustees themselves, who would take charge of managing their clients' personal data. After all, if you entrust your money to someone, it is likely that you can also trust them with your data. This requires that we identify legal models for data trustees to create the necessary trust. Law is the key tool for this, similar to its trust-creating function in the financial markets. It is interesting to observe that more and more models for data trusts are being worked on worldwide.[10] At MIT, Professor Alex Pentland refers to the US Credit Unions, which are organized as cooperatives and to which 100 million Americans belong, as possible data trustees of the future.[11]

Another task is to introduce and promote efficient platform models oriented towards public interests, especially in those areas where the public interest is particularly high, such as in education, administration, and health. It is precisely in these areas that Europe has traditionally been stronger than the United States.[12] So far, these areas have not yet been fully occupied by US platforms. But we must act in haste, as can be seen from the run on the health sector by Google. In the end, 'software eats it all' may well apply to these sectors as well.[13] The question remains: will European companies, including public and non-profit enterprises and the public sector, with the support of politics, manage to develop and successfully market software themselves? A European approach to digitization will be demonstrated precisely by whether, in these sectors, Europe is capable of transfer the traditional strengths of the European social model into systems of software and AI.

And the development of the Smart City should not be left to Google and the GAFAM companies,[14] but must become a central pillar of European democracy policy.[15]

SEPARATION OF DIGITAL POWERS

To prevent certain corporations dominating too many realms of public life.

The sociologist Heinrich Popitz in his *Phenomena of Power*[16] already stated that the linchpin of all power control in modern societies is the control of technical action. He recommends that we examine the innovations of the modern consti-tutional state in terms of capabilities to control power to see whether they could also contain technical power in such a way that safeguards democracy, the rule of law, and fundamental rights.[17]

Here we can borrow from the principle of separation of powers, which is imple-mented in many constitutions in two ways, namely in the form of a horizontal and a vertical separation of powers. The horizontal separation of powers describes the functional division of state power between the legislative (legislation), executive (government), and judicial (courts). In addition, the fourth power is the free inde-pendent press, which controls power through critical reporting, inquiries, and in-vestigations, and free and independent science, which also has a critical function.

The vertical separation of powers in Europe describes the division of respon-sibilities between the European Union, the central governments, regions, and municipalities. In the federal states, no level may 'rule through', no one has all the power.

But is it conceivable to introduce a general principle of sharing technical power by law, just as the constitutional state shares power strictly vertically and horizontally?

This idea may sound revolutionary at first sight. However, it is already reality in the field of media law in a number of countries. In order to ensure the plurality of public opinion, which is essential for democracy, media law limits the technical reach of magazines and radio and television stations and/or the market share that a media group can hold, and this is without proof of abuse, as is necessary in com-petition law.

The purpose is to prevent the emergence of predominant power able to influ-ence public opinion by measures to ensure diversity. In principle, this is a hori-zontal separation of powers according to functions, i.e., within the press.

A very topical question is whether social networks and search engines, which have become a very important source of political information, should conse-quently be treated like media within the framework of media concentration law and thus be subject to the separation principle of media concentration law.[18]

Nothing really holds us back from this approach. Especially because these plat-forms are not passive but rather create content actively in some cases, and in all situations arrange and display it, i.e., automate editorial functions or, more re-cently, have these performed by journalists, as in the case of Facebook.[19]

They exercise power of opinion by deciding what information appears on the first hit page. Their algorithms of automatic editing and curating are not, and cannot be, value-neutral, since they influence essential areas of public communication.

Because the GAFAM networks and the search engines themselves aggregate political news and disseminate it tailored to personal profiles accumulated by them, they themselves have become key actors of the electronic public sphere. Therefore, the media law that protects the function of the public in democracy must also be applied to them, at the very minimum in the form of the media con-centration law.[20]

In fact, they compete with newspapers and television for advertising, but also for attention.[21] In the discussion on the question of whether Facebook should distribute political ads and whether it has a role in verifying advertising claims, Facebook described itself as a medium of the press.[22]

The new German draft State Media Treaty (see chapter 7) which replaces the State Treaty on Broadcasting, is a step in the right direction in that it requires these intermediary platforms to disclose how and according to what rules they aggregate news and present it to users. But media concentration law still needs updating.[23]

One conceivable additional option for regulation is to require windows on search and social networking sites to display a uniform, non-personalized selection of news of the day in news feeds to all users. It should also be possible to diversify these locally. The selection and compilation of sources could be based on competition between reputable, professional media sources, under the control of the self-regulatory bodies of the press or the state media authorities. At the same time such a mechanism must guarantee the necessary distance to the state and the independence of the used media sources. This would be a modern variant, so to speak, of the existing 'window regulation' in the German Interstate Broadcasting Treaty, which ensures a minimum of political relevant information and diversity in private television.[24] In America, Facebook itself has chosen the news sources, including the right-wing extremist propaganda website Breitbart.com. In addition, Facebook retains the personalization with its own algorithms. Both are detrimental to the democratic public space. These examples confirm that this matter must be regulated by democracy and cannot be left to the GAFAM companies.

In addition to the goal of ensuring diversity, which has the task of defending against predominant power of opinion and which is as important today as it was in the age of mass media, the goal of securing a democratic public sphere that can be viewed and reviewed by all must be added. The radical personalization by the GAFAM business model must be limited when it comes to the public exchange of information. Otherwise, this common public sphere and thus the most important prerequisite of a democratic society may be lost in personalization without any common elements left.

A GENERAL DATA PROTECTION REGULATION (GDPR) FOR AI

Using GDPR as a model for creating legislation for AI.

Just a few fundamental issues should be considered when drafting a general regulation on artificial intelligence. In this area of very rapidly advancing technology, it is not now a question of enacting technology-specific, small-scale or sectoral rules. Because these could be obsolete again tomorrow and will leave large areas of potentially risky AI completely unregulated. Rather, it is a question of laying down some few basic general legal rules for AI in binding form, which are formulated in a technology-neutral and future-oriented manner. Technology-neutral rules retain their regulatory content when technology and business models are developing rapidly. There dynamic interpretation allows to update their practical relevance in the light of new circumstances.

The law has the great advantage in that it is written for people who can think for themselves. This is an important distinction between the law and technical code. You can interpret and apply the law again and again in line with new challenges, provided that the legislator makes good use of the open texture of the language and does not get lost in the details or even buzzwords of the times, as is often demanded by lobbyists. This is possible without calling into question legal certainty today.

That law in the technical age must be rewritten, just as computer programs receive updates, is a fallacy of the engineering view of the world. Computer programmes need new, rewritten versions of code because the code was written for stupids—namely for machines—which, unlike humans, are not in a position to constantly reinterpret anew the text of the law—the code—by thinking themselves.

All the arguments now being put forward against AI legislation have also been put forward against data protection legislation, in the years before 1995, when the first Directive on the protection of personal data was introduced in the European Union, and again from 2012 to 2016, in the four years of negotiations on the GDPR. None of these arguments convinced the legislator—and rightly so:

The assertion that law cannot develop as fast as technology and business models is contradicted by technology-neutral law in Europe. The GDPR is a modern example of technology-neutral law whose meaning and relevance changes with the progress of technology, including AI.

The assertion that a law is fundamentally not precise enough to regulate complex technologies, and that a law that lies beneath the detail, precision, and usability of good code is not a good law and should therefore not be passed by the legislature, is another fallacy of the technical world view. By definition, a law passed in the democratic process requires compromise. The GDPR was negotiated between the co-legislators of the European Union, with almost 4,000 amendments laid by the European Parliament. Compromise texts of laws that have been drafted through a democratic process are the noblest expression of democracy. And a democracy that has lost the ability to negotiate compromises is in crisis. Compromise texts of laws in democracy usually fulfil their function, because the compromise reached, ideally after long public deliberation, is a social advance towards a consensus—never fully reached—on the rules we want to live by.

And these compromise laws are not written to be applied by machines and automation—like code. Laws are created to be applied by people who can justify their own decisions. And in case of dispute, they are there to be interpreted by reasonable judges who are expected to provide reasons for their judgment and are usually neither alone nor without appeal.

It is this process of openness of the law and the legal process for later interpretation by wise and independent judges with the help of independent science[25] that gives the law the flexibility to cope with the demands of constant technical innovation and constantly evolving business models. This can be done without having to rewrite the laws like a code that has to be constantly revised since version 1.0.

The GDPR has shown that Europe can set global standards with democratic laws that are bound by fundamental rights. The claim by neo-liberalism and technological ideology, innovation, growth, and freedom are best served without any democratic laws affecting technology is simply false.

Just as the 'greening of General Electric' and industry in general has come about because environmental legislation has created incentives for innovation towards environmental sustainability, the European Union's DPAs will now be able to drive innovation for a way of collecting and processing personal data that respects individual rights and the importance of privacy in democracy. The same will happen with regard to well-regulated AI. And just as the European economy has achieved market leadership in many areas of sustainable technology through environmental technology and sustainable industrial products, thanks to green regulatory pressure, so will it be successful worldwide with high data protection standards and regulated AI, in which the basic values of the Enlightenment and constitutional democracies are incorporated from the outset.

PLATFORM IMPARTIALITY AND INTERCONNECTIVITY OBLIGATIONS

To protect against platform political partisanship and ensure simple transfer between platforms.

Net neutrality as laid down in EU law, transparency obligations for intermediaries, as now laid down in the German draft Interstate Media Treaty, and the principle of separation as described earlier, will not suffice to ensure the functioning of the democratic public in an age of power concentration in the GAFAM.

It will probably be necessary to introduce an additional political impartiality requirement for platforms and search engines with market power. The current discussion in the United States about the political one-sidedness of the platforms gives a foretaste of the problems of the concentration of power among the platforms in a democratic society.

We therefore need a legally established political impartiality obligation for large platforms and search engines to complement net neutrality and the other principles already described. Of course, control of the political impartiality of platforms must not be placed in the hands of the state, for example a 'Ministry of Truth'. But the platforms can and should be obliged to participate in the forums of self-organization of the press, like Germany's Press Council. It should be the responsibility of these forums, which are far removed from the state, to monitor the impartiality of the platforms.

In addition, the systemic tendency to dominance in the platform economy through the winner-takes-all effect must be tackled. An interconnectivity obligation can serve to reduce the winner-take-all effects in the platform economy and thus create new opportunities for competitors to enter the market.

The obligation to interconnect will lead to the creation of a new uninterrupted connection of services with each other, both between services of the same function and across functions, e.g., between social networks, search, cloud services and messenger services, and many new combinations of interconnection.[26] This increases competition between providers, as network effects no longer occur only at one company in a closed system, which in turn becomes the starting point for achieving dominance in subsequent areas. Rather, the benefits of the network accrue at all competitors, at least as far as networking with the members of all competing networks is concerned. The rules applied to members of networks in such interconnected systems should always be those of the provider with which the members have contracted. In such a way, different networks can compete in their offer, for example with free or paying services, different content additions and different ways of collecting and treating, or not, personal data.

The decisive factor will probably be that networking will always only take place according to the rules of the network on which the user is registered, and that smaller networks will in any case be allowed to reserve their exclusive content and functionalities for their users, which go beyond a minimum level to be defined by law. They should not be obliged to open these to users originating from other networks. The centrality of differentiation between the initial profile on each platform will ensure that the interconnectivity obligation actually results in a wider range of service design and content. We consider it conceivable that precisely the combination of social network and exclusive content could become an attractive business model for the content producers such as publishing houses to provide social networks, if these conditions are met.

JOINED-UP REGULATION AND JOINED-UP REGULATORS FOR THE PLATFORM ECONOMY AND ALL-PURPOSE TECHNOLOGY

To deal with platforms operating in many markets simultaneously and using all-purpose technology.

The problem with competition law is that it allows companies to achieve economic size and even dominance per se. Only the abuse of the dominant position can be sanctioned. And the definition of abuse is constrained to effects on the market, i.e., competitors and consumers, but does not include effects on democracy.

There are already doubts as to whether the limited instruments of competition law are sufficient to maintain competition in the market and, above all, the decentralized innovative power in the economy. This is because so far, no recourse is available against practices such as the systematic buying up of smaller, innovative start-ups[27] or the legal imitation of innovation. A report by scientists to the EU Commission makes initial recommendations for reform and shows how more can possibly be done with existing law, including through new interpretation.[28]

However, it is all the more true for democracy that the concentration of power will always be a serious problem, even if no abuse within the meaning of competition law can be established.

Competition law as it stands today is therefore not sufficient to address the problem of the concentration of power in GAFAM in such a way that decentralized innovation and democratic compatibility of further development are ensured.

New ways to make use of existing law and reforms of law must therefore be explored. A reform of German competition law is moving forward to enable the competition authority to determine the market power of platforms more easily, not least because of certain corporations having exclusive access to competition-relevant data, in particular, but not exclusively, personal data.[29] Under certain circumstances, the refusal to give access to data to other actors is to be regarded as an abuse of market power. The disclosure of data may become mandatory, although this must be done in accordance with the GDPR.

It is also important that the cooperation between the competition authorities, data protection authorities, and other regulators is facilitated through a legal basis which expressly authorizes the exchange of information.

Fragmented regulators must learn to deal, through cooperation, with platforms operating in many markets simultaneously. It will be necessary to consider whether the current set-up with multiple structurally fragmented economic regulators is appropriate, or whether it should be abandoned. This is because in the digital platform economy in the age of AI, problems clearly defined by sector or topic—as in the economy of the last century—are becoming increasingly rare. If platforms become multilateral, thus operate in many sectors simultaneously, and use general-purpose technology such as AI, this should also be reflected in the structure of the authorities, especially since the subject of regulation, platforms, data, and AI will thus also become a common topic in many areas of law and for all supervisory authorities. It will become increasingly difficult to explain why public prosecutors' offices for criminal law prosecutions are organized in a unitary manner, across the broad diversity of crimes, but the supervisory authorities for business regulation remain fragmented by law into many small authorities and are less flexible at adaptation, even though they are all increasingly confronted with the same powerful platforms and groups. Enforcement in the different areas of law in question may become more effective in unitary structures also for economic regulation. The FTC, which unites competition law, consumer law, and privacy enforcement, has already demonstrated that privacy enforcement benefits from being under the same roof as competition enforcement, as one could see in the $5 billion fine imposed on Facebook for privacy breaches. Clearly, the traditionally fine-shy privacy and data protection enforcement in the United States benefitted from the closeness to competition law enforcers in this case. The independent Data Protection Authorities in Europe have not yet been able to come up with such a significant fine, as they do not benefit from proximity to competition law enforcers under the same roof. They thus are slower to learn the rigour and resolve necessary to successfully enforce the law from their older and in matters of fining and litigation, more experienced competition law colleagues. It is now time for them to catch up.

SECURING INDEPENDENCE FOR JOURNALISM AND SCIENCE

To secure sustainable funding and freedom from interference for the fourth estate and independent research.

Finally, for technological power to be accountable and for democracy to be robust, we need to see a strengthening of the independent institutions of journalism as the fourth estate and of science, which are free and equipped to work independently. Journalism that is dependent on the repeated operating aid of the digital giants and a science which is trained to seek research funded by digital giants or other large corporations cannot claim the credibility as truth-generating institutions that democracy requires.

So, let us begin, step by step, to break the comfortable friendship with the digital giants. Let us make it clear that scientists, journalists, publishers, and media houses that take operating aid from them cannot be free in the long run. The only exception to this rule are genuine capital foundations, in the management of which the founding companies have no stake and from the income of which journalism or science is permanently financed without the founding companies having any influence. So, let us say yes to capital foundations, but no to donations in the form of operating subsidies, which are temporary and create dependencies. Because at the latest when the operating aid is used up or expires, you have to go begging again. This creates dependency and an incentive to be willing to be useful and to please the donors. The GAFAM companies seek this dependency because it promises them influence, at least in the form of the anticipatory holds in the minds of those who know that they will soon have to ask for money again and will therefore curtail any criticism.

However, it is also important to abolish the incentives for non-transparent cooperation between scientists and companies. The pressure in science to acquire third-party funding, regardless of how and from which sources, must be reduced. Strict transparency rules must oblige the scientists and institutes applying for funding to disclose in all their events and publications which companies supports their work, and the conditions for this support. Just as publishers must make visible any newspaper content that is advertising or otherwise purchased, publishers should also be required to disclose when they receive money from corporations, for example through the Google[30] or Facebook journalism initiatives.[31] The dependencies that arise here are less transparent than advertising that a reader sees. What is needed, then, is transparency at least as great as that of advertising in newspapers. At present, there is no complete transparency as to where EUR 15 million from Google has gone in Europe.[32]

More importantly, however, is to find a way to give back to journalism the advertising revenue that Google and Facebook have taken away from it.

It is astonishing how the democracies in the United States and Europe have stood by and watched as the GAFAM companies threaten to destroy the fourth power in the state, privately financed journalism, with their enormous profits. For the cacophony on the Internet is no substitute for the contribution of investigative, reflective, and critical journalism to the control of public and private power in free societies.

The copyright directive of the European Union,[33] which regulates, among other things, the ancillary copyright for journalistic products, was a first attempt to repair the imbalance between the profits of the GAFAM companies and the destruction of a pillar of democracy. As we are now seeing in France, however, Google is resisting the application and simply says: we are not paying.[34] It will therefore be necessary to tighten up the copyright directive and make any links to press content for Internet platforms and social networks of the scale of GAFAM liable to pay, while at the same time setting up a binding rights collection system. After all, delivering publishers to individual negotiations with Google and other GAFAM companies will not work.

Google's business model is based on processing data free of charge from three sources: content available on the Internet, users' personal data, and cloud data storage. This model must take a back seat to the interests of democracy in maintaining a free press, the protection of personal data, and thus individual freedom and human dignity. If this happens, i.e., if Google has to pay for press content, adheres properly to the GDPR, and is no longer allowed to record and track users on press websites, Google will still remain highly profitable and innovative. But democracy and the rule of law will then have a chance to stay alive through a functioning fourth power.

It would indeed be important to simply prohibit the collection of reader data by third parties on publishing and press pages, insofar as these third parties themselves collect advertising and at the same time collect the personal data of readers. If only the publishers themselves were allowed to insert advertising alongside their content and process reader data with their consent, and if at the same time the GAFAM companies were no longer able to use the content free of charge, the publishers and journalists would once again be at the economic centre of the advertising market. A larger part of the advertising cake would once again reach them, thus further enabling the plurality of the free, privately financed press.

It is urgently necessary to prevent profits from press activity from accruing to Google and Facebook from the outset. They must remain with the many media outlets whose decline is lamented everywhere, but most loudly in America.[35] In addition, thought will also have to be given to increasing support for journalism through foundation models and other measures.[36] In any case, Europe needs a holistic policy for press freedom and press plurality for the sake of democracy.[37]

Regulating the GAFAM platforms is a key element of any democracy policy today. Democracy will have to do more to secure the private financing of its fourth estate than we have seen so far in member state media policy and at the EU level. Just as resolutely as Facebook and Google are increasing their profits year after year at the expense of the free press, so must the European Union and its member states resolutely ensure that journalism and publishers still have a chance against these giants. At stake is a diverse and locally based press and free, critical journalism with the ambition to control power. Of course, the publishers and journalists themselves must also be innovative. But with the current asymmetry of power relations, appeals alone for faster digitization and more innovation in the press will not be enough. A telling example of this is provided by the Reuters Institute in Oxford, which itself receives millions from Google and therefore wisely does not propose anything that could affect Google's profitability.

Political action at EU level is now required. This starts with the necessary taxation of the digital giants, goes on to copyright and media-like responsibility for illegal content, and finally to specific rules in the competitive relationship between platforms and the press.

CONCLUSION: A NEW TOOLBOX OF CONTROL OF TECHNOLOGICAL POWER IN THE AGE OF AI

In this second phase of the digital revolution we are currently in, we can no longer afford to make mistakes like those made in the early days of digital technology and the global Internet. Technology and knowledge seem to be exploding. Some speak of an exponential increase.

This is contrasted by the intentionally slow processes of change in deliberative democracies. The reason for this is that experience has shown how important it is to include reflection and discussion in questions of the human exercise of power in democracies before opinion forming and decision-making. A consequence of this insight is also the separation of powers.

We believe that the question of who will rule in the future and who will make the decisions must be asked today. Whoever wants to answer it in the spirit of democracy must bring the representatives of technology and democracy into a new discussion. And this dialogue must be underpinned by a new critique of technological power, which draws on the Frankfurt School and Hans Jonas's precautionary principle as much as on principles of competition law and media law. For democracies to prevail, a holistic approach to curtailing digital dominance is necessary, which looks not only at the functioning of the market, but also at the functioning of democracy. There is not one golden bullet, but a coherent package of measures must be put in place to curtail the different, mutually reinforcing emanations of digital power in the hand of the GAFAM, in order to secure the good functioning of democracies and markets and to protect individuals against the overreach of economic power.[38]

NOTES

1. This paper is based on our book *Prinzip Mensch—Macht, Freiheit und Demokratie im Zeitalter der Künstlichen Intelligenz* (Nemitz and Pfeffer 2020a); an enhanced English edition titled *The Human Imperative —Power, Liberty and Democracy in the age of Artificial Intelligence* is forthcoming (Nemitz and Pfeffer 2022b). The authors thank Nyasha Weinberg for her contributions on substance and language. They don't necessarily represent positions of their employers or clients.
2. Jonas (1985).
3. TFEU and European Commission, European Political Strategy Center (2016, p. 3 in the box).
4. This was the thought expressed by Michael Veale, author of another chapter in this book, to Paul Nemitz at a conference in Budapest in 2019.
5. Forrester Research (2019).
6. Castells (2019).
7. University of Potsdam (2019).
8. Kronfli (2020).
9. 'Report of the Data Ethics Commission [in German]' (2019, 133 ff.).
10. See Delcroix and Lawrence (2019) and several websites: https://doi.org/10.1093/idpl/ipz014; https://www.polypoly.eu/; https://theodi.org/article/what-is-a-data-trust/; https://www.slideshare.net/peterkwells/launch-of-odi-2019-data-trust-pilots-work; https://mydata.org/; https://hello.elementai.com/rs/024-OAQ-547/images/Data_Trusts_EN_201914.pdf; https://digitalpublic.io/; https://www.cigionline.org/articles/what-data-trust; https://radicalxchange.org/blog/posts/2019-10-24-uh78r5/; https://pacscenter.stanford.edu/research/digital-civil-society-lab/trusted-data-intermediaries/; https://www.midata.coop/en/home/.
11. Walsh (2019).
12. Nemitz and Kwiatkowsky (2019).
13. Andreessen (2011).
14. Tett, (2019).
15. See on this https://decodeproject.eu/; Decode (2018); European Commission. (n.d.); Green (2019); https://colab-digital.de/koki/; Lewin, (2018), Prager (2019).
16. Popitz (2017, 180).
17. In the same direction Wu (2011).
18. See on this already Council of Europe (2011, para 15 last sentence of the Appendix).
19. Palmer (2019). For a differentiating earlier analysis, see Tambini and Labo (2016).
20. Tambini (2018).
21. See in detail Lobigs and Neuberger (2018, 69ff.).
22. Goodman and Kornbluh (2019).
23. Gounalakis (2018); on the activities of the CEC, see https://www.kek-online.de/.
24. See § 30 f of the former RSTV.
25. In a society increasingly dominated by private sector markets and technologies, it is essential to increase the share of public funding for independent science in order to safeguard its orientation towards truth and public interests and its independence, and to avoid it being dominated by private interests.
26. Further approaches to the commitment to interconnectivity and to enabling dynamic data portability: Antitrust Digest (2019); Yale School of Management (2019);

Digital Competition Expert Panel (2019); Crémer et al. (2019); Kommission Wettbewerbsrecht 4.0 (2019).

27. https://en.wikipedia.org/wiki/List_of_mergers_and_acquisitions_by_Microsoft; https://en.wikipedia.org/wiki/List_of_mergers_and_acquisitions_by_Alphabet; https://en.wikipedia.org/wiki/List_of_mergers_and_acquisitions_by_Facebook; https://en.wikipedia.org/wiki/List_of_mergers_and_acquisitions_by_Apple; https://en.wikipedia.org/wiki/List_of_mergers_and_acquisitions_by_Amazon.

28. Crémer et al. (2019).

29. Federal Ministry of Economics and Energy (2019). See, for more on this, Sara Hartmann and Bernd Holznagel in this volume.

30. Google (n.d.) and Newsgeist (n.d.).

31. Facebook (n.d.).

32. Dachwitz (2018).

33. European Union (2019).

34. Fanta (2019); Hanfeld (2018); Niemeier (2019).

35. Sullivan (2019); Brauck(2019); see also the collection on #Newspaper Death at the TAZ, https://taz.de/Zeitungssterben/!t5028783/.

36. DAFNE (2019); Klomp (2019); Karstens (2017).

37. Nielsen et al. (2019); see also Nemitz (2019).

38. Postscriptum: There is a transatlantic consensus emerging on the need for legislation (see the Manifesto in defence of Democracy and the Jule of Law in the age of Artificial Intelligence, published by leading academics from the EU and the US at the occasion of the EU-US Summit in Brussels in June 2021, https://www.aiathens.org/manifesto). The Eurpean Commission has proposed five draft regulations which address parts of the challenges set out in this book, namely the Data Governance Act, COM 2020/767of 25.11.2020, https://eur-lex.europa.eu/legal-content/EN/TXT/?uri=CELEX:52020PC0767; Digital Services Act, COM 2020/825 of 15.12.2020, https://eur-lex.europa.eu/legal-content/en/ALL/?uri=COM:2020:825:FIN; Digital Markets Act, COM 2020/842 of 15.12.2020, https://eur-lex.europa.eu/legal-content/en/TXT/?uri=COM:2020:842:FIN; Artificial Intelligence Act, COM 2021/206 of 21.4.2021, https://eur-lex.europa.eu/legal-content/EN/TXT/?uri=CELLAR:e0649735-a372-11eb-9585-01aa75ed71a1; and an amending Regulation to the framework for a European Digital Identity, COM 2021/281 of 3.6.2021, https://eur-lex.europa.eu/legal-content/DA/TXT/?uri=COM:2021:281:FIN. Legislative proposals on civil liability for Artificial Intelligence and on the protection of elections are announced for autumn 2021. The legislative negotiations between the Council, representing the governments of EU Member States, and the European Parliament, representing the people, are accompanied by heavy lobbying. You can follow the progress of the legislative procedure by inputing the COM document number into the legislative observatory database at https://oeil.secure.europarl.europa.eu/oeil/search/search.do?searchTab=y. The tasks of building a coherent corpus of enforceable rules on how the Internet and Digital Technologies must serve Democracy, Fundamental Rights of individuals and functioning markets remains on the table and requires broad engagement. Shaping these rules cannot be left alone, or in the first place, to the corporate lobbyists and the techno-scientific intelligenzia, as these rules,

admittedly of very technical content, will shape how our democracy and markets function in the future and how fundamental rights of individuals are respected—or not.

REFERENCES

Andreessen, Marc. 2011. 'Why Software Is Eating the World'. *Wall Street Journal*, August 20. https://a16z.com/2011/08/20/why-software-is-eating-the-world/.

Antitrust Digest. 2019. 'Stigler Center (University of Chicago) Report on Digital Platforms', July 12. https://antitrustdigest.net/stigler-center-university-of-chicago-report-on-digital-platforms/

Brauck, Marku. 2019. 'Newspaper Death—The Year 2019 Will Be Bitter'. Spiegel online, February 26. https://www.spiegel.de/kultur/gesellschaft/dumont-vom-zeitungssterben-und-einem-wankenden-geschaeftsmodell-kommentar-a-1255220.html.

Castells, Manuel. 2019. 'La revolucion 5 G'. *La Vanguardia*, March 30. https://www.lavanguardia.com/opinion/20190330/461329107516/la-revolucion-5g.html.

Council of Europe. 2011. 'Recommendation CM/Rec (20110 7) of the Committee of Ministers of the Council of Europe to Member States on a New Notion of Media'. https://www.osce.org/files/f/documents/1/f/101403.pdf.

Crémer, Jacques, Yves-Alexandre de Montjoye, and Heike Schweitzer. 2019. 'Competition Policy for the Digital Era'. European Commission. Luxembourg: Publications office of the European Union. https://ec.europa.eu/competition/publications/reports/kd0419345enn.pdf.

Dachwitz, Ingo. 2018. 'News Initiative: Where Google's Millions for the Media in Germany Go'. Netzpolitik.org, September 26. https://netzpolitik.org/2018/news-initiative-wohin-googles-millionen-fuer-die-medien-in-deutschland-fliessen/.

DAFNE. 2019. 'Journalism Funding in Europe', June 26. https://dafne-online.eu/news/conference-report/journalism-funding-in-europe/.

Decode. 2018. 'Reclaiming the Smart City', July 18. https://media.nesta.org.uk/documents/DECODE-2018_report-smart-cities.pdf.

Delcroix, Sylvia, and Neil Lawrence. 2019. 'Bottom-Up Data Trusts: Disturbing the "One Size Fits All" Approach to Data Governance'. *International Data Privacy Law* 9(4): 236–52. https://doi.org/10.1093/idpl/ipz014.

Digital Competition Expert Panel. 2019. 'Unlocking Digital Competition: Report of the Digital Competition Expert Panel', March. https://assets.publishing.service.gov.uk/government/uploads/system/uploads/attachment_data/file/785547/unlocking_digital_competition_furman_review_web.pdf.

European Commission. n.d. 'Smart Cities'. https://ec.europa.eu/info/eu-regional-and-urban-development/topics/cities-and-urban-development/city-initiatives/smart-cities_en.

European Union. 2019. 'Directive (EU) 2019/790 of the European Parliament and of the Council of 17 April 2019 on Copyright and Related Rights in the Digital Single Market and Amending Directives 96/9/EC and 2001/29/EC'. OJ L 130, 17.5.2019. http://data.europa.eu/eli/dir/2019/790/oj.

Facebook. n.d. 'Journalism Project'. https://www.facebook.com/journalismproject.

Fanta, Alexander. 2019. 'EU Ancillary Copyright Law Threatens to Fail Even Before It Is Launched'. Netzpolitik.org, September 26. https:// netzpolitik.org/2019/eu-leistungsschutzrecht-droht-schon-vor-dem-start-zu-scheitern/.

Federal Ministry of Economics and Energy. 2019. 'Draft of a Tenth Act to Amend the Act against Restraints of Competition for a Focused, Proactive and Digital Competition Law 4.0 (GWB Digitisation Act)', October 7. https://www.d-kart.de/wp-content/uploads/2019/10/GWB-Digitalisierungsgesetz-Fassung-Ressortabstimmung.pdf.

Forrester Research. 2019. 'Predictions 2020: Edge Computing Makes the Leap'. ZD Net. December 2. https://www.zdnet.com/article/predictions-2020-edge-computing-makes-the-leap/; https://www.forrester.com/report/Predictions+2020+Edge+Computing/-/E-RES157595.

Goodman Ellen, and Karen Kornbluh. 2019. 'How Facebook Shot Themselves in the Foot in Their Elizabeth Warren Spat'. *Guardian*, October 15. https://www.theguardian.com/commentisfree/2019/oct/15/facebook-elizabeth-warren-regulation.

Google. n.d. 'News Initiative'. https://newsinitiative.withgoogle.com/.

Gounalakis, Georgios. 2018. 'The Law on Media Concentration Is No Longer Up to Date: Interview with the Chairman of the Commission on Concentration in the Media (CEC)'. medienpolitik.net, August 26. https://www.medienpolitik.net/2018/08/medienpolitikdas-medienkonzentrationsrecht-ist-nicht-mehr-zeitgemaess/.

Green, Ben. 2019. *The Smart Enough City*. Boston: MIT Press. https://mitpress.mit.edu/books/smart-enough-city.

Hanfeld, Michael. 2018. 'Europe under Google—Defenceless'. FAZ, September 28. https://www.faz.net/aktuell/feuilleton/medien/europa-unter-google-leistungsschutzlos-16406524.html.

Jonas, Hans. 1985. *The Imperative of Responsibility: In the Search of an Ethics in the Technological Age*.

Karstens, Eric. 2017. 'The Media Philanthropy Space in 2017'. Alliance, December 5. https://www.alliancemagazine.org/feature/media-philanthropy-space-2017/.

Klomp, Biba. 2019. 'Six Ways to Boost Media Philanthropy in Europe', June 26. https://medium.com/we-are-the-european-journalism-centre/six-ways-to-boost-media-philanthropy-in-europe-e3ffce78a0c6.

Kommission Wettbewerbsrecht 4.0. 2019. 'Globalisierung und Digitalisierung verändern unsere Wirtschaft und Gesellschaft', September 9. https://www.wettbewerbsrecht-40.de/KW40/Redaktion/DE/Artikel/kommission-wettbewerbsrecht-4-0.html.

Kronfli, Basil. 2020. 'Huawei's Plan to Escape Google Could Fix Android for Everyone'. *Wired*, February 26. https://www.wired.co.uk/article/huawei-appgallery-android-open-source.

Lewin, Amy. 2018. 'Barcelona's Robin Hood of Data: Francesca Bria'. *Sifted.eu*, November 16. https://sifted.eu/articles/barcelonas-robin-hood-of-data-francesca-bria/.

Lobigs, Frank, and Christoph Neuberger. 2018. 'Meinungsmacht im Internet und die Digitalstrategien von Medienunternehmen'. Gutachten für die Kommission zur Ermittlung der Konzentration im Medienbereich (KEK). https://www.kek-online.de/fileadmin/user_upload/KEK/Publikationen/Gutachten/Meinungsmacht_im_Internet_ALM51_web_neu.

Nemitz, Paul. 2019. 'In a Pincer Movement between Artificial Intelligence and Populism?—Democracy and the Fourth Estate in Europe under Threat'. In *Press and Media Freedom in Europe—A Fundamental Right under Threat?* Center for Applied European Studies (CAES), January 16. https://www.frankfurt-university.de/fileadmin/standard/Forschung/CAES/Dokumente/FRA-UAS_CAES_Presse-_und_Medienfreiheit_in_der_EU_ebook_01.pdf.

Nemitz, Paul, and Arndt Kwiatkowsky. 2019. 'Why Europe Needs Public Funding for Platform Development'. *Delphi*, September 2. https://doi.org/10.21552/delphi/2019/2/9.

Nemitz, Paul, and M. Pfeffer. 2020a. *Prinzip Mensch—Macht, Freiheit und Demokratie im Zeitalter der Künstlichen Intelligenz.* Bonn: Dietz Verlag. www.prinzipmensch.eu.

Nemitz, Paul, and M. Pfeffer. 2022b. *The Human Imperative—Power, Liberty and Democracy in the age of Artificial Intelligence.* Forthcoming.

Newsgeist. n.d. 'Exploring the Future of News'. Website. https://www.newsgeist.org/exploring-future-news/.

Nielsen, Rasmus Kleis, Robert Gorwa, and Madeleine de Cock Buning. 2019. 'What Can Be Done? Digital Media Policy Options for Strengthening European Democracy'. Reuters Institute, November. https://reutersinstitute.politics.ox.ac.uk/sites/default/files/2019-11/What_Can_Be_Done_FINAL.pdf.

Niemeier, Timo. 2019. ' "Rape Knighthood": Publishers Complain Again about Google'. DWDL, October 24. https://www.dwdl.de/nachrichten/74653/raubrittertum_verlage_beklagen_sich_erneut_ueber_google/?utm_source=tm_medium=tm_campaign=tm_term=

Palmer, Annie. 2019. 'Facebook Is Hiring Journalists to Curate Its News Tab'. CNBC, August 20. https://www.cnbc.com/2019/08/20/facebook-is-hiring-journalists-to-curate-its-news-tab.html.

Popitz, Heinrich. 2017. *Phenomena of Power: Authority, Domination, and Violence.* New York: Columbia University Press. English translation of the original *Phänomene der Macht*, 2nd ed., 1992, Tübingen.

Prager, Alicia. 2019. 'Francesca Bria: Europa Cannot Rely on Silicon Valley'. *Euractiv*, May 8. https://www.euractiv.com/section/digital/interview/sam-francesca-bria-europe-cannot-rely-on-silicon-valley/.

'Report of the Data Ethics Commission (in German)'. 2019. https://www.bmi.bund.de/SharedDocs/downloads/DE/publikationen/themen/it-digitalpolitik/gutachten-datenethikkommission.pdf?__blob=publicationFile=3.

Sullivan, Margaret. 2019. 'The Death Knell for Local Newspapers? It's Perilously Close'. *Washington Post*, November 22. https://www.washingtonpost.com/lifestyle/style/the-death-knell-for-local-newspapers-its-perilously-close/2019/11/21/e82bafbc-ff12-11e9-9518-1e76abc088b6_story.html.

Tambini, Damian, and Sharif Labo. 2016. 'Digital Intermediaries in the UK: Implications for News Plurality'. *Info* 18(4): 33–58.

Tambini, Damian. 2018. 'Parliament, People and Platforms'. *Intermedia* 46(3). https://www.iicom.org/intermedia/intermedia-oct-2018/parliament-people-platforms/.

Tett, Gilian. 2019. 'Google's Smart City: Dystopian Nightmare or Model for the Future'. *Financial Times*, November 13. https://www.ft.com/content/9fbd70da-05a7-11ea-9afa-d9e2401fa7ca.

TFEU and European Commission, European Political Strategy Center. 2016. 'Art. 191 (2): Towards an Innovation Principle Endorsed by Better Regulation', June 30. https://ec.europa.eu/epsc/sites/epsc/files/strategic_note_issue_14.pdf.

University of Potsdam. 2019. 'Augsburger Allgemeine—Interview mit Prof. Pousttchi', January 30. https://www.uni-potsdam.de/de/digitalisierung-prof-pousttchi/aktuelles/aktuelle-artikel/augsburger-allgemeine-interview-mit-prof-pousttchi.html.

Walsh, Dyland. 2019. 'How Credit Unions Could Help People Make the Most of Personal Data'. MIT Sloane School. Ideas Made to Matter, July 8. https://mitsloan.mit.edu/ideas-made-to-matter/how-credit-unions-could-help-people-make-most-personal-data.

Wu, Tim. 2011. 'The Separations Principle'. In *The Master Switch: The Rise and Fall of Information Empires*.

Yale School of Management. 2019. 'Prof. Fiona Scott Morton Leads Call for Greater Competition among Digital Platforms', May 21. https://som.yale.edu/news/2019/05/prof-fiona-scott-morton-leads-call-for-greater-competition-among-digital-platforms.

16

Reconceptualizing Media Freedom

DAMIAN TAMBINI ■

INTRODUCTION: MEDIA FREEDOM AND THE NEW MEDIA CONTRACT

There is a consensus among a growing number of experts that the power of new Internet intermediaries, their role in the circulation of speech and opinion in democracies, and harms associated with their services, require democratic polities to forge new social contracts[1] of regulation and accountability with these new communication gatekeepers. The notion of a social contract builds on previous notions of the 'social responsibility' of media[2] and promises to reconcile liberty (a contract freely entered into) with an ethic of responsibility (voluntary self-regulation) by building new institutions of governance that foster media accountability whilst maintaining autonomy of the media from the state.

There are however, deep and enduring differences between the legal and policy approaches taken by democracies to new media on the Internet, and particularly between the United States and Europe. Such differences undermine international consensus on the desirability and design of any new settlement for Internet-based media. This chapter argues that contrasting regulatory approaches in the United States and Europe are rooted in philosophical, legal, and historical differences that must be overcome if successful new social contracts for the platforms are to be agreed.[3]

The chapter identifies two main underlying philosophies:[4] First, a negative rights approach to media freedom which proposes that media should be considered speakers like any others and that media and speech freedom exists through constraint on state incursion into the speech field. Second, an international human rights approach according to which media freedom requires not only protection against state capture but also positive state intervention to promote expression rights of individuals through media, and special privileges to promote democratic media as a socially beneficial form of speech.

The US Supreme Court is the leading proponent of the first theory. The UN Human Rights Council, and the UN Special Rapporteur on freedom of expression, along with the Council of Europe and regional human rights courts broadly adopt the second. These two theories yield divergent approaches to the regulation of Internet intermediaries and is in danger of constituting a new fissure in the 'splinternet' of differing global regulatory approaches to the Internet.

Observers in the United States are increasingly aware of the importance of these international human rights standards in designing a new regulatory settlement for Internet media. It is by now a cliché to observe that it is Europe, with its transnational human rights regime, that is leading the movement for regulation of Internet intermediaries.[5] But the European/international view, which forms the intellectual backdrop to the EU Digital Services Act (DSA), clashes with the US theory, which is the default approach of the tech companies themselves. Many of the regulatory approaches that derive from the US negative rights approach are restricted to voluntary, consumer-oriented approaches that are based on competition between platforms; precisely the regulatory framework that Europeans argue will not suffice, and which the DSA proposes should be backed by statutory regulation.

I argue that a new, international theory of media freedom is needed, to bridge the widening divide between negative rights approaches and international human rights approaches.[6] Without progress on the underlying normative theory, policymakers will continue to talk across one another: conflating media freedom with freedom of expression, resisting necessary regulation of intermediaries on mistaken media freedom grounds, and underestimating the conceptual and normative differences between a US-oriented, First Amendment tradition and a positive rights, European and international human rights perspective. The first stage in successful regulation is a theoretical synthesis that brings together these two traditions and forges a new approach based on the advantages of both, and a realistic assessment of their weaknesses. Whilst the negative rights view has served the United States and the world well in the post-war period in which broadcasting dominated democratic communication, it will not reconcile the next phase of global media development with democracy. Until theoretical advances are made, policy debate will be a dialogue of the deaf between protagonists for whom the same terms—such as freedom of speech, press, and the media, have profoundly different meanings and implications.

US EXCEPTIONALISM: THE ORIGINS AND CONSEQUENCES OF A NEGATIVE RIGHTS APPROACH

The distinction between negative and positive rights theories of media freedom is well established.[7] Both are explained with reference to the historical context of their emergence.[8] The negative rights approach to freedom of the press emerged during the American Revolution at the end of the eighteenth century, which was profoundly suspicious of any attempt by public authorities—starting with imperial Britain—to control media, speech, and debate through censorship and particularly through taxation.[9] This view of media freedom is reflected in strong public condemnation of media accountability mechanisms supported by law or the state. On the other hand, international human rights approaches, created in mid-twentieth century Europe and through the UN, were driven by suspicion of the corporatist, authoritarian merging of public and private power, that occurred during fascism, and the links between private monopolization of media and the failure of democracy.[10] They built on a positive rights tradition dating back to the French Revolution which sought to achieve citizenship through law, not against, or in spite of it.[11] Post-war human rights approaches are centrally concerned with preventing authoritarian control of democratic communication, which explains why an international human rights perspective is concerned also with 'private censorship'—the restriction of speech by private media, whereas in strict terms this is not an issue for the First Amendment. This has profound implications for the role of Parliament and the state in fostering a new 'social contract' which under the 'exceptional' US approach cannot be coerced or encouraged by the law.

The American Revolution, partly motivated as a reaction to English censorship, was the crucible of a mistrust of state actions which led to a taboo on discriminatory taxes[12] which were used to silence or control media. This led directly to the wording of the First Amendment in terms not of a positive statement of a right, but of a negative prohibition on state action. Hence: "Congress shall make no law respecting an establishment of religion, or prohibiting the free exercise thereof; or abridging the freedom of speech, or of the press; or the right of the people peaceably to assemble, and to petition the Government for a redress of grievances." American 'exceptionalism' thus casts free speech and media freedom in terms of a content neutral, viewpoint neutral, negative rights prohibition on censorship profoundly mistrustful of positive state actions to shape media systems. The content-neutral negative rights approach therefore is not only enshrined in a series of constitutional judgements in the United States, particularly since the 1920s, but also deeply imbued in US political culture.[13] Fundamentally the First Amendment theory is that the state best serves speech and democracy by inaction. This has profound implications for the role of Congress and the state in fostering a 'social contract': it cannot be coerced—or even encouraged—by the law.

In contrast, the international human rights approach that emerged later, during the post-war broadcasting era, is concerned not only with avoiding state censorship but also with a positive construction of a plural, pro-democratic media system, including through state action, partly due to the experience of twentieth-century authoritarianism in which media used their autonomy to develop a propaganda model fatal to democracy. The UN and the Council of Europe declarations,[14] which positively assert human rights to communicate both through speech and receiving ideas, were based on the urgent need to structure communication to avoid *both* state capture of speech *and* the corporatist concentration and merging of media and political power.[15] Legal doctrines such the European Convention on Human Rights' (ECHR) positive obligation to promote media pluralism[16] originate in this conscious attempt to create 'pro-democracy' media systems: in the European Charter of Fundamental Rights media pluralism has equal status as a 'corollary' of media freedom.[17]

As Victor Pickard points out in this volume, the negative rights theory is not unanimously supported even in the United States. There is a strong strand of both theory and case law that seeks to question this approach to regulation[18] and set out a positive approach to public accountability of media and the necessity of inter-vention to create the necessary conditions for enjoyment of speech rights. Even in the twentieth century, and particularly in broadcasting, public-interest regulation of speech has been justified by reference to its social consequences, for example through the 'fairness doctrine' of the Federal Communications Commission. The fairness doctrine was however eventually struck down as contrary to the First Amendment, and the negative rights philosophy still holds sway in most First Amendment jurisprudence.[19]

In Europe, and in the international human rights system, the negative rights approach of the United States has long been eschewed. Freedom of expression is subject to qualifications and restrictions under the relevant UN declarations and the European Convention of Human Rights, and much of the legal argument is concerned with how to determine when such restrictions are justified. This is in-deed why the United States, rather than simply ratify international human rights law on freedom of speech, has entered a number of reservations.[20] This reflects a fundamental difference of philosophy: under international human rights stand-ards, media freedom is a qualified, instrumental right,[21] which exists to promote other goods and interests, including democratic communication itself, also by re-stricting private constraints on speech.[22]

These philosophical differences have important consequences when it comes to current policy discussions. A wide range of *legal* reforms, including in rela-tion to distribution, prominence, intellectual property, spectrum, and media law liability and standards are seen as necessary and are being actively contemplated in Europe.[23] For example both in North America and in Europe new proposals are being considered to transform the liability of intermediaries, and incentivize new technologies to sort, sift, label, and prioritize the content that flows through the main Internet gateways.[24] The proposed EU DSA will create a number of new obligations on large online platforms to meet standards of transparency, responsi-bility, and self-regulation. Under the proposed rules, social media companies have to make their recommendation systems transparent, and be subject to auditing of their risk management, codes of conduct, and self-regulation.[25]

Because solutions like these conflict with both the spirit and the letter of the First Amendment, private solutions tend to be favoured in the United States, at least thus far. But within the international human rights sphere, and particularly Europe, such market solutions are not only seen as inadequate but also seen as inherently inferior because they lack the legitimacy of being 'prescribed by law', which is required of restrictions to freedom of expression in the Council of Europe.[26] The international community, particularly in Europe, looking back at the formative experience of the twentieth century, is acutely aware of the dema-gogic potential of the new media and the dangers that concentrations of opinion forming power present to democracy.[27] Many argue that the antidemocratic 'populist turn' in the past decade is evidence of the lack of social responsibility of the platforms, which in turn is due to a lack of oversight.

Another important difference between the First Amendment and the international human rights perspective is that current interpretations of the US First Amendment tend to treat freedom of speech and of the press as indistinct (medium as speaker) whereas in international human rights, media freedom is distinct from the human right to freedom of expression (or speech). In some respects media freedom is more important because of the amplificatory role the media play in democracy, and in others less important because expression has inherent— rather than merely instrumental—value.[28]

The philosophical basis of the distinction between human rights to free speech and expression on the one hand and media or press freedom on the other lies in two arguments:

1. The fact that as *human* rights, arguments for freedom of speech see the basis of human autonomy as a good in itself—the psychological benefits that underlie the Kantian notion that human autonomy, including through speech, is a part of the fundamental notion of humans as ends in themselves rather than means to other ends. Media and press freedom are primarily means to other ends—such as the search for truth and democracy, and providing the platform for the self-expression of humans.[29]

2. In democratic theory, it is asserted that the media, because they constitute key bottlenecks and gateways in communication of fact and opinion, carry particular *responsibilities*, including for the potential detrimental and beneficial effects their actions have for democratic deliberation and legitimacy, to truth as a value, and also ongoing specific privileges and protections.[30] This is reflected in the 'watchdog doctrine' of the European Court of Human Rights, according to which the media can enjoy special protections and privileges, including for example source protection, over and above those rights and protections afforded to other speakers. The ECHR states that the exercise of free expression *'since it carries with it duties and responsibilities*, may be subject to such formalities, conditions, restrictions or penalties as are prescribed by law and are necessary in a democratic society'. These duties and responsibilities have been interpreted as particularly onerous in the media, in an approach that contrasts with the approach of US courts, which tends to reject special rights for the media.[31]

In international human rights terms, both freedom of expression and freedom of the media should be subject to restrictions if these are necessary, proportionate, and for a legitimate aim in a democratic society,[32] but the law on restrictions has developed a particular framework for what can be considered necessary and legitimate restrictions of the media. In relation to broadcasting, for example, these include the justification of licensing, whereas in the press they do not. It is unclear what is the basis of these distinctions, but there is a marked contrast between the United States on one hand and the European and international human rights system on the other: broadcast licence requirements have been gradually chipped away by the First Amendment in the United States,[33] but in Europe they are explicitly bolstered by Article 10.1, which states that 'this Article shall not prevent States from requiring the licensing of broadcasting, television or cinema enterprises'. This raised fundamental questions about the accountability framework for new media which are not mentioned in these laws. If the justification of media regulation is based on spectrum scarcity (the use of a scarce public resource that limits channels) then it can be rolled back with the shift to digital, but if it is based on the social features and consequences of media distribution then the rationale for regulation may persist, for example if certain players remain dominant in economic terms.[34]

The culture of Internet companies in the United States aligns with the negative rights approach. It tends to be libertarian, based on a deeply held assumption that state or legal regulation of communications is inferior to market allocation of communicative resources.[35] There is a natural affinity between the 'negative rights' approach, and the self-regulatory approaches of the tech giants who have devised elaborate self-regulatory schemes such as Facebook's Oversight Board, and Google's Right to be Forgotten Panel, their AI ethics panel, and Community Standards and a range of other initiatives,[36] which they argue are more compatible with freedom of speech than would be a system of licensing or regulation by public authority, such as that being developed in Germany and the United Kingdom, for example.[37] Such a self-regulatory approach, based on a theory of democratic communication according to which the greatest threat is state censorship, runs with the grain of the prevailing philosophy of freedom of speech in the United States.

The long-term impact of the rejection of positive state intervention, and particularly any state support of democratic media is illustrated by the US approach to media taxation. US courts have opposed application of tax law in ways that discriminate amongst newspapers or between the press and other areas of economic activity. An important US Supreme Court case from 1983[38] reversed a decision to uphold a tax law that targeted several larger newspaper publishers. Rather than simply applying the general sales tax that applied to everyone, newspapers were exempted from sales tax but taxed via a specific tax on paper and ink, which only larger newspapers were liable for.[39] The reasoning of the court was that it was not in fact necessary to find that the state had tried to use tax to censor the press, merely that the state, in imposing the tax was discriminating in the sense of going beyond the general purposes of tax (e.g., generating revenue) and was applied in a way that discriminated against the press: 'A power to tax differentially . . . can operate as effectively as a censor to check critical comment by the press, undercutting the basic assumption of our political system that the press will often serve as an important restraint on government'.[40] This interpretation of the US constitution actively prevents application of taxation law with the potential to lead to a 'censorious' use of taxation against newspapers. The judgement is clear that such a motive on the part of legislators was neither evident nor indeed necessary in this specific case; the potential for such a purpose is enough. Justice White makes it explicit in his concurring opinion: 'The fear is that the government might use the tax as a threatened sanction to achieve a censorial purpose'. The fear of slippery slopes to censorial purpose permeates First Amendment doctrine, which makes it inherently opposed to building institutions of accountability which may impact speech and the press. As we shall see in the next section, the US First Amendment approach threatens to strangle an incipient new 'social contract' with dominant digital platforms at birth.

THE POLICY TOOLKIT

The chapters in this book show that dealing with digital dominance through a new policy settlement or 'social contract' will require a range of new, interconnected policy interventions, including new taxes and subsidies,[41] new approaches to antitrust and competition enforcement,[42] new approaches to content regulation,[43] online liability,[44] data protection,[45] and media law reforms. Each of these proposed policy interventions is problematic from the perspective of a negative rights, content-neutral approach, and will be opposed on that basis in public policy, in courts and in public opinion in the United States.

Taxes

Taxation policy can be used as part of a wider settlement in order to penalize harmful outcomes (such as disinformation or hatred) and subsidize the good (veracity and deliberation). Clearly such interventions could be abused to control media, but this should not preclude their administration by genuinely independent and transparent agencies such as media funds and charity trusts.[46] Tax breaks for journalism, news, and media are well established in Europe, but as we saw not in the United States, as the First Amendment is particularly hostile to discriminatory taxation of media and communication companies.

Subsidies

Many of the proposed solutions to the crisis of journalism involve subsidies to news and journalism. In France and Scandinavia subsidies for media outlets, awarded using independent bodies that apply objective criteria,[47] have been a constant feature of media systems that acknowledge that, particularly in small markets or threatened languages, quality media outlets may not be sufficiently supported by the market. The US Supreme Court has been profoundly suspicious of all forms of subsidy including spectrum.

Content Regulation/Liability

US approaches eschew content regulation by public authorities and therefore social demands of accountability and protection from harm are redirected back to the gatekeepers and publishers of content considered harmful to individuals or to the public interest. By contrast, content regulation online has been seen by the Council of Europe and other international human rights bodies as harmonious with international human rights standards. Long struggles and international differences over press regulation testify to this fact.[48] The debate about new media on the Internet has focused on the question of legal liability, but given the volume of content, the division of labour between courts, self-regulatory bodies and the moderation practices of gatekeepers themselves will remain in flux until and enduring policy settlement to replace the limited liability regime is found.[49] Negative rights approaches will be used to scupper attempts to move from self to co-regulation by backing voluntary codes with law.

Licensing is a point of particular contrast. The gulf that separates the United States from the rest of the human rights community is particularly wide in relation to broadcasting: In the United States, the conflict between public-interest broadcasting standards and First Amendment ultimately resulted in the failure of the Fairness Doctrine.[50] In contrast, UN General Comment 34 (s39) positively states that signatories of the International Convention on Civil and Political Rights (ICCPR, to which the United States has entered multiple reservations) have a positive obligation to ensure that frequencies are provided equitably between 'public, commercial and community' broadcasters,[51] which as a minimum will require public authorities to discriminate between those categories. The ECHR explicitly *permits* licensing of broadcasters in article 10.3. The reservations and declarations made by the United States thus reflect the long tradition of 'US exceptionalism' in which the United States claims to have higher standards of freedom of expression than other countries, and reserves the right to maintain these higher standards. The particular sticking point for the United States was Article 19.3 of the ICCPR, which sets out the restrictions of speech which are to be considered justifiable. The United States considers these to be too widely drawn and permissive of too broad a scope for censorship:

> 19.3. The exercise of the rights provided for in paragraph 2 of this article carries with it special duties and responsibilities. It may therefore be subject to certain restrictions, but these shall only be such as are provided by law and are necessary: (a) For respect of the rights or reputations of others; (b) For the protection of national security or of public order (ordre public), or of public health or morals.

Whilst there are some distinctions,[52] the standards of the ICCPR are very similar to those of the Council of Europe, and the policy approach of the European Union is aligned with the fundamental rights standards. In short, the new social contract will require a 'meta-policy' which links together incentives in all of these legal areas. The EU DSA goes some way towards outlining what such a framework would entail. Such an overarching approach to regulation of these new media would be applicable in a US context only if the normative theory that underpins the negative rights approach was rejected.

DIGITAL DOMINANCE AND FREEDOM OF THE MEDIA

It is the market power of Internet intermediaries that imbues them with their gatekeeping power, and arguably the ethical responsibilities of media. But the US and the international approaches offer contrasting strategies on how to check gatekeeping power and enforce the ethical responsibilities that it entails.

The rise of powerful Internet gatekeepers creates institutions with media capabilities and functions outside the social compact of rights and duties that mainstream media, however imperfectly, evolved. Attempts have been made to accommodate ideas of freedom of the media with the new reality. Oster (2015), for example, posits a role for a new functional definition of media which bears some similarity to the approach of the Council of Europe (2011)[53] in setting out new rights and duties for the media, and defining the new Internet intermediaries as media on the basis of their size and function.

Although Hartmann and Holznagel point out (in this volume) that in legal systems such as Germany they are traditionally separate, there is a strong interrelationship between issues of competition/market structure and media law/freedom of expression. The question for example of whether content takedown by private actors constitutes effective censorship—or merely the exercise of editorial discretion—will depend on the size and market power of that platform. Whether, for the purposes of awarding privileges of prominence,[54] discoverability, or distribution, for example, an intermediary or content provider should be considered 'media' will also depend upon, amongst other things, the size and market position of that intermediary.[55] These abstract principles are playing out in practice: the EU DSA, and the implementation of new standards on the responsibility of video providers make clear that expectations will differ according to the size and the nature of the service and that particularly onerous responsibilities will apply to a new category of 'very large on-line platforms'.[56] The Digital Markets Act, which was published by the Commission at the same time as the DSA, sets out a new set of rules to promote competition in digital markets, which also protect media pluralism.[57] In Germany, which has the most advanced law in Europe in this respect, an important goal of competition law is to maintain communicative opportunities and media pluralism.[58]

So whilst market dominance might in theory bestow particular media freedom privileges on intermediaries because of the 'watchdog' role they play,[59] they also entail particular duties. It is the interplay of these rights and duties, which is encapsulated in the wording of the ECHR (but not in the first amendment), which constitutes the social contract of dominant platforms. A central question for both platforms and legacy news providers is which of them are to take on which of the privileges and responsibilities that come with being designated 'media'.

In international human rights systems such as the Council of Europe, media pluralism is the *corollary* of media freedom.[60] This is because liberal democracies have learned from history that powerful media institutions, whilst they must be autonomous from the state, also have the potential to destroy democracy because they can exert a powerful influence on public opinion. When media concentration enables public opinion to be shifted and controlled by powerful media gatekeepers, the democratic process loses its legitimacy. This is why media freedom is accompanied in all mature democracies by structural controls on ownership, mergers, and control of media companies that are well reflected and embedded in international legal standards.[61] These are delivered through competition and company law, but have specific objectives separate from the normal objectives of competition law, namely the protection of democratic deliberation and the prevention of concentration of power.[62]

Media pluralism, or media diversity as it is called in the United States,[63] the principle that the concentration of media markets should be limited, and that democracy is served by a plurality of media outlets, content types, and viewpoints is a well-established principle in Europe and North America. It forms part of the EU Charter on Fundamental Rights[64] and the Federal Communication Commission (FCC) rules in the United States.[65] It is implemented in antitrust and merger rules in the media sector and can also be conceived of in terms of autonomy: the necessity of avoiding a situation in which large media players—think of the Murdoch empire—are so dominant that they obtain power over government actors. Of course, none of these laws and frameworks is perfect, but there is a long history in liberal democracy of trying to use them to draw a line, and to protect media freedom. Media freedom and media pluralism are also direct corollaries in the sense that a reduction of media plurality would justify less media freedom in order to check power. With power comes responsibility.

The notion of media pluralism is thus a core principle of media freedom: who is free, and to what extent they are free, is determined by considerations including their power over public opinion and the public resources they use. The principle is simple: those media institutions that are most powerful should be subject, according to a sliding scale based on their size and dominance, to more checks and balances of that power, and guarantees of responsibility. If News International, the BBC, or indeed Facebook decide to promote an issue, or suppress a viewpoint, this matters a great deal more than if a humble blogger does so. Ultimately, it is the principle of size and power rather than public or private that should govern decisions about whether private actors or public authorities should be considered censors or editors, regulators or speakers. This is why competition and other regulatory issues are so closely linked, and why policies such as the European DSA, and the Online Safety Bill in the United Kingdom set out thresholds and a graduated approach: tougher restrictions apply to larger, more influential platforms.

The question of which structural rules and design principles need to be applied in a democracy must thus be posed afresh as new Internet intermediaries, such as social and search companies, take on the role of mediating intermediaries in the new media system, displacing the companies and services we previously thought of as 'media'. This is particularly important because the new Internet media differ in major ways to the old media, and particularly in their ability to tailor and target media content to the interests, needs, and vulnerabilities of particular audience segments and even individuals.[66] This poses the problem of propaganda (the extent to which media are able to shape public opinion) in a new setting in which the doctrines, and also the precise rules, thresholds, and measures to protect media diversity and pluralism need to be revised:[67] it may be the case that even a company that controls a small part of the overall media market can have a damaging effect on the process of deliberation and the legitimacy of elections, if it controls enough personal data to target messages effectively to a swing constituency and chooses to do so. Co-regulatory codes of conduct should set out a framework of voluntary self-restraint so that new media commit to refrain from propaganda.[68] This process has already started, for example with self-imposed limits on political advertising being considered by Twitter, Facebook, and other platforms, but regulators such as the UK Information Commissioner's Office and various parliamentary committees have called for further restrictions including an industry-wide statutory code.[69]

Large-scale commerce in personal data, together with powerful machine learning and AI change the nature of propaganda and open the prospect for highly targeted and manipulative agents capable of compromising the autonomy of humans by controlling their information inputs. This is manifest in the widespread social concern about filter bubbles and targeted propaganda, which we can dub 'surveillance democracy'.[70] From the point of view of media freedom this shift is important, because it heightens the need for limits and conditions to be placed on media power and also changes the nature of those limits and conditions. Media freedom or freedom of expression is cited as a reason to reject algorithmic accountability or AI ethics (for example in relation to the imposition of transparency requirements, or qualifications of liability exemptions under the Digital Millennium Copyright Act or the E-Commerce Directive), and this will, and should increasingly be seen as a concern for human autonomy within the context of control by nonhuman agents, not merely as a concern for expressive rights and the abstract value of liberty of the 'media'.

THE DANGERS OF NEGATIVE RIGHTS

At a time of rapid technological change, modernizing media systems may require new forms of accountability and regulation of media. But new interventions have been seen as conflicting with the First Amendment. Legal doctrines such as content neutrality[71] are a case in point. According to this doctrine the state should not interfere in speech in ways that discriminate among sources or forms of content, for fear that state actors will abuse their power to shape opinion in their favour.

Those adopting this approach view with suspicion all forms of public institution-building with regard to the media. All forms of support, but particularly subsidies, tax breaks, content regulation, and distribution support tend to be seen as inevitably subject to capture and control and therefore to be avoided. In short, content neutrality may make it more difficult for states to control democratic media, but it also stops the state supporting the media.[72] Negative rights approaches, prevalent in the United States, tend to favour a market-oriented approach, neglecting the needs of poor and excluded minorities, which are less attractive to advertisers or less likely to pay for media services. The negative rights, market approach of the 'mainstream media' in the United States has not served minorities well.

At a time when all but the most powerful media, or those backed by industrial interests cannot survive without some form of public support, such a position is untenable. The US approach to the First Amendment has paved the way for the spread of democracy during the twentieth century, and the prevention of authoritarian concentrations of power to manipulate opinion by the state. But it has been less effective in controlling the manipulation of speech and opinion by private actors.

Negative rights approaches favour self-regulation over government or legal regulation. As a result, media ethics, both in the form of professional standards and in formal self-regulation, has been adopted through codes of conduct and professional standards. However, the level of public awareness of self-regulation and ethics remains very low:[73] media users, particularly in social media, rarely have sufficient information on which to base their judgements of what to believe and why: what processes of verification and commitment to what theory of truth lies behind the content they are reading from this social media source, or that newspaper or broadcaster. In response to pressure over the past two decades from governments, from civil society, and from international organizations, private actors are self-regulating, but this creates confusion over the nature of this regulation and its origin. To what extent are for example codes of content on terrorism and hate speech, sponsored by the European Union and encouraged by the DSA, voluntary? To what extent are UK journalism codes backed by a Royal Charter[74] voluntary, and to what extent should they be?

Confusion over the motivation and origin of self-regulation, and the growth of opaque structures of complex co-regulation compounds problems of public trust and transparency.[75] The procedural dimension of media policy: ensuring that building new institutions of ethical standards and codes are transparent, inclusive and accountable to civil society becomes increasingly important.[76]

THE DANGERS OF POSITIVE RIGHTS AND INTERNATIONAL HUMAN RIGHTS APPROACHES

Positive approaches on the other hand also contain dangers. Isiah Berlin warned against positive interventions to support 'freedom to', arguing that they would lead to curtailment of freedoms.[77] Similarly, the US Supreme Court has been against a view of the free press that gives positive privileges to media across a range of legal areas, arguing that their administration chills speech.

The positive interventions permitted under the international human rights approach, including subsidies, tax breaks, and content regulation carry with them the danger not only of pre-publication censorship, but of subtle systems of reciprocity and 'understandings' and a tendency to favour a pro-regime, pro–status quo approach through self-censorship, which can be particularly difficult to detect. Public broadcasting systems, notions of 'impartiality', 'objectivity' or 'media pluralism', for example, can in the wrong hands form cornerstones of systems of soft censorship, excluding non-mainstream, anti–status quo views. The core issues to resolve in both cases are transparency, trust, and conditionality. How to provide information about the system to ensure that the media receive 'due trust' appropriate to their ethics?[78] How to engage real conditionality and accountability to the publics served by media, but also maintain autonomy of the state and other interests?

It is crucial to note, however, that a new settlement on freedom of the media will not equate to a chilling of speech across society. This is because of the distinction between freedom of the media and freedom of speech: the duties and responsibilities of the media only apply to the media, and the ethical compact of enhanced responsibility—for example that reflected in the DSA in the European Union—only applies to those powerful gatekeepers that provide a platform that accelerates and amplifies speech. Contestation and dissent can be more open and vibrant and viral on the wider Internet than it was in the age of print media.

The dangers of positive rights approaches are real, but they are not insurmountable and they require new approaches to guaranteeing separation of state and media power. So when proposals, for example for new approaches to data regulation, taxation, or protections from legal liability that seek to offer a subsidy to quality journalism for example are considered, they must be administered and awarded by a legitimate, transparent, inclusive, and cross-party manner.[79]

The approach of international human rights is not to prohibit positive interventions, it is to constrain them, for example by creating standards of independence of regulation, which the Council of Europe has done,[80] and which membership of the European Union increasingly requires.[81] Rather than the abstract concept of negative liberty, the requirement of structural and operational separation between media and state is increasingly important.[82] Where the application of positive approaches falls short—as for example in contemporary Poland and Hungary—it is when it is not forcefully and decisively implemented, rather than due to the deficiencies of the approach itself.

REFORMING REGULATION: THE PROCEDURAL DIMENSION OF A NEW SOCIAL CONTRACT

Within the constraints of global legal norms of freedom of expression and of the media, and national constitutional frameworks, each democratic media system should agree a 'social contract' for the new media, as Pickard points out in his contribution to this volume. Policy initiatives such as the Digital Markets Act and the DSA of the European Union offer an opportunity to recast the institutions of the past and reform media systems in order to provide robust support to the legitimizing function of media and their role in truth seeking and democratic deliberation.

The US-led, content-neutral, negative rights, libertarian approach has curtailed state capture of media and direct control by government, but it has also hindered accountability and institution-building that would enable civic and public accountability of media. On the other hand, the positive rights approach has been vulnerable to capture and conflict of interest, but it has enabled media to cover a plurality of viewpoints even in small markets and segments that may struggle in a free market.

The coming social contract for new media requires a new philosophy of media freedom, and one that should be conducive to the creation of independent institutions with structures of accountability not to government or even parliament, but to civil society. It should incorporate strong commitments to transparency and procedural standards to prevent capture by both public and private interests. This should start with the process of media policymaking itself.[83] This means fostering public debate about this social contract. The contract should ultimately not be between government and the media, it should be between civil society and the media. Successful liberal democracies ensured that the key junctures of policymaking were led by transparent and independent policy commissions that could not be controlled or captured by specific political parties or interests,[84] and future policymaking also needs to root legitimacy in civil society.

It should by now be clear that the various rules and institutions involved in the governance settlement for the media are tightly intertwined and interdependent. The rationale for content regulation of platforms for example depends on their size, power, and scope. They should be more regulated for plurality and diversity if they are more dominant, and at the same time, a private platform for speech can operate as a more effective censor of speech if it is more dominant in any given market. In practical terms this means that policy debates bleed into one another: for example the current global debate about the appropriate competition framework for digital media platforms[85] focusses mainly on the direct economic implications of platform dominance on price, quality, and consumer interests, but inevitably will need to take into account the wider social and political implications, just as the previous competition framework developed sector specific structural and behavioural rules that established specific limits on media structures to protect not competition or consumer welfare, but democracy and citizen welfare.[86]

This is why the appropriate public policy vehicle to resolve these questions is not a policy review focussing only on competition, only on market structure or only on content standards, but a single review that encompasses all of these. Adopting a positive, human rights approach is based on the media providing support for the right to receive ideas, which might entail positive intervention to create privileges to support media. Conditionality of media privilege is a complex matter. As a general principle media privileges should be granted in order to incentivize truth-seeking and deliberative inclusion, but these should not be in the gift of state or other interests.

In international human rights it has been established since the major post-war declarations that freedom of expression carries with it 'duties and responsibilities' and this has been institutionalized in a wide range of complex co- and self-regulatory ethics. The notions of 'responsible journalism' and 'watchdog journalism' establish conditionality between privileges (such as liability and source protection) and duties. Underlying the notion of reciprocity is precisely the instrumental nature of the right: media are free not because of their inherent value to human autonomy, but because of their value in achieving other values, including truth, democracy, and human autonomy. The operation of conditionality can be seen as one of the key dividing lines between positive rights approaches and negative rights approaches which undermine mechanisms of conditionality and accountability.

CONCLUSION

The positive approach to regulation of internet intermediaries in the European Union conflicts with the current "negative rights" approach of the First Amendment, but it is likely that the EU framework will become a default global standard for democracies.[87] Internet intermediaries are emerging as the new 'media' of the Internet, but they are not subject to the same framework of conditional duties and responsibilities as established media, nor do they enjoy the same privileges. A new theory of media freedom is needed. This chapter has argued for an updated positive rights approach.

Both the US First Amendment approach, and the approach of international human rights are flawed. The libertarian approach of the United States has afforded too much power to private media owners, in a way that undermined the conditions for democratic deliberation. Positive rights approaches on the other hand evolved out of the state-captured media systems, and public broadcasters, for example, struggled to escape the clutches of the state. As a result, both the negative rights version and the positive rights version failed to deliver the independent truth function for democratic deliberation, and liberal democracies suffered frequent crises of legitimacy and trust. With the crisis of sustainability of traditional media this has become more profound and urgent.

The negative rights theory of media freedom is insufficient. Control of discourse by the state or other centres of power is clearly incompatible with democracy, but regulation by the market alone is unable to maintain the legitimacy of democracy. It is becoming evident that active development of intermediate structuring institutions of democratic deliberation in complex democracies is a matter of urgent public policy concern. The question is: who or what should regulate communication; why, and how? As we move from a stable, media-specific legal framework to a converged, data-driven, AI-powered, Internet-mediated one, there is very little agreement on the fundamentals, and long-established philosophical and legal doctrines, such as established ideas of media freedom, rightly come into question.

A growing number of commentators and experts are becoming aware that the content-neutral negative rights approach of the United States is not sustainable, because it undermines the ability of public authorities to take the necessary steps to update their media systems in order to support the emergence of ethical, truth-seeking media which are necessary for democracy.[88] Various forms of public intervention may be necessary in order to transform and update the media systems of liberal democracies in the United States as elsewhere, and it *is* possible to design them (for example subsidies, tax breaks or content regulation) without creeping state control of discourse. Partly as a result of the commitment in Europe to the positive approach of international human rights, European countries have been more keen to propose regulatory reforms for Internet media, including new regulatory frameworks for internet intermediaries such as the EU DSA.

In order to modernize media governance and strike a new compact of conditional rights, inter-related structural, behavioural, infrastructure, and content issues need to be discussed together, and conditionality imposed through a system of regulation and credible threats. There is a high danger of corporate capture of policymaking. The central challenge is a procedural one: to ensure that the policy process itself genuinely responds to a broad set of pro-democratic, civil society concerns, meets standards of transparency, and is not captured by any sectoral interest. This is easier said than done, but could be facilitated by agreement on a common theory of media freedom among democracies. This could entail:

- New models and standards of policymaking process. The Council of Europe has outlined a new standard for media governance which highlights the need for procedural standards of inclusion and transparency as the new social contract is agreed, to avoid the opaque deal-making and reciprocities that will otherwise arise.[89]
- Further international standards. A successor to UN General Comment 34 could advocate technology-neutral media rights and procedural standards in policymaking in the media sector reflecting the unique challenges for media policymaking in democracies. Ensuring that governance is independent, both of individual companies and of the state, is fundamental.
- Procedural standards on policymaking are important in this respect because often it is not the nature of a subsidy, tax, or content regulation framework, but the threats and controls exerted in discussion of such a framework that act as a more powerful check on the media. The Council of Europe (2021) has initiated work to set out new standards on media-state relationships in this respect.
- Active standard setting by media industry actors. The media, in particular news media, are powerful in the policy process, and not only by shaping public debate editorially. They can also refuse to be involved

in policy decisions such as standard setting and consultation, thereby denying it legitimacy, and boosting standard setting by international organizations, as can the platforms themselves.

- Oversight and commentary by international IGOs and NGOs such as the Council of Europe and the UN Human Rights Council. I have argued that human rights standards should play a leading role but that they should be updated and applied more precisely to new technologies.
- Human rights impact assessments, such as those developed under the Ruggie Principles should also take into account media freedom as a fundamental right (Oster 2015) and they should not be used to 'chill' institution building.

International Human rights approaches were established with the strong support of the United States in the years following World War II. But the United States diverged from these standards, ostensibly to maintain higher standards of freedom of speech. I have argued that the coming period will represent particular challenges to the US approach to positive interventions. Those that believe in liberal democracy should work actively to build a converged theory of media freedom that offers a workable compromise between US exceptionalism and human rights standards, whilst protecting media governance institutions from capture by sectoral interests.

As Habermas (2006, 411) points out, 'mediated political communication in the public sphere can facilitate deliberative legitimation processes only if a self-regulating media system gains independence from its social environments' and develops a 'truth-tracking potentia'. A new social contract based on positive media freedom may enable it to do so.

NOTES

1. See Pickard (2014) for a discussion of the notion of social contract, and Pickard (this volume) for an application. See also Tambini (2012), Ward (2005).
2. Hutchens Commission (1948); Siebert et al. (1963).
3. I here draw on institutional approaches in law, economics, and political science. For institutionalists, ideas matter in social and political change, as they constitute institutionalized path dependencies that explain the enduring nature of legal and political structures. See Hall and Taylor (1996), Powell and DiMaggio (1991), and North (1990); see also Colin Hay (2004).
4. This distinction is not new, it is well established in the literature. See Stein (2004), Kenyon and Scott (2020), Baker (2007), and Pickard (2015).
5. The international adoption of the EU General Data Protection Regulation as a default global standard illustrates the important role of international policy adoption in setting global standards.
6. I develop this theory further in Tambini (2021).
7. See especially Baker (2007), Sunstein (2000), Stein (2004), and, for a discussion, Kenyon (2014), Kenyon and Scott (2020).

8. This point is made forcefully by Dieter Grimm (2005, 119–20), according to whom the distinction between the negative and positive function of fundamental rights in general should be understood in terms of the distinctions between the French and the American revolutions: 'The different circumstances under which these two revolutions operated and, caused by these circumstances, the different purposes of the American and French Revolution can supply an explanation: While the American Revolution aimed at independence from the motherland and at self-government, the French revolution aimed at a different social and legal order'.

9. See Starr (2004).

10. Humphreys (1994) describes the case of post-war Germany, where the German Basic Law and the Interstate Broadcasting Treaties set out a positive approach to media freedom.

11. Grimm (2005).

12. See Tambini (2021), Starr (2004), and Pickard (2015). The historical interpretation finds its way into the reasoning of judges: for example, in the Grosjean judgement of the supreme court, the judges held that 'From the history of the subject, it is plain that the English rule restricting freedom of the press to immunity from censorship before publication was not accepted by the American colonists, and that the First Amendment was aimed at any form of previous restraint upon printed publications or their circulation, including restraint by taxation of newspapers and their advertising, which were well known and odious methods still used in England when the First Amendment was adopted'. *Grosjean v. American Press Co., Inc.*, 297 U.S. 233 (1936).

13. Sunstein (2018), Healy (2013).

14. Universal Declaration of Human Rights/ European Convention on Human Rights.

15. See Ash (2016) for a discussion.

16. See the ECtHR case: *Manole and Others v. Moldova* (Dec.)—13936/02 Decision 26.9.2006 [Section IV], see also Council of Europe (2018).

17. European Charter of Fundamental Rights Article 12.

18. See, especially, Lichtenberg (1990), Baker (2007), and Stewart (1975).

19. Pickard (2015).

20. For example, the United States entered a number of reservations (did not fully sign up) to article 20 of the International Covenant on Civil and Political Rights on the grounds that they were not compatible with US commitments to freedom of speech and of the press. https://scholarlycommons.law.northwestern.edu/cgi/viewcontent.cgi?article=1018&context=njihr

21. According to the US Senate: (138 Cong. Rec. S4781-01 (daily ed., April 2, 1992).

III. The Senate's advice and consent (to the ICCPR) is subject to the following declarations:
'(1) That the United States declares that the provisions of Articles 1 through 27 of the Covenant are not self-executing.
(2) That it is the view of the United States that States Party to the Covenant should wherever possible refrain from imposing any restrictions or limitations on the exercise of the rights recognized and protected by the Covenant, even when such restrictions and limitations are permissible under the terms of the Covenant. *For the United States, Article 5, paragraph*

2, *which provides that fundamental human rights existing in any State Party may not be diminished on the pretext that the Covenant recognizes them to a lesser extent, has particular relevance to Article 19, paragraph 3, which would permit certain restrictions on the freedom of expression.* The United States declares that it will continue to adhere to the requirements and constraints of its Constitution in respect to all such restrictions and limitations' (Emphasis added).

22. Article 19.3 of the International Convention on Civil and Political Rights and Article 10.2 of the European Convention on Human Rights, for example, set out some categories of reasons why states might justifiably restrict free speech.

23. See the reforms introduced in the introduction to this volume, such as the DSA and the Audiovisual Media Services Directive.

24. For a discussion, see Mazzoli and Tambini (2020) and Gillespie (2018).

25. The Draft EU DSA (2020).

26. ECHR Article 10 sets out a three part test for restrictions on freedom of expression to be permissible: they must be necessary in a democratic society, for a legitimate aim, and prescribed by law.

27. See, for example, Solon Barocas (2012) and Daniel Kreiss (2012). The EU DSA proposals form part of the EU Democracy Action Plan (2020), a set of reforms that aim to protect democratic institutions.

28. See Barendt (2005, 424).

29. See Barendt (2005).

30. See Habermas (1989), Lichtenberg (1990), Keane (1991), and Moore (this volume).

31. In the Jersild case the court underlined the institutional role of the press. 'The punishment of a journalist for assisting in the dissemination of statements made by another person in an interview would seriously hamper the contribution of the press to discussion of matters of public interest and should not be envisaged unless there are particularly strong reasons for doing so' (see Dommering 2008, 46). By contrast, the US Supreme Court holds that there are no special duties and responsibilities for the media as opposed to speakers generally.

32. This is the three-part test under the European Convention on Human Rights article 10.2.

33. The demise of the 'Fairness Doctrine' in US broadcasting law for example, see Tambini (2021).

34. See Sunstein (2000).

35. See Gillespie (2018).

36. See Gillespie (2018).

37. For an argument about the free speech implications of self-regulation, which attempts to seek legitimacy for a pure model of self-regulation by referring to International Human Rights Standards see Article 19: Social Media Councils (2019). https://www.article19.org/social-media-councils/. The Netz DG law (2018) in Germany and the UK Online Safety Bill (2021) offer a contrasting approach.

38. *Minneapolis Star Tribune Company v. Commissioner*, 460 U.S. 575 (1983).

39. According to the judgement: 'Commentators have generally viewed [a previous case that established limits on press taxation] Grosjean as dependent on the improper censorial goals of the legislature. See T. Emerson, The System of Freedom of

Expression 419 (1970); L. Tribe, American Constitutional Law 592 n. 8, 724 n. 10 (1978). We think that the result in Grosjean may have been attributable in part to the perception on the part of the Court that the state imposed the tax with an intent to penalize a selected group of newspapers. In the case currently before us, however, there is no legislative history and no indication, apart from the structure of the tax itself, of any impermissible or censorial motive on the part of the legislature'.

40. Opinion of the court at 6, Minnesota Commissioner of Revenue, 460 U.S. 575 (1983).

41. The response to the crisis of journalism revenue has led to multiple new proposals for tax breaks and subsidies, see Downie and Shudson (2009) The question of platform taxation has been approached both as a revenue question (OECD) and as a social policy issues. See also Brogi et al., this volume.

42. See the report of the UK Competition and Markets Authority (2019), Feld (2019), and Furman (2019).

43. See Article 19; Hartmann and Holznagel (this volume).

44. Intermediaries are being brought into a new co-regulatory regime in Europe. The DSA will create incentives for member states to hold intermediaries to account for protecting their users, in an approach broadly similar to the proposed Online Harms legislation in the United Kingdom, which will introduce an intermediate category between conduits and publishers. At the same time the AudioVisual Media Services Directive creates a new category of regulatory subject: the video-sharing platform.

45. Graef (2018), Napoli (this volume), and Balkin (2016).

46. Levy and Picard (2011). See Brogi and Carlini (this volume).

47. See Schweizer et al. (2014).

48. Tambini et al. (2008).

49. The European approach of the Ecommerce Directive 2000 art 14, and the US DMCA S230 are currently rather similar, offering some liability protection for hosts and conduits with no knowledge that content they transmit or host infringes rights. The DSA proposes to leave this in place, but incentivize self-regulation by platforms and third parties.

50. For a discussion, see Sunstein (2000), Yoo (2003), and Krasnow and Goodman (1998, 618–19).

51. United Nations Human Rights Committee (2011). General Comment 34 on the Rights to Freedom of Opinion and Expression, S39.

52. See, for a discussion, McGonagle (2015, 19).

53. Council of Europe (2011). Recommendation on a New Notion of Media.

54. Mazzoli 2020; Mazzoli and Tambini (2020).

55. The Council of Europe (2011) argues that designation as media should be based on a combination of size, professional standards and self-designation. Oster (2015) offers a similar set of criteria.

56. EC (2020a).

57. EC (2020b).

58. Hartmann and Holznagel (this volume).

59. Lichtenberg (1990) and Oster (2015).

60. EU Charter of Fundamental Rights article 12.

61. For example, the Council of Europe (2018).

62. Craufurd-Smith and Tambini (2015).
63. Napoli (1999).
64. Article 11.2: 'The freedom and pluralism of the media shall be respected'.
65. See Napoli (2015), in Valcke et al. (2015): https://link.springer.com/book/10.1057/9781137304308.
66. Barocas (2012), Kreis (2012), and Helberger (2018).
67. Craufurd-Smith and Tambini (2015).
68. See Marsden et al. (this volume).
69. See Marsden et al. (this volume).
70. See Zuboff (2019) and Moore (2018).
71. Annany (2018, 29).
72. See Baker (1989, 2007).
73. See Reuters Institute (n.d.).
74. The United Kingdom passed a Royal Charter on the Press in 2013, but it has never been enforced. See Heawood (2019).
75. See Tambini (2021) for a development of this argument.
76. See Council of Europe (2021, section 2.2).
77. Berlin (1958).
78. Onora O'Neill suggested that media accountability should aim for 'assessibility' to ensure that media users know how news is made (O'Neil 2002).
79. This is the position for example of the Council of Europe (2021) recommendation on media governance, which the author was involved in authoring.
80. See Craufurd Smith et al. (2017) and Council of Europe (2020).
81. See for example the Revised Audiovisual Media Services Directive (2018) article 30.
82. Council of Europe (2020, 2021).
83. Council of Europe (2021).
84. This was never perfect, but processes such as the Hutchens Commission, the UK Royal Commissions on the Press, and other open and transparent policy processes helped ensure that single parties or interest did not shape media governance institutions in their favour.
85. See in particular Furman, Competition and Markets Authority, Feld (2019), Hartmann and Holznagel (this volume).
86. Khan (2018).
87. Bradford (2020).
88. Pickard (this volume), Council of Europe (2011, 2021).
89. Council of Europe (2021).

REFERENCES

Ananny, M. 2018. *Networked Press Freedom: Creating Infrastructures for a Public Right to Hear*. Cambridge, MA: MIT Press.
Balkin, J. M. 2016. 'Information Fiduciaries and the First Amendment'. *UC Davis Law Review* 49(4): 1183–1234.
Baker, C. Edwin. 2007. *Media Concentration and Democracy: Why Ownership Matters*. Cambridge: Cambridge University Press.

Barendt, E. 2005. *Freedom of Speech*. 2nd ed. New York, NY: Oxford University Press.

Barocas, S. 2012. 'The Price of Precision: Voter Microtargeting and Its Potential Harms to The Democratic Process'. In *Proceedings of the First Edition Workshop on Politics, Elections and Data*, 31–36. ACM.

Berlin, I. 1958. *Liberty: Incorporating Four Essays on Liberty*. Oxford: Clarendon Press.

Bradford, A. 2020. *The Brussels Effect: How the European Union Rules the World*. New York: Oxford University Press.

Council of Europe. 2011. 'Recommendation on a New Notion of Media'. Council of Europe, Strasbourg.

Council of Europe. 2018. 'Recommendations: Resolution (74) 43 on Press Concentrations; Recommendation CM/Rec (2018)1[1] of the Committee of Ministers to Member States on Media Pluralism and Transparency of Media Ownership'. Council of Europe, Strasbourg.

Council of Europe. 2020. 'Recommendation of the Committee of Ministers to Member States on the Independence and Functions of Regulatory Authorities for the Broadcasting Sector', December 20, 2000. Council of Europe, Strasbourg.

Council of Europe. 2021. 'Recommendation of the Committee of Ministers to Member States on Principles for Media and Communication Governance'. Council of Europe, Strasbourg.

Craufurd-Smith, R., Y. Stolte, E. Psychogiopoulou, and D. Anagnostou. 2017. 'The Freedom and Independence of Public Service Media in Europe: International Standards and Domestic Implementation'. *International Journal of Communication* 11: 1936–55.

Craufurd Smith, R., and D. Tambini. 2015. 'Measuring Media Plurality in the United Kingdom: Policy Choices and Regulatory Challenges'. *Journal of Media Law* 4(1). 35–63.

Dommering, E. 2008. 'Article 10 ECHR (Freedom of Expression)'. In *European Media Law*, edited by O. Castendyk et al., pp. 35–84. Alphen aan den Rijn: Kluwer Law International.

Downie, L., Jr., and M. Schudson. 2009. 'The Reconstruction of American Journalism'. *Columbia Journalism Review*. October 2009.

EC. 2020a. 'Proposal for a Regulation on Digital Services Act 2020'. https://ec.europa.eu/info/strategy/priorities-2019-2024/europe-fit-digital-age/digital-services-act-ensuring-safe-and-accountable-online-environment_en.

EC. 2020b. 'Proposal for a Regulation on Digital Markets Act 2020'. https://ec.europa.eu/info/strategy/priorities-2019-2024/europe-fit-digital-age/digital-markets-act-ensuring-fair-and-open-digital-markets_en.

Feld, H. 2019. 'Digital Platform Act. Public Knowledge'. Accessed July 27, 2020. https://www.digitalplatformact.com/.

Furman, J. Unlocking Digital Competition. Report of the Digital Competition Expert Panel. 2019. London HMSO.

Garton Ash, T. 2016. *Free Speech: Ten Principles for a Connected World*. New Haven: Yale University Press.

Gillespie, T. 2018. *Custodians of the Internet: Platforms, Content Moderation, and the Hidden Decisions That Shape Social Media*. New Haven: Yale University Press.

Graef, I. 2018. 'When Data Evolves into Market Power: Data Concentration and Data Abuse under Competition Law'. In *Digital Dominance: The Power of Google, Amazon,*

Facebook, and Apple, edited by M. Moore and D. Tambini, 71–97. Oxford: Oxford University Press.

Grimm, D. 2005. 'The Protective Function of the State'. In *Science and Technique of Democracy*. Strasbourg: Council of Europe (European and US Constitutionalism). Pp. 137–155.

Habermas, J. 1989. *The Structural Transformation of the Public Sphere*. Cambridge: Polity.

Habermas, J. 2006. Political Communication in Media Society: Does Democracy Still Enjoy an Epistemic Dimension? The Impact of Normative Theory on Empirical Research. *Communication Theory* 16(4). 411–426.

Hall, P. A., and R. C. R. Taylor. 1996. 'Political Science and the Three New Institutionalisms'. *Political Studies* 44(5): 936–57.

Hay, Colin. 2004. 'Ideas, Interests and Institutions in the Comparative Political Economy of Great Transformations'. *Review of International Political Economy* 11(1): 204–26.

Heawood, J. 2019. The Press Freedom Myth. London: Biteback Publishing.

Helberger, N. 2018. 'Challenging Diversity—Social Media Platforms and a New Conception of Media Diversity'. In *Digital Dominance: The Power of Google, Amazon, Facebook, and Apple*, edited by M. Moore and D. Tambini, 153–75. Oxford: Oxford University Press.

Humphreys, P. 1994. *Media and Media Policy in Germany: The Press and Broadcasting since 1945*. Oxford: Berg.

Hutchens Commission. 1947. *Report of the Commission on Freedom of the Press*. Chicago: University of Chicago.

Kenyon, A., and A. Scott. 2020. *Positive Free Speech: Rationales, Methods and Implications*. Oxford: Hart.

Khan, L. 2018. 'Amazon—An Infrastructure Service and Its Challenge to Current Antitrust Law'. In *Digital Dominance: The Power of Google, Amazon, Facebook, and Apple*, edited by M. Moore and D. Tambini, 98–132. Oxford: Oxford University Press.

Krasnow, E. G., and J. N. Goodman. n.d. 'The "Public Interest" Standard: The Search for the Holy Grail'. Federal Communications Law Journal. 50(3) 33: 605–633.

Kreiss, D. 2012. 'Yes We Can (Profile You): A Brief Primer on Campaigns and Political Data'. *Stanford Law Review Online* 64: 70.

Levy, D. A. L., and R. G. Picard, eds. 2011. *Is There a Better Structure for the News Providers: The Potential in Charitable and Trust Ownership*. Oxford: Reuters Institute for the Study of Journalism.

Lichtenberg, J., ed. 1990. 'Foundations and Limits of Freedom of the Press'. In *Democracy and the Mass Media: A Collection of Essays*, 102–35. Cambridge Studies in Philosophy and Public Policy. Cambridge: Cambridge University Press.

Mazzoli, E., and D. Tambini. 2020. 'Prioritization Uncovered'. Strasbourg: Council of Europe.

McGonagle, T., and Y. Donders, eds. 2015. *The United Nations and Freedom of Expression and Information: Critical Perspectives*. Cambridge: Cambridge University Press.

Napoli, P. 2015. 'Assessing Media Diversity in the U.S.: A Comparative Analysis of the FCC's Diversity Index and the EU's Media Pluralism Monitor'. In *Media Pluralism and Diversity, Concepts, Risks and Global Trends*, edited by Peggy Valcke et al. London: Springer. Pp. 141–151.

North, D. C. 1990. *Institutions, Institutional Change, and Economic Performance*. Cambridge: Cambridge University Press.

O'Neil, Onora. 2002. *A Question of Trust*. The BBC Reith Lectures. https://www.bbc.co.uk/programmes/p00ghvd8

Oster, J. 2015. *Media Freedom as a Fundamental Right*. Cambridge: Cambridge University Press.

Pickard, V. 2014. *America's Battle for Media Democracy: The Triumph of Corporate Libertarianism and the Future of Media Reform*. Communication, Society and Politics. New York: Cambridge University Press.

Powell, W., and P. Dimaggio. 1991. *The New Institutionalism in Organisational Analysis*. Chicago: University of Chicago Press.

Reuters Institute. n.d. 'Trust in News in a Digital World'. https://reutersinstitute.politics.ox.ac.uk/what-we-think-we-know-and-what-we-want-know-perspectives-trust-news-changing-world

Schweizer, C., et al. 2014. 'Public Funding of Private Media'. LSE Media Policy Brief. http://eprints.lse.ac.uk/56427/.

Scott, A., and A. Kenyon, eds. 2020. *Positive Free Speech*. London: Bloomsbury.

Siebert, F. S., T. Peterson, and W. Schramm. 1963. *Four Theories of the Press: The Authoritarian, Libertarian, Social Responsibility and Soviet Communist Concepts of What the Press Should Be and Do*. Urbana: University of Illinois Press.

Starr, P. 2004. *The Creation of the Media: Political Origins of Modern Communications*. New York: Basic Books.

Stein, L. 2004. 'Understanding Speech Rights: Defensive and Empowerment Approaches to the First Amendment'. *Media Culture and Society* 26(1): 102–20.

Sunstein, C. R. 2000. 'Television and the Public Interest'. *California Law Review* 88(2): 499. doi: 10.2307/3481228.

Sunstein, C. R. 2018. *#Republic: Divided Democracy in the Age of Social Media*. Princeton: Princeton University Press.

Tambini, D., et al. 2008. *Codifying Cyberspace: Communications Self-Regulation in the Age of Internet Convergence*. London: Routledge.

Tambini, D. 2012. 'Financial Journalism and Conflicts of Interest in Hong Kong'. *Journal of Mass Media Ethics* 28(1): 15–29.

Tambini, D. 2021. *Media Freedom*. Cambridge: Polity.

Ward, S. J. A. 2005. 'Philosophical Foundations for Global Journalism Ethics'. *Journal of Mass Media Ethics* 20(1): 3–21.

Yoo, C. S. 2003. 'The Rise and Demise of the Technology-Specific Approach to the First Amendment'. *Georgetown Law Journal* 91: 245–356.

Zuboff, S. 2019. *The Age of Surveillance Capitalism: The Fight for a Human Future at the New Frontier of Power*. London: Profile Books.

17

A New Social Contract for Platforms

VICTOR PICKARD ∎

HISTORICAL LESSONS FOR THE DIGITAL AGE

Today we face a global dilemma. Democratic societies around the world are grappling with unprecedented concentrated power in a small number of platform companies. No firms have ever wielded such control over so much of our information and communication infrastructures. Recent years have witnessed a rising public backlash against the platforms, especially Facebook and Google, for amassing too much unaccountable power and for causing severe social harms across the planet. Both corporations routinely abuse their market power, extract wealth from users, communities, and media producers, and afflict societies with tremendous negative externalities. In addition to harming democratic processes all over the globe, these firms are also depriving societies of reliable information by financially starving journalistic institutions while proliferating misinformation throughout our media ecosystems (Vaidhyanathan 2018; Pickard 2020a).

Yet, despite all of these problems—many of them worsening by the day—our current moment is also one of exciting possibility. History shows us that periodically the status quo is jolted, creating openings for new ideas and experiments. Arguably, we are in such a moment now. Given how crises cast policy options into stark relief, now is a window of opportunity—most likely a fleeting one—for bold plans and structural reform. If ambitious policy recommendations seem far-fetched—even utopian—at this moment, it is nonetheless important to establish such lofty visions now by creating the normative foundations that make progressive change possible in the future.

Looking to historical parallels when similar debates over media firms' normative role can help guide our thinking about our own era and expand the political imaginary of what might be possible. Such an analysis might also provide cautionary tales of what can go wrong and how we might learn from previous mistakes. One such instructive moment occurred in the post-war 1940s in the United States during a number of policy battles concerning broadcasters' social responsibilities. This period witnessed a feisty media reform movement attempt to establish a more democratic media system. Then, as now, several media firms commanded tremendous power over news and information systems. Attempts to rein them in and impose public interest protections were admirable, but ultimately undermined by red-baiting and an ascendance market fundamentalism in the United States. The public trustee model of broadcasting that emerged shows both the promises and perils of such policy debates. Ultimately, it was a lost opportunity. Why did the post-war settlement fail, and what are the implications of this outcome for current debates over platform social responsibilities? What lessons can be learned from this historical episode and what would new power relationships look like?

In addressing these questions, this chapter proposes that we frame the problems caused by platform monopolies as facets of a broader structural problem— concentrated and unaccountable power over our core information and communication infrastructures. The likes of Facebook and Google have assumed this power before societies were able to receive meaningful democratic obligations in return. Now the time has come to correct this power imbalance and redress social harms. We therefore need to forge a new 'social contract' between the platforms, regulators, and society writ large.

After providing a cursory overview of some of the social harms—especially their damage to journalism and to the integrity of news and information—I discuss the concept of the social contract and its usefulness as a framework towards redesigning our news and information systems. To help us imagine how this process might unfold, I draw attention to earlier policy battles around broadcast monopolies during which similar power struggles took place. Finally, I begin to sketch what such a new contract might look like.

PLATFORMS' SOCIAL HARMS

Coinciding with the precipitous decline of traditional news media, platform monopolies—Facebook most notably—are attaining levels of media power unprecedented in human history. As an algorithm-driven gatekeeper over a primary information source for more than 2.5 billion users, Facebook wields tremendous political economic control over core infrastructures and causes considerable social harms, from facilitating hate speech against vulnerable and marginalized groups to propagating fascistic propaganda. In recent years, Facebook has mishandled users' data, spread dangerous misinformation and propaganda, destabilized elections in places such as the Philippines, enabled foreign interference in democratic elections in places such as the United States, and even facilitated ethnic cleansing in Myanmar (Silverman 2016; Vaidhyanathan 2018; Stevenson 2018). Nations around the world are scrambling to protect their elections from being compromised by disinformation that is magnified through Facebook's network. In the United States, for example, where Americans increasingly access news through the platform, Facebook's role in presidential elections is drawing well-deserved scrutiny.

In addition to well-documented online harms, Facebook's deleterious impact on democracy is increasingly apparent in how it (along with Google) corrupts the integrity of our news and information systems. One of the biggest threats to news media's business model is the duopoly's abuse of their market power over digital advertising. Facebook (which dominates social media) and Google (which has a dominant market position in search) are devouring the lion's share of digital advertising revenue. This means that the duopoly is displacing revenue for the traditional news media that provide quality news and information. There is a sad irony given that, at the precise moment these platforms expect journalists' help with fact-checking against the misinformation they circulate, they are financially snuffing them out (Kafka 2018). By taking as much as a combined 85% of all new US digital advertising revenue growth, the Facebook-Google duopoly are threatening journalism's financial future (Shields 2017). By some calculations, these two companies control 73% of the total online advertising market.[1] Considering the role that these same companies play in amplifying misinformation, they should be bolstering instead of starving news outlets. With journalism under threat around the world—from oppressive governments and market failure—the platforms' culpability in hastening the demise of news media's advertising-dependent business model deserves more attention.

Thus far, the platforms have responded with very modest gestures towards aiding journalism in any substantive way (I expand on this later). Their efforts largely amount to window dressing. In fact, it is unrealistic to expect anything more unless the platforms are forced to compensate for their significant social harms by, for example, directly subsidizing public media and discontinuing behaviours that are good for their bottom line but bad for democratic society. Ultimately, these social problems necessitate *structural* reforms; they cannot be solved by simply shaming digital monopolies into good behaviour or by tweaking market incentives. We need a new social contract.

SOCIAL CONTRACT AS METAPHOR AND FRAMEWORK

The idea of a 'social contract' gives us purchase on a number of challenges as we try to make the case not only that platforms must be more socially responsible but also that the public should have some control over these affairs. As a starting point, the social contract concept helps make explicit the power relationships between communication/media firms, regulators, and members of the public. It also underscores the contingent and conditional aspects of these relationships (e.g., media firms can enjoy such tremendous privileges only as long as they adhere to specific public service obligations). Most importantly, it clarifies the normative understanding that media firms' purpose is not merely to accumulate profit but also to support democracy. And finally, it establishes criteria for media firms' continuing benefits; failure to adhere to these criteria will result in termination of the contract and even potential punitive measures. For these reasons and more, a social contract is a useful framework through which we can clarify understandings and advance the general discourse around these power relationships.

When we think of a contract, it typically calls up associations with legal documents or signing off on terms of service. A social contract can connote a legally binding agreement, but its articulation by earlier philosophers, from Rousseau to Hobbes, treated it more as a mutual understanding. At the very least, a social contract signals a higher purpose—a collective agreement that upholds a normative ideal for democratic society. We see glimpses of this type of implicit contract in our understanding of 'natural monopolies' or public utilities that are 'affected with a public interest'. We also see traces of it in the concepts 'information fiduciaries' in the United States and 'duty of care' in the United Kingdom. The assumption is that, given these firms special position in the market (typically monopolistic networks) and the special purpose of the service they deliver (typically essential public services such as transportation, electricity, water, or, in the case of the platforms, information and communication), they must deliver on specific democratic obligations to society.

But many vexing questions remain. What are the procedural standards and who designs the contract? How do we even start such a process? Is it simply a rhetorical device? How do we make sure there is adequate public trust in the process and ensure that the government does not have too much control over it? Most of all, we need to make sure that this social contract is democratically deliberated, but in what forum? Should we look to multi-stakeholder frameworks such as the Internet Governance Forum or the European Union, or international bodies connected to United Nations? Can we use such already-existing institutions or must we create something new?

Establishing a social contract is obviously a very complex endeavour. It is also worth underscoring that the subject of the contract—namely, the responsibilities of the platforms—is of such high importance, that it necessitates a *collective* agreement (hence the modifier 'social'). We are not merely discussing an individual user agreement for a particular software program. Rather, we are defining the terms for how the world's most central communication and information infrastructures are governed, and, in doing so, ensuring that public interests are protected and codified. Moreover, this discussion is unfolding within the context of a global pandemic, making these infrastructures and systems even more vitally important and raising the stakes considerably. Indeed, we must also take into consideration the 'crisis communication' aspect of these networks.

Adding to this urgency is the broader notion that we may be living through what previous historians have termed 'critical junctures' (McChesney 2007) or 'constitutive moments' (Starr 2004). Such inflection points are especially significant because policy decisions made during these periods could very well have an inordinate impact on the trajectory of communication and information systems for generations to come.

The stakes of these discussions, therefore, are considerable. As we ponder how we exact such conditionality, determine points of decision-making, and decide upon the institutional frameworks that should be involved, we might turn to an earlier moment in communication, a critical juncture in which a series of contestations determined the contours of a major communication medium. In particular, we might look to US media policy debates in the 1940s, which determined the social responsibilities of radio monopolies.

LESSONS FROM THE POST-WAR MOMENT

The post-war 1940s witnessed a series of decisive US policy battles as government officials, social movements, and communication industries grappled over defining the normative role of news and information in a democratic society. What were media companies' social responsibilities? And, as significant, what was government's role in managing this relationship between media and society? Put differently, what were the government's affirmative duties in assuring that democratic society had access to reliable news and information? What, if any, regulations were legitimate and necessary?

An important social context at this time was the social-democratic formation of a media reform movement of grassroots activists and progressive policymakers. This coalition emerged to challenge the commercial interests consolidating control of US media, particularly broadcasting. One key initiative borne out of this movement was the 1946 Federal Communications Commission (FCC) Report on Public Service Responsibilities of Broadcast Licensees—better known as the 'Blue Book', given the colour of its cover. This policy initiative was high-water mark for FCC progressive activism that mandated meaningful public service obligations for broadcasters in return for their use of the public airwaves.

Another key policy forum, this one aimed at the news media in general, was 'The Commission on Freedom of the Press'—better known as the 'Hutchins Commission'—which issued a general report in 1947 that codified journalistic ethics. During the immediate post-war years, these initiatives posed significant challenges to the reigning libertarian paradigm for media regulation. However, an industry-led backlash focused on red-baiting tactics ultimately defeated the policy initiatives outlined in the Blue Book and Hutchins Commission, and the 1940s media reform movement was largely contained.

The outcome of these norm-setting policy debates gave rise to a kind of social contract between media institutions, US regulatory regimes, and the polity—what I refer to as a 'post-war settlement' for US media (Pickard 2015). This settlement was characterized by three tacit assumptions: Media institutions should remain only lightly regulated, practice industry-defined social responsibility, and be protected by a negative freedom of the press (Berlin 1969). Such renderings conceive freedom of the press in a way that privileges the rights of media owners over those of listeners, readers, and the broader public. In other words, it elevated a libertarian freedom *from* government regulation over the public's freedom *to* a diverse and informative media system.

Throughout much of my work I have referred to this paradigm as 'corporate libertarianism' because it simultaneously normalizes corporate power over our media system (going so far as to treat corporations as people under the law), while delegitimating particular kinds of government intervention (generally, policies that benefitted communities at the expense of corporate profits). This settlement consolidated an industry-friendly regime that largely foreclosed on alternative models, and prefigured normative expectations—an arrangement that has had, in my view, a very negative impact on the integrity and democratic potential of the American media system for decades (Pickard 2015).

Not only did these resolutions combine to consolidate commercial ownership and control of key institutions of the press but also they solidified a forced settlement that continues to define US media's social obligations today. These power relationships continue to undermine a constructive regulatory role for government while leaving de facto governance to marketplace relationships, which permanently elevate profits over democratic imperatives. Radio monopolies went from being terrified in 1945 of imminent government intervention to being assured in 1949 of near-complete autonomy. However, had the progressive media reformers in the post-war 1940s triumphed, things may have gone quite differently. Instead, the commercial system emerged even stronger than before. Instead of serving as the foundations for US media policy, the Blue Book and Hutchins Commission were largely forgotten.

This failure stemmed partly from the broader political context—a growing anti-communist hysteria that rendered even moderate regulatory efforts off-limits—to ideological weaknesses such as a residual libertarianism that assumed broadcasters were arguing in good faith and that market forces would self-correct for commercial excesses. Absent strong structural reform—in particular the creation of public alternatives that were not market-dependent and profit-driven—left regulators at the mercy of shifting political winds. Media corporations were able to take advantage of red-baiting discourses to discredit regulatory reforms and were hence able to grab yet more power. Furthermore, in this discursive context, the radio monopolies were able to capture the First Amendment and use it as a shield against progressive government intervention.

Designed to push back and contain media reform movements, this corporate consolidation of power over American media systematically obscured structural critiques, and kept in place a lightly regulated media system. The movement against commercial media had been contained, and under the new settlement, media would be 'socially responsible' and the American people were meant to feel secure in this knowledge. This settlement would impact much of what Americans would encounter in their media for decades to come. The post-war settlement for US media marked a failure for reformers' vision of a more democratic media system, one that emphasized public access over corporate profits and diversity over commercial values. This was not inevitable or natural—nor must it be permanent.

We must aim to not recapitulate such an outcome in our current policy debates over the social role of platform monopolies.

Indeed, there are many lessons to be gleaned. One is the subsequent erasure of power from those early debates. The way this historical development often is narrated today is very technocentric—that, for example, chaos reigned on the airwaves and it had to be managed according to a scarcity rationale. Often left out of these narratives is that the initial impulse to regulate broadcasting was borne from a recognition that these broadcast monopolies had a tremendous amount of power that needed to be countervailed (Moss and Fein 2003).

Another lesson from this time that holds important relevance for current debates is that simply breaking up monopolies was found to be insufficient. The FCC actually forced one of the two major broadcasters (NBC) to divest itself of one of its two major networks (what later became become ABC). However, going from two big players (the other one being CBS, with a much smaller MBS also in the mix) to three did not noticeably democratize the media landscape. Another lesson was that regulation—most notably, the Fairness Doctrine, which mandated some degree of local accountability—also proved to be an insufficient means of reining in the broadcast monopolies. If breaking up and/or regulating media firms prove to be suboptimal, the creation of *public alternatives* would appear to be the last, best option.

Today, as neo-liberalism comes under increasing strain and begins to collapse beneath the weight of its many structural contradictions, this earlier paradigm shift holds much relevance for the crises facing us. The implications of these historical lessons are that regulation and antimonopoly measures are not enough. Perhaps the actual lesson to be learned from this period is that we need bold structural reforms—reforms that change the underlying logics and business models that drive so much of our heavily commercialized news and information systems. These could range from creating new institutions to radically removing market pressures from our communication infrastructures. Anything less runs the risk of merely shoring up the platforms' power for the long-term.

TOWARDS A NEW SOCIAL CONTRACT

As the platforms have accumulated tremendous power and extracted wealth from local communities—while also creating tremendous social harms around the world—we should be talking more about what they owe society in return for the many benefits they receive.[2] More specifically, we should renegotiate the social contract between platforms and society. What might this new contract look like?

Creating a public alternative to Facebook would be optimal in many ways, but thanks to network effects and path dependencies, it probably is not feasible to create something entirely new. This conclusion, then, raises the question: Could we transition the existing order into something like a public utility or a public benefit corporation? This possibility is certainly worth considering. The Internet is clearly an essential public service, a core infrastructure, thus moving towards a public utility model should at least be on the table. Even the market-libertarian US government briefly nationalized AT&T during World War I. But it is exceedingly difficult to imagine how we might similarly nationalize a network that is not national, but global.

While meaningful competition to Facebook is unlikely to develop in the near-term, regulators around the world are seriously considering a variety of interventions. Over the past number of years, a growing number of scholars have levelled critiques about Facebook's business model and technological design (see, for example, Taplin 2017; Gillespie 2018; Vaidhyanathan 2018; Zuboff, 2019). This criticism is rapidly growing amid increased public scrutiny for the misinformation Facebook amplifies and from which it profits.

Facebook's social, cultural, and political imprint comes with enormous privileges. Historical precedent and mainstream economics justify aggressive regulation, especially towards dominant firms for which it is socially beneficial that one operator controls an entire sector or service. Such arrangements are common to specific industries, especially networks such as communication and transportation systems dominated by one centralized entity. This often happens due to the considerable high fixed costs of building such systems, but also because of potential efficiencies and higher profits for the respective monopoly. Like public utilities, such firms offer core services and infrastructures like electricity and water.

Given that such services are both expensive to maintain and essential for the public good, societies tend to buffer them from direct market forces. In such cases, governments typically use regulatory incentives and punitive measures— short of breaking them up—to prevent such monopolies from abusing their market power. Nonetheless, despite ample historical and international lessons for why such protections are necessary, the United States has allowed monopolies and cartels to capture many sectors of its economy. Antitrust and pro-competition laws and regulations—and the disciplinary power they wield by merely being on the table as a credible threat—have long protected competition and encouraged innovation. These have ranged from the government forcing AT&T to share its patents free of charge to leasing its wires to competitors at fair rates (Schiller forthcoming).

Beyond historicizing this problem to consider what policy interventions have been deployed in the past, it is also worthwhile to consider other democratic nations' reform efforts. European countries have levelled a wide range of fines and penalties, and a number of countries are considering taxes and levies on the platforms to help fund local journalism (Pickard 2020). Reining in Facebook will require a well-equipped toolbox of regulatory instruments. In addition to antitrust measures, interventions may include mandating data portability and operability; banning all advertising from dark-money groups; demanding radical transparency of all advertising on the platform with respect to origin, funding, and targeting; and enforcing public oversight of algorithms and data collection.

Some scholars and advocates have argued that we should establish a new social-media regulatory agency (Feld 2019) or a 'social media council' (Tworek 2019). Other ideas include treating platforms as 'information fiduciaries' (Balkin and

Zittrain 2016) or insisting that they practice a 'duty of care' (Tambini 2019) based on legal obligations such as harm prevention, risk assessment, and public accountability. Another compelling argument is that the aggregate user data that platforms depend on should be treated as a public resource (like spectrum) that triggers public interest regulations (See also Napoli 2019a, 2019b). Despite proliferating proposals and already-existing frameworks for actionable law and policy, the notion that we must regulate platform companies is still controversial and a consensus has still not been reached. Nonetheless, while some experts see Facebook as a kind of Frankenstein monster beyond social control or reform (Vaidhyanathan 2018), self-regulation is clearly insufficient, and we should not let Facebook shirk responsibility for the social harms it has created around the world, especially since we pay dearly for these services with our data, labour, and attention.

Thus far, discussions have focused mostly on regulating user privacy, advertising transparency, and platform moderation, which are all, of course, vitally important issues. However, we also should consider a broader, bolder vision for what these platform monopolies owe society in return for the incredible power we have allowed them to accumulate. Fortunately, recent years have witnessed growing vitality and an expanded political imaginary evidenced by lively debates over how we should confront concentrated corporate power. These could be divided between neo-Brandeisians who call for smashing up the monopolies (Stoller 2019; Wu 2018), and those who call for some form of regulation. The former position might see anything short of aggressive antitrust enforcement as an accommodationist approach.

It is unreasonable to assume, however, that all media-related problems are resolvable by simply reducing the size and multiplying the number of commercial outlets that depend on surveillance advertising, disseminating low-quality content, and undervaluing democratic concerns. An implicit assumption of the growing anti-monopoly movement is that markets provide for the ideal allocation of resources—as long as we manage them well enough with clear 'rules of the road' to maintain adequate competition. However, much historical evidence suggests that over time regulatory capture and policy failure squelches such checks and balances (Pickard 2015). Furthermore, this record shows that a purported emphasis on pluralism, diversity, and competition do not create the conditions for sustainable systems of democratic communication. Such a goal requires a more deliberate institutional design. Moreover, as I noted earlier, many of these problems are not actually monopoly problems; they are capitalism problems. Therefore, a core part of social contract might focus on taking aspects of our information and communication infrastructures out of the market—to essentially de-commodify them.

A PUBLIC MEDIA TAX

An altogether different approach would be to mandate that the platforms help maintain a publicly owned supply of news and information. Previously I proposed that platform monopolies such as Facebook and Google be forced to pay into a public media fund (Pickard 2018, 2019, 2020). The basic argument is that as part of that contract could mandate that they help fund the very infrastructures that they profit from so handsomely. This means that they should fund news, but we also could have the platforms pay into a fund that supports the build-out of digital infrastructures.

This proposal seems eminently reasonable when we consider that the platforms pay precious little in taxes. However, countries around the world are beginning to consider taxing them, and some already are. From April 2020, the UK government has introduced a new 2% digital services tax on the revenues of search engines, social media platforms, and online marketplaces, which derive value from UK users. This money will go towards underwriting key services and infrastructures. Other countries around the world, most recently Australia, are beginning to tax the platforms and/or compel them to share more advertising revenue with news publishers. The Organization for Economic Co-operation and Development also has issued similar tax proposals, and even the United States has begun to call for a more equitable distribution.

While platform monopolies have not single-handedly caused the journalism crisis, they have exacerbated and amplified communication-related social harms. Beyond regulating and penalizing these firms, we should require that they help undo the damage they have caused. Not only do they bear some responsibility but also these firms have tremendous resources at their disposal. Despite this state of affairs, a general unease about policy interventions in this arena have long stymied meaningful action. Much of this inaction, especially in the United States, stems from the four 'isms'—techno utopianism, First Amendment absolutism, market fundamentalism, and corporate libertarianism—which combine to render structural policy interventions off-limits (Pickard 2020b). Nonetheless, policy scholarship has long established that media markets produce various externalities (see, for example, Baker 2002). It is the role of government policy to manage them— to minimize the negative and maximize the positive externalities for the benefit of democratic society. Even the relatively libertarian United States redistributes media power with public access cable channels, the universal service fund, and subsidized public broadcasting, to name just a few examples. Policy analysts also have proposed various schemes for taxing platforms in the US context.[3]

Internationally, policymakers and advocates have proposed a number of similar models. For example, in the United Kingdom, the Media Reform Coalition and the National Union of Journalists proposed allocating capital raised from taxes on digital monopolies to support public service journalism. The Labour Party echoed this plan by calling for digital monopolies to pay into an independent 'public interest media fund' (Corbyn 2018). Similarly, the Cairncross Review, a detailed report on the future of British news media, called for a new institute to oversee direct funding for public-interest news outlets (Waterson 2019). Another proposal has called for establishing a $1 billion international public interest media fund to support investigative news organizations around the world, protecting them from violence and intimidation (Lalwani 2019).[4] According to this plan, the fund would rely on capital from social media platforms as well as government agencies and philanthropists. Platform monopolies should not be solely responsible for funding public media, but the least they could do is support the investigative journalism, policy reporting, and international news coverage that they are complicit in undermining.

Taxing platforms like Google and Facebook, to force them to help offset their considerable social harms (proliferating misinformation, violating users' privacy, and gobbling up digital ad revenue) seems inherently fair. However, Google and Facebook have thus far focused more on perception management than substance. In recent years, each promised $300 million for news-related projects. For example, Google has pledged this money towards its News Initiative,[5] and Facebook has sponsored several projects, including its $3 million journalism 'accelerator' to help 10–15 news organizations build their digital subscriptions using Facebook's platform (Ingram 2018). Another program, Facebook's 'Today In' app section, aggregates local news in communities across the United States, but it ran into problems when Facebook found many areas already depleted of local news (Molla and Wagner 2019). More recently, Google has announced that it would tailor its algorithms to better promote original reporting (Berr 2019), and Facebook has promised to offer major news outlets a license to its 'News Tab' that will feature headlines and article previews (Fussell 2019). Nonetheless, these initiatives are insufficient given the magnitude of the global journalism crisis—efforts that one news industry representative likened to 'handing out candy every once in a while' instead of contributing to long-term solutions (quoted in Baca 2019).

Redistributing revenue towards public media could address the twin problems of unaccountable monopoly power and the loss of public service journalism. Facebook and Google (which owns YouTube) should help fund the very industry that they both profit from and eviscerate. For example, these firms could pay a nominal 'public media tax' of 1% on their earnings, which would generate significant revenue for a journalism trust fund (Pickard 2018).

Such a tax would yield hundreds of millions of dollars annually in the United States. Combined with other revenue streams—for example, philanthropic and government contributions—this money could go far in establishing an endowment for independent public media (Pickard 2020a). The media reform organization Free Press (full disclosure: I sit on their board) similarly calls for a tax on digital advertising more broadly, which would generate approximately $2 billion per year for public service journalism (Karr and Aaron 2019, 8). These firms can certainly afford such expenditures, especially since they pay precious little in taxes.

Another area where the platforms should better manage negative and positive externalities is in the curating of information. The notion that these firms are neutral platforms has long been debunked (Gillespie 2010). Periodically they have recalibrated their algorithms to privilege some information in mind. With this technological capability in mind, the platforms could be compelled to 'signal boost' reliable news and information by privileging public media in their news feeds and search engines algorithmically. Similar to public interest requirements traditionally placed on broadcasters, these social obligations could be mandated

by democratic countries as part of a new quid pro quo for the many benefits that
are conferred on them.

Unfortunately, it seems that we are not moving in this direction, with most
reform proposals centring on self-regulatory methods. As a cautionary sign, we
might recall the influential Article 19 proposals on a social media council (and
the fact that the director then moved to Facebook). More recently, the so-called
Supreme Court for Facebook moderation also seems like a thinly veiled attempt
to keep regulation largely in house. Ultimately, historical experience from earlier
policy debates such as the Hutchins Commission shows us that the social responsibility model for platforms, based purely on self-regulation, will fail just as the
social responsibility model for the press ultimately failed in the 1940s. Democratic
societies around the world must aim to do much more.

THE CRISIS IS ALSO AN OPPORTUNITY

At perhaps no other time has the need for reliable, fact-based, and well-resourced
journalism been more acute. The pandemic crisis has intensified already-existing
structural problems and inequities in our media systems. At the same time, we
are growing more dependent on these platforms, even as they seek to amass yet
more political and economic power (Dwoskin 2020). It is also true that Amazon
and other firms are also becoming powerhouses in these communication and information spheres. Furthermore, any new social contract for the digital age will
have to address different layers of the 'stack' including Internet service providers
(Pickard and Berma, 2019).

Nonetheless, we must not let this crisis 'go to waste'. What is required is a new
normative foundation for the media we need. While governments around the
world grapple with media failures and policy problems, we all should dare imagine what an alternative system might look like in the future, even as we advocate
for new standards that can be backed up by enforceable policies. If we are to have
a democratic media system, these should be non-negotiable terms. But more than
regulating already-existing media institutions to become more socially responsible, we need to usher in structural alternatives. This still requires policy interventions, but interventions that seek to do more than simply tweak and police the
incumbents. We must create new institutions and systems. By declaring that as
our ultimate goal, we can reorient our policy approaches to the major communication and information crises facing democratic societies today.

NOTES

1. Calculations vary to some degree. For example, this report places the duopoly's
    share at slightly less: 'Looking Beyond the Facebook/ Google Duopoly', *eMar-
    keter*, December 12, 2017, https:// www.emarketer.com/ content/ exploring- the-

duopoly- beyond-google- and-facebook. Amazon is gradually becoming a third significant player in digital advertising.
2. Parts of this section draw from Pickard (2020b).
3. For earlier articulations of this idea, see Pickard (2016), Waldman (2017), Bell (2017), and Pickard (2018).
4. All dollar values in US currency.
5. See https://newsinitiative.withgoogle.com/.

REFERENCES

Baca, Marie C. 2019. 'Google and Facebook's Latest Efforts to "Save" Journalism Are Sparking Debate'. *Washington Post*, September 20. www.washingtonpost.com/technology/2019/09/13/google-facebooks-latest-efforts-save-journalism-are-already-getting-eye-rolls/.

Baker, C. E. 2002. *Media, Markets, and Democracy*. New York: Cambridge University Press.

Balkin, J., and J. Zittrain. 2016. 'A Grand Bargain to Make Tech Companies Trustworthy'. *The Atlantic*, October 3. https://www.theatlantic.com/technology/archive/2016/10/informationfiduciary/502346/.

Bell, Emily. 2017. 'How Mark Zuckerberg Could Really Fix Journalism'. *Columbia Journalism Review*, February 21. www.cjr.org/tow_center/mark-zuckerberg-facebook-fix-journalism.php.

Berlin, Isaiah. 1969. 'Two Concepts of Liberty'. In *Four Essays on Liberty*. Oxford: Oxford University Press.

Berr, Jonathan. 2019. 'Is Google's Embrace of "Original Reporting" Good News for Publishers?' *Forbes*. https://www.forbes.com/sites/jonathanberr/2019/09/12/is-googles-embrace-of—original-reporting-good-news-for-publishers/.

Corbyn, Jeremy. 2018. 'Alternative MacTaggart Lecture'. https://labour.org.uk/press/full-text-jeremy-corbyns-2018-alternative-mactaggart-lecture/.

Dwoskin, Elizabeth (2020). 'Tech Giants Are Profiting—And Getting More Powerful—Even as the Global Economy Tanks'. *Washington Post*, April 27. https://www.washingtonpost.com/technology/2020/04/27/big-tech-coronavirus-winners/.

Feld, H. 2019. 'The Case for the Digital Platform Act: Breakups, Starfish Problems, and Tech Regulation'. Washington, DC: Public Knowledge.

Freedman, D. 2014. *The Contradictions of Media Power*. London: Bloomsbury.

Fussell, Sidney. 2019. 'Facebook Wants a Do-Over on News'. *The Atlantic*, August 22. https://www.theatlantic.com/technology/archive/2019/08/facebooks-news-tab-will-be-run-humans-and-algorithms/596554/.

Gillespie, Tarleton L. 2010. 'The Politics of "Platforms"'. *New Media and Society* 12(3): 347–364.

Gillespie, Tarleton. 2018. *Custodians of the Internet: Platforms, Content Moderation, and the Hidden Decisions That Shape Social Media*. New Haven: Yale University Press.

Hubbard, S. 2017. 'Fake News Is a Real Antitrust Problem'. *Competition Policy International*, December 19. https://www.competitionpolicyinternational.com/fake-news-is-a-real-antitrustproblem/.

Ingram, Mathew. 2018. 'The Media Today: Facebook Tosses a Dime at Local Journalism'. *Columbia Journalism Review*, February 28. https://www.cjr.org/ the_ media_ today/ facebook-local-news-funding.php.

Kafka, Peter. 2018. 'These Two Charts Tell You Everything You Need to Know about Google's and Facebook's Domination of the Ad Business'. *Recode*, February 13. https:// www.recode.net/ 2018/ 2/ 13/ 17002918/ google-facebook-advertising-domination-chart-moffettnathanson- michael-nathanson.

Karr, Timothy, and Craig Aaron. 2019. 'Beyond Fixing Facebook: How the Multibillion-Dollar Business behind Online Advertising Could Reinvent Public Media, Revitalize Journalism and Strengthen Democracy', February 25. Florence, MA: Free Press. www.freepress.net/policy-library/beyond-fixing-facebook.

Kornbluh, Karen, and Ellen Goodman. 2020. 'Safeguarding Digital Democracy Digital Innovation and Democracy Initiative Roadmap'. German Marshall Fund.

Lalwani,Nishant.2019.'AFreePressIstheLifebloodofDemocracy—JournalistsMustNotBe Silenced'. *TheGuardian*,July5.www.theguardian.com/global-development/2019/jul/ 05/a-free-press-is-the-lifeblood-of-democracy-journalists-must-not-be-silenced.

McChesney, R. 2007. *Communication Revolution: Critical Junctures and the Future of Media*. New York, NY: The New Press.

Molla, Rani, and Kurt Wagner. 2019. 'Facebook Wants to Share More Local News, but It's Having Trouble Finding It'. *Vox*, March 18, https://www.vox.com/2019/3/18/ 18271058/facebook-local-news-journalism-grant.

Moss, David, and Michael Fein. 2003. 'Radio Regulation Revisited: Coase, the FCC, and the Public Interest'. *Journal of Policy History* 15(4): 389–416.

Napoli, P. 2019a. *Platform News and the Public Interest: Why the Algorithmic Marketplace of Ideas Fails and What Can Be Done about It*. New York: Columbia University Press.

Napoli, P. 2019b. 'User Data as Public Resource: Implications for Social Media Regulation'. *Policy and Internet* 1(4): 439–59.

Pickard, V., and D. Berman. 2019. *After Net Neutrality: A New Deal for the Digital Age*. New Haven: Yale University Press.

Pickard, Victor. 2010. 'Reopening the Postwar Settlement for U.S. Media: The Origins and Implications of the Social Contract between Media, the State, and the Polity'. *Communication, Culture and Critique* 3(2): 170–89.

Pickard, Victor. 2015. *America's Battle for Media Democracy: The Triumph of Corporate Libertarianism and the Future of Media Reform*. New York, NY: Cambridge University Press.

Pickard, Victor. 2018. 'Break Facebook's Power and Renew Journalism'. *The Nation*, April 18. www.thenation.com/article/break-facebooks-power-and-renew-journalism/.

Pickard, Victor. 2019. 'Public Investments for Global News'. The Centre for International Governance Innovation, October 28. https://www.cigionline.org/articles/ public-investments-global-news.

Pickard, Victor. 2020a. *Democracy without Journalism? Confronting the Misinformation Society*. New York, NY: Oxford University Press.

Pickard, Victor. 2020b. 'Restructuring Democratic Infrastructures: A Policy Approach to the Journalism Crisis'. *Digital Journalism* 8(6): 704–719.

Shields, Mike. 2017. 'CMO Today: Google and Facebook Drive 2017 Digital Ad Surge'. *Wall Street Journal*, March 14. https://www.wsj.com/ articles/ cmo-today-google-and-facebook-drive-2017-digital-ad-surge-1489491871.

Silverman, Craig. 2016. 'This Analysis Shows How Viral Fake Election News Stories Outperformed Real News on Facebook'. *BuzzFeed News*, November 16. https://www.buzzfeed.com/ craigsilverman/viral-fake-election-news-outperformed-real-news-on-facebook?utm_term=kyNMQ7pa8#.uqEVNx5kd.

Starr, P. 2004. *Creation of the Media*. New York, NY: Basic Books.

Stevenson, Alexandra. 2018. 'Facebook Admits It Was Used to Incite Violence in Myanmar'. *New York Times*, November 6. https://www.nytimes.com/2018/11/06/technology/ Myanmar-facebook.html.

Tambini, D. 2019. 'The Differentiated Duty of Care: A Response to the Online Harms White Paper'. *Journal of Media Law* 11(1): 28–40.

Taplin, J. 2017. *Move Fast and Break Things*. New York: Little Brown & Co.

Tworek, H. 2019. 'Social Media Councils'. Centre for International Governance Innovation. https:// www.cigionline.org/articles/social-media-councils.

Vaidhyanathan, Siva. 2018. *Antisocial Media: How Facebook Disconnects Us and Undermines Democracy*. New York: Oxford University Press, 190–195.

Waldman, Steve. 2017. 'What Facebook Owes to Journalism'. *New York Times*, February 21. www.nytimes.com/2017/02/21/opinion/what-facebook-owes-to-journalism.html.

Waterson, Jim. 2019. 'Public Funds Should Be Used to Rescue Local Journalism, Says Report'. *The Guardian*, February 11. www.theguardian.com/media/2019/feb/11/public-funds-should-be-used-to-rescue-local-journalism-says-report.

Wu, T. 2018. *The Curse of Bigness: Antitrust in the New Gilded Age*. New York: Columbia Global Reports.

Zuboff, S. (2019). *The Age of Surveillance Capitalism: The Fight for a Human Future at the New Frontier of Power*. New York: Hachette/PublicAffairs.

Conclusion

Without a Holistic Vision, Democratic Media Reforms May Fail

MARTIN MOORE AND DAMIAN TAMBINI ∎

Since we finished working on the previous volume of this series—*Digital Dominance: The Power of Google, Apple, Facebook and Amazon* (2018)— there have been seismic shifts in attitudes towards the technology platforms. A global consensus has emerged that big tech is unduly powerful and needs reining in. From the United Kingdom to Germany, from France to Australia, governments have sought ways in which to reduce the power of the platforms and address some of the negative externalities that have come with the rising dominance of a few. China, whose government already had much greater control of its tech platforms than any other country in the world, continues to go further (Yu and Go 2020). Perhaps most surprising is the relative bipartisan consensus in the United States in favour of greater regulation. In a country riven by partisanship on almost every issue, regulation of big tech has emerged as one of fragile cross-party agreement. Democrats and Republicans differ in their assessment of the problems associated with dominant technology corporations, and therefore the rationale for regulation, but share the belief that 'something must be done'. During the 2020 presidential campaign, candidates Biden and Trump—different in so many ways—both echoed the refrain 'Revoke Section 230' (of the Communications Decency Act [1996]). This relative political consensus was mirrored across much of the mainstream media, and in numerous public opinion polls. Even the platforms themselves recognized—and in some cases encouraged—greater regulation. Mark Zuckerberg wrote columns in the *Washington Post* and the *Financial Times* arguing that the Internet needs new rules and laying out some of the questions regulation might address (Zuckerberg 2019, 2020).

Though the Facebook CEO was careful to emphasize that it had to be the 'right' sort of regulation.

There have also been significant shifts as regards conceptual thinking around regulation and the accountability of big tech. We have started to move beyond some of the unhelpful twentieth-century analogies and premises that constrained initial policy responses. No longer do we have to keep comparing digital information intermediaries to publishers—in the twentieth-century sense, at least. Lorna Woods and William Perrin have made a constructive contribution in moving our thinking forward by comparing them instead to commercially run public spaces—like sports stadiums, theatres, or parks—where the owners have a *duty of care* with regard to those who use those spaces, while not having direct control over what they do or say when they are in them. Similarly, the neo-Brandeisians—most notably Lina Khan (a version of whose seminal *Yale Law Review* article was published in the previous volume) are moving us beyond the narrow definition of 'harm' that had come to characterize US competition law. Khan and others have shown that basing competition action solely on pricing theory ignores many other individual and collective harms that result from commercial dominance. As such, they have also reduced the ability of the platforms to avoid scrutiny by using the parallel currency of data. Similarly, Harold Feld has helped to reconceive our understanding of dominance by introducing the concept of the 'Cost of Exclusion' to assess the extent to which digital platforms constitute critical social infrastructure (Feld 2019).

Despite the growing consensus around the need to rein in the power of big tech, and new theories that have allowed us to move beyond the railway tracks of twentieth-century thinking, a wide range of potential policy approaches remain. Once you move beyond the sloganeering of 'Revoke S230', 'Break Up Big Tech', or 'Own your own data', there emerges a very broad spectrum of perspectives about what ought to be done and with what end goal. Policy responses tend to be siloed and piecemeal—from those who favour returning to the golden era of antitrust and want to embark on a mission to separate technology companies into smaller constituent parts, to those who would regulate big tech like natural monopolies and impose on them positive obligations as well as negative restrictions. Even within each of these camps there is a wide diversity of views.

One problem that this volume attempts to address is that policy is fragmented because the underlying thinking is siloed. Economists, who have given extensive thought to consumer welfare and anticompetitive behaviour, have given less thought to privacy and other rights. Privacy experts, who have given great consideration to the collection and use of personal data, have thought less about free speech. Free speech scholars have thought carefully about the opportunities and threats to free speech online via regulation, but less about elections or national security. And so on. And yet, the platforms' influence spreads across all these areas and beyond. Action in one area will, inevitably, have repercussions elsewhere. Force social media platforms to reduce the amount of disinformation and abuse publicly available on their services, and one should not be surprised when they nudge their users towards private, encrypted services. Pressure intermediaries to intervene and control speech on their platforms, and those who want to express hyperpartisan views and exchange conspiracy theories will migrate elsewhere (from Twitter to Parler, for example). Redress the balance of market power between platforms and news publishers, and it may be less necessary to tax platforms or offer more favourable copyright terms to publishers.

Responses to the power of big tech need to be more holistic. They need to see the links between responses. They need to recognize, for example, that statutory regulation of the platforms does raise vital issues about free speech and therefore take account of how it can be protected. They need to see that antitrust action may make the problem of disinformation worse rather than better, if people disappear to smaller platforms where different rules apply. Nothing illustrates the links between responses better than the complexity of personal data. The collection and use of personal data by these companies is, simultaneously, a competitive issue, a civil liberties issue, a privacy issue, an electoral issue, a security issue, and a democratic issue. When it comes to competition, data can be used by these companies to protect and grow their competitive advantage, to move into new industry sectors, or to track emerging competitors (Barwise and Watkins 2018). In terms of civil liberties, constant surveillance can chill speech, compromise journalistic investigation, and compromise political action (Angwin 2014). On privacy, thanks to data collection, these companies know more about our personal communications and behaviours than our closest friends and relatives. Electorally, data can be used to bypass existing electoral laws and protections (Tambini 2018). In terms of security, personal data can be acquired and used by foreign powers to demoralize and polarize, as the Mueller Inquiry found (Mueller 2019). Politically, surveillance capitalism poses a threat to personal autonomy and to our political freedoms (Zuboff 2019).

At the time of going to press, Europe and the United Kingdom are ahead of the United States in terms of the detail and the progress of their proposals for regulatory reform, particularly with regard to two EU legislative initiatives—the Digital Markets Act (DMA) and Digital Services Act (DSA), though the US administration is under pressure to adopt a more radical approach. These proposals do start to link competition, data, and other concerns, and seek to empower public authorities to coordinate their responses. Both the DMA and DSA adopt a graduated and differentiated approach in which the size and dominance of digital gatekeepers determines the behavioural obligations that they need to meet. Both bring together concerns with personal data with an attempt to place limits on the power of platform gatekeepers (as was proposed by Tambini and Moore 2018, 404). In the European Union, the United Kingdom, Germany, and elsewhere, competition regulators such as the Competition and Markets Authority explicitly retain the ability to propose 'structural remedies'—i.e., break-up or operational separation of platform companies, and have indicated that there is a strong prima facie case for this (CMA 2020), though how they would do it is not clear.

Significant steps, then, are being taken towards a new compact with platform gatekeepers, but they are incomplete and entail dangers. They risk locking in dominant players by raising barriers to entry; they may institute opaque and illegitimate complex systems of co-regulatory speech control, and they may regulate—but not replace—a business model of surveillance capitalism. These new approaches may extract more money from these companies, but not in ways that address negative externalities such that they genuinely reflect the citizens' view of the public interest. In order to avoid these risks and failures, policymakers need to focus on procedural concerns such as regulatory independence and they need to take a more holistic approach.

To be more holistic, responses to big tech need to go beyond siloed responses to platform power, and have a coherent vision of what a future digital political economy should look like. Not a concrete prescription of the future, but acknowledgement of where we are now, what the most significant problems are with respect to digital dominance, and where we would like to get to within the next decade or two. What is the future of the European 'mixed system' of communication for example? Is democratic resilience served by maintaining a plurality of public, private, and community-owned gatekeepers? How might it be possible to balance information sovereignty with the international flow of speech and ideas? Only by having an idea of the direction of travel will it be possible to see how regulatory responses can help get us there. Clearly there is no one end point. There are many—and many forks in the road. People with different political views will have different aims and distinctive goals. This is both inevitable and natural. Yet each needs to sketch out a map of their preferred direction of travel. Having no map is the problem, not differing views.

For illustration, here we map out three alternative visions. Though these are not mutually exclusive, each would lead to a radically different future and presents distinct challenges. The first envisages a far more competitive digital world, one in which few large firms dominate, where the market acts as the chief corrective to concerns about power, partisanship, and plurality. The second imagines a world dominated by a handful of large technology platforms, similar to the one we live in now, but in which these platforms are regarded as natural monopolies and regulated as such. The third envisions a mixed digital environment, where fiscal policy, far-sighted legislation, and positive public intervention seek to limit the scale and influence of technology platforms, and where for-profit platforms compete with a mix of cooperative, community interest, non-profit, and publicly funded services.

A route to the first vision would require assertive antitrust action against each of the dominant tech platforms. It would involve breaking these companies up, almost certainly into their component parts. This would include, for example, separating Google Search from other services within Alphabet (including the separate elements of its advertising business). It would mean breaking Amazon down into an online retailer, an offline logistics service, and a cloud service. It would mean separating Facebook from WhatsApp, Instagram, and Messenger (as appeared to be the intention of the legal action launched by the US Federal Trade Commission and more than forty US states against Facebook in December 2020). This approach has a natural appeal to those, like US Senator Mark Warner, who compare the Internet to the wild west, and see legislators as modern-day marshals, using antitrust to force a showdown with the baddies to bring them to heel. The antitrust reality will be less cinematic. Legal action will take years, involve tortuous negotiation, and eventually result in complex compromise. The companies that emerge at the end of it will be the products of legal process, not democratic design.

Such antitrust action would address problems with the companies themselves, but not the system that enabled these companies to grow so powerful. As such, even if a dominant intermediary company is broken up, without parallel action to counter the effects of the system, one or more of the constituent parts of each company could quickly rise to the size and dominance of the parent. To prevent this would require not only the structural separation of dominant digital organizations but also legislation to limit the future sectoral or infrastructural spread of the newly formed organizations.[1] It would require laws that prevent the undue accumulation of data and consequent advantages associated with it. And, it would mean the development of shared data and technical standards that would facilitate straightforward sharing and interoperability between services. The challenges of pursuing this route are legion. Beyond the reinterpretation and potential revision of competition law, the redefinition of sectoral markets, and legislation to ensure separation of digital powers, it would require radically new approaches to data collection and use. Yet, following this route allows one to avoid some of the even harder questions posed by the second vision.

The second vision concludes that the main services provided by these tech companies function better as monopolies. It assumes that search is best performed by one (or perhaps two) dominant companies, as is social networking, as is retail logistics, as are mobile operating systems. It assumes, in other words, that these services are natural monopolies analogous to the provision of water or electricity. If one assumes this, then these companies would need to be regulated as such. This would mean putting legal obligations on these companies, both negative and positive, creating methods of oversight, and ensuring effective sanctions for failure and non-compliance. The companies would need to have negative obligations to protect users from harm, and positive obligations to support certain standards and to provide particular services (such as information in a public emergency). There would have to be measures in place to ensure the rights and safety of users (and oversight of those measures). There would need to be rules in place to guarantee fair trading to other businesses who rely on the platform (such as news providers on Facebook) and fair access (to the material available on the platform). Equally, given the powers of these tech giants—most notably to surveil—there would have to be explicit protections to prevent governments or other actors from using these platforms to pursue their own ends. Since, were the surveillance capabilities of a company like Google available and accessible to a national government, it would give that government unprecedented powers to control its citizens and curtail their freedoms.

For those who fear the power of big government even more than the power of these tech superpowers, the dangers of this route would outweigh the benefits. Such a route would by necessity mean much closer connections between the state and these firms. It would mean statutory controls over speech and privacy online. It would therefore require a high degree of trust in government, coupled with trust in the newly regulated tech monopolies, to act in the public interest, and confidence that neither would overextend or abuse their powers. In many democratic countries such trust and confidence is in short supply. Moreover, once considered to be natural monopolies, these companies would quickly evolve into national monopolies, since it would be national governments who would monitor, regulate, and castigate them. This would propel the Internet in the direction of digital sovereignty, and choke the existing transnational flow of data and services. Some countries, like China and Russia, would applaud a move towards this sort of nationalized Internet, but most democracies would view it as a regression from the openness and accessibility that have characterized the last three decades. This is, however, a route that governments could find themselves travelling in by default, if they do not consciously choose a different path.

The third vision aspires to a mixed digital ecosystem, where large technology companies compete with mid- and small-sized firms, and where citizens can choose between a variety of search, social, and online retail platforms, including a variety of business and ownership models. The history of broadcasting, particularly in Europe, suggests that democratic resilience is served by offering consumers a genuine choice between commercial, genuinely independent public service, community, and value-driven trusts. The same deep plurality, involving structural diversity on multiple dimensions, may require sustained policy that permits evolutionary development of a variety of new and existing institutions. To achieve such a mixed digital ecosystem requires action on multiple fronts simultaneously, with value-driven policy, including public funding, social policy taxation, competition tools, and new forms of multi-stakeholderism and complex co-regulatory and self-regulatory content standards enforcement. It means seeing each action as part of a larger whole, as a component part of a broader plan to shift towards a distinctly different digital future than the one we currently experience. In this vision, action against any single company is only constructive if it fits within this wider program. The hammer and chisel of antitrust are only useful insofar as they are used in coordination with regulation and incentives. Taxes are helpful when they reduce the capacity of platforms to surveil citizens or undercut smaller competitors, but not when they consolidate the surveillance capitalism business model or can simply be incorporated into the price of doing business. The policy levers available to realize this vision include competition law, taxation, self- and co-regulation, and the creation of new methods and institutions of oversight, along with positive interventions in the public interest. Such a route would likely include, for example, incentives to encourage the development alternative digital platforms, redistributive taxation, fair access requirements, and positive public interest interventions. It requires, in other words, a whole toolkit of measures used in parallel, but with a shared vision of what they are intended to achieve.

The chapters in this book are intended to provide elements of this toolkit. Together they show how regional or national policymakers, and the technology platforms themselves, can move towards this more mixed digital ecosystem. They indicate, for example, how technology platforms can be made accountable for some of the harms and negative externalities they have induced. This can be done by imposing a 'duty of care' on them, analogous to the duty borne by those responsible for commercial public spaces (Woods and Perrin). Such a duty ought to protect people using their services, without jeopardizing those users' freedom to self-publish. Greater accountability can also be achieved by applying existing data protection law more severely, such that it can limit—perhaps even end—automated targeting on the basis of intimate personal data (Phillips and Mazzoli). At the same time, platforms could be redefined as public trustees such that they have to treat personal data as a public resource (Napoli), and ex ante regulation could be introduced to safeguard personal data, as well as the inferences derived from that data (Pasquale). Moreover, some of the negative externalities caused by the business model of the platforms can be ameliorated through the reinvestment of a small proportion of their surplus into public goods, such as journalism (Brogi and Carlini).

Yet the toolkit is about more than just giving these platforms greater responsibility for the harms already identified. It should illuminate ways in which the platforms can make more beneficial contributions to politics and society. This can be done, for example, by giving them positive obligations similar to those which applied to public service broadcasters in the twentieth century (Rowbottom). It can be done by obligating the platforms to make their video content more universally accessible (Noam). Or, it could be done through the development of alternative digital public spheres, for example to support election campaigns (Moore). In each of these—and similar—interventions, democratic governments will need to be conscious of the centrality of freedom of expression, particularly when taking action against disinformation (Marsden, Brown and Veale).

Alongside the actions designed to increase platform accountability and positive contributions, structural interventions will be needed if we are to move towards a more mixed digital ecosystem. This could be done through changes to the law and fiscal policy to incentivize alternative platform ownership. Nathan Schneider shows how straightforward such changes would be, provided there is the political will. Governments could go even further, 'embracing concepts such as co-creation and market shaping towards value creation' to ensure that 'collectively created value serves collective ends', as Mariana Mazzucato and Joshua Entsminger argue in Chapter 2. This would mean interrogating the business model of the platforms in ways that have not been done to date, with the aim of challenging their commodification of public content production and personal data. Equally, states should learn from one another, for example in seeing how competition law and media law can be used together to preserve opinion plurality, as in Germany (Holznagel and Hartmann).

A mixed digital ecosystem will also require institution-building and strengthening. Chapters in this volume highlight the problems that institutions need to address and sketch out what such new and evolved institutions might look like. To deal with the failures of global digital governance, Bob Fay proposes a digital stability board, modelled on the Financial Services Board established after the global financial crisis of 2008. To overcome the opacity of data collection and use, Ben Wagner and Lubos Kuklis propose the creation of an independent data auditor. To ensure that platforms take greater care of personal data, Paul Nemitz and Matthias Pfeffer suggest taking the lead of Germany's Data Ethics Commission and setting up a group of data trustees.

Adopting any of the three routes outlined earlier, or alternative ones, cannot be done in a vacuum. Technological developments, political circumstance, and public support will each play a crucial role in the direction travelled. Yet, the greatest obstacle to progress will be the tech superpowers themselves. In addition to their vast wealth and reach, each now has formidable political lobbying power (Satariano and Stevis-Gridneff 2020). Moreover, their command of our digital world gives them numerous levers they can pull if they feel threatened by government. In Australia, Google and Facebook initially warned that their services would be at risk if the government there went ahead with a proposed law that would force them to pay for links to news, though only Facebook followed through on its threat, and only for a brief period (Easton 2020; Silva 2020; Easton 2021). In the United Kingdom, Facebook reportedly told UK Parliamentarians that it would pull its investment out of the United Kingdom if they persisted in their criticism of big tech (Chapman 2020). Despite the sound and fury however, once legislation is passed the platforms do adapt, as shown in Germany after the NetzDG law came into force. Still, going into negotiation with the platforms without a vision or route map will hamper policymakers' ability to draw red lines, to connect different negotiating outcomes, or to see the systemic effects. Without potential routes and intended destinations, complemented by an understanding of the ramifications of each, states will condemn themselves to constant knee-jerk responses and their inevitable unintended consequences. Without committing to a direction of travel, many states will default to the easiest and least expensive options—which will favour further outsourcing of regulation to the platforms themselves (as is already happening with the regulation of elections), and lead to the confirmation and consolidation of the power of these platforms, rather than its diminishment.

Both the second and third routes will be more difficult for the United States to follow, unless it adopts a less fundamentalist approach to the First Amendment than it has done in the last half-century (Franks 2019). Both approaches require the imposition of certain constraints on the largest technology platforms that would be inconsistent with contemporary US interpretations of free speech. By contrast, in Europe each of these approaches can be done in ways which are consistent with Article 10 of the European Convention on Human Rights, since this recognizes that the exercise of freedom of expression 'carries with it duties and responsibilities, may be subject to such formalities, conditions, restrictions or penalties as are prescribed by law and are necessary in a democratic society'. US fundamentalism on this issue is, as Damian Tambini writes in this volume, exceptional and becoming democratically unsustainable in the digital era, 'because it undermines the ability of public authorities to take the necessary steps to update their media systems in order to support democracy' (Tambini). Unless the

United States adapts its position then it becomes almost inevitable that the universal Internet will splinter along regional and national lines. The chapters in this volume favour a route that is therefore more accessible to Europe than the United States, even though some of the authors are themselves writing from America.

Planning a holistic and systemic response to the problems posed by the tech giants may seem ambitious—perhaps even idealistic. Yet, as Victor Pickard writes in the final chapter, we now have 'most likely a fleeting—window of opportunity for bold plans and structural reform'. This is a moment when the drafting of a new social contract is possible. However, this moment will pass, and any decisions made—or not made—now, will likely influence the digital direction of much of the rest of this half century.

NOTE

1.   This corresponds to Tim Wu's argument in *The Master Switch*, where he wrote: 'It is crucial to recognize . . . the importance of the Separations Principle for the information economy . . . [by which] I refer to the idea of maintaining a salutary distance between differing functions' (Wu 2012, 304).

REFERENCES

Angwin, Julia. 2014. *Dragnet Nation: A Quest for Privacy, Security, and Freedom in a World of Relentless Surveillance*. New York: Macmillan.

Barwise, Patrick, and Leo Watkins. 2018. 'The Evolution of Digital Dominance: How and Why We Got to GAFA'. In *Digital Dominance: The Power of Google, Amazon, Facebook and Apple*, edited by Martin Moore and Damian Tambini. New York: Oxford University Press. Pp. 21–49.

Chapman, Matthew. 2020. 'Revealed: Mark Zuckerberg Threatened to Pull UK Investment in Secret Meeting with Matt Hancock'. *Bureau of Investigative Journalism*, December 8. https://www.thebureauinvestigates.com/stories/2020-12-08/revealed-mark-zuckerberg-threatened-to-pull-uk-investment-in-secret-meeting-with-matt-hancock.

Easton, Will. 2020. 'An Update about Changes to Facebook's Services in Australia'. Facebook, August 31. https://about.fb.com/news/2020/08/changes-to-facebooks-services-in-australia/.

Easton, Will. 2021. 'Changes to Sharing and Viewing News on Facebook in Australia'. Facebook, February 17, updated February 22. https://about.fb.com/news/2021/02/changes-to-sharing-and-viewing-news-on-facebook-in-australia/.

Feld, Harold. 2019. 'The Case for the Digital Platform Act: Market Structure and Regulation of Digital Platform'. Roosevelt Institute and Public Knowledge, CC BY-NC-SA 4.0.

Franks, Mary Anne. 2019. *The Cult of the Constitution*. Stanford: Stanford University Press.

Mueller, Robert S. 2019. 'Report on the Investigation into Russian Interference in the 2016 Presidential Election'. Washington, DC: US Department of Justice.

Satariano, Adam, and Matina Stevis-Gridneff. 2020. 'Big Tech Turns Its Lobbyists Loose on Europe, Alarming Regulators'. *New York Times*, December 14. https://www.nytimes.com/2020/12/14/technology/big-tech-lobbying-europe.html.

Silva, Mel. 2020. 'Update to Our Open Letter to Australians'. Google. https://about.google/google-in-australia/an-open-letter/.

Tambini, Damian. 2018. 'Social Media Power and Election Legitimacy'. In *Digital Dominance: The Power of Google, Amazon, Facebook and Apple*, edited by Martin Moore and Damian Tambini. New York: Oxford University Press. Pp. 265–293.

Wu, Tim. 2010. *The Master Switch: The Rise and Fall of Information Empires*. New York: Alfred A. Knopf.

Yu, Sohie, and Brenda Go. 2020. 'China Ups Scrutiny of Tech Giants with Draft Anti-Monopoly Rules'. Reuters, November 10. https://www.reuters.com/article/china-regulation-ecommerce-idUSKBN27Q0JB.

Zuboff, Shoshana. 2019. *The Age of Surveillance Capitalism: The Fight for a Human Future at the New Frontier of Power*. London: Profile Books.

Zuckerberg, Mark. 2019. 'Mark Zuckerberg: The Internet Needs New Rules. Let's Start in These Four Areas'. *Washington Post*, March 30. https://www.washingtonpost.com/opinions/mark-zuckerberg-the-internet-needs-new-rules-lets-start-in-these-four-areas/2019/03/29/9e6f0504-521a-11e9-a3f7-78b7525a8d5f_story.html.

Zuckerberg, Mark. 2020. 'Mark Zuckerberg: Big Tech Needs More Regulation'. *Financial Times*, February 16. https://www.ft.com/content/602ec7ec-4f18-11ea-95a0-43d18ec715f5.

For the benefit of digital users, indexed terms that span two pages (e.g., 52–53) may, on occasion, appear on only one of those pages.

Tables and figures are indicated by *t* and *f* following the page number

Aaronson, Susan Ariel, 257, 262
accountability
    media, US, 329
    new media, framework for, 303–4
    platform, 344
accountability reforms
    intermediaries, Internet, 299, 300
    policy proposals for, 338
advertising, online
    ad platforms, restrictions and bans, 114
    capitalizing on consumer data, 112
    Covid-19 and, 132
    data targeting and profiling, 112, 128
    in elections
        conclusion, 248
        digital media, 238
        electoral disinformation, 207–9
        introduction, 235
        media law in, 235, 236
        policy considerations, 243
        technology companies, public service
            style obligations, 246
    media dependence on, results of, 325
    microtargeting, 114
    political, regulation of, 205–6
    professional media, supporting the, 240
    revenues, impacts of optimizing, 112
    revenues, need to maximize, 110, 112
    targeted, 243

aggregate data
    benefits of, 157
    eliminating via edge
        technologies, 281–82
    government ownership of, 159–60
    as public resource, 155–59, 330–31
    public trustees of, 155–59, 162
    as a source of market power, justifying
        structural interventions, 151
Agriculture Department, US, 83
Airbnb, 75
airline industry, 176–77
Alaska Permanent Fund, 81
algorithmic rents, 25–27
Amazon, 132, 224. *See also* GAFA
        (Google/Alphabet, Apple,
        Facebook, Amazon); GAFAM
        (Google/Alphabet, Apple,
        Facebook, Amazon)
anti-money laundering (AML) rules, 175
antitrust actions, 2–3, 18, 20–21, 30–31,
        83, 151
Apple, 132, 281–82. *See also* GAFA
        (Google/Alphabet, Apple,
        Facebook, Amazon); GAFAM
        (Google/Alphabet, Apple,
        Facebook, Amazon)
Applications Programs Interfaces (APIs),
        60, 62–63

Arendt, Hannah, 214–15
artificial intelligence (AI)
    data trustees in development of, 282
    disinformation identification, 205
    legislation, using GDPR as a model
        for, 285
    regulating, need for, 280
attention markets / attention cost, 140, 141
audiovisual industry, 137–39
Australia, 4, 138–39, 210, 332, 338–39, 345

Baidu (China), 118–19
Balkin, Jack, 151–52, 158–59
Barlow, John Perry, 76–77
Bauwens, Michel, 83
Belt and Road initiative, 257
Benkler, Yochai, 199, 239, 244–45
Benn, Tony, 84–85
Berlin, Isiah, 310
Beyer, Jessica, 95–96
Biden, Joe, 338–39
big data imperative, 180
big tech, a new social contract for, 12
big tech, policy proposals to regulate. See
    also platforms
    accountability reforms, 338
    antitrust actions, 2–3
    competition law, changing to shape
        market structure, 2–3
    competitive behaviour controls, 3–4
    decentralizing through code and
        technological architecture, 7–8
    ethical codes and rules, 6
    fundamental rights, developing, 10–11
    global and regional coordination, 11–12
    globally shared norms and methods of
        coordinated action, 10–9
    growth and acquisitions, greater
        limitations on, 3
    harms, new protections for citizens and
        consumers from, 6–7
    infrastructure, reconfiguring to reduce
        platform power and enable a more
        mixed ecosystem., 7
    legislation
        copyright and patents, 5–6
        illegal content, defining, 5

    liability and content, 5
    new offenses, introduction of, 5
    to protect against misuse of platforms
        by malign actors, 5–4
    media literacy, coupling with consumer
        empowerment, 9
    moat-building, methods to prevent, 4
    new models of ownership,
        incentivizing, 8
    personal data, greater control of, 6–7
    political and social issues, developing
        specific rules and obligations
        around critical, 9–8
    power abuses, preventing, 3
    prominence obligations, 10
    self-regulation, new structures and
        legitimacy strategies for, 6
    size and growth, limiting, 2–3
    taxation, strategic use of, 8–9
Bing (Microsoft), 118–19
Blogger, 101
Bolsonaro, Jair, 225–26
Brazil, 138–39
Brin, Sergey, 26–27
British Broadcasting Company, 230
broadcast media
    public service obligations, 327
    public trustee model of, 323–24
broadcast media, election-related
    regulation
    digital media, 238
    framework for, 240
    media law in, 236
    policy considerations
        digital advertising, 243
        digital platforms, responsibilities
            of, 242
        professional media, supporting the, 240
        public service obligations, 246
    regulatory framework, function of, 235
broadcast spectrum, 157–58, 159
Brogi, Elda, 8–9, 129, 142n.1, 143n.19
Brown, Ian, 10, 195, 198, 210
Bruns, Axel, 225

Canada, 198, 205, 210, 258, 271
Canada, US, Mexico trade agreement, 259

Canada-France Joint Partnership on
    AI, 258
capitalism, digital, 19
Capper-Volstead Act, 83
Carlini, Roberta Maria, 8–9
Castells, Manuel, 282
censorship
    ethical codes and rules, 6
    by monopoly platforms, 114–15
    negative rights prohibition on, 301, 304
    political, 77–78, 272
    positive rights approach, 311
    private, 212, 245, 300–1, 307
    protections, 5, 212
    state, 204, 301–2, 306
Chase, Daniel, 156
child behavior, predicting, 187
China
    digital platforms, governance of, 257
    direct access to relevant data, 171–72
    disinformation, correcting, 171–72
    disinformation tactics, 196–97
    Great Firewall, 77–78
    Great Firewall national champions, 257
    online platforms, regulating, 171–72
    WeChat use statistics, 222
Citron, Danielle, 152–53
Clinton, Hillary, 195–96
Cold War, disinformation tactics, 196–97
Communications Decency Act (US), 152–
    53, 259, 271, 338–39
community-owned business success,
    policy undergirding, 75
community-owned platforms
    constraints on, 76–78
    examples of, 81, 84–85
    financing, 75, 77
    introduction, 74–76
    market share, 75
    order of operations, 84–85
    vectors for advancing
        coordination and collective voice,
            enablers of, 82–84
        incorporation and membership,
            versatile statutes for, 78–79
        scalable financing for diverse
            communities, 80–82

Community Standards (Facebook), 259
competition, policy proposals to
    regulate, 3–4
competition law
    definition of harm in, 339
    European, 35
    limitations of, 288
    reforming, 289
competition law, German proposal for
    reforming
    a competition authority, 289
    data protections, 289
    defining the material scope according to
        market status, 47–48
    introduction, 35–36
    media regulation merged with elements
        of competition law, 45–49
    plurality measures, 48
    positive safeguards for public interest
        content, 46–47
    a singular authority, creation of a, 48–49
    summary and conclusion, 49–50
competition law, German responses to
    digital dominance
    evaluation, 43–45
    federal antitrust Act (GWB), 36, 37, 38–
        39, 45–46, 47–48
    introduction, 36–39
    market dominance, redefining, 38
    market tipping, measures to
        prevent, 36–37
    super-market rulers, abuse controls
        for, 37–38
consumer empowerment, coupling media
    literacy with, 9
Cooperative Platform Economy Act
    (CA), 78–79
copyright, 5–6, 137–39, 291, 292
Copyright Designs and Patents Act, 105
corporate dominance of public life,
    preventing, 283
corporate libertarianism, 328
Cost of Exclusion concept, 339
COVID-19 pandemic
    DSTs and, 135
    failures exposed with, 74
    Infodemic, 272

COVID-19 pandemic (*cont.*)
  infodemic associated with, 131–32, 195–
    96, 223, 272
  infodemic relating to, 195–96
  information regarding, public trust
    in, 180
  Internet use during, 221–22
  journalism funding, 139
  media pluralism and, 131–33
  misleading information, production
    of, 223
  reliance on digital technologies and,
    221–22, 255
  simple declarations, 181–82
  surveillance data to identify infection
    precursors, 181–82
crowdfunding, 78

Dahlgren, Peter, 225
data. *See also* user data
  as a collective good, 157
  decentralizing control over, 281
  for predictive analysis, 26–27
data capitalism, extractive, 19
data economy, distrust of the, 180
data exploitation, 68
data extraction
  ad-supported media, 160–61
  competitive economy based on, 27
  in platform-driven markets, 19, 21–
    22, 29–30
  sources of, 157
data hoarding, 21–22
data infrastructure, 180–81
data liquidity, 187
data management in the interest of the
    individual, 282–83
data minimization principle, 115
data personalization, active vs. passive, 114
data privacy and security, 152, 157, 340
data profiling, 26–27
Data Protection Act (UK), 210
data protection authorities (DPAs), 174
data protection law, 209–10
data protection rights, 282–83
data protections. *See also* GDPR (General
    Data Protection Regulation)

changes in the landscape of, 180
competition and media law, German
    proposal for reforming, 289
health data, 187
political exemptions for
    disinformation, 209–11
from wide access, 68
data targeting, 110–11, 112, 114–17, 128
data trustees and platforms in the public
    interest, 282
data trusts, 283
defamation laws, 203
democracy
  concentration of media ownership
    and, 127
  crisis of, 199
  digitally dominant platforms and, 281,
    289, 291, 292
  digital media and, 238
  electoral systems, vulnerability of, 196–
    97, 199, 225–26, 235
  freedom of expression and, 211
  GAFAM's power, effect on, 281
  institutional balances, 1
  Internet impact on, 1, 110, 114, 203–4
  journalism, an independent, 290
  media freedom and, 303
  media pluralism and, 132
  media's power in a, 308–9
  new media, power of, 302–3
  online advertising, impacts on, 114
  science, independent, 290
Democracy Club (UK), 229
Democracy Works (US), 229–30
democratic future, determining our
  AI legislation, 285
  conclusion, 292
  data trustees and platforms in the public
    interest, 282
  decentralized mobile operating
    systems, 281
  introduction, 280
  joined-up regulation and regulators
    for the platform economy and all-
    purpose technology, 288
  mobile operating systems,
    decentralized, 281

platform impartiality and
    interconnectivity obligations, 287
securing independence for journalism
    and science, 290
separation of digital powers, 283
democratic knowledge and
    participation, 228–30
Designing Accounting Safeguards to Help
    Broaden Oversight and Regulations
    on Data Act, 157
digital advertising. *See* advertising, online
digital economic rents, 25–27
Digital Economy Partnership
    Agreement, 259
digital intermediary tax
    the audiovisual precedent and the
        copyright debate, 137–39
    benefits of, 141
    conclusion, 141–42
    the digital tax schemes, 133–35
    an EU digital tax to support
        journalism, 135–37
    free goods and public goods, 140
    introduction, 127
    voluntary funding vs., 139
Digital Market Act (DMA) (EU), 4, 129,
    257–58, 307, 340
digital powers, separation of, 283
Digital Services Act (DSA) (EU)
    advertising rules, 113
    duty of care requirements, 5, 105–6
    on media freedom, 300, 308, 311
    modernizing the digital services
        framework, 257–58
    new social contract framework, 12
    obligations of online platforms, 302
    regional and global coordination, 11
    responsibility of video providers, 307
    scope, 174
    transparency requirements, 49
    US proposals compared, 340
Digital Services Taxes (DSTs), 132
Digital Stability Board (DSB) for global
    governance
    framework, 256, 265
    funding, 269
    model for, 256, 264

    objectives, 265
    political mandate, 268
    proposal, 264
    reasons for, 266
    social media platform governance, 271
    standard setting for big data, AI, social
        media platforms, 270
direct marketing, 210
disinformation. *See also* electoral
    disinformation
    artificial intelligence (AI) in
        identifying, 205
    automated filtering of, 205
    defined, 195–96
    introduction, 195–98
    misinformation vs., 195–96
    pre-Internet, 196–97
    public concerns, 223
    regulatory responses to, 199–200
disinformation consumption, political
    viewpoint in, 199
disinformation laws, 203–4
DuckDuckGo, 118–19, 120
duty of care, obliging platforms to accept a
    based on legal obligations, 330–31
    categories of harm identified, 98
    codes of practice, 102–3
    conclusion, 105–6
    criminal law in, 100
    for disinformation, 153
    enforcement and sanctions, 104–5
    government-enforced (UK), 153
    introduction, 93–94
    overview of the duty, 98–100
    regulation, platform not content as
        focus of, 94–98
    regulatory interlock, 103–4
    risk identification and
        management, 99–100
    scope of services, 101–2
    statutory model, selecting a, 96–98
    for voter manipulation, 153

economy, the online
    economic democracy for the, 75–76
    Internet startups, 77
    tech startups in the, 76–77

Edelman, Gilad, 201
edge computing, shift towards, 281
election campaigns
    attempts to manipulate online, 225–28
    broadcasting regulations and, 236
    digital media, effect on, 238
    ethics in, 245
    mass media communications, impact
        on, 236
election information, online, 228–29
election regulation, media law in,
        235, 236
election-related broadcast regulation in the
        digital era
    conclusion, 248
    digital media, 238
    introduction, 235
    media law in, 235, 236
    policy considerations
        digital advertising, 243
        professional media, supporting
            the, 240
        technology companies, public service
            style obligations, 246
Electoral Act (South Africa), 206
electoral advertising
    online
        conclusion, 248
        digital media, 238
        disrupting campaign rules, 199
        electoral disinformation, 207–9
        increase in, 199
        introduction, 235
        media law in, 235, 236
        policy considerations, 243
        technology companies, public service
            style obligations, 246
        via social media, 246
    regulation, UK, 236
    voter data for, 197
electoral disinformation
    Code of Practice to combat, 208
    data protection political
        exemptions, 209–11
    by domestic political actors, 196–97
    electoral outcomes, effect on, 197,
        199, 211

by foreign state actors, 196–97,
        199, 225–26
    global increase in, 197
    implementing best practices against, 198
    inference and, 198–201
    introduction, 195
    online behavioural advertising
        and, 207–9
    regulating
        complexity of, 198
        recommendations for further
            action, 211–15
        social media, 204–7
        US, partisanship in, 199–200
    regulating big tech, challenges of
        data protection law, 196
        election law, media law, 196
        mass communications regulation, 196
        targeted online advertising, 196
    research on, 195
    on social media, 199–200, 204–
        7, 324–25
    troll factories for, 199
electoral disinformation laws, 203–
        4, 206–7
electoral public spheres, creating
        new, 221–30
electoral systems, vulnerability of, 235
Employee Stock Ownership Plan (ESOP)
        (US), 79, 81, 84–85
entrepreneurial ecosystem
        development, 18
equity compensation, 75
Entsminger, Josh, 3, 344
European Convention on Human
        Rights (ECHR), 301–2, 303, 306,
        307, 345–46
European Union
    audiovisual precedent, 137–39
    content regulation and liability, 306
    copyright debate, 137–39
    digital platforms, governance of, 257–58
    digital tax to support
        journalism, 135–37
    DST proposals, 135–37
    financing community-owned renewable
        power, 81

Statute for a European Cooperative
    Society, 79
targeted advertising policy, 112
Everett v. Comojo, 97

Facebook. *See also* GAFA (Google/
    Alphabet, Apple, Facebook,
    Amazon); GAFAM (Google/
    Alphabet, Apple, Facebook,
    Amazon)
average user data points, 161
competition, function-oriented, 21–22
content governance, 259
digital advertising, results of media
    dependence on, 224–25
digital advertising revenue growth, 325
duty of care, obliging from, 101
election disinformation, 196–97, 199–
    200, 259, 324–25
evolution of, 224
function in establishing, 224
harms done by, 324–25, 333
market share, Germany, 36
Oversight Board, 163, 304
power of
    market power, abuse of, 325
    over core infrastructures, 324–25
    over the media, 139, 224, 290–91, 333
    political, 345
    privileges accompanying, 330
privacy fines, 289–90
real name policies, 227
regulating, 330
self-regulatory approach, 304
taxation proposal, 333
transparency data fine, 170
user statistics, 222
Fairness Doctrine (US), 302, 306, 329
fake news, 196–97, 199
Farm Credit Act, 75
Farm Credit System, 80
Fay, Robert, 256
Federal Antitrust Act (Germany), 4, 9
Federal Communications Commission
    (US), 327, 329
Federal Communications Decency Act
    (US), 259

Federal Radio Commission (US), 159
federated learning, 115–16, 118
Feld, Harold, 19, 153, 339
fiduciary, defined, 151–52
Financial Stability Board (FSB), 256,
    264, 269
First Amendment (US), 152, 153, 154,
    158–59, 201, 301, 302, 305,
    306, 310
First Amendment fundamentalism,
    153, 345–46
5G technology, 282
Forum on Information and Democracy
    Working Group, 259
France, 119, 138–39, 258, 305, 338–39
Franks, Mary A., 153
Fraser, Nancy, 222
freedom of expression
    defined, 177, 196
    democracy and, 211
    duties and responsibilities, 345–46
    European Union restrictions, 302
    fundamental right of, developing, 10–
        11, 177
    governance of, privatization of the, 177
    international human rights approach,
        300, 302, 303
    media freedom vs., 303
    protections, 171–72, 212, 272
    regulating, 211–12
    regulators to strengthen, 177
    restrictions on, 207
    state controls, 196, 203, 213
    vulnerability of, 10
freedom of information, 1
freedom of opinion, 196
freedom of speech. *See also* First
    Amendment (US)
    freedom of the media vs., 311
    international human rights approach,
        301–2, 303
    media, role of, 299, 300
    open video systems, access
        rights, 65, 66
    regulating, justification for, 302
    suppressing, 199–200
freedom of the press, 222–23, 310

free expression of the will of the
    electors, 196
Friendly Societies Act, 78

GAFA (Google/Alphabet, Apple,
    Facebook, Amazon)
  dominance, challenging the, 282
  market positions, 18
  power of
    effect on democracy, 281
    regulating, 280, 284
GAFAM (Google, Apple, Facebook,
    Amazon, Microsoft)
  democracy, impact on, 1, 289, 292
  incumbency advantages, 1
  market capitalization growth, 1
  operating subsidies, creating
    dependence on, 290
  power of
    democracy and, 289
    monopoly position, 292
    threats to destroy, 291
  regulating, democracy and, 292
Gal, Michal, 140
gatekeepers, 129, 257–58, 307, 340–41
General Data Protection
    Regulation (GDPR)
  data harvesting, regulating, 115–17
  enforcement and sanctions, 104–5
  implementation, Irish data protection
    authority, 171
  limiting mechanisms disclosure, 172
  as a model for AI legislation, 285
  obligations imposed by, globally, 257–58
  obligations of platforms accumulating
    user data, 151
  privacy, emphasis on, 102
  property rights over user data, 156
  reporting standards, international
    linkages, 176
  targeted advertising, impact on, 113
Germany. See also competition, German
    proposal for reforming; media law,
    German proposal for reforming
  cooperative association
    membership, 82
  election information, online, 229–30

Interstate Broadcasting Treaty
    (Rundfunkstaatsvertrag
    (RStV), 39–41
gig economies, 74–75, 78–79
Gillibrand, Kirsten, 74–75
Girard, Michel, 260, 270
Gitlin, Todd, 225
Global Initiative on Ethics of Autonomous
    and Intelligent Systems (The IEEE
    Global Initiative), 260
Global Partnership on AI, 258
Goldwater, Barry, 186–87
Good Samaritans Act (US), 152–53, 162
Google. See also GAFA (Google/Alphabet,
    Apple, Facebook, Amazon);
    GAFAM (Google/Alphabet, Apple,
    Facebook, Amazon)
  ad platforms, restrictions and bans, 114
  business model, democracy and, 291
  content governance, 259
  data extraction, 161
  digital advertising revenue growth, 325
  function in establishing, 224
  harms done by, 333
  market share, Germany, 36
  power of, 333
    market power, abuse of, 325
    over the media, 139, 224–25, 290–
      91, 292
    political, 345
  publishers, agreements with, 141
  real name policies, 227
  self-regulatory approach, 304
  taxation of, 333
  verticalization of digital services, 22
Google Gmail, 222
Google Search, 118–19, 120–21
Graef, Inge, 151
Great Financial Crisis (GFC), 256
Green New Deal, 75–76

Habermas, Jurgen, 222, 224–25, 230, 315
harm, defined in competition law, 339
harms
  categories identified, 98
  duty of care regarding, 153
  ethical codes and rules, introduction of, 6

medical inferences and predictions,
180–92
new protections for citizens and
consumers from, 6
personal data, greater control to
prevent, 6–7
platform monopolies, 324
regulating, 153
self-regulation of, new structures and
legitimacy strategies, 6
services as natural monopolies, 333
by social media, 93–94, 153, 324–
25, 333
Hartmann, Sarah, 307
hate speech laws, 203
Helberger, Natali, 111–12
"The Hidden Cost of Free Goods:
Implications for Antitrust
Enforcement" (Gal &
Rubinfeld), 140
Hildebrandt, M., 116
Holyoake, George Jacob, 78
Holznagel, Bernd, 307
homes, connected, 186
"How Big Data Enables Economic Harm"
(Newman), 181
human rights
AI and, 258
to communicate (see freedom of
expression; freedom of speech)
duty of care and, 99
post-war, 300–1
regional and global coordination, 11
standards for respect of, 271
Human Rights Act, 99
human rights law, 196, 203, 211
Humprecht, Edda, 239
Hutchins Commission (US), 327

illegal content, proposals to regulate, 5
The Imperative of Responsibility
(Jonas), 280
indexing and search functions, search
engines, 118–19
India, 206
inequality, increases in, 1
infant industry argument, 280

infodemic, 131–32, 195–96, 223, 272
information ecosystem, 223
information fiduciaries
defined, 151–52
digital platforms as, 151–53
facilitating regulatory interventions
related to privacy and security of
user data, 152
duties of, 151–52
innovation, 18–21, 289
innovation systems, 27–30
intellectual property rights, 3, 8–9, 66
intermediaries, information
business models for, 61–62
deficiencies of, 223
functions of, 60–61, 61f, 222–23
normative public sphere, acting as, 223
open video systems
business models for, 61–62
functions of, 60–61, 61f
intermediaries, Internet
defined as media, 307
regulating, 308–9
regulation and accountability reforms,
299, 300
intermediaries, verifying platform
data by
access, determining limits of, 175
benefits of, 172–73
conclusion, 177
introduction, 169–70
misuse of for strategic national
interests, 175–76
problem defined, 170–71
proposal, 171–74
public or private? 173–74
scope and limitations, 172–73
standard setting for online platform
transparency reports, 176–77
International Co-operative Alliance, 82
International Data Standards Board
(IDSB), 262
International Grand Committee on
Disinformation (ICG), 269
International Telecommunications Union
(ITU) Global Symposium for
Regulators, 260

Internet
    addiction by design, 21–22
    authoritarian approaches to
        governance, 171–72
    Covid-19 and use of the, 221–22
    democracy, impact on, 1, 110,
        114, 203–4
    negative rights approach to media
        freedom, 304
    political campaigning, 198
    power over elections, 203–4
    regulatory history, 204–5
Internet Engineering Task Force, 270
'Internet Governance Forum Plus, 262
Internet of Things (IoT), 281, 282
Internet startups, 77
Interstate Broadcasting Treaty (TStV)
    (Germany), 39
Interstate Media Treaty (MStV)
    (Germany), 39, 287
intervention, GWB in lowering thresholds
    for, 36–37
Italy, 82, 84–85

Johnson, Boris, 238
Joint Partnership on AI (Canada and
    France), 258
Joint Technical Committee Number 1
    (JTC1), 260
Jonas, Hans, 280, 292
journalism
    securing funding and freedom from
        interference for the future of
        democracy, 290
    social media as a medium of, 284
journalism funding
    digital tax for, 135–37
    large platform controls on, 139, 290–91,
        292, 333
journalist ethics, 327

Karpf, David, 197, 211
Kattel, Rainer, 3, 19–20
Kaye, David, 196
Keane, John, 238–39
Kelso, Louis, 81, 84–85
Kelso, Patricia Hetter, 81

Khan, Lina, 25–26, 339
Kuklis, Lubos, 11, 344–45

Leblond, Patrick, 262
Legacoop (Italy), 82
Leiser, Mark, 95
Lessig, Lawrence, 94–95
liability and content legislation, 5
Liebling, A. J., 222–23
life, digitalization of everyday, 21–22
Limited Cooperative Association statute
    (CO), 78–79
LinkedIn, 21
Lippmann, Walter, 127
Lyft, 77–78

Main Street Employee Ownership
    Act, 84–85
Main Street Employee Ownership Act
    (US), 84–85
Maréchal, Nathalie, 268
market dominance
    GWB evaluation criteria for, 37–38
    redefining, 38
market power
    abuse of, 325
    data aggregations as source of, 151
    intermediary, GWB new criteria for, 38
    online video
        regulatory responses to, 59
        submarkets, concentrations
            of, 56–59
    online video submarkets, concentrations
        of, 57t
    platform power and, 21–23
    platforms, digitally dominant, 18,
        323, 325
    user choice in, 60
market tipping, GWB measures to
    prevent, 36–37
Marsden, Chris, 223
mass media
    as gatekeeper, 222–23
    impact on election campaigns, 236
    platforms as gatekeepers of, 129
Mastodon, 101
Mazzoli, Eleonora Maria, 6–7, 343–44

Mazzucato, Mariana, 3, 8, 17, 18, 19–20,
        24–26, 224, 344
McKinsey Global Institute, 270
McQuillan, Dan, 184–85
Medhora, Rohinton P., 255–56
media. *See also* journalism
    ad-supported, 160–61
    audience data, monetizing, 160–61
    concentration of ownership, risk to
        democracy, 127
    elections, impact on, 236
    as gatekeeper, 222–23
    gatekeepers, 129
    Internet intermediaries defined as, 307
    journalism
        securing funding and freedom from
            interference for the future of
            democracy, 290
        social media as a medium of, 284
    journalism funding
        digital tax for, 135–37
        large platform controls on, 139, 290–
            91, 292, 333
    new Internet media, 308–9
    new media
        accountability framework, 303–4
        dangers of power to
            democracy, 302–3
        social contract for the, 311
    new media contract, 299
    news media economy, 129, 130t–31t,
        132, 135–37
    news online
        automated systems and
            recommenders, 111
        commercial pressures on, 111–12
        costs, covering the costs of, 112
        self-regulatory mechanism, 113
        user access, changes in, 128
    newspaper industry, market trends, 129,
        130t–31t
    power of the
        actively guide and shape
            individuals, 111–12
        in a democracy, 308–9
        regulating, 308
        to shape public opinion, 308

    power over the
        large platform controls, 139, 290–91,
            292, 333
        online advertising, dependence
            on, 325
        social media, 139, 224–25, 290–91, 333
    social responsibility of, 299
    TV media, transition to third
        generation, 55
    United States
        accountability, 329
        broadcast monopolies, power of, 329
        corporate consolidation of power
            of, 328–29
        lessons from the post-war moment,
            323–24, 327
        media reform movement, 328–29
        public trustee model of
            broadcasting, 323–24
        social obligations, 328–29
media, traditional
    digital media and the, 239
    disinformation, impacts on, 199–200
    election coverage, 238, 239
    impoverishment of, 129–31, 132, 325
    legacy business model, 128
    regulation, 100
media concentration law, 284
media ethics, 310
media freedom
    conclusion, 313
    digital dominance and, 307
    international human rights approach,
        299, 300–2, 303–4, 310
    media pluralism and, 307
    negative rights approach
        consequences of, 300
        dangers of, 309
    the new media contract and, 299
    new social contract, procedural
        dimensions of, 311
    policies, international differences in,
        299, 300
    policy interventions for
        content regulation/liability, 306
        subsidies, 305
        taxes, 305

media freedom (*cont.*)
  positive rights approach
    dangers of, 310
    historically, 300–1
  regulation reforms
    new social contract, procedural
      dimensions of, 311
media law
  in election regulation, 235, 236
  in online advertising
    in in elections, 235, 236
  technical power, controlling, 284
media law, German proposal for reforming
  a competition authority, 289
  data protections, 289
  defining the material scope according to
    market status, 47–48
  media regulation merged with elements
    of competition law, 45–49
  plurality measures, 48
  positive safeguards for public interest
    content, 46–47
  a singular authority, creation of
    a, 48–49
  summary and conclusion, 49–50
media literacy, coupling with consumer
  empowerment, 9
media market, main players in the, 128
media pluralism in a digital environment
  the Covid-19 effect, 131–33
  digital intermediary tax to support the
    public good
    the audiovisual precedent and the
      copyright debate, 137–39
    benefits of, 141
    conclusion, 141–42
    the digital tax schemes, 133–35
    an EU digital tax to support
      journalism, 135–37
    free goods and public goods, 140
    public service obligations, 223
    voluntary funding vs., 139
  the great disruption, 128–31
  as media freedom, 301–2, 307
  principle of, 308
  protecting, 308–9
  threats to, 128, 129

media regulation, German responses to
  digital dominance
  Internet platforms, 41
  Interstate Media Treaty (MStV), 39, 41–
    42, 45–46
  introduction, 39–45
  media intermediaries, 41–42
  must-carry rules, 40–41, 43
  negative behavioural duties, 42–43
  new categories of media services,
    introduction of, 41–42
  non-discrimination rules, 40–41, 42–43
  open network platforms, 41
  OTT (over-the-top) cable bundling
    services, 42
  platform regulation, evolution of, 39–41
  positive safeguards obligations, 43
  smart TV devices, 42
  summary and conclusion, 49–50
  transparency in, 42, 43
  user interfaces, 41
media taxation
  to penalize harmful outcomes, 305
  public media tax, 331
  to support the public good
    the audiovisual precedent and the
      copyright debate, 137–39
    benefits of, 141
    conclusion, 141–42
    the digital tax schemes, 133–35
    an EU digital tax to support
      journalism, 135–37
    free goods and public goods, 140
    public service obligations, 223
    voluntary funding vs., 139
  US approach to, 304–5
medical inferences and predictions from
  non-medical data
  conclusion, 187–88
  data collection
    by inference, basic and multifactor,
      182, 184–85
    by simple declaration, 181–
      82, 183–84
    by somatic tells, 182, 186–87
    categories of information, 181–82
    health data protections, 187

mandated by law, 183
of mental health data, 186–87
rules of consent for, 183
sale of data, 183–84
types of action from, 182–83
diversity of, 181
examples of, 181
harms done by, 181, 186
interventions, key recommendations
for, 188
managing, 182
mental illness, 186–87
Microsoft, 132. *See also* GAFAM (Google/
Alphabet, Apple, Facebook,
Amazon)
microtargeting, 207–8
misinformation
defined, 195–96
public concerns, 223
on social media, 200*f*
misleading information, production
of, 223
Mitchell, Joe, 229
moat-building, methods to prevent, 4
mobile communications, 281
mobile operating systems,
decentralized, 281
Models for Platform Governance
(CIGI), 271–72
Molk, Peter, 80
money laundering, 175
monopolies, platform
harms done by, 324
levels of media power, 324–25
a public media tax for, 331
Montreal Declaration on the Responsible
Development of AI, 259
Moore, Martin, 224, 225, 227, 340, 344
must-carry rules and obligations, 40–41,
43, 44–45, 242
My Society (UK), 229

Nadella, Satya, 131
Napoli, Philip M., 155, 156, 159,
160, 163–64
National Cooperative Business
Association, 82

National Institute of Standards and
Technology (US), 272
Naver (South Korea), 118–19
Neil, Andrew, 238
Nemitz, Paul, 7–8, 293n.1
Netflix, 221–22
net neutrality, 287
Network Enforcement Act (Germany),
162, 170, 174
Network Enforcement Law
(Germany), 176
network rents, 25–27
Netz DG (Network Enforcement Act)
(Germany), 5, 170, 171–72,
176, 345
New Deal legislation, 75–76, 81, 83, 84–85
new Internet media, 308–9
Newman, John M., 140
Newman, Nathan S., 181
new media
accountability framework, 303–4
dangers of power to democracy, 302–3
social contract for the, 311
new media contract, media freedom and
the, 299
news and information ecologies
Internet, impact on, 1
News Media Bargaining Code, 4
news media economy, 129, 130*t*–31*t*, 132
digital tax to support
journalism, 135–37
news media production
concentration of ownership, democracy,
risk to, 127
new social contract for new media, 311
new social contract for platforms
crisis as opportunity, 334
historical lessons for the digital
age, 323
moving towards a, 329
news online
automated systems and
recommenders, 111
commercial pressures on, 111–12
costs, covering the costs of, 112
self-regulatory mechanism, 113
user access, changes in, 128

newspaper industry, market trends, 129,
     130t–31t
Niaros, Vasilis, 83
Nissenbaum, Helen, 184
Noam, Eli M., 47–48, 64–65, 70n.1, 239
non-contagion of misfortune
     principle, 183–84

Occupier's Liability Act, 97
OCEANIS— The Open Community
     for Ethics in Autonomous and
     Intelligent Systems, 260
Office of the Data Protection
     Commissioner (Malta), 210
online behavioural advertising (OBA)
     disinformation and, 207–9
     targeted, data sources for, 207–8
online ecosystems, 18
Online Safety Bill (UK), 5, 308
Online Harms legislation, 5
online platforms. See platforms
online video
     market power
          regulatory responses to, 59
          submarkets, concentrations of, 56–
             59, 57t
     market structure of, 55–58
     negative aspects/significant
          problems, 55
Open Data Charter, 258
open video systems
     access arrangements, 62–63
     access pricing, 64–65
     access provision, 64
     administration, 63
     information intermediaries, business
          models for, 61–62
     information intermediaries, functions
          of, 60–61, 61f
     market definition, 63–64
     options to reduce digital
          dominance in, 59
     overview, 60
     self-regulatory mechanism, 63–64
open video systems, access rights
     API arrangements, 60, 62–63
     compulsory licenses, 65–66

conclusion, 69–70
conditions, governance of, 60
to content platforms, 66–67
to content producers and
     aggregators, 65–66
to data, 68
to infrastructure platforms, 67
intellectual property rights, 66
to last-mile transmission service, 67–68
operating directions, 65
privacy protections, 68
purpose of, 60
seller-required bundling (tying), 66
speech rights, 65, 66
subscription platforms, 66
Organization for Economic Cooperation
     and Development (OECD), 133–
     35, 141–42, 258, 267
outrage industry, US, 199
Owen, Taylor, 255–56

Page, Larry, 26–27
Parcu, Pier Luigi, 132
Partnership on AI, 258
patents, 5–6
Pasquale, Frank, 7, 74–75, 188–89n.2,
     189n.10, 190n.15
Pathway for Prosperity Commission
     Digital Roadmap, 263
Pentland, Alex, 283
Perrin, William, 339
Pfeffer, Matthias, 7–8, 293n.1
Phenomena of Power (Popitz), 283–84
Phillips, Angela, 6–7, 78–79, 112
Phillips, Linda, 78–79
Pickard, Victor, 141, 302, 311–12
Pigouvian tax, 140
platform, defined, 18
Platform Accountability and
     Consumer Transparency Act
     (PACT), 271–72
platform data, auditing intermediaries for
     verifying
     access, determining limits of, 175
     benefits of, 172–73
     conclusion, 177
     introduction, 169–70

misuse of for strategic national
  interests, 175–76
problem defined, 170–71
proposal, 171–74
public or private? 173–74
scope and limitations, 172–73
standard setting for online platform
  transparency reports, 176–77
platform data, unverified
impacts of, 169
in transparency reports, 170
platform-driven digital markets, reshaping
conclusion, 30–31
governing platforms as innovation
  systems, 27–30
introduction, 17–18
from market power to platform
  power, 21–23
platform economies, politics of
  innovation in, 18–21
proposal, 18
value creation and value
  extraction, 23–27
platform economies
joined-up regulation and regulators for
  the, 288
leveraging, 22–23
politics of innovation in, 18–21
platform governance, 18, 19
platforms. See also duty of care, obliging
  platforms to accept a; social media
  platforms; specific platforms
accountability and positive
  contributions, increasing, 344
advantages to scale in, 56
alternative visions for
  antitrust actions, 341
  mixed digital ecosystem,
    343, 345–46
  services as natural monopolies,
    342, 345–46
civil liability protections, 152–53, 259
concerns associated with using, 255
Covid-19 and use of, 255
elements shaping, 18–19
embedded nature of, 17, 19
evolution of, 18

extractive behavior of, 19, 21–22, 23,
  27, 29–30
function-oriented competition, 21–22
harms done by
  to democracy, 323
  responsibility for, 344
as information fiduciaries, 151–53
interference by foreign state actors
  in, 196–97
obligations
  behavioral, size and dominance
    affecting, 340
  to contribute to politics and
    society, 344
  impartiality, 287
  interconnectivity, 287
  proposals for, 302
  protect against misuse by malign
    actors, 5–4
off-line involvement, 21–22
public backlash against, 323
transparency reports, 170
transparency reports
  standards, 176–77
universal scope of concern, 28
value chain, 255
verticalization of digital
  services, 22–23
platforms, digitally dominant. See also big
  tech, policy proposals to regulate
allocative efficiency, 29
censorship of content, 114–15
challenging the, 282
content moderation practices,
  reporting, 170
democracies, impact on, 1
disinformation regulation, 204–7
dominance of public life, 283
fourth estate, threats to destroy, 291
as gatekeeper, 257–58
GWB abuse controls for, 37–38
incumbency advantages, 1
market capitalization growth, 1
market power, 18, 323
operating subsidies, creating
  dependence on, 290
political advertising regulations, 205–6

platforms, digitally dominant (*cont.*)
  power abuses, preventing
    competitive behaviour controls, 3–4
    moat-building, methods to prevent, 4
  power of
    concentrated, lack of regulation, 280
    democracy and, 281, 289
    global monopoly, 292
    infrastructure, reconfiguring to
      reduce, 7–9
    market-shaping, 21–23
    monopoly position, 118, 119
    power of opinion controlled by,
      regulating, 284
    regulating, 280
    results from, 323
  regulating, 19, 280, 292
  societal impacts of, 118
  transnational
    dominance of, limiting reporting
      by, 171
platforms, global governance of
  artificial intelligence (AI), 256, 257,
    258, 270
  big data, 256, 257, 270
  challenges of, 257
  conclusion, 273
  current regulatory situation, risks of
    the, 260
  Digital Stability Board (DSB) for
    framework, 256, 265
    funding, 269
    model for, 256, 264
    objectives, 265
    political mandate, 268
    proposal, 264
    reasons for, 266
    social media platform
      governance, 271
    standard setting for big data, AI,
      social media platforms, 270
  international cooperation, recent
    initiatives on, 256
  introduction, 255
  solutions proposed
    Digital Stability Board (DSB),
      256, 264

  global and regional
    coordination, 11–12
  International Data Standards Board
    (IDSB), 262
  'Internet Governance Forum
    Plus, 262
  Pathway for Prosperity Commission
    Digital Roadmap, 263
  shared norms and methods of
    coordinated action, 10–9
political campaigning, digital, 198
political partisanship, protecting against
  platform, 287
politics, digital platforms influence on, 284
Popitz, Heinrich, 283–84
Pousttchi, Key, 282
power, technological, controlling, 283
precautionary principle, 280, 292
Principles on Artificial Intelligence
  (OECD), 258
privacy
  contextual integrity, 184
  decentralized mobile operating systems
    for, 281
  protections, limitations on, 171–72
  social value of, 184
  unitary structures for
    enforcement, 289–90
Privacy Framework (APEC), 258
privacy law, 257–58
Privacy Policy (Google), 259
Privacy Principles (OECD), 258
privacy rights, 10–11, 157, 340
propaganda, 5, 308
property law (US), 156
property rights over user data, 156–57
Protection from Online Falsehoods and
  Manipulation Act (Singapore), 203
Protection of Personal Information Act
  (South Africa), 210
prudent man rule, 75
public broadcasting, 119–20
public health initiatives, 180
public life, preventing corporations from
  dominating, 283
public service obligations
  media law in election regulation, 235

media pluralism, digital intermediary
tax to support the public good
of, 223
public services, protecting against big techs
domination of, 282
public service search engine, 117–21
public sphere, 222–23, 230
public trust doctrine, 154–55, 157–58
public trustees, treating dominant digital
platforms as
aggregate user data as public
resource, 155–59
application and limitations, scope and
thresholds, 159–62
conclusion, 162–64
introduction, 151–54
responsibilities of, 154–55
public trust model
applying to dominant digital
platforms, 155–59
public trustee, qualifying as a, 160–61
public trustees, types of, 154–55
trust property in the, 153, 154, 155, 156

quantum Internet, 282
quantum Internet, enabling a, 281
Qwant (European-French), 118–19

Radio Act (US), 159
Reddit, 99–100
Regan, Priscilla M., 155
Reidenberg, Joel R., 94–95
rents/rent-extraction, 24–27
Representation of the People Act
(India), 206
Rid, Thomas, 199, 211
ride-sharing, 76–78
right of self-determination, 196
Roberts Biddle, Ellery, 268
robotics systems, in-home, 186
Roe, Sym, 229
Romer, Paul, 140
Rowbottom, Jacob, 223
Rubinfeld, Daniel, 140
Rural Electrification Act, 75, 80, 84–85
Russia, electoral disinformation, 196–
97, 225–26

Schneider, Nathan, 8, 74–75, 79, 81–
83, 344
science, securing funding and freedom
from interference for the future
of, 290
search engines
active vs. passive personalization, 114
indexing and search functions, 118–19
political impartiality requirement, 287
search engines, de-linking from
commercial imperatives
data targeting, regulating, 110–
11, 114–17
introduction, 110–11
opaque ranking systems, 111–13
public service search engines, 110–
11, 117–21
summary and conclusion, 121–22
systemic change, requirements
for, 113–21
security law, 257–58
Settle, Jaime, 246–47
Shaw, Chris, 229
Sherman Act, 35
Singapore, 198
Smart City, 283
Snow, Jon, 223
Snowden, Edward, 225
social contract
as metaphor and framework, 325
new social contract for new media, 311
new social contract for platforms
crisis as opportunity, 334
historical lessons for the digital
age, 323
moving towards a, 329
social distancing, 74
social-media cooperatives, 74–75
social media platforms. *See also* duty of
care, obliging platforms to accept a;
specific platforms
ad archive standards, 208–9
concerns, 93
Covid-19 and use of, 221–22
disinformation, 131–32, 196–97
electoral disinformation on, 199–200,
204–7, 208–9, 211, 324–25

social media platforms (*cont.*)
  extreme material, search engines
      prioritizing, 111–12
  global rule setting by, 259
  harms done by, 93–94
  immunity from liability, 152–53, 162
  misinformation on, 200*f*
  modifying user behaviour to maximize
      revenue, 95–96
  obligations to carry speech, 201
  power of opinion controlled by, 284
  public role, 131–32
  regulating, 93–94
    electoral disinformation, 204–7
    harms done by, 93–94
    paid advertising on, 245–46
    the use of for electoral
        disinformation, 204–7
    transparency in political advertising
    voluntary commitment to, 208
South Africa, 206–7
Soviet Union, 196–97
Spain, 82
Stanford University, 83–84
Starmer, Keir, 245
State Media Treaty (Germany), 285
stickiness, 21–22
surveillance
  giving in to, 74
  to identify infection
      precursors, 181–82
  robotics systems, in-home, 186
surveillance capitalism, 95–96
surveillance democracy, 309

Tambini, Damian, 195
Target, 181
taxation
  digital intermediary tax
    the audiovisual precedent and the
        copyright debate, 137–39
    benefits of, 141
    conclusion, 141–42
    the digital tax schemes, 133–35
    an EU digital tax to support
        journalism, 135–37
    free goods and public goods, 140

  introduction, 127
  voluntary funding vs., 139
  on the media, 304–5, 331
  policy proposals to regulate, 8–9
Tech new Deal, 75–76
technical power, controlling, 283
technological and democratic future,
    determining our
  AI legislation, 285
  conclusion, 292
  data trustees and platforms in the public
      interest, 282
  decentralized mobile operating
      systems, 281
  introduction, 280
  joined-up regulation and regulators
      for the platform economy and all-
      purpose technology, 288
  mobile operating systems,
      decentralized, 281
  platform impartiality and
      interconnectivity obligations, 287
  securing independence for journalism
      and science, 290
  separation of digital powers, 283
technology, all-purpose, 288
technology law, 280, 281
technology platforms
  public service style obligations in
      elections, 246
  public sphere of, 222
technology super-platforms
  elections, effects on, 225–28
  nation states, relationship with, 225
  public sphere functions of, 221–30
  real name policies, 227
  responsibilities, regulating, 223
  self-regulatory mechanism, 304
tech startups, 76–77
Tisne, Martin, 157
Toronto Declaration on Human Rights in
    Machine Learning Systems, 259
tragedy of commons, 140
Transparency and Accountability Centre
    (TikTok), 259
Trump, Donald, 84–85, 163, 186–87, 200,
    201*f*, 201, 202*f*, 213, 338–39

truth, political, 201
Tucker, Christine, 21–22
Turley, Anna, 93–94
TV media, transition to third
    generation, 55
Twitch, 101
Twitter, 201*f*–2*f*
    ad platforms, restrictions and
        bans, 114
    duty of care, obliging from, 101
    electoral outcomes, effect on, 211
    fact-checking Trump, 200–1
    function in establishing, 224
    real name policies, 227
    self-regulatory mechanism, 259
    user fake news exposures on, 199
Twitter Rules, 259

Uber, 25–26, 75, 77–78
United Kingdom
    Community Shares model, 80
    cooperative associations, 83
    Friendly Societies Act, 78
    workplace safety, duty of care, 97–98
United States
    AI regulation, 258
    anti-money laundering (AML)
        legislation, 175
    broadcasting standards, 306
    Capper-Volstead Act, 83
    civil liability protections for platforms,
        152–53, 162, 259
    Cold War disinformation tactics, 196–97
    cooperative associations, 78–79, 80–
        81, 83–84
    digital platforms, governance of, 257
    equity crowdfunding, 80
    exceptionalism, 301
    First Amendment protections, 152, 153,
        154, 158–59, 201, 301, 302, 305,
        306, 310, 345–46
    freedom of the press, 310
    Main Street Employee Ownership
        Act, 84–85
    privacy and data protection
        enforcement, 289–90
    property law, 156

social media
    civil liability protections, 152–53,
        162, 271
    policy recommendations for
        dominant, 163–64
    Russian election interference
        via, 196–97
    transparency and reporting
        requirements, 271–72
    user data policy, 152
    worker ownership, 83, 84–85
United States media
    accountability, 329
    broadcast monopolies, power of, 329
    corporate consolidation of power
        of, 328–29
    diversity, 308
    lessons from the post-war moment,
        323–24, 327
    media reform movement, 328–29
    negative rights approach to media
        freedom, 300, 309
    public trustee model of
        broadcasting, 323–24
    reform movement, 323–24, 327
    social obligations, 328–29
    subsidies, 305
    taxation, 304–5
universal Internet, splintering the, 345–46
USA JOBS Act, 80
user data, 207–8. *See also* data
    ambiguous character of, 156
    collective ownership of, 157, 160
    economic value of, 157
    monetization of, 160–61
    ownership of, 115–16, 156–57
    personal, complexity of, 340
    platform obligations, 151
    privacy and security of, 152, 157, 340
    for profiling, 26–27
    property rights over, 156–57
    protections, 68, 74, 115–16
    as public resource, 155–59
    regulating, 6–7, 110–11, 114–17
    responsible use of, ensuring, 282
    targeting, 112, 114–17, 128
    targeting, regulating, 110–11, 114–17

value, public, 27–30
value-extraction, 24
Veale, Michael, 10, 293n.4
voter data, 197
voting information, online, 228–29

Wagner, Ben, 11, 170, 171–72, 174,
        177, 333
Wardle, Claire, 223
Web Foundation Contract for the
        Web, 259
WeChat, 222
WhatsApp, 225–26
Wheeler, Tom, 163
Wiener, Jason, 78–79
Woods, Lorna, 339

Wordpress, 101
Working Group on Infodemics, 259
workplace safety, 97

Yahoo, 118–19
Yandex (Russia), 118–19
Yang, Andrew, 159
Young, Lord of Graffham, 98
YouTube, 114, 221–22
Yugoslavia, 84–85

Zimbabwe, 202–3
Zittrain, Jonathan, 151–52
Zuboff, Shoshana, 26–27, 95–96, 157
Zuckerberg, Mark, 222, 338–39
Zuma, President of South Africa, 206